THE FURTHER THOUGHTS OF CHAIR MANN

by

ANTHONY MANN

TROUSER PRESS

©Anthony Mann 1999

Cover Design by Jill Wadsworth

Typesetting and "Colouring-In of cover" by Tim Harvey

Published by Trouser Press

First published 1999

British Library Cataloguing-in-Publication Data
A catalogue record for this book is available from the British Library

ISBN
09516501-7-3

Printed and bound by
The Guernsey Press Co. Ltd., Guernsey, Channel Islands.

ACKNOWLEDGMENTS

Firstly, my thanks to all the newspapers I have perused, both national and local, for their reporting of news events, without which the world would surely have stopped revolving.

I must also thank my wife, Maureen, who (almost) uncomplainingly typed the text, adjusted the syntax and reassembled any infinitives which may have been split.

FORWARD - OR EVER ONWARD

So, it's you. I wondered when that moment of curiosity would raise itself to the point where you felt compelled to examine the contents.

Have we ever met before? - maybe not literally, but as reader and writer. Or are you a Trouser Press virgin? Preferably around 20 years of age, with a 40" bust! That, however, is the trouble with the ageing process, one's fantasies become more fanciful whilst reality becomes ..... well, acceptable.

Now then, a few do's and don'ts before proceeding:

PLEASE check to see that your hands are clean. I don't want any paw marks or dog-eared corners.

DO NOT flick through in the hope of finding a section of glossy pages of photos - it's all words, and although it is not joined-up writing, some contain more than one syllable. Please note!

DO NOT proceed if you are from the lower classes, or a single parent or you are on benefit. Chances are I'm paying for your copy, which defeats the object of the exercise. So kindly replace it and finger Jeffrey Archer instead. On second thoughts, take it. After all, I subsidise your cigarettes, alcohol, lottery tickets and children. Oh, and by the way, for those who are used to getting something for nothing out of life, try something novel - like paying for it on the way out! Who knows, you might just learn a little (there, hope that doesn't sound too pompous).

NOTES: The word "gay" is used only in relationship to being happy. If I mean "homosexual" I'll say "homosexual!"

Any offence that may be taken is purely intentional.

This may be taken as read for those of a namby-pamby, pinko liberal persuasion, and those who wish to fill our over-populated islands with more refugees (free with every lorry arriving at Dover) who have never contributed to any benefit they will naturally receive once having set foot on our soil.

Right, the above are the ground rules, so stay with me whilst we discuss, analyse or simply mull over a whole range of topics from the insignificant announcement that yet another famine has prompted millions of Westerners to donate cash that's being eaten up (not literally) by the same military junta that caused the problem in the first place, to the truly earth-shattering - such as the news that Budgen's Store in Ash Vale, Surrey, no longer has a deli.

OUTRAGED? YOU COULD BE!

CONTENTS

CHAPTER ONE

NOW WHERE WERE WE?

It's been over seven years since "*As I Was Saying*" took to the bookshelves. Some things, however, never change. Judges are still handing out ludicrously short sentences, Social Services are still "learning" while yet another round of child abuse cases hit the headlines, animals are still being hunted to extinction and to cap it all, at the time of going to press Lord Longford is still with us - so no good news there either!

It's 1.22 pm here in beautiful downtown West London and I've just unzipped the plaid patterned cold box that holds the key to my afternoon survival. Half a Scotch egg, two rounds of cheese and pickle sandwiches, two tomatoes and a yoghurt. Yes, after 29 years of marriage, Maureen still gets up and makes the sandwiches irrespective of the time I leave for work. You may ask why she doesn't make them the night before and pop them in the fridge, but with the number of nightly soaps to watch, catch up on, plus falling asleep in the chair, there's just not the time.

I've just finished reading a short article in the *Telegraph* concerning the rising standards in our schools. Who *are* they kidding? William came home last night and informed us that his English teacher was impressed with his mock GCSE attempt and is looking for him to attain a B grade. He can't spell, has no knowledge of punctuation, other than a full stop, and even worse, no real interest. I suspect 50% of all marks are freely given for just turning up. It will be interesting to see where years of appalling teaching standards and equally appalling lethargy on William's part positions him in the all-important passport to work tables.

Last Saturday, Maureen and I visited one of those electrical stores. Whilst it is good to take advantage of any "Buy Now Pay Later" scheme, the down side is that you have to suffer reams of form filling and questions. As I said to the assistant, "I've only got the rest of my life left and time is rapidly running out, sitting here". The young, fresh-faced assistant who served us was pleasant enough, but failed after the "Sec" in "Secretary" in his ability to spell the word. After several fruitless attempts he asked Maureen how it was spelt. I have no doubt that he still attained the highest marks possible in his English exams.

Listening as one does, to *Radio 4*, on the journey up this morning, I was amused to hear that there is still a battle royal taking place regarding marriage vows for homosexuals. One vicar was talking of his blessing being given to a couple called Matthew and David. One is a lecturer in art, the other a nurse. The little lovebirds told of their desire to "solemnize their vows" - I did hear right, didn't I!

I am looking out of the car whilst I munch one of the cheese and pickle sandwiches. It's still raining. There is a park to my right, surrounded by faded green spear-fencing. At this particular spot a large tree has "exploded" through the railings to such a degree that they have literally been eaten up, the lower sections now being quite contorted - and very photogenic it is too (not by me, I hasten to add. The last film I took is still jammed in the camera). Anyway, back to the *Telegraph Business Section*. It looks as if we are about to lose yet another brewery. Wolverhampton & Dudley Brewers appear determined to buy out Marston, Thompson and Evershed. I've no doubt we'll hear all the same old platitudes about the brewery continuing to survive and customers not being the losers. The only guarantee is that the shareholders will be the winners.

Let's see, now. What else is newsworthy. Ah, yes. There's a photo of a Scottish borders fox hunter, who rejoices in the name of Raymond Shiels. Apparently, he's in intensive care after guzzling a mouthful of sheep-dip instead of whisky! His wife said he had been handed the bottle whilst the hounds were "searching after a fox". Seems he earlier got confused with the choice of bottles in his car - probably too busy dreaming of guts and entrails. Upshot is, that he started hallucinating, had to be helped off his horse, taken to hospital and is now in intensive care. However, doctors have stabilised his condition and everything is functioning okay now. One Wat Jeffrey, the Jed Forest Huntmaster, said that Mr. Shiels was "a popular member of the hunt" - (now there's a surprise) and that he "appears to have come out of this safely". It's terrifying to think how all this could have ended - you know, as dead as one of his foxes!

Right, well that's that, nobody famous in the obituary column. I've just finished the last sandwich and the half Scotch egg (home-made). I'm now going to listen to *"The Archers"* and wend my way back to work - talk to you later.

You've guessed - it's now later. Maureen's watching *"Coronation Street"* and I've just had one of those conversations with William that is designed to shock. Only a few days short of his sixteenth birthday, and once again "on report" at school for either doing something, or not doing something - whatever. His science teacher earlier today had the benefit of a discussion with him on sperm. William informed us that she said she was very pleased that he was taking such an interest in science, well, certain aspects anyway! This announcement follows on from his coming down the stairs smelling like an Essex brothel, in an attempt to win over some girl. His hair, now parted in the centre, forms horns around his forehead. He tells us girls like him being "horny". I'm not rising to the bait.

I have to admit, William has become easier to handle as he's got older. Complaints from neighbours are down to a trickle. I remember once, about a year ago, answering the doorbell to find a complete stranger standing in front of me. "What's he done now?" I enquired before the lady could utter a word. "Who?" she replied. "William!" I assumed she didn't know his name. "Presumably, you've come to complain about him?" "No", she replied, looking somewhat perplexed. "I'm here to collect the Christian Aid envelope". Which wasn't good news for her, as the announcement gave me the green light for a discussion as to why I wouldn't contribute to her cause. She stood on our doorstep three minutes short of an hour - good listener.

One Christmas, William was given a bike. Straight round to his best mate's house, he rode. At about 8.30 a.m. Maureen pulled back the sitting-room curtains, only to see the "man with the neat lawn" who resides in a neighbouring street, finger-wagging our offspring. Maureen quickly closed the curtains.

The people who bought our old cottage across the road were never keen on William. The wife - a tad of a snob - once (sorry, more than once) sent her husband across to complain about him. I countered his list of accusations with a retort that at least he could shut his door at night, we had to live with William. I don't think this placated his wife. As I write, the cottage is empty. They moved out a couple of months ago. The same prospective purchaser came back to view a few times, but we haven't seen him again. Maureen and I - hang on a minute, William's interrupting ....

Back again, guess what? He needs money to go to the pictures. He's meeting a girl from Mytchett outside the Robin Cinema in Camberley.

9

Her father's bringing them home - what was I saying? Oh, yes - last weekend, Maureen and I took a walk around our old cottage and were surprised to find that the curtains we left were still hanging from the patio doors, and another familiar pair hung from the bedroom windows. Our ex-neighbours were either careful with their money, or they liked our taste in soft furnishings! - who knows? Who cares? .....

People are funny, aren't they? How many times do we get a chance of life on this earth, other than coming back as a rabbit, aardvark or black box? - Once, twice, twenty eight? As far as I know, it's once. Why, oh, why, these priests put themselves through that tortuous, traumatic, self-denying life, I cannot fathom. There is a case currently going through the courts concerning a Father Noel Barry who, though admitting to having been tempted to have sex with an ex-nun, apparently didn't, despite their sharing the same hotel room. This indecent (sorry) incident took place during the eighties, at which time he was also supposed to be having an affair with a 50-year old headmistress. Now this lady is suing the *Sun* newspaper over allegations of a sexual relationship story being made public thirteen years ago. The point is, that when push comes to shove, does it matter? Both "other parties" were over the age of consent, which is unusual in the priesthood, and both were female - another pleasant surprise. Some people make problems.....

William is back, he's more impressed with the father's mode of transport than the girl! He drove the pair of them home in a four wheel drive something, "he drove it really fast, I talked to him about boxing and cars - he was okay". Funny how other people's parents can be fully paid up members of the human race, but not their own.

Staying with the family, Glyn, now in his late twenties, is still at home and has grown into a really nice chap. He moved out a couple of years ago, went to live above a pub. A few months down the line and he came home again - just after I'd re-decorated his old bedroom as a guest room - typical! He's talking about moving out after Christmas to share a house with a couple of friends, so maybe we'll get our room back. Then again .....

Deborah was married three years ago. Have to say, it was the best day of my life. Proud dad, happy couple, warm, sunny day and a great reception venue. Glad to report she was not overly keen on a disco so we employed the services of a female pianist who played background music throughout the meal. This was rounded off by a very enjoyable evening at the groom's parents' house. Wedding car was a royal blue 1950's Bentley, whilst the bridesmaids and Maureen travelled in a 1930's London taxi - you know, the one where the hood comes down at the back. Yes, you do know, you've seen them in the Poirot movies and they're always outside Victoria Station. James, my ex-car trading colleague in Bracknell - now turned full time wedding car provider - owns three of them, two maroon and one blue. All round, a very happy day. It was just over four years ago that Deborah told us that her boyfriend would be coming round early on Saturday. We had no idea that he was going to ask - and he did ask permission - to take her hand. We were genuinely taken aback. I remember saying something predictable and fairly inane about "it's all or nothing, you're not just having her hand". Oh, well.

As I write the couple are alive and well and living in Church Crookham, Fleet. She gave me a bit of a shock the other day. Rang up and said she had something important to discuss. "You're not pregnant, are you?" I groaned, before she could say any more. "No, why?" She sounded slightly affronted. "Well, we've just bought a new carpet and I'm not fussed on hearing the gurgling of a baby while it's being sick all over it!"

What did she want? Oh, only someone to record *"Friends"* since they would be recording something else on their own video. Luckily, her request was for something really important!

Right, that's enough, it's time to take Muttley for a walk. I just have to say, "Do you ..." and the ears pick up. Then I get to "Do you want to go ....." and she's up from her slumber. Then it's, "Do you want to go and get your lead and ....." She's off, at the speed of light, to sit at the front door while I put my shoes on. See you tomorrow.

Morning! Back to priests, I'm afraid, which is less safe than facing them, but there we go. Transferring the balance of wrongdoing fairly back in the realms of the obvious, one Father John Lloyd, a friend and aide to the Most Reverend (how can anyone live with such a handle?) John Ward, Roman Catholic Archbishop of Cardiff, has been found guilty of child abuse. No new story, no real surprise and it's not so much the continual wheedling out of these people from the woodwork, but the effort by religious authorities to cover their employees. Surely this goes against everything they purport to stand for.

One woman, raped by Father Lloyd over twenty five years ago, reported the matter to the Archbishop - you know, the Most Reverend etc. She told the jury that he was "curt and angry" with her. So we know where his loyalties lay. Fortunately, she had the guts to keep going and reported Father Lloyd to the police, who supported her. The defendant was yesterday sentenced to eight years for rape and five years for serious sexual assault. He got another twenty one months for one indecent assault and three years for yet another ten indecent assaults. These sentences are to be served concurrently when his *current* sentence is concluded in a couple of weeks' time. He was sentenced last February for assaulting a 13 year old girl, having just baptised her. Perhaps he's dyslexic, confuses abuse with anoint.

For the Vatican to demand an investigation into the handling of the affair is good news. You just don't trust their motives. Are they serious, or just after a damage-limitation result? - and people wonder why I detest all religions!

What was I saying about Social Services never learning? A boyfriend - it always is (well, nearly always a boyfriend) beats a 5 year old girl to death. The next door neighbour has a tape-recording made previously of the girl telling her that "Daddy hits me in the stomach", etc. She told Social Services, she told the police. Guess what happened? Oh, that's right - nothing! David Wright, Director of Norfolk Social Services, said that the same mistakes could be made again because of the immense number of domestic violence cases his department has to deal with. "We failed in our duty and for that I'm truly sorry".

The police say that they have changed their procedures following the little girl's death and there is now more rigorous highlighting of suspicious cases to Social Services. Well, that's all right, then. They've all learned from their experience. Are you confident they've "learned" once again? No, neither am I.

I'm sitting in what was William's bedroom - the box room and now my writing room. When Debbie moved out on her wedding morning, William moved in. In fact, he literally moved in on her wedding night, claiming squatters' rights, which freed up the smallest of the bedrooms for me to make my winter quarters for writing purposes. From a window one can see across the main Reading-Redhill railway line that runs behind our house. For the ten years we have lived here, the view has been one of woods. They are bordered by a triangle of railway lines. Entrance to these woods was via a narrow under-bridge off Lakeside Road, itself ending just east of a single tunnel before exiting onto the busy Vale Road. Many years ago, Guildford Borough Council made a compulsory purchase of the few homesteads that lay amongst the hundreds of silver birch, oaks, etc. that formed this unspoilt area. Human intrusion was minimal due to access. It had for many years been designated as a "potential development site" but remained at the bottom of the pile. The mid-nineties saw it rise to prominence and despite protests - yes, you've guessed - GBC saw fit to sell the land. Access was to be via a roundabout from Lakeside Road that would tunnel under the main Guildford to Aldershot line, which forms the southern side of the triangle. The old entrance would be made pedestrian-only.

One of the sticking points over the last few years has been the single tunnel access to the Vale Road itself. This was *always* going to be widened as part of any "future development strategy". I, like many others, attended local council meetings and this policy was upheld periodically over a twenty year period. Time and policies change, however, and I'm currently listening to tune of the Barratt Homes "development march" in bulldozed flat. Only last year, one could not see through the first few feet of trees, so dense were the woodlands. Birds of many nations, foxes and occasional deer would present themselves close to the railway line, unperturbed and unopposed. Off of Lakeside Road from the site of the new roundabout the inexorable tunnelling under the railway lines continued until daylight appeared. Even as recently as August, the only houses one could espy were by driving to the show house and wandering around the pavement-less site. They all seemed to be sold as quickly as they were being built. Four hundred and forty houses are planned for the 40-odd acre site.

Almost overnight our woods were lost. It is now a muddy flat acreage bordered by 20 feet - yes, 20 feet! - of silver birch and very little else. That is the boundary Barratts and Guildford Borough Council have deemed acceptable to separate houses from railway. We can now see through to the railway line on the far side. As I write, roof struts, building blocks and piles of earth form the view to our left, with phase 6 of the development to our right.

The autumn witnessed the felling of hundreds and hundreds of trees. The creaking, almost human crying of wood giving out its last gasps during those defiant death throes were constant as a hard-hat with a hard heart and chainsaw destroyed one after another after another.

This slaughter of one more small corner that was England coincided with a programme on neighbours feuding - or feuding neighbours - whatever. Many of the programme maker's tales relied heavily on boundary issues, especially hedges. The tree that came in for the greatest lambasting was the Leylandii (we've just had an argument over the spelling of this tree - and I was right! Wouldn't have mentioned it if

I was wrong of course). The complaints were that it grows too bushy, too high, can't see anything within a couple of years. Great!! Sounds just the thing. So out we went, and ordered twenty of the blighters. I've planted them at 2'6" intervals, and I'm now watching them grow daily.

Anyway, guess what? Guildford Borough Council decided that the volume of traffic generated by this massive development no longer required the tunnel in Lakeside Road to be widened! Four hundred and forty houses must generate at least six hundred cars at a conservative guesstimate. They cannot go anywhere else but turn left (towards the aforementioned bridge) and Vale Road or turn right towards the army road into Aldershot. It's funny, isn't it, how with all the increase in road traffic nationally, since this development was first mooted nearly thirty years ago, it no longer warrants money being spent by any of the interested parties, that's Barratts, GBC or Railtrack. It stinks. Still, it's saved someone a few bob, hasn't it.

Out of curiosity, I once again ventured around the site some weeks ago. It really is quite sickening the "subtle" lengths these developers will go to in their attempt to woo their prospective punters. The roundabout leading to the tunnel has been landscaped by Barratts. There's a notice telling you so. I understand some houses are to be built between this roundabout and the tunnel. They will not be developed until last, as it gives a more open perspective to the estate approach. On the left is a sign erected to advertise the development. It reads:-

Barratts
"Old Farm Place"
Premier Collection
A "stunning" development of
2,3, and 4 bedroom houses"

The words "premier collection" appear as part of a flowery logo that wouldn't look out of place complementing the wrapping around prize-winning sausages or Laura Ashley's curtains. A painted vintage plough sits above the words "Old Farm Place" as if to endorse the rustic charm.

Once through the tunnel one is confronted on one's right by black, wrought iron spear-fencing, topped off in gold - very traditional. The fencing fronts the show homes, surrounded by bedding plants, shrubs and the soothing sound of water, as it is pumped around a garden pond. The left hand side of the road hosts a small bed of plants fronting a board which states, "This is a reserved ecological area in accordance to the local authority requirements for the benefit of future generations". I think it means that Barratts were not given permission to build on it! Well, not yet anyway. On entering the main show house one is confronted by a model of the development. Interestingly, the railway lines are not denoted as lines but by a triangular stretch of green paint, upon which lay small white printed slips stating the word "railway". Whilst waiting for one of the two green-suited assistants to complete discussions with her prospective punter, I flicked through the list containing details of the range of houses available. There was the "Chatsworth", the "Richmond", "Jedburgh", "Lauderdale", "Edinburgh", etc. By the time I'd witnessed (suffered!) the conversation concerning the benefits of living there, I was seething.

"Can I help you?" enquired a green suit.

"Yes, have you got details of phase 6, please?"

"No, the land has not yet been released", GS replied, adding, "Are you interested in buying a property in that area?"

"No, I'm one of the poor sods who lives opposite, on the other side of the railway line and I'd like to know what class of person is going to be living across from me".

She looked slightly taken aback, my tones had not been over-friendly. I continued.

"Are they going to be flats or houses?"

"Oh, houses along the railway line".

The other Green Suit was still discussing £160,000 worth of building with a young middle-class family, which gave me some hope.

"Where are the ne'er-do-wells going?" I enquired.

"Sorry?"

"You know, the vagrants, itinerants, those who do not contribute. The social scroungers, where are they going?"

She looked flustered, but she understood. I had, by now, gained the attention of the other Green Suit and the middle-class family who were quickly being coaxed out into the sunlight. The flustered one continued:

"We are obliged by law to provide 10% social housing. It's over here". She pointed on the model to the south-east corner of the development, already built but now hidden away behind more recent construction.

"Nice names", I pontificated, pointing to the house style list. "Psychological marketing. I don't suppose I'll find any called the Gravesend, the Neasden or the Toxteth".

She didn't seem overly impressed. I then went "into one", the exact words of which I do not remember, but I concentrated my venom towards the destruction of habitat, the ghetto, as opposed to estate, that

I felt was being created and I then enquired as to who exactly it was who decided that the widening of the tunnel in Lakeside Road was no longer required after all.

To be fair, there was absolutely no point in my carrying on like this at all. It just made me feel better. It's the "con" of rural life I dislike so much. For instance, builders rarely develop across from the show house - at least not initially. In this case, that condescending sign I referred to earlier stands testimony to their disregard. Before Guildford Borough Council sold its local ratepayers down the River Blackwater once again, it was *all* a conservation area.

Builders have too much clout and too little respect, but then, as we know to our cost, respect doesn't bring profit..... Timed that just right, Maureen's just called up to me. It's shopping time. Only two Saturdays left before Christmas, and this is the first of them.

"What?" - "Yes, I'm coming".
She doesn't understand. I can't be rude and leave you in the lurch without saying cheerio, you'd have no idea how long I was going to be.

"Yes, yes, I'm ready. Coming." That woman has no patience. Byee.

Can you think of anything worse than a Saturday afternoon spent in Aldershot? Well, there is. Just add rain. D'you remember my going on about the perfectly acceptable, original and genuine Victorian Arcade we had? You do? Good. Well, the one they've replaced it with, at great cost, and a pale plastic imitation to boot, is still virtually empty. Just to recap, the old one had a sandwich shop, a grocer's, pawnbroker's, hairdresser's, toy shop, plus several others, and all independents. What is available since its senseless destruction? I think I'm right in saying that at no time in the intervening years have more than five shops been let at any one time. At present we have shops selling lingerie, football kits, a print shop, key cutters and a hairdresser. It's difficult to find another town that has been so let down by so many councils over so long a period. I'm not going to go on, it's all too depressing. See books 1 and 2 for further details.

Some good news, however, Manchester United could only draw at Spurs. It's a joyous occasion whenever United fail to win. It's funny, but looking back I never thought I could despise a team so much. I've tried analysing why, because years ago they represented everything that was good about Britain. I'm sure many of their overseas army of fans first heard about them due to the Munich disaster and stayed with them, as we did in Britain. United may not have been one's local side but due to that air crash, there is always a place in our heart for them. So what went wrong? The love affair generally carried on through the sixties to the eighties, then another disaster struck. This time it was money. The desire to earn, almost at any price, has cost them a lot of fans. Oh, I know they seat 55,000 plus each week, and could probably fill it ten-fold, but their arrogance has alienated them from those who saw the danger signs, as well as those who despised seeing the gaping, chattering chops of a man chewing gum. Why can't Alex Ferguson shut his mouth when he chews? And why does *"Match of the Day"* insist on showing his tonsils.? While we're on *"M.O.T.D."* why, when they've edited out 60% of the main match, are we still subjected to the sight of players spitting or even worse, ejaculating mucus from their nostrils. As soon as I spot a digit roving nose-wards, I look away. Some producers and editors I assume have a warped sense of the viewable highlights.

Getting back to Man.U., a four letter word (almost) if ever I heard one. The greedy move to change strips for each competition irritated many, as quickly as it filled their coffers. The intimidating motions of Beckham, Schmeichel, Keane, etc. to officials every time a decision goes against them doesn't help.   It's no surprise that Johnsen, Beckham, Butt, Sheringham and both Nevilles have been booked. So what was wrong with Keane? He's normally one of the first. Hang on, G. Neville has been sent off as well. So what's Mr. Ferguson got to say for himself?

Well, nothing actually. An official has just announced that Mr. Ferguson won't be coming into the Press Room. One can only assume that he's slightly miffed.

I do hope that the other cause of resentment doesn't go through. I refer to the planned takeover of Manchester United by that world-dominating organisation "Greedy Media Bastards plc" (or *BskyB* as they prefer to call themselves). It's all money. I have no qualms concerning any sport financing itself but it should be for the benefit of all. While the big six simply take stock of their riches Oxford, Brighton, Portsmouth and Chester, among many others, wonder where the money is going to come from just to pay the bills. With the ever increasing number of imported players, the smaller clubs are less relied upon to nurture today's youngsters into tomorrow's internationals.

Nearly forgot! Manchester United again. This is the team that likes to get around rules by bringing in foreign players who would not have been given work permits for this country. They've now decided to "adopt" Royal Antwerp, the second division Flemish team, in their efforts to side-step regulations. This legal scam comes about because rules in Belgium are more relaxed than here, so Royal Antwerp bring a

17

player from outside the EC, play them for the required minimum period and then transfer them to United. I have no doubt that this practice will soon be copied by others, but once again, it's the Old Trafford outfit which push back the barriers first.

We've got friends coming for dinner tonight. You can always tell we have friends coming, as the toilet paper in the downstairs loo is colour-co-ordinated. No Tesco value white tonight!

Right, there's a lot to do now, like lighting the fire, chilling the wine, turning down the lights - it's all go. Maureen, of course, will be taking it easy. Just cooking, laying the table and putting on her make-up.

Usual mid-day space by the side of the park. It's Tuesday, it's cold and the traffic on the M3 this morning was bloody dreadful. I leave at 7 o'clock in order to get to West London by 8.30. Including the return journey, that's three hours out of my life, every day, and for what? If I could earn enough money from the sale of books I'd give it all up tomorrow - no, now - but it's a catch 22 situation. I need to work to bring in the money that pays the mortgage, so I can't concentrate fully on writing. And I can't afford to take the chance of writing full time until the mortgage is paid. The writing, however, does pay for the replacement white goods, such as the dishwasher, fridge, freezer, etc. - oh yes, and the holidays. But all this full time work will change after Christmas. I'm going part-time with my present contractors and taking on two more contracts (part-time again) which should enable me to have a little more time to write.

At the moment, I am attempting to write two books at once. Good move, actually as when I dry up on a storyline in the novel, I can carry on with this. The novel, incidentally, is entitled "*Remember To Turn Off The Gas*". It's about a group of characters who meet on a tour of America. I've based one or two on people I met a few months ago when researching material in America. I travelled by rail from coast to coast, but more of that later. Indeed, I require an evening without interruption to relate that story. But I will, promise.

I thought it would help with promotion and signing sessions, etc. if I had two books out at the same time. The problem is that I use the pen name for this series and my real name for the novels. Oh, well, I'm sure it will sort itself out. Now, let's tuck into these inviting egg mayonnaise sarnies. A joint effort between Mattesons and Maureen!

Didn't have any trouble with the sandwiches, but the tomatoes have spilled over onto the tie. Oh, sod it, I'll give it a wash later. Now, to the papers and a sight which makes the cockles of the heart glow. There's a story here that confirms what I said years ago, and yes, I do feel a slight sense of preening coming on. There's a report stating that the Commission for Racial Equality is everything I said it was, i.e. "Destructive and dangerous" in its approach to race relations. Apparently, and this is no surprise, much of its £15 million pound budget is spent on securing its very existence rather than resolving racial issues. The report has been written by a black female, one Blondel Cluff. So no trace of white interference thus far. She concludes that there is a "promotion of an aggressive and hostile race relations ethos. Greater encouragement is given to litigation than conciliation" , and that there is an "unwillingness to embrace self-help solutions to problems faced by ethnic minority groups".

Ms. Cluff, a city lawyer, contends that any dissent at meetings of the CRE are met with total disdain by those in charge, while sympathisers are likely to give a pat on the back, but say nothing themselves.

One area of concern she highlights is the fact that young people are encouraged to take legal steps by issuing a "youth card". This is to help them win discriminatory cases. Her most damning comment is that "if you disagree with the CRE they can really become quite thug like". Does all this come as a surprise? No. I still maintain that by disbanding this self-perpetuating group of overseers and taking away its toy, all £15 million pounds of it, race relations in this country would be a lot better served. These people thrive on confrontation. They do not want good relations, only winners, ethnic winners at that.

A nice story, now. I was pleased to see that Diane Blood, the lady whose husband died before giving consent for his sperm to be used, has successfully given birth to a little boy. The lengths that woman had to go to before being allowed to "conceive" was alarming. Here we have a situation where some "ethical commission" comes down against her wishes when logic, common sense and love are all on her side. This at a time when you can clone virtually anything, bugger about with genetics, re-event the guagga and buy and sell babies, but have one yourself, by your own husband's sperm? Not without a fight, apparently. Again, who are these people who have so much power and so little common sense? Did any of us elect them? No, we never do.

I've turned to page 8 of the *Telegraph*. Now this annoys me - another tradition gone. I was somewhat irritated when the Speaker of the House of Commons, Betty Boothroyd, decided not to continue tradition by wearing a wig. If she objected so strongly, she shouldn't have taken the job. Now, that conceited puffed-up apology for a Lord

Chancellor, Lord Irvine, has turned his back on the sartorial elegance of yore by discarding the black breeches, white stockings and black-buckled shoes and gone in for a black court jacket and tails over a pair of trousers and black shoes. Who told him he could change uniform?

Turning back to the cover page, there's a rather nice photo of Hilary Clinton. I have to tell you, I quite fancy that! However, if she rings asking me to engage in an affair, I shall have to politely decline. Much as I find her attractive, you wouldn't want to go where Bill's been, bearing in mind where else Bill has been! Have to say, there's another photograph of her on page 13 and she doesn't look awful there either. Right! That's the yoghurt finished, must get back to work and clean my tie. Oh, before I go. D'you remember John, my mate from Pewsey? Well, he upped sticks and toured the world. Missed out Harpenden, mind you, before settling in a little town in Bohemia, Czech Republic. Maureen and I went over there for four days last year. I'll tell you about that holiday later, as well. It's all right, there's not hordes of photos to wade through. However, John and Hana, his girlfriend, are currently in England and will be staying with us overnight.

Same place, same time, only a day later. Maureen and I slept on sofas last night while John and Hana stayed in our room. Have you not remembered John yet? He was the one I went to Holland with, during that infamous weekend during the eighties. The reason he came over this time with Hana, who runs a small restaurant/B & B (I'll give you the address later) is that he's trying to set up a small travel company. He's bought a 10-seater minibus, taken out one seat for the luggage and now conveys guests on tours of the local sites and towns. He took us when we went across last year. Slight difference, though. He didn't have the minibus. In fact, he didn't have a driving licence either! Drink and drive - and didn't get it back until two months after we'd returned to England. When we arrived at Prague Airport, having not seen each other for some five years, I held aloft a sign stating the "Manns from Surrey". Thought those arriving should redress the balance of signs offered by those waiting. John thought it was funny, anyway. He now offers up his own board as clients appear in Arrivals. His states, "Pink Helmet Tours" or, now that he's put on a bit of weight, "Fat Bastard Travel - A Division of Pink Helmet Tours". All good fun, I say.

You'll like this. Well, Mel Brooks would. Some time ago John was working for a Jewish entrepreneur. He carried out a lot of work for him and there was quite a bit of travel involved. Upshot is, John never got paid. In conversation last night, I asked him if he ever did get his money. "No", replied John wistfully, "but I do feel I got my own back. Some months ago Hana and I visited Auschwitz so I sent him a postcard - Wish you were here'". Forget the down side, that is a closing line and a half, and an extremely funny one as well.

It looks as if the future of yet another brewery is in doubt. Vaux, the famous north-eastern brewer, has decided to turn its back on its founding industry and plump for the lucrative leisure market, focusing on its Swallow Hotel chain. The Vaux name has been around for 161 years. The group are to sell off the brewing side and whoever buys (if anyone buys) the name will fortunately go with it. They are not the first and will definitely not be the last to throw off the manufacturing arm and concentrate on areas of greater profit generated more quickly. Let us hope there is a management buy-out. Ushers, Highgate and Tolly Cobbold Breweries have all been successful examples over the last few years where people who care have put their money where their gullet is and succeeded. Good luck to them, I say.

Hang on, I've just read a tad more in the Quester Column of the *Telegraph Business News*. Swallow Hotels wish to make their hotels more "women friendly", so as to attract the growing proportion of female business travellers, so I'll be looking out for unsmiling strutters in severe suits next time I'm up north. One presumes that there will be male prostitutes and lesbian escorts waiting in the foyers while male guests complain of harassment. Oh, how the tables of society turn. Should be fun, though.

Before I go back to work, I thought I'd tell you why I'm here in the first place. Back in 1992, while I was writing *"As I Was Saying"*, I decided to conclude my car sales business. I sold my last car in November of that year. I had, earlier in the year, received a phone call from my associate in Bracknell - you know, the one who now has the wedding cars. He informed me that a locally based motoring magazine publisher was looking for a part-time merchandiser and asked if I was interested. Well, yes, part time work equalled part time income and allowed me to finish writing in time for a September publication date. The two mornings a week merchandising shortly turned into two days, which in turn rose to four days a week. During December, the company discussed with me the possibility of mounting a "New Car Show" in 1993. The idea was for me to find a site, negotiate fees with the local council and generally set it up and run it. The result was that I organised one show that year in Swindon. Between 1994 and 1997 I was involved in the organisation of a further twenty one shows. We had a good team and a fair number of laughs.

I remained self-employed and took on a couple of other commissions, including working for a puzzle magazine publishing house, and interviewing and selecting security and driving staff for a car auction. One particular aspect of the former job was that I had to visit virtually every holiday camp and caravan site from Hastings to Penzance before turning east, via Newquay and Barnstaple, and finally ending my journey in "Deliverance country", otherwise known as north Somerset.

I was in the middle of arranging this year's shows when, during early February, I was approached by my old boss, Jack, from the late seventies. He had just been appointed MD of a new car superstore in West London. Whilst fully occupied managing his own mini empire, there was still the desire to rise to new challenges. Another colleague from all those years ago was just starting off as a buyer with this new company, so I went up for a chat and came away agreeing to join in two weeks' time.

The motoring magazine publishers were becoming serious about putting me on the books as a full time employee, with company car, pension and all that goes with it. The sticking point, however, was money. To be fair, they accepted that they were not the greatest payers in the world, but working full time meant literally taking a pay cut, compared to my remaining self-employed on an hourly rate. So, given the choice, I decided to work in west London and continue with my self-employed status.

Working here has proved to be more of an adventure and an experience, due to all the internal politics. One's expectations will never be achieved but I've certainly learned a lot and in the months from March, when I started, to July, I actually felt that the company could create quite a niche for itself in the supermarket sector. July proved to be the turning point as far as I, and many others, could see as Jack, our Managing Director, was shown the door. The Directors turned their collective backs on the one person who could make it work. Still, as long as they think they know best.

Perversely, the atmosphere is now far more relaxed, but then so are the standards. Sales staff regularly ask me how Jack is getting on and would I pass on their regards, etc. Despite being a task-master, with little humour during working hours, they would still rather that he was in the driving chair. They knew where they were. You might get a bollocking, but once over and done with, life went on, and you certainly would learn from your mistake. Our ship is currently rudderless, drifting on a sea of indifference, buoyed by the ego of a management who believe that their titles are an indication of their ability. As someone once said, "If you think you're good, you're comparing yourself to the wrong person".

Anyway, just five weeks to go and then it's part-time.

It's Saturday, 19th December, the last week before Christmas, and no, I haven't bought one present yet. All in good time, all in next week!

Supermarkets are much like developers, aren't they? Whenever a decision goes against them, which is rare, they don't just hold up their corporate hands and say "fine", they appeal. The East Riding of Yorkshire Planning Committee have voted 14-5 against the building of a Tesco superstore on the site of a cattle market in the historic town of Beverley. Three hundred people demonstrated against the development during the meeting, shopkeepers fear the demise of their town centre, but Tesco are to appeal to John Prescott. Why are they allowed to? Surely the folks who live in Beverley should decide. Did they not vote in these councillors to make these decisions and should that decision not then be final? Apparently not.

Here's one that's been simmering for a few months. I first read about it last February. Under the heading "Plan to charge for parking at work" the story unfolded of the desire to raise more than £3 billion a year by charging companies who provide car parking for staff and customers. There followed details of proposed costs per space. Also included were supermarkets based in out of town locations. Who are these people who plan to impose charges almost in retrospect of the planning? They were quite happy to grant permission knowing that part of the attraction to the motorist is that they will not incur even greater parking costs, but now they want yet another slice of the motoring cake. The issue went quiet for a few months, but this week I read that ninety five councils are planning to charge for work parking places, whilst another forty authorities wish to introduce road tolls.

I have no doubt that many of these councils are run by Lib-Dems. Their shallow ideology never ceases to amaze me. Do they really expect the money raised to go directly into funding public transport? John Prescott, speaking on the subject, was continually pressed to state that this would be the case, but he could not commit himself to that principle other than "in the short term".

Interestingly, the proposal concerning supermarkets appears to be up for a rethink. I assume it's the old marketing ploy of making public all the bad news, then making it more palatable by deducting one of the more contentious proposals. It then all seems so much more acceptable, while the Government gets what it wanted in the first place.

I was surprised to note that Phil Redmond, creator of *"Brookside"*, has stated that "The lives of the professional classes do not provide interesting television" and that "working class drama is simply a lot more interesting than middle class drama". Is he saying that the inhabitants of the Close are all working class? I would have thought that families who are portrayed were mainly middle class - it's just that they have a regional accent. I think the nub of his distaste is the accent portrayed by the character "Max Farnham", which is distinctly Home Counties South. It's a pity that Phil (still battling for the under classes) Redmond doesn't get his priorities right and do something about his hair (like cutting it). Now I'm not against long hair per se, it suits some, like Laurence Llewelyn Bowen, but not our Scouser. And you could never call me bitchy.

Now here's a story that makes you mad. Here we have a certain Mrs. Halfpenny who starts work with a company in 1988, becomes pregnant in 1994, when working as a regional administrator and quote "linchpin" of its Cheshire office. Linchpin by the way means she's indispensable, which of course nobody ever is. Back to the story. Her pregnancy develops problems, so she takes paid leave from August, 1994, to March, 1995, when she starts her maternity leave. Her baby is born in April and she notifies the company of her intention to return to work in October. Surely long enough for anyone. But no, she has to postpone her return because she is suffering from post-natal depression. I always think of it as a bit like bach-ache - it's never easily identifiable, but you can row the financial boat out for months, or even years.
Now her employers accept that she is legally entitled to extend her maternity leave by four weeks until the end of November. Guess what? She's unable to return even then. So they sack her. She claims unfair and wrongful dismissal, along with sex bias (whatever that means) - have you ever heard of a man claiming post-natal depression? Her case is rejected, but no, she can't leave it there, so off to the appeal court goes Mrs. H. where the judges unanimously allow her appeal on the grounds that she gave her employers notice of her intention to return to work. This notice apparently revived her suspended contract, which was still in force at the end of November, 1995. I'd like to know who paid for this case and the subsequent appeal. I just presume it was us again?
Outside the court, having won the Lottery (sorry, the case!) and

24

£100,000 to boot, Mrs. H. said it was "the best Christmas present I could have", and that it was "a victory for women everywhere". It's certainly a victory for all those who wanted money for nothing. The implications of her winning this case are that the floodgates are apparently wide open for hundreds of other mothers who said "sod it, I'm not going in today" then looked in the mirror and thought, "perhaps I'm suffering from something - headache? No, post-natal depression? No. Lazy-itis - yes, but we'll go to court on a PND charge". Could you imagine women taking a case like this to court years ago. There wouldn't have been the money to finance them for one thing, and for another, they just wouldn't have got away with it.

Footnote to the story, and why I'm not surprised, is that Mrs. Halfpenny (and that is exactly the sum of money I'd have given her if forced to find in her favour) is now in her second year as a law student. She is hoping to specialise in discrimination and employment law. God, or somebody, please save us from these people!

Now, I'm going to be busy for the next week or so, what with Christmas nearly upon us, etc. so I'll bid you good-day and hope that Charlton Athletic get back to winning ways and move off of the 16 points they have accumulated thus far and seem to have been stuck on for ages during their inexorable slide down the greasy Premier pole.

So, have a nice Christmas - or if you're Jewish, Muslim or anything else, have a nice holiday.

It's Monday, 28th December, and I've just returned from taking mum and dad back to their home in Wallington. Normally dad drives down but they've both been suffering from a bad bout of flu and bronchial trouble, so I collected them on Christmas Eve. On Christmas morning I took them both a cup of tea - that's once each, obviously - only to find dad in great pain with his left knee. It was badly swollen. After much thought and a phone call I managed to get him into the car and drove down to the local surgery where a very pleasant doctor prescribed a course of anti-inflammatory tablets that would at least relieve the pain. Home once more and getting close to turkey-eating time Maureen and I drove to Safeways in Southwood and collected his prescription. The outcome was that Christmas dinner was not a success. He and mum sat in the small sitting room, as dad could not move, and with mum still suffering from the effects of flu she was not at all hungry. Maureen, Glyn, William, Debbie, Tim and I sat around the dining table, the meal was disjointed with no Christmas pudding, as Maureen's parents and sister arrived mid-meal. Not their fault, we were late, but I've had better Christmas dinners. I never did get Kylie Minogue in my stocking, although given the choice, I would have preferred her in her own stockings. But never mind, I did get a coach for my model railway.

Talking of railways, I see that the term "driver" is being dropped along with that of "conductor" and "steward". All are to be known as "customer care representatives". Maintenance depots will in future be renamed "train care facilities" It won't, of course, make the trains run on time or give the passenger, as opposed to customer, cleaner windows. In fact, it will help nobody who pays for the service but it will give work to people who really should go out and get a proper job.

Last night Maureen announced that both sinks in the kitchen were blocked. The proceeds from the dishwasher would not flow away. Being a DIY natural (not!) I unscrewed the pewter coloured plastic cap under the sink, having first inserted a bowl underneath. What I didn't take account of was the fairly dramatic pressure that the water created. It went everywhere. Not content with flooding the cupboard, the kitchen floor and everyone's feet, I gamely tipped the bowl into the sink, only to find it ejecting once more into the cupboard and ultimately back over me. What a pillock. Yes, I'd forgotten to screw the cap back on. Giving it up as a bad job I stumbled upon a tin of drain cleaner. Sprinkling the contents down the sink, along with a cup of water (having by now secured the cap) we retired for the night.

This morning, unfortunately, it was no better, so I tried forcing cold water down the sink, only for it to fill up once again. Again the bowl, again the cap removed, but gently. One bowl filled, no wet patches. Blow me if I didnt do exactly the same as I'd done the night before! Down the sink it went, straight back over me. I'm fed up with being wet.

Desperate times call for desperate actions. I eventually managed to break the seal on the U-bend and discovered a blockage of enormous proportions. There was some four inches of congealed fat, well it wasn't mine - I grill the bacon.

The last week or so has provided some interesting reading. It seems that a lesbian campaigner (and as you know, I have nothing against lesbians other than another woman. Sorry about that!) is likely to be honoured for her pains. Ms. Angela Mason apparently led the fight for the equal age of consent for homosexuals. Not surprisingly, previously regaled Ian McKellen, ex EastEnder bender Michael Cashmore and a number of MP's want her to be made a baronness or a CBE. Why?

I have to tell you that I find the whole procedure for handing out awards for people who have just done their job, and often not that well, to be amazingly unfair. Thousands of people work at their job for a pittance, look after elderly parents, the sick, etc. with no recognition throughout their lives, but some woman who champions the proposed lowering of age of consent is apparently fair game for a knighthood or letters. Doesn't make sense. What has she done for conventional relationships?

This 53 year old and her "partner" of 25 years standing are now going to challenge the law of adoption. They "had" a daughter fourteen years ago when Ms. M. was artificially inseminated. By whom? Now seeking the same rights as heterosexuals, i.e. proper people, she insists that under the new human rights laws she and her partner are being discriminated against and that this is a breach of family life. Family life! That's a joke. Look around you, Ms. M. Family life consists of a mummy bear and a daddy bear and little baby bears who have been born because daddy bear and mummy bear spent nights upstairs in bed listening to Chris de Burgh before making teddies. Unlike Ms. M. they did not choose someone's sperm from a bank. Like everything for minorities I've no doubt it's made easy for them. No hospital visits, no doctors' appointments, there's probably a web site: *Les-Sperm.co.@minorityrights.UK*. Still, as long as they're unhappy.

While on the subject, I'm reminded of an article way back in March when midwives had to promise to be more respectful to lesbian mothers. Another sop to the deranged. As I've said, I have no problems with lesbians - if they're good looking I'll willingly pay to see them put on a show. (Sorry, just slipped out, which it probably would, of course. Sorry again). It's just (being serious now) that the two mothers' act is a truly selfish one. I have absolutely no doubt that the child is there for their convenience. Where does it benefit? Children should have one mother, and one father - preferably their own. If not, adopted or foster mums and dads. Here endeth the lesson.

Last week saw the back of meddlesome Mandelson. Wouldn't he make an ideal Nazi - just add a moustache! Also gone is side-kick Geoffrey Robinson. He who said "I merely considered myself someone in a position to help a friend". Bloody good friend! "How much d'you need, old boy?" "Oh, £373,000". "No probs. I'll just get out the petty cash tin. Lucky I've just been to the bank".......

It doesn't matter which political party they are in, they are, with a very few honourable exceptions, in it for their own ends. Some ends more than others! What I find amusing is that Mandelson is being lorded as an honorable cove because he resigned immediately. What tosh! He only resigned because he was found out. It wasn't a coincidence.

There was an interesting little article concerning a teenager sent home by his school for wearing Brylcreem. Staff are concerned that his hair will catch fire. Health & Safety inspectors must be rubbing their hands. Another case worthy of investigation, another waste of public money. The makers of Brylcreem say that their product is not flammable and that it "has been used for years without problems". Well, someone must know. It either is or isn't.

There appears to be a distinct lack of humour at the *BBC*. Around ten members of the religious affairs team decided to celebrate the festive season at a local restaurant in Manchester. Having been offered £100 as an incentive, Abigail Saxon, aged 34, who is a *BBC* producer, got undressed in the ladies' toilet, reappeared in the restaurant and began streaking around the tables, wearing only her socks. After completing two laps of the tables - I mean she ran around them, not sat on them - she gave a final lap of honour, shouting "This one's for free".

Harmless fun, you'd think? No, not a bit of it. Reports raced back even quicker than our streaker to the Reverend Ernest Rea, head of the BBC's religious affairs, who stated that he was "absolutely appalled". Why? Because he wasn't invited? The Beeb are now investigating the matter and will take the "appropriate disciplinary action". What's that? Six of the best with the knickers down? There's a photo of Abigail (hope you don't mind if I call you Abby) and she doesn't look that awful. At 34 it's nice to find someone game enough to show off their body. I sincerely hope she keeps her job and she lets me know the next time she feels the need to express herself in that way. The Reverend Rea must be a humourless soul - in fact, wait for it - a very dire Rea!

Teletext has just announced that Chelsea have held Manchester United to a 0-0 draw. Over the last two years Glyn has become quite a Chelsea fan. This has resulted in the takings of Aldershot's "Fountain" public house increasing, since he likes to down a few pints whilst watching his favourite team on the large Sky screen. I say the "Fountain", it's actually now known as "La Fontaine". Why? On returning home one can tell the result, if not the whole story, by Glyn's facial features and expressions. It seems that in this match Lebeouf was lucky to stay on the pitch. No doubt United's gum chewing, mouth gaping manager will be on about that now. Still, both teams did better than Charlton, who lost *again*. So nil points over the weekend for them.

It's strange how Glyn, who was never really interested in football, has become a passionate supporter of the game - well, Chelsea anyway. When he was a child I took him to see Aldershot and Newport County as often as he wanted to. Well, to be honest, I used to drag him along with me. Reminding him of this recently, he concluded that those early experiences retarded his enthusiasm by twenty years!

William went through a phase of football. He needed a kit but having paid out fortunes for other "must do's" only to see the gear discarded after a couple of months, I'm now a bit more selective about the financial commitment we make.

Coming home from the shops William was eager to wear the new kit that Maureen and I had purchased. He wasn't best pleased with the boots as they were bereft of the all-important Nike tick on them. I tried to fool him by buying "Nicks" instead. "God, these are so sad" was all he said as he looked disdainfully down towards his feet. Worse was to come. He said nothing as he tried on the shorts and top. "Which team wears these colours?" he eventually asked. "Arsenal, Chelsea, Spurs, Liverpool" and so on. I nodded negatively to all suggestions. His shoulders slumped. "It's not a team that's not in the premier, is it?" "Well, what's wrong with that?" I replied, seeking support from Maureen, who was by now displaying the "I told you so" look. As he muttered something about "Everyone else will laugh" I told him that black and gold looked very smart. He gave vent to a few other towns before giving up. "It's Newport County's colours" I joyfully informed offspring No. 3. To say he was less than underwhelmed would be to put it mildly.

The following day, and £60 lighter, he was attired in Manchester United's away strip. William played for a local side for just one season before boredom set in and another "must do" which had affected everyone's evenings and Sunday afternoons came to a close for good. The down side is that he never learned the skills that United players undoubtedly possess. But then, neither did he lambast or intimidate the referee, so some good came of it.

Nursing, in all its forms, is a thankless task these days. I've just read of a crew of paramedics called upon to try and save the life of a dying gipsy. Instead of being able to treat the man, who had suffered a heart attack, they had to retire to the ambulance whilst a group of some thirty fellow itinerants battered the side panels of the vehicle. A passer-by was then attacked, presumably for just being there. The mob made their way to the hospital where the man later died. This poor, deprived ethnic minority was apparently angry over the treatment being given to their compatriot by the paramedics. I'd have thought it should have been they who were complaining about the treatment meted out by the great unwashed and unwanted. The wrong in all this is that these people have a right to complain so strongly and I bet a pound to a penny that they've never contributed in their lives.

Well, I'm back to work tomorrow. Hopefully the traffic shouldn't be too awful. It's 10.35 pm now so I'm going to charge my glass with Glayva, and then to bed. Goodnight.

It's New Year's Eve. I'm writing this as Maureen is watching Angus Deayton take us almost into 1999. All in all, it's not been a bad year, certainly an interesting one. The aim now is to get this book finished by May, then borrow the son-in-law's computer (oh, and the son-in-law, of course). He has one of these super-duper, all-singing, all-dancing modular thingies that spell-checks, paginates and spills out 150,000 words, all correctly aligned onto one disk, which can then be sent to the printers. I then hope to have this in the shops by late September. By going part-time, I'll hopefully be able to resurrect contacts that I haven't spoken to for over a year. That's the problem with working for one company from one location. You can't visit all the WH Smiths, Waterstones , etc. But then, the money from a decent contract does come in handy for those little essentials in life, like survival. As I said earlier - catch 22, or what?

Without seeing a customer face to face for over twelve months, I'm surprised, and not a little delighted, that the first three titles are still being ordered by retail outlets and libraries. I spent four hours one evening last month, just packing copies, either singly or in multiples. The third book, published late in 1995, was my first novel. You may know that I belong to a local railway club. During one of our regular meetings in 1993, I was chatting with a fellow member who suggested that I should "write a book about this place". I chewed over the possibility on the way home. A year and a half later several thousand copies of *"The Club ..... An Everyday Story of Trainspotters"* landed in pallets in the drive. I had previously sent a copy of the front cover and synopsis to the humour buyer at WH Smiths. Fortunately, they seemed reasonably impressed, rang back and ordered 1000 copies "to start with". That gave me 50% of my confidence, as their order paid for 50% of the printing costs!

Incidentally, the first two books took thirteen and fourteen months respectively to break even, *"The Club....."* took nine weeks. No, it has never become a best-seller, and no, I have not yet succeeded in selling the rights to television, although with some help from a well-known television writer I have been very close on two occasions.

You cannot measure the thrill of receiving a call from a bookshop, asking for more copies or being asked to partake in a signing session. Two other spin-offs, from which I derive great pleasure, are giving talks to ladies clubs, writing groups, etc. and being invited onto local radio. I remember my first "chat" was during the launch of *"From Where I Sit"* shortly before Christmas, 1990, on *County Sound Radio*, which is based in Guildford. My heart was in my mouth. I felt desperate to talk and yet full up and slightly sick at the same time. My knuckles were white from where they had virtually clamped the side of the desk. I was always conscious of keeping my head in the position prescribed by the sound engineer. I also sweated like a pig. As I walked outside at the conclusion of the interview, I remembered all the things I should have said, hadn't said, and then concerned myself with all the "um's" that had escaped.

Maureen had taped the interview and there were indeed several "ums". But it got better. Now, I'm glad to say, I get wheeled in, especially on BBC local radio, when they want me to take part in a discussion on a certain subject, or if they have a space to fill and need someone at short notice. You don't get paid, but they do allow you to publicise the books. All good fun, and you get to meet some nice and interesting people.

When *"The Club"* was launched I was invited onto *LBC* and given some 20 minutes to chat to Frank Bough. Very gentlemanly and very professional. It was peak time listening, around 10 a.m on a weekday. I was sandwiched between the late, great Benny Green and Jimmy Greaves. As the only "unknown" it could have been a tad daunting, but I was made very welcome. The same could be said of Austin Mitchell, who howled Basil Brush like at virtually every comment made. That interview was during the early days of publicising the second book, *"As I Was Saying"*.

Right, let's travail the columns of the papers on this last night of the year before Mr. Deayton goes off air and I go off to bed.

Here's a sinister example of how far down the politically maladjusted path we have travelled. The Royal Shakespeare Company have removed all references to religion and all anti-Semitism from a new production of medieval mystery plays. The line "I am a Jew and I want to kill you" is replaced by "I am a member of the religious authorities and frankly, I wish you would go away". Now, you could understand and relate quite easily to the latter line being uttered by Sgt. Wilson to the troops in *"Dad's Army"*, but this re-writer of Shakespeare's work, a chappie called Kemp, states that he is also against anti-Islamic and sexist material as well. So, in an attempt to offend nobody, there is not one mention of Jews, Christians, Muslims, or any other belief. He re-writes history. Now this is dangerous. Changing Shakespeare, Dickens or the bible is no different. It will end in tears.

How petty can you get? A soccer fan aged 47 has had his rattle confiscated by Reading Football Club on the grounds that it is an offensive weapon. Clive Doyle, Reading FC's Safety Officer (now there's a job and a half!) describes it as "quite large" and posing a threat to other supporters. He wouldn't allow the rattle to be returned until the end of the match. It really is quite astonishing. They let in the scum of the earth every Saturday at every ground in the country, but a genuine fan with an elderly rattle is perceived as a threat! I'm surprised Mr. Doyle didn't require counselling for being confronted with such a big one.

I had a quick look at the New Year's Honours List and as you know, I feel this is one tradition that should be ditched. What a farce. Over the years, just over half the 1966 World Cup winning team, which was England, by the way, have been awarded medals. Why not all of the team? After all, it was a team effort.

I enjoy Robert Carlyle's acting as much as anyone but should success in the *"The Full Monty"* and *"Trainspotting"* qualify him for an OBE? Maureen Lipman and - heaven preserve us - Lenny Henry have both been awarded CBE's. I couldn't find any obvious mention of Ms. Mason, remember? From a few pages back! The lesbian. Oh, you do? Fine, fine!.......

Maureen's just pointed to the clock. It's 11.45 pm. I'm locking up. I'll say goodnight to the dog and then to bed. Should be tucked in by 11.58 pm, so Happy New Year and see you tomorrow.

CHAPTER TWO:

NEW YEAR, NEW CURRENCY, OLD HABITS

I've just come back from the paper shop. Glyn has obviously returned from his night out on the New Year tiles as the door was bolted. William's still asleep, he could sleep for England if required. Why are the young always so tired?

I noticed that all the headlines of today's papers are of a similar theme. *The Daily Telegraph* "Wishes for a happy new Euro". Strange, but it doesn't say "Best wishes" or state who they're from. Certainly not me! I remember back in 1989 and later in 1992, when writing the first two books, I asked (of anyone really) "Why do we continue to proceed down this federal highway". I still maintain it will result in chaos. Why have we rolled over? Certainly not to be tickled on our collective undercarriages. The irony is that the Germans have got what they wanted without a bullet fired in anger - or pleasure in their case. The French continue to nuzzle up to the Krauts like a bitch on heat. I don't know why we bothered to save them - should have left them there to rot.

All the soundbites, the clichés, the rhetoric generated by the Europhiles is met with British Government denial that closer integration is a foregone conclusion. Methinks those in the know speak with multi-forked tongue.

I do not understand the long-term logic of our surrendering sovereignty. Do not forget that we are talking about a group of Europeans who will stop at nothing to nullify the power of erstwhile national governments, not just ours. I'm sure this is fine for countries such as Italy, whose government and currency credentials are always a little lacking, but not us, not Great Britain. Japan does not need a club and seems to get by, so why are we intent on signing over our world to those egocentric manipulators who have never been elected by the populations they purport to serve. And that is really the nub, isn't it? We elect an MP to represent a constituency in a British parliament who serves; these European commissioners make rules without reference. The whole show smacks of corruption and a total lack of democracy. Is it really only a minority of us who can see what is staring all in the face?

The only grain of comfort is the thought that what goes round comes round. By that I mean that life is cyclical. There is no such thing as "old fashioned", something is either "in" or "out", but it is never old. Christian names, skirt lengths, holiday destinations, yo-yo's, their popularity ebbs and flows. There will come a day when people demand to take back their national identity and another round of local democracy will ensue, but until then we will have to suffer the indignity of closer ties, more interference with higher taxes and more unnecessary laws emanating from Brussels - bastards!

While I think of it, the phrase "what goes round comes round" is appropriate for another reason. Bear with me, it is appropriate, *really*! You may recall that whilst enjoying a fairly successful period trading cars during the mid-eighties, I was "turned over" by someone I took to be a friend. If you didn't know, you do now! The event took place during the summer of 1986 and I spent the next six years attempting to get this ex-business associate to court. Difficult of course, when he is residing in Spain. Details of these early years can be found in *"From Where I Sit"*. During the period when I was writing the follow-up in 1992, Maureen received a phone call one night from an old acquaintance. He tipped me off that the chap concerned was back in this country. I was at the railway club, involved in a committee meeting. Maureen rang me at the club. I made my excuses and left. I came home and rang back the contact immediately for further details. He informed me that Pat Connolly was back and staying with his daughter, for just four days, Friday to Monday, since she was to be married on the Saturday. She was living - wait for it - only two roads away. I had not seen her for ages, but a trip next morning (Friday) to the local library and a brief glance through the Electoral Roll gave me her address. You have to understand that at this stage we were pretty badly off financially. Between us we had one ageing Mini. I used to take Maureen to work in Farnham and then trundle around, attempting to buy cars (cheap cars!) and do the merchandising for the motoring magazine publisher. All this hassle, whilst trying to finish *"As I Was Saying"*. Anyway, I remember I happened to be remarking on the case when I received the phone call. I was unable to comment any further on the situation, particularly as the case could come to court. Therefore, no further mention was made in book two.

Looking back, the situation was straight out of a Brian Rix farce. Returning home with the daughter's address, I rang Farnborough CID, who throughout the intervening six years had been extremely helpful and supportive. Sod's law dictated that the one morning when I really needed help, nobody I knew was available. A little pleading, well fairly desperate if my memory serves me rightly, provoked the powers that be to take details and make a promise to call me back. They did. "Yes", they said, "we are prepared to arrest him if he is definitely at the address you have given us, but we have to make sure he's there". They asked me if I had checked. I replied that I had not. Did I have a mobile phone? That was a joke, we could barely afford the BT landline. I received my instructions. I was to sit close by the house in question and observe. The police station was short-staffed (no, that's not a joke). Then, if I espied the aforementioned bastard, I was to ring them, keeping them informed of times, movements, etc.

It's at moments like these that you find out who you're friends are. A local garage in Ash, with whom I had previously done a lot of business, offered me the loan of an old banger for the weekend, plus one of the director's mobile phones for the same period. The vehicle was a two-tone (red and rust) R-plated VW Golf, without tax but with a very squeaky door. Remember, it's a 1977 "R" not the 1997 variety. I sat just out of sight, alongside a small piece of green for around 20 minutes before Connolly walked out from the porch and stepped into a car with someone I did not recognise. I slumped in my seat for fear of being spotted. Slowly raising myself after several seconds, I looked in the rear mirror, then remembered that it didn't have one, before turning and looking over my shoulder up the road.

The seeds of doubt were setting in, did I see him? Did I just want to see him? I pulled myself together. Of course it was him. My sticky fingers punched the keypad on the mobile phone. The police said they'd " have a think about it and call me back". They did add one piece of very good news - in between our previous call and this one, they had contacted the Crown Prosecution Service who agreed to the continued support of my case, should it get to court. Whilst I am reliving this part, where I am waiting for the police to call back, I'll explain that the porch was very prominent and I could not see the front door being opened or closed, without making myself too obvious.

I alighted from the car and stood behind an advantageously placed bush that stood on this very small area of grass. Hang on, it's the phone. The police said I was to remain at my post and continue to report in. They said they would not arrest him at the moment as he might "leg it" over a neighbouring garden. I thought they had been watching too much of *The Bill* but it was difficult to argue! They did have one good suggestion and that was that I, or someone, trawl through the list of local churches to find out which was to perform his daughter's wedding ceremony. I sat there all day. A lamp-post stood tall beside me. Attached to it was a notice advising all concerned that this was a Neighbourhood Watch area. It was a hot, May day. A local neighbour, in shorts, tirelessly walked his mower back and forth, up and down his front lawn. Not once did he look at the rusting Golf, which was ultimately to sit there for some 14 hours in total, with me either inside, sitting proud, slumped or standing outside, looking most suspicious behind the aforementioned bush.

When Maureen arrived home from work she rang to ask if I was hungry. "What do they do in "The Bill" when they're doing this surveillance lark and they want a pee?" I enquired. Maureen reminded me that it was only TV and they weren't really on surveillance. I appreciated both her sarcasm and her sandwiches, pork pie and the tomato she brought me. Our cars passed at the top of the road. She surveyed while I went home for a pee. Ten minutes later, sarnies etc. having been exchanged, I was back in position. It was shortly after 7.15 pm. I remember, because Maureen said that as much as she wanted to help, "Coronation Street" was about to start so other than an arrest, I was not to disturb her!

At around 7.40 pm I received a phone call. No, it wasn't the police, it was John, my mate from Pink Helmet Tours. At that time he was still living in Pewsey and had just called in to our house on his way home. Maureen had brought him up to date on the situation, but typically John insisted on "dropping by". We were talking between mobile phones when, in the drooping wing mirror, I caught sight of his light coloured Mercedes.

"I've got a customer for one of these". John was enthusiastic and serious.

"What, a heap of crap like this", I replied.

He was slowly approaching the driver's side of the Golf.

"What's the near side like?" he enquired, as he passed, waving manically.

Bearing in mind the intensity of my situation, this cameo was quite surreal. I started the engine, drove down the road, reversed into someone's drive, thus turning the car around and then drove back to park in the same position but with the nearside now on display to John. He passed me once more.

"That side's even worse!" he muttered.

Slumped in my seat, I responded,

"D'you want it or not?"

"£100", John offered as his Mercedes passed at walking pace.

£175", I replied.

£140, that's my best offer".

The atmosphere was tense.

"£150".

"Oh, all right", said John.

The whingeing sound of resigned acceptance meant that he was on to a good profit. I had, in time-honoured motor trade fashion, previously taken the precaution of asking the garage how much they wanted for it before taking the car on loan. They'd said they would sell the rust bucket for £100. John dropped the £150 off with Maureen, adding that he would visit us the following Monday to pick up the Golf when it had finished its active service, along with the appropriate paperwork.

During the period of porch-watching I spotted Connolly come and go on two occasions before phoning Farnborough Police Station at around 8.30 pm. They suggested I went home and concentrated on the wedding locations. I phoned several churches, posing as a guest who had lost his invitation and knowing only the date. No luck. Maureen and I took the dog for a walk, passing the daughter's house twice, before retiring for the night. The dog was very confused, as once you get to the top of our road we always turn left, along the main road and back round the block. This evening we'd turned right. Muttley kept giving me the "are you sure about this" look. I felt it would take too long to explain the situation and anyway, the loss of our money hadn't really affected her, she still got her eight biscuits every morning and a tin of Pal every night.

The next day, Saturday, I was again outside their house, parked beside the bush by 7 am. This time I was in our green Mini. Within half an hour I was aware that the man in the shorts, who had spent all day mowing his lawn, was out and furtling around in his drive. Within minutes he had commenced picking up grass cuttings left from the previous day's exertions. I kept in contact with the police and waited for events to unfold. Between 10.30 and 11 am a flower shop delivery van arrived. I hid behind the bush. Posies and other creations were extracted from the van's rear before the lady driver left and headed up the road, with me and the Mini in hot pursuit. I flashed her at the junction with the main road. She looked in the mirror and I could see her putting on the hand-brake. I dashed out and ran over to talk to her. I cannot remember exactly what I said, but it was something about being a surprise guest - touch of irony there, I thought. She was very helpful, confirming Connolly's daughter's name but unable to give me the church address.

I rang the police. Now there was to be some action. A detective sergeant and a D.C. were to drive from Farnborough Police Station to close to where I was parked. My instructions on espying their black, unmarked Cavalier, was to move my Mini out of the immediate area and walk "slowly" to the Cavalier and step into one of the rear doors. It seemed an age before they arrived and I now truly felt that we had a chance of having him arrested. It was during this wait that I had a heart-stopping moment, as Connolly himself walked swiftly out of the porch, got into a car and drove out of the drive and passed me (still in the bushes, and somewhat surprised). I leapt into the Mini and took up my binoculars. At this point I quickly learned that it's best to adjust them before commencing this type of covert operation. I hadn't adjusted them and by the time I managed to see through the lens, he'd turned into the main road and gone. I also realised it is always a good idea to take off one's own sunglasses and the lens cap before attempting to use binoculars! "What if he's seen me, what if he's not coming back", I thought .... But he did, and before the police arrived.

The Cavalier flashed as it pulled somewhat short of the house in question. I reversed my Mini into a drive and drove past the policemen, acknowledging them in the process. Having parked up and locked the vehicle I walked "slowly" towards their car. Both the D.S. and the D.C. emerged, asking me to point out the house in question. As I did, they indicated that I should sit out of sight in the back "just in case". With that, the man in the shorts, who by now had spent some four hours in the garden, never having seemingly noticed my continual movements twixt car and bushes, strode across and asked both policemen what they were doing, as they "looked suspicious". The two officers extracted their ID cards before the said neighbour could enquire as to the nature of their visit.

"Just surveillance work, sir, nothing to be concerned about".
The neighbour looked very smug, obviously having convinced himself that something suspicious was going on.

We sat for some half an hour or more, with my being asked to check and re-check photographs of the suspect. I confirmed that they were of Connolly. All of a sudden, wedding cars ambled by, passing us before turning right into the drive. There was much conversation, kissing and shaking of hands, before the entourage slowly made its way towards the main road. The unmarked Cavalier reversed into a side street. I was told to keep my head down and we proceeded within the cortege. Turning right at the top of the road we passed several church options, before turning towards Tongham. The policeman in the passenger seat kept me informed of our movements, as all I could see was the sky. St. Paul's Church, Tongham, was the only one I hadn't contacted. Why not, I cannot answer, I must have just missed it out. Anyway, opposite the church at that time was a BT depot, with a convenient off-street entrance. We parked there and I was allowed to watch father and daughter emerge from the wedding car. The police once again extracted the photographs. Connolly and the bride were asked by the photographer to stand together for the camera. Luckily, that meant with their backs to the church, facing us. I was asked to identify Connolly, which I did. The police seemed happy with my verification. The key turned, the engine started up.

"Where are we going", I enquired.

"Home", replied one of the officers. "You don't think I'm making an arrest and having you two in the back together, do you? We'll drop you off and arrange to arrest him a little later".

Our wait at home seemed like an eternity. The phone call was received shortly after 2 pm, confirming that Connolly was in police custody and that he was "not best pleased". It transpired that the police, having dropped me off where my Mini lay parked, returned and waited by the BT depot until the ceremony was over. They witnessed the photo call, the hugs, the tears, the confetti and the waving away of the bride and groom. Connolly then opened the door of the bridesmaids' car, escorting them to their seats. As he was about to join them a hand clutched his shoulder and an enquiry was made.

"Are you Mr. Connolly, Mr. Pat Connolly?"

His answer was in the affirmative. The D.S. then said,

"Guess who's not going to have their vol-au-vents?"

Now that is straight out of *The Bill*!

Over the proceeding couple of months Connolly appeared several times in Aldershot Magistrates Court where he was given bail. Maureen and I sat a couple of benches behind his family. It was all quite tense. A date was set for my case, along with a number of others that were to be taken into consideration for trial at Winchester Crown Court. The CPS endeavoured to enlist the help of a major car auction which had also been defrauded by Connolly at the same time, but as they had written off the money and considered there was little chance of recovery, were not interested in attending the court. I did ring them myself to see if they would at least appear in order to back up my case, but their interest was less than minimal.

On the day of the trial, I travelled down to Winchester Crown Court in a Fiat Regatta Estate that I had been loaned. The price of the petrol and the car parking was deducted from the month's housekeeping. Connolly was sitting in the corridor with his son. Eye contact was made but no words were exchanged.

Legal eagles on both sides stood sombrely discussing what I took to be the finer points of the case. Of the various charges Connolly was pleading guilty to around half - mine was not one of them. The CPS were, however, so convinced of my case and my suitability as a witness that what happened next struck me like a bolt of lightning. I remember the police, who had been sitting with me, being called into the CPS office. The circuit judge was already there, along with lawyers and other officials. The door closed. Some minutes later all reappeared. The police were glum. I knew instinctively that I was to be the loser. "You're not going to like this", said the D.S. but apparently we have the softest judge on the list today and they're going to do a deal".

It appeared that if the CPS proceeded with the Not Guilty cases, Connolly had been advised to change his guilty pleas to the others to ones of Not Guilty. So to save time, and more importantly money, the other charges were to be dropped and I was not even going to be called. After all the lows - and there had been many, interspersed with a sprinkling of highs - I felt gutted. I watched this legal farce from the confines of the public gallery. I have to tell you I took in very little. The whole of this part of the proceedings was really a blur. How could the system do this to me, I who had lost £45,000? Connolly was sentenced to 240 hours Community Service.

I later walked, along with the police, into the canteen where we sat drinking tea. They attempted to explain the machinations of the law. I didn't understand. I heard what they said, but I took in little. The door opened and Connolly entered with his son. They sat across the room. He avoided eye contact.

Now, I'm back to my old self. Confident, strong willed and potentially stupid. If it were now, and not seven years ago, I would flatten the bastard and to hell with the consequences. But back then, I had never ever felt quite so low. The police half expected me to create a scene but I felt totally devoid of fight and spirit. I remember the son receiving a phone call on his mobile phone, before the two police officers and myself walked out of the cafeteria, out of the building and into a sea of drizzle. Once onto the rain-swept concourse we stopped. Final pleasantries were exchanged. The two policeman, in biscuit-coloured raincoats, collars turned up, and me in a jacket, watched Connolly and his son walk towards a Mercedes, which came and parked close by to whisk them back from whence they came. He didn't look at me as he entered the car. I watched them drive off and thought that within two hours I'd be giving the Regatta back to its rightful owner.

"It's not fair", I uttered dejectedly.

"Life's not fair", replied one of the officers, before adding ruefully, "At the end of it all, it's just a game ...."

We shook hands. I thanked them for their efforts, they shrugged their shoulders. I never saw them or Connolly again.

I did hear that due to a bad back he completed a token number of hours of Community Service before being signed off. He returned to Spain. I heard no more until a chance encounter with a mutual colleague during 1995. She informed me that they had met accidentally and that she could "find out" his new address in England if I so desired. I promised to pop back, but I never did. Just before Christmas, 1997, whilst on business for the motoring magazine publishers, I came face to face with the chap who rang Maureen all of five years previous. "What goes round, comes round". I have to tell you that the last thing I wanted was to discuss Connolly. Such is my bitterness that I still find it hard to talk about the incident without irrational rage consuming all other thoughts. His opening gambit, however, made me curious indeed. He explained that Connolly was racked with constant pain. He couldn't put his finger on the name of the illness, but said it was a slow, crippling one. It was without doubt one of the best Christmas presents I received, and from such an unexpected source.

Starting here at the car superstore in West London last March was the first time I have been so closely involved with "the trade" for years. Dealers and traders popped in to either buy or sell. I attempted ever so hard not to come into contact with any of them, lest they bring up the subject. One trader, we'll call him Tony, started talking about the old times one afternoon and circumstances made it impossible for me to walk away without appearing to be rude. We hadn't met for several years and I dreaded the moment when the inevitable question would arise.

"Didn't you lose a lot of money once to Pat?"

I quickly replied "yes" and hoped the subject was concluded, but life isn't like that.

"Saw him recently", said Tony.

"Please don't tell me he's doing well", I thought. "I really couldn't stand that".

Tony continued.

"Saw him in hospital some little time ago. He's very ill".

"This is good news", I thought. "Two sightings of him in distress".

"Let me know if you see him there again", I asked.

"You going to visit him, then?" Tony's eyebrows furrowed.

"Oh, yes", I replied, "But only to sneer. I want to see that bastard suffering. I'll also be going to his funeral, whenever that is".

Literally spitting on his grave won't account for the money, which with interest, as I said before, totalled some £45,000, but it would help...

I've been keeping some notes on computer and social work speak, which may be of interest. Certainly was to me, but then, I'm the sad sap who enjoys taking train timetables to bed with him.....

The following is a written question and answer situation courtesy of a local council employee.

Secretary Q:

Do you know why the printer puts through blank sheets on every report I do?

Computer Expert A:

Yes, I think so. What you're probably not doing is to bring your .h1, .h2 etc. up from the second page of the report, i.e. when you type the first page, you push the .h1 (header) down when you reach the second page, until it's at the bottom of your typing, but when you've finished typing you should mark a block at the beginning of the .h1 (Ctrl KB) and at the end of .h3 or .h4 (Ctrl KK) then move the .h numbers up to the top of page 2 and press Ctrl KV to move.

In fact, I've noticed that on your reports you get a header and footer on each page. Think we were told to use the header and footer on the first page only and that's why you either make a note of when you get down to the second page so that you don't have to move the .h1 etc. up or take no notice and just move it up when you get to the end of the report.

Well, I hope the above makes sense to all you readers. Oh, don't tell me, you understood every word - I do hate cleverclogs.

The next piece is extracted from a letter sent to me by a major bookseller, whose covering letter required written assurance that I was "Year 2000 comformity acceptable". Having explained (that's a joke) in the first paragraph that problems can arise, resulting in "equipment or products, including embedded control logic failing completely or malfunctioning, causing data to be corrupted", it then sets out three main rules.

Rule 1 includes phrases such as "general integrity", "roll over between all significant time demarcations", and adds that "current date means today's date as known to the equipment or product".

Rule 2 is concerned with "date integrity", "functionality", leading to paragraph 5, which states that "no equipment or product shall use particular date values for special meanings: eg, "99" to signify "no end value" or "end of file" or "OO" to mean "not applicable" or "beginning of file". Rule 3 deals with explicit/implicit century.

I won't go on, but you've got the idea. I registered my acknowledgement and told them that providing WH Smiths can still provide me with an order book and an invoice book in duplicate for around £4 each, I should be Year 2000 compatible well into the next century. I haven't had a reply!

One more from the computer itself. This is what Maureen received on the screen when she pressed the wrong button.

"This application has violated system integrity due to execution of an invalid instruction and will be terminated. Quit all applications, quit Windows, and then restart your computer".
Sor-ry!!

Here's a few extracts from supporting papers, setting out the background for "Community Office Assistant" applicants. The council in question is South Somerset District.

"This is an opportunity for you to act as the public face' of the three partner councils'.

"You would need to be able to operate in a flexible environment' as new ideas are tested ...."

"..... may involve outreach activity ...."

"You have to be able to demonstrate that "you have an ability to empathise with people's problems".

But what does all the above mean? I think it means that the applicant says, "Oh, I know" to everything and then does bugger-all about it. Apparently, the Community Office will give information to individuals who will be known as "friends". You have to "make things happen at a micro level".

"You act as an advocate and problem chaser for individuals lost in bureaucracies, including our own." - yes, it actually says that.

"You have to be an oiler of wheels by assisting groups in the community to develop their own skills and to recognise mutualities of interest". - don't they go on?

"You also co-ordinate significant institutional players, as well as individual movers and shakers".

Anyway, there was more tosh than that extracted, some seven pages in all. If I was an aspiring applicant I think the prospect of unemployment would suddenly take on the option of healthy alternative. What say you?

Now then, as it's New Year's Day I thought I'd highlight a few stories that for me stuck out as "pretty good".

Here goes -

Pretty good sea-going story.

Lt. Commander David Bellingham, or PWO Underpants as he was reportedly known, was fined £2000 and severely reprimanded for having a sexually explicit conversation with a Wren. He was, however, cleared of seven charges of harassment of Wrens under his control (I'm resisting all temptation to add, cheap, tit and shag jokes. Honest!) He was also found not guilty of three charges of touching Wrens and "scandalous conduct". (After watching several episodes of "Oh, Dr. Beeching" I'm surprised this charge isn't more common).

There were four Wrens who made allegations against the above-named chappie. One of them is said to have lost four stone due to the case. But look on the bright side, dear, at least you've saved the fee of a Weight Watcher's course!

Pretty good "there's a surprise" story.

Glenys Kinnock's tax disc was found to be out of date when she was stopped by Wiltshire police. Now this offence is considered by the DVLC to be a serious one, with penalties rising to £1000. It comes as no surprise to read that the Kinnocks' explanation went down well enough with the police for them not to prosecute. They therefore forfeit not one penny of their joint £200,000 per annum income. Good to know that justice is dead and buried. I know it's only a small matter but would you or I got away with it. Did I hear someone say no?

Pretty good execution story.

On 3rd February Karla Fay Tucker, aged 38, was executed in Texas. She was the first woman to be put to death in that state since 1863. Nevertheless, she thanked her lawyers and said she was sorry for killing a woman with a pick-axe in 1983. So that's all right, then. Apparently, there were demonstrations outside of the prison, some chanting for a reprieve, others chanting for the authorities to get on with it. Good job they don't go in for panto in the U.S.A. Can you imagine all the calls from the pro-executionists. "Off with her head", followed by, "Oh, no you can't" from those against, followed by "Oh, yes you can" .... It's when the witnesses to the execution join in with "Behind you" that it starts to get a bit tacky.

On a serious note, I read that the EC stuck its collective Euro snout into the trough by snorting condemnation and appealing for clemency for Ms. Tucker. Can anyone tell me what it has to do with Brussels?

Pretty good non-murder story.

Murder in Brooklyn, New York, took the week off. Not a single killing was reported between 8th and 15th March. That's nice!

Pretty good nostalgia story.

A Mr. King from East London bought a 1951 Ford Anglia (sit up and beg variety) from a scrap dealer for £5 when he was 17 years of age. He then started to court a girl from Barnsley, they travelled everywhere in the car. Finally breaking down on a trip up north, it was consigned to a scrap yard in Barnsley during the early seventies. He and said girlfriend got married and set up home in the aforementioned town, with little thought being given to the Anglia, until last year, when passing that same scrap yard, he noticed a pile of motors had been removed, only to bring to light their old Ford, still sporting radiator grille and bumpers. Mr. King has since repurchased the car for £6, the sum he was paid by the scrap yard all those years ago. He now plans to restore it and present it to his wife as a Silver Wedding anniversary present. I like that!

Pretty good "surprised it was only third" story.

It was announced that Aldershot took third place in the most depressed town in Britain survey. (I prefer to think of it more as a competition, as you have to try pretty damned hard to become this depressing). For the record, Bridgewater, Somerset, was second and Dartford in Kent came top, winning a day out to Sudbury in Suffolk to see how it is done.

Pretty good new accident black spot story.

The Angel of the North was stood on its own two feet during February in an attempt to put Gateshead on the map. By standing for ten minutes it became more successful than its football team did in years. Since then, however, there have been rear-enders galore, as motorists who pass by gawping, fail to keep their eyes on the road. Still, the breakdown services are doing very nicely, thank you!

Pretty good proper politician story.

It was reported that Jack Straw, the Home Secretary, refused to accept special VIP treatment for Blackburn Rovers' away match against West Ham United. Instead, he appeared very content to sit in public seating alongside other visiting supporters. Apparently, it's the same at Blackburn when he's watching home matches. You could assume that he is either being extremely politically correct, transparent, desperately scared of muddying his reputation, etc. or, you could consider him a genuine supporter. For once I go with the latter.

Pretty good "biggest waste of money since the Millennium Dome" story.

This goes to the Lord Chancellor - or Lord Irvine, whichever you prefer. How the man had the gall to attempt to defend his shelling out £60,000 of tax-payers' money on wallpaper and associated bibs and bobs when refurbishing his official residence defies logic. When you think that that money could have been used to insulate pensioners' houses, or plant trees, or treat Lord Longford to a lobotomy - a million and one things really, but there, much better it goes to someone who's already loaded.

Pretty good lingering death story.

After building 2.2 million of them, Rover (sorry, BMW) have dropped the Metro. 1980-1998. How on earth did it last for so long?

Pretty good titbit story.

An American couple paid £17,300 for a small piece of wedding cake at an auction of royal memorabilia. The cake in question was that of the Duke and Duchess of Windsor - or if you prefer, our ex-king and that dreadful American woman.

Pretty good most-surprising advert.

On Saturday, 21st February, 1998, there ran a full page ad in the *Daily Express*, offering six CD's or four extended length cassettes. Special price only £19.99. "Of whom?" I hear you ask. The Cliff Adams Singers and the Jack Emblow Quartet. "Sing Something Simple!" Did *you* know it's still going. Every Sunday, late afternoon, for over thirty five years. I couldn't stand them when I was a teenager, I can't stand them now. They have the uncanny knack of making every song they sing sound like ....well, the last one, and the one before, and the one that's coming next. Half the ad is devoted to listing each title under various headings. There's "Sing Something Unforgettable", followed by "Sing Something Sing-a-long" which immediately reminds one of Max Bygraves. Then you come to "Sing Something Romantic", fifties, forties, sentimental, before ending up with "Sing Something Golden Showcase". I think "Sing Something Forgettable" would have been more appropriate. There's a picture of the singers and the quartet. I have to say some of them look young enough to still be breathing - thirty five years - bloody incredible!

Pretty good non-story.

This goes to the *Wales on Sunday's* report by Jason Lamport about a lady who resides in the border town of Ross-on-Wye. Her name is Diana Spencer. She says that in 1981 when Prince Charles and the better known Diana Spencer announced their engagement, the Ross-on-Wye Di became the toast of the town. Neighbours curtsied and colleagues referred to her as Lady Di. She says she enjoyed the attention and played up to the "hordes of teasing royalists" (sounds a rather sad life so far).

Anyway, things are different these days. Ross-on-Wye Di now tries to keep her name a secret. She states that "the moment she died, the joy went out of my famous name. People thought I was either taking the mickey or looked at me as if they wanted me dead". (Slight insecurity problem?) For some inexplicable reason, she began wondering why she wasn't killed instead of the other Di. Well, she wasn't travelling by car through a tunnel in Paris, that's why! She says she felt guilty that she had the same name but was still alive!! She goes on (and on) "Strangers had their barriers up as soon as they heard my name. Conversations stopped and people turned their backs on me". She now just introduces herself as Diana and ends the article with the peculiar comment, "Sometimes I feel it would have been easier if this Diana Spencer had died instead of the other one". The woman's either a tad paranoid or she has some funny friends. She's 51 years old apparently, so it could be the change of life. If so, I advise her to get a new one!

There's no title for a piece so sad as the following, but I felt compelled to re-tell it. In March, a retired chap of sixty found himself answering the door to the police for the third time in his life. The first was in 1978 when the police arrived to tell him that his 11 year old son had been knocked down and killed as he crossed the A1 road near his village. A year and a day later, the police called for a second time. This time their other son, aged 17, had died in a road accident whilst riding his bike. The third visit was to inform him that his wife had been killed in a head-on collision ...... Wife, both children, family gone. So where was his God?

There was a small article in the *Telegraph* last week that brought a smile to my face - an ironic smile, you understand, not a gut-wrenching side-splitter - just so long as you get the picture. Apparently, the poor and out of work in South Africa are blaming immigrants for their situation. They want to curb the influx of job-seekers from neighbouring African states. Police say that "illegals" make an impact on the crime rate because they are unable to find work and then they turn to crime. Hawkers and street pedlars have come under attack from the native population. Doubtless white do-gooders would put the actions within the volatile fledgling state down to its white imperialist past, the white man's current influence, white business owners paying low rates for immigrants, etc. Could you imagine attacks like that happening here? More legislation, more rights, more power and a whopping increase in the budget for the CRE.

Maureen's standing at the office door. She's holding a small piece of paper. "What's that? It came with the ironing board?" Maureen has successfully opened the new ironing board purchased from our joint account, but to be used exclusively by her. Isn't it nice to know that there are still jobs they can do which men wish not to interfere with ....Washing up is another!

Anyway, like most women she did not find it difficult to open, adjust and find the correct height, or seek out at which end the iron sits. This example comes with a note illustrating a woman holding a half-opened ironing board. The note reads " To open. 1. Stand the board vertically - nose nearest the floor. 2. Hold the top foot with the left hand, squeezing the height adjustment level with the right hand whilst opening the board. 3. Once fully opened, lower to the required height whilst squeezing the adjustment lever. To close. Grip the board firmly in the centre. Squeeze the height adjustment level and lower to the ground.

And if you couldn't follow all that and you didn't have the nous to open without instructions, it then goes on to give you a help line telephone number in case of difficulties. Unbelievable.

I remember an article some little time ago that highlighted examples of the way in which manufacturers treat their purchasers as complete and utter tossers. Is it that they think the majority of us are generally in need of such assistance and advice, or are they scared to extinction that someone will sue unless they convey the obvious?

For instance, Rowenta, makers of electric irons, warn "Do not iron clothes on body".

Another - Marks and Sparks warns purchasers of its bread and butter pudding, "Take care - product will be hot after heating" - really!

Sainsbury's peanuts' packet label advises anyone who didn't know that they contain nuts.

There is a camera on sale where the instructions advise that it will only work when there is a film inside.

Another one? Okay. There is a chainsaw on sale with the timely warning, "Do not stop it with your hands".

I'll finish with one from America, because this really takes the biscuit, or in their case the cookie. Some American car rear view mirrors carry a warning label explaining that "the image you see is actually behind you". Can you believe it? I have to say I would not - until I visited America, and yes, I would now.

Here's a heart-warming story.

Wilkin and Sons, the jam makers from Tiptree in Essex, are setting up an employees' trust fund in a bid to keep the big conglomerates from mounting any takeover bids and we all know what happens then. The small independent gets closed down, the good guys and gals lose their jobs, a more efficient, cheaper product with greater profit but less taste goes on sale in its stead. But back to the story. Peter Wilkin is the fourth generation of his family to head the company. He apparently has no direct heirs, and although he is not contemplating retirement the "Employee Benefit Trust" has purchased slightly more than 50% of the company's shares.

Unusually, and very pleasant to read, Mr. Wilkin describes the company's success as being down to the workers who are his most valuable asset. Many of the staff's forefathers and mothers have worked for the Wilkins. The company owns some 1000 acres of farmland, of which half is used for fruit growing. Sixty six houses, built by the firm's founder for the workers and their families, are still in company ownership. It shows that occasionally, just occasionally, one's faith in people can be restored. So remember, Wilkins of Tiptrees jams next time you shop in Safeway, Sainsbury's, Tesco's....... Frankly, we love em.

You know what I said about MBE's, CBE's etc. Well, here we have two examples of what I mean in this week's local paper. A nurse at Frimley Park Hospital has been made an MBE. She has worked there for eleven years. So? A lollipop lady of twenty five years standing - and she has done some standing - has also been awarded the MBE. Again, so? Or why? I have nothing against either lady and I'm sure they've given great service with a smile, stretching all those years. But then so have many others.

They both got paid for their jobs, didn't they? You might as well give an award to anyone who does their job properly. It all sounds so hit and miss. And for what? The really sad thing is that they all seem so flushed with gratitude. Oh, well.

Hugh Walton, in the *Daily Telegraph*, reviewing last night's television, informed his readers that Dame Thora Hird performed her maiden appearance the same year as the Titanic performed its disappearing act. (Not his words, but the point was made). In "Lost for Words" where she played Deric Longden's mother, her acting was on another plain. Pete Postlethwaite played Deric. If you didn't watch it, do so when it's repeated. I doubt you'll find a more brilliantly acted, funny, yet dramatic piece all year. Mr. Walton describes it in much better terms than I possibly could. A whole column, in fact, but I echo his sentiments entirely. It was brilliant.

There is still no conclusion to the proposed takeover by Wolverhampton and Dudley Breweries for Marston, Thompson and Evershed, other than the latter have now made a counter-takeover for the former. Why can't they just leave each other alone and allow the customer to continue purchasing their extremely good ales.

We've just received another letter from William's school. They are seeking our consent to keep him in for something or other. I told them when he moved to this school that they had our permission to flog him within an inch of his life, but no, they just want to keep him in. There were no letters, no partnerships with parents when I was young. They just got on with it. Walloped you, kept you in to write a thousand lines. It was all so simple. The parents didn't sue for the child's trauma either - or their own, come to think of it.

William actually left his last school at the age of 14 and transferred to his present seat of learning (I jest) but it's not all the fault of the teachers. The headmaster of his previous school talked a good school, when we sat alongside other parents at the Open Evening. We felt it would be good for William at the age of eleven. However, discipline was sadly lacking, while bullying went on unpunished. Any mention of this to the school was met with a strong denial. Apparently it just didn't happen and that to us was the worst aspect.

William became very unhappy. The company that ran the school bus service actually declined to renew their contract due to the continued vandalism of the bus. Seat belts torn, seats slashed, objects thrown - you've got the picture. One day the driver returned to the school, complete with children, because he'd just had enough. We complained loudly one time when William was burnt by a cigarette thrust on his hand by some thug. We got nowhere. So we moved him to his present school. His behaviour is certainly better, but, well put it this way, his brother and sister were definitely easier to manage.

Five years ago, during my holiday camp trips for the puzzle magazine publishers, I had occasion to stay overnight in Minehead. The guest house in question was one I had stayed at on two previous occasions. Not having had a holiday, or even a weekend away for three years, this weekend seemed like the perfect getaway for Maureen and William to join me. At that time we were still working our collective socks off to repay the bank. It was, in fact, some time during 1995 that we celebrated the lowering of our overdraft with the Midland Bank to under £10,000. I received a statement which read "OD £9998.86. We were elated. You've got the picture, life was still far from easy, but the light at the end of the tunnel was beginning to shine somewhat brighter.

Having arrived in Minehead on the coldest and wettest May day in years, I introduced Maureen and William to the B & B's owner. He pointed upstairs to the family room I had agreed to take for two nights on my last visit. As we turned on the stair landing and the owner was about to enter his private rooms downstairs, William espied the thermostat and exclaimed, "*They* have their heating turned up high". I saw the landlord stop in his stride. Maureen then added, "18 degrees, we don't have it that hot, even in the winter". Thank you for your support, I thought.

Later that day we had tea in a small, pleasant restaurant where one pays at the counter, having first consumed the meal. William followed me. I asked for the bill which was issued forthwith and I commenced writing the cheque. "How much was it", enquired William. "It doesn't matter", I replied, giving him the look that says "shut up". "Have we been conned?" he persisted. "You enjoyed it, didn't you?" I barked. He nodded, still moving awkwardly and placing his hands all over the counter. With cheque checked and bank card returned I asked for a receipt. "D'you need that in case one of us is ill and you need to sue?" he exclaimed loudly. The little git was only eleven - love im!

Talking of schools, which at one point we were, I see that teachers are likely to be issued with radios "in case of attack". This suggestion follows in the wake of Philip Lawrence, the headmaster (I so hate the word head teacher) who died over two years ago. According to a survey conducted by the Suzy Lamplugh Trust, one in ten schoolchildren carry weapons. The government (it matters not which political colour) as usual come lumbering behind with their latest aid for teacher welfare. In just under four months' time, teachers will be able to use "reasonable force" to restrain pupils in certain circumstances. Advice on how and when will be issued later! Smacks of stable doors, bolts and little bastards to me.

The teaching "profession" - I'll pause while you titter - have shot themselves many times in their collective feet over the past two decades. They wanted no responsibility for their charges before school, lunch times or after school. They actively supported the decline of the school uniform, citing that most pathetic of arguments that parents could not afford them. When I was at school, parents of the children at Spencer Park Secondary Modern on Wandsworth Common managed to afford it, out of much lower wages than those taken home today. Also there was no supplementary benefit paid out to the social scroungers, the self-unemployed and other witless characters who buy designer trainers, clothes and caps (worn backwards). These are the very people who can afford the uniforms, not those who work, pay taxes, council rates and mortgages. They generally tend to struggle.

Basically, teachers relinquished all responsibility and with it all respect. And now that their misguided actions have rebounded on them, they don't like it.

I recall an article concerning the fiftieth anniversary of a school headmaster. His name is Normal Hale and he runs Milbourne Lodge in Esher. He became owner and head in 1948 and has stuck to the same curriculum ever since. Latin is taught from the age of 8, Greek for the top set at 10. It is a mixed school, with low fees and high attainments. Mr. Hale comments that they do not use their computers for learning and that they do not go in for that "craft, design and technology nonsense". Good man, good results. I agree that these fringe activities are a sop to youthful attention and a diversion from subjects with substance. The requirement now is purely to attain good exam results. Remember, as the achievements rise every year, the ability to speak properly falls in relationship.

Only last year the Schools Minister, Stephen Byers, announced targets for improvements in English. The "buzz" phrase is "teach reading traditionally". All local authorities must strive to achieve their new targets. I suspect far below what we had in the sixties. But, still! The only exception - now here's a surprise - is where English is not used as a first language. So you come to this country, you cannot be bothered to learn the native language, and frankly, why bother, when you have local government notices and welcoming signs in the town halls that are in every language known to Mohammed. Even Southall Railway Station is in sub-titles. Your rent's paid for you by those who work, Social Security treats you like royalty - well, it has to or they're taken to the CRE as another test case. There really is little incentive to integrate and educate.

The following sums up the insecurity, the guilt and the lack of vision that this country suffers from. A new school is opening up in Milton Keynes. The school governors voted for it to be called "Walton High". Labour and Lib-Dems on Bucks Council state that the name sounds too much like a grammar school and wish it to be named "The Walnut Tree Secondary School". Heaven forbid that a school should appear to display its values within its title. Typical Labour, the "everything's too good for me" mentality, and typical of the wishy-washy Lib-Dems who ebb and flow with every tide. The only certainty with the latter is that they spend council tax income like its going out of fashion and given a quarter of a chance, they would sell Britain to Brussels at the stroke of a pen. Yellow certainly is an appropriate colour for their party.

Perhaps all teachers are Lib-Dems. There are some disturbing stories regarding bullying that back up our own experience regarding teachers and headmasters not wishing to know in case their school gets a bad name. The church and abuse, schools and bullying - similar lack of courage, isn't there?

It appears that at least two hundred families per month take their children out of school because of bullying. Over fifty thousand children are now taught outside of our national schools system. This is a disgrace. You can have all the reports, the surveys, the committees, the recommendations, they'll all nod their heads and agree, but until we return to the days when discipline was seen to be fair, respect for teachers was the norm and parents never considered suing because little Johnny had had his nose tweaked (thus infringing on his human rights) we are basically on a highway to anarchy. There are no lay-by's, no side roads, no short cuts. It needs a commitment from government, unlike any commitment they've ever made before, because if they do not alter the attitude of these thugs and vandals, society as we knew it is finished.

Just as I finished the above, I took a look at the *Daily Mail* dated yesterday, 5th January, and read an article about an 8 year old girl found hanging from her skipping rope after being bullied at school. Her father died when she was 5 and the girl had suffered bullying and hurtful words ever since. Indeed, the school in Salford has confirmed that during the previous term two incidents of bullying were brought to the school's attention by the girl's mother. You cannot begin to imagine the pain and suffering that causes one so young to take her own life.

Oh to be a Roman Catholic priest in Beijing's prisons. The Chinese authorities have denied accusations by the Vatican that priests are being "tortured". Now there's torture and there's pleasure and sometimes the two are as intrinsically linked as cops and robbers - you know, never knowing which is which. This accusation centres around apparent attempts to force "illegal" Catholics, loyal to the Pope, to break their vows of chastity, enabling them to join the Chinese Patriotic Catholic Association.

Some priest, with an unpronounceable name, sorely lacking in the humour stakes, comments that he was forced to endure "sexual torture with a prostitute". The object of the exercise was to destroy his morality by making him break his vows. So being forced to have sex is a problem? Providing the prozzy, as I suspect they say in *"Brookside"*, issued him with a condom, I don't see a problem! Christ Almighty - to name just one of their heroes, it wasn't long ago a red hot poker was used in the name of decency and cleansing. Then you could have agreed that he had something to whinge about. As I said about priests earlier, some people make problems.

What's that? You're having your tea soon. Well, that's fine with me. I'm going to catch up with some shut-eye for a while, then when you're back, I'll tell you a joke..... No, you'll have to wait, your tea's getting cold.....

Right, I'll begin. Oh, if at any time you say to yourself "heard it", move on.

We move across the pond to the USA where native tribes roamed the land in freedom, buffalo abounded and no-one had ever considered inventing the Austin Allegro. Anyway, there are these plains Indians who are hungry, thirsty and desperate. The squaws are whining, the children screaming, the dogs scratching and dying. It is not a happy place.

"What are we going to do?" asks everyone of the Chief.
He looks around him, the ground is dry, there has been no rain for weeks. Another dog drops. He beckons over his medicine man.

"You're going to have to pull something out of the fire. It's getting pretty desperate".

(He says "you're going to" as opposed to "you're gonna" because it's awfully American and they haven't arrived in any great numbers yet!) The medicine man thinks.

"I know", he replies, "I'll go into one of my trances".

So off into a trance he goes, dancing around in a circle, "Hey-a-way-a, hey-a-wey-a", arms akimbo. A crowd establishes itself around him. They are excited. Some, however, merely raise their eyebrows as they've seen it all before. His record isn't wonderful. Out of the trance he comes, bright eyed and bushy of metaphorical tail. He points,

"Over the hill, into the next valley is a bacon tree that will feed all of us".

They all jump for joy, women hug men, children hug each other, while the stepfather at No. 22 with the rather funny family hugs the pet moose ....Anyway, off they go over the hill and into the next valle y. They stand and look around. There is absolutely bugger all there. It's as deserted as the one they left and they've spent an age getting there. In fact, they've spent the same amount of time it takes getting from Heston Services to the Hanger Lane gyratory system during rush hour. Sloping shoulders, crest-fallen crests, they look a miserable bunch. The Chief looks at his medicine man.

"All right, I'll go and have another trance".

"You do that", says the Chief.

55

So he ups pick-axe, or whatever Johnny native calls it, and with a "hey-a-way-a, hey-a-way-a", round and round he jaunts upon the scorched earth. Out of the trance he comes.

"I've got it", he shouts at last. "It wasn't this one, it's the next valley".

"Are you sure?" queries the Chief.

"Honest Injun", the medicine man replies. (His jokes aren't very good either).

So off they trudge towards the rim of the next hill, someone swears they can hear the theme music to the "Big Country". Once again, the square root of bugger all. In fact a square root would have been an improvement. They stare at the barren landscape, broken only by the skeletal remains of animals amid bleached stumps.

"So where's your bacon tree?", asks the Chief.

"I don't know", replies the medicine man, as he wipes his hand across his face in desperation. "It was there in both visions.
He slumps to his knees. (Pretty powerful stuff this). When suddenly a bugle is heard in the distance. Der-der-der-der-der-der-der-der-der-der-der-der-der (you go up a note when you get to the bold type). Try it again. Just wait a second. Right, you've got it now? Good. A dust bowl descends upon them and they are surrounded by the boys in blue. The Unionists fire their guns. They take no prisoners and they bugger off. Now that's what's meant by ethnic cleansing! Dogs are dead, children are dead, squaws are dead and all the braves are dead. Only two are left, barely alive. The Chief and the medicine man. Each clutch their chests, only feet apart, as they stifle their pain, for they are proud and brave chappies. The Chief turns his head to the right and asks, "So where was this ere bacon tree, because you've really ballsed up this time". The medicine man turns his head to the left and refusing to do any gags about medicine balls says, "I was so close". "Close" comes the incredulous reply. "Close, we're all bloody dead. How close is that?"

"Well, it wasn't a bacon tree I saw in my vision. (*Wait for it*). IT WAS AN AMBUSH"!

I'll just wait for the guffawing to die down. No, you can't reprise a joke, however good it is.

I bring the following up at this point for no other reason than I'm in that kind of mood. In last year's edition of "*Who's Who*", a chap by the name of George Salmond, a professor of molecular microbiology, listed among his past-times, "the daily avoidance of assorted professional

56

beggars, alcoholics and deranged individuals in the streets of Cambridge". Now whilst you and I would see nothing surprising about this, the poor and the homeless have taken exception to his comments. You know, in the same way as you and I take exception to the poor and the homeless. Now there's a charity called "Winter Comfort", which doshes out food for those without homes. Ruth Wyner, its director, considered it surprising that "*Who's Who*" can print things like that, adding "It is ghastly and does not sound like the comment of an intelligent person". It sounds ghastly to me that someone who is as educated as Ms. Wyner could waste so much of her own time on people who rarely help themselves. Take away their benefit, fags and alcohol and they'd soon find jobs. Final word goes to an ex-inmate called Barry, who said that "the professor has got money and he thinks he can say these things. If he fell on hard times like me, he would not talk that way". I suspect that if the Hon. Prof. fell on hard times he'd get on his bike and look for work. After all, there are a number of bikes in Cambridge. Come to think of it, there's a number of bikes in Aldershot, but then they've got two legs, usually parted!!

By the by, I've just received through the post two tickets for Sunday week's game between Charlton Athletic and Newcastle United. Glyn's coming to see the match with me. It's been some thirty five years since I last visited The Valley but Charlton's results are generally one of the first I look for, along with Cardiff, Swansea, Wrexham, Merthyr Tydfil, Newport and Aldershot. I also take a special note of Crewe and Brechin City, but then these are the ramblings of a very sad person, I know, but backing the underdog comes naturally to the true Brit. Not for me the sheep-like devotion to "bought success", no, for me it's has-beens, losers and want-to-be's. Anyway, I do hope Charlton stay up. If only their team survive the first year's promotion, then there should be hope of a more permanent place in the Premier.

I generally tend to take an interest in a club whose managers are not endowed with a bottomless money pit and who come across as genuine people. One of the reasons why I have re-warmed to Charlton. Alan Curbishley, Dario Grady, John Rudge (late of Port Vale), Martin O'Neill of Leicester, appear to be examples of good, honest people, trying to do an often thankless task when faced with the cheque-book mentality of the Manchester United's of this world. I cite them and not their rich compatriots, purely out of the need to feel vindictive.

Still on football, I read with interest that *BskyB* are to launch a "pub and club only" football service. They are considering offering half-time films to keep drinkers watching instead of buying drinks or chatting. I can see the brewing industry taking kindly to the idea of not buying drinks.

I can honestly say, hand on heart, that I have yet to visit a public house for the purpose of watching a football match. To be fair, they very rarely show Newport County and I have not had satellite installed either. Frankly, I prefer to listen to *Radio 5* than contribute towards that antipodean's coffers. Mind you, quite how long the *BBC* are going to be able to retain live football is questionable, now that commercial radio stations have jumped on the band wagon. It's bad enough with all the adverts, but the hype, the over-stated excitement - it's an insult to my intelligence. I don't need anyone "selling" a match to me, I want an unbiased, informed report, not a vehicle with which to promote their own egos. What's that? You could say the same about me and this book? Go away and buy me a pint - straight glass, please!

Nice photo and story in today's *Express*. There's a chap called Ernest Goode who bought a Vauxhall 10 in 1938 and is still driving it. The car cost £172 new and apparently was one of the country's most advanced vehicles at the time. It has a 10 hp engine and a top speed of 60 mph. Mr. Goode has clocked up over 133,000 miles. It was of interest to note that in the sixty years that the car has been on the road, Mr. Goode has been let down only twice - once in 1948 and again five years ago, when the top hose went. Not exactly a major problem. Mr. Goode is hoping to keep his beloved Vauxhall on the road until 2003, the company's one hundredth anniversary year, when he intends donating the car to the Science Museum.

Compare the 10 hp above to the announcement that Aston Martin's new limited edition DB7 has 335 of our four-legged friends. Interestingly, the article describes "exploiting Austins (sic) full 335 horse power engine". Obviously the writer is still subconsciously hankering after a GT Allegro! This DB7, incidentally, will be limited to one hundred examples and will incorporate such goodies as an ebony cigar humidor, silver plated Dunhill cigar cutters (non-smokers may request a grooming kit instead) and matching Dunhill pens. Even the hub caps are in the shape of a Dunhill watch case. So, at £97,500 for the convertible, it's a close run thing, but I think the mortgage repayments are going to be the biggest expense we have this month!

Now then, what have we here? That wonderfully august body the EC have been accused of deliberately covering up examples of fraud and financial irregularities. It amuses me the way newspapers announce that it involves vast sums of taxpayers' money. Where else would it come from? This has all come to light due to a senior EC auditor sending copies of his findings to Euro MP's. This rare and fine upholder of the truth is now suspended for four months (that's longer than Roy Keane, Dennis Wise or Eric Cantona have ever had to serve) and is put on half-wages. Many of the allegations concern some woman called Edith Cresson, who regales under the title of Science, Research and Education Commissioner.

Not surprisingly, Jacques Santer, that poor misguided Euro-fool, is vigorously defending the commission - well, it is his baby. Six commissioners have been named. The French Cresson woman, plus a Finn, Italian, Swede, Spaniard and a Greek. Pity, there should always be a German in the line-up and by Christ, do those Germans know about line-ups (against the wall and be shot type) - do I have to spell it out?

Poor Mr. S. He concedes that there has been management problems but "to question the Commission's work as a whole is intolerable". Why? Is no-one allowed to question these people? Are they above investigation? I suspect they are not but will make it bloody hard for anyone to try. These unelected clones would be unemployable outside of their cosy, club-like world. No wonder they cling on so dearly, the salary, perks, pensions, expenses. They must laugh at the populace over whose lives they control and whose money they spend - bastards!

And just to illustrate another example of the Euro snout being poked once more into matters that do not concern it, I give you the following.

No longer can you travel from Leeds to Holmfirth on route 484 directly, as the journey is just over 30 miles long. What's that got to do with the price of eggs, I hear you ask. Well, I shall elucidate. A new Euro law states that all drivers on routes longer than 30 miles must work shorter hours and have longer breaks.

Seventy-two year old Lilian Brunton, who has ridden the route directly for thirteen years, must now (wait for it) alight from the bus, now route 482, at Wakefield, which is half-way along the run, and then get back on the bus again after the driver has changed the route number to the old 484. It's apparently okay for the same bus to be used by the same driver, providing it stops on one route number and starts on another. That is the only way they can get round the regulations. To add insult to the tedium of getting off and back on again, Mrs. Brunton also has to pay twice as they are considered two separate journeys for payment purposes, thus doubling her fare. And there's bugger all she, or anyone else, can do about it.

Examples of the stupidity these people display is all around us. There is no incentive for children to be responsible and independent. It is now illegal for youngsters to help milkman to deliver milk. This law has been passed on the dubious grounds of safety. This has nothing to do with safety and everything to do with control.

The case in question concerns a young lad who has been helping the same milkman in Barnsley for four years since he was ten. The milkman received a letter from Barnsley Council warning him to stop using young helpers or face a fine of up to £1000. Under the European Directive 94/33, councils are instructed to amend their laws, making it illegal for children to deliver milk. The milkman's wife said the letter made them feel like criminals. The lad's dad said his boy loved the job, but no, another avenue of personal freedom has gone. As for the sheep-like Barnsley Council, their spokesman stated, "We are simply carrying out an EC directive". Doesn't sound as if he comes from Yorkshire, does he? Whatever happened to all that northern guile, guts and grit?

We'll stay with Europe for a while. One of the reviewers for either *"From Where I Sit"* or *"As I Was Saying"* considered off-handedly that I was xenophobic. It is all very simplistic and easy to off-load a description of someone' views in one clichéd word, but like all opinions, you don't arrive at them for no good reason. I resent more than anything the power of those that have never been elected. It goes against all the basic, democratic principles that apply to the western world. MEP's may be elected but they are merely drones. The real queen bees are in the shape of that Cresson woman - that's the *French* Cresson woman. I've seen a photograph of her. You'd trust Arthur Daley more than her. She looks such a humourless soul n all. Can't imagine her telling the one about the Kraut, the Iti and the Frog!

Take UK beef. Banned from Europe and to be fair, if its quality is questionable, then fine, but one reads reports of BSE in European cattle. Are they just better at covering up than we are? I have a feeling that the British are more cynical, more questioning of what we are told than those on the Continent and certainly more so than the American public, who believe in Uncle Sam and apple pie unerringly. Anyway, take beef. We are allowed to send it to the Channel Islands, the Isle of Man, Canvey Island, but not the Falklands. Although it is a dependency, it is apparently not that dependent. So for all the killing and fighting that went on to retain its status as "British", £2,400 worth of prime steaks and sirloin had to find another market and the intended destination, Shorty's Diner, in Stanley, had to seek out alternative supplies in Brazil and Guatemala.

While I'm in the mood to let vent, I recall the EC aiming to do some good by phasing out driftnets over one and half miles long by the end of 1994. Now in this instance, the British were not whiter than white (oops - smacks of a racist overtone there - wash my mouth out). In fact, it was down to the donkey-baiting, monkey-torturing, bull-fighting Spanish to cut British and French driftnets during the mid-nineties. They used techniques which catch fewer tuna but do not kill thousands of dolphins and whales that get caught and die an extremely slow and painful death. Despite our changing sides, Ireland, France and Greece supported Italy, so there was no overriding majority in favour at last year's meeting, despite the original agreement back in 1992. The Italian fishing industry has three thousand workers. Their ships comprise 90% of the driftnet fleet. What is so debilitating is that 80% of all their catch goes back because it's either unwanted or inedible. It all comes down to a nation's desire to look after its self interest. Italians with nets, French with their language, Germans with their beach towels ......

There's nothing worse than a sneak - other than a misguided sneak. I refer to a chappie called Jack Cooper, a volunteer ticket inspector with the North Yorkshire Moors Railway, who has reported seeing Geoff and Jenny Bramley and their two foster daughters on one of his trains. The Bramleys have been on the run for four months since being told by Cambridge Social Services that they would not be allowed to keep the girls, as they could not provide the "special home" they needed.

This case has hit the headlines once more due to the discovery of the Bramley's Honda Concerto car in York last Wednesday.

When the pressure is really on, I mean *really* on, you just need someone like the fat controller, the ex-Reverend Cooper. Not content with this coup, he then describes the couple and children he claims to be the Cambridge Four. He comments that the two adults seemed inadequate in coping with the children. Still not content, he adds that the "woman was just sitting there watching and the man was trying to get them to be quiet, but he didn't seem to be making much of a job of it". He goes on to tell how the children were disturbing other passengers and that the adults did nothing to stop them. Enter our "hero" who told the little girls a story about how noisy children frighten sheep, and they soon calmed down. "I turned to the parents and half-jokingly said that I hadn't lost my touch" (a dangerous thing for someone in the clergy to say, I thought!). "The man looked a bit put out but woman didn't say anything". We then get a description of how thin the adult female was. You do get the feeling that the ex-man of the cloth is making sure he gets his two thirds of a page of glory.

Interestingly, the *Mail on Sunday* in its summary of the case, states the ex-rev as claiming he saw one of the children screaming uncontrollably, whilst the other looked restless.

Frankly, having read that the little girls' mother felt unable to cope, one cannot help but feel the sisters would have a better life with the runaway couple than in the hands of a Social Services department. Would you trust them to make a logical decision based on love and affection, as opposed to politics and personal egos?

It must be desperate for a couple, unable to have children of their own, to foster these girls for around fifteen months, only to be told that they were going to be taken away. Not surprisingly, public reaction has been to support the Bramleys and not social services. This view is backed up by the police, who confirm that their requests for information have brought little response, stating that "misguided sympathy is discouraging witnesses". The five year old girl's natural father is demanding an investigation - naturally.

I've just seen a photograph of Liz Railton, the director of Cambridgeshire's Social Services. Short hair, long neck that suits dangly ear-rings. I may be wrong but she appears to ooze left-wing ideology and has political correctness written all over her, and you know me, never one to make a snap decision.

It will be interesting to see what happens.

Right, dinner's ready. Roast beef, Yorkshire pudding and all the trimmings. I think I'll open a bottle of the darkest and earthiest red I can find. See you! .....

Well, that went down a treat. I like to think I did my bit for the family dinner. I opened the wine and I also praised Maureen's culinary skills. Leading on from the ex-vicar who poked his nose in where it wasn't wanted, we now look at a priest who poked in more than his snout! Another one of their ilk, a certain Canon Roger Williams, is a very forgiving man. So forgiving in fact that he takes in a former canon, the Canon Knight, after he has been released from prison. This Knight in not so shining armour has just served 21 months of a three and a half year sentence for indecently assaulting boys aged between 11 and 14. This odious, bearded and bespectacled person invited the boys home with him and then gave them alcohol. These offences happened over a ten year period, finally ending in 1985.

What starts to make it seem like the usual old pals' act is when the Church of England allow him to remain in the ministry, whilst the powers that be knew of his offences. Now that he is out, old pals' act number two comes into play. The good and forgiving Canon Williams knew Knight when they were at Lichfield Theological College nearly forty years ago.

Why would anyone wish to shelter a convicted paedophile, even for a couple of nights? The arrogance of the church, however, is easy to witness. Canon Williams never once sought the views of his own flock, many of whom have children. Indeed, such is the feeling that three members of the parochial church council resigned.

It's interesting as to why Canon Williams pleaded forgiveness for the paedophile, but refused to marry a local lady because her husband was a divorcee. It would appear, therefore, that being divorced is a far more heinous crime than the abuse of children. Well, that's the church for you.

But, shaking heads in disbelief and wonderment, involves parents too. The owner and headmaster of Sherborne Preparatory School finally stepped down last May, handing over the running of the school to a trust. For twenty five of his thirty years in charge, he abused children at the school. There was an official investigation, two police enquiries, six social services enquiries, spanning twelve years, plus complaints from a teacher thirteen years ago. All of these authorities were frustrated in their efforts, however, by parents who either out of blind trust or selfishness refused to co-operate. This blind trust stems from the classic paedophile behaviour of befriending the parents. They only see the school's academic achievements. The selfishness stems from parents' desire for their offspring to pass Common Entrance exams to schools such as Millfield and Eton.

Even pupils had complained. But, no, the parental hindrance went on. I won't go into the unsavoury activities (you never know what kind of pervert might read this book!) but it doesn't say a lot for some of the parents. All money and blind eyes.

I just managed to complete the above sentence before Maureen shouted, "Are you ready?" We're off for that great expedition to Sainbury's. It would cost so much less if she went by herself - no beer or wine, only one jar of Branston pickle, instead of the three other varieties "we've just got to try" or that less convincing argument that I always put forward, "It's got a nice label, looks classy". Am I a pushover, or what?

It's all right, the phone's just rung. Maureen's picked it up. I can tell from the tone of conversation that it's my mother, so that'll give us another couple of minutes.

D'you know, just over a year ago, a Scout leader, described by the judge as predatory, was jailed for eighteen years, so with good behaviour he'll probably be out in about six months. Anyway, David Stanley always picked vulnerable young boys while he was with the Scouts and whilst working as a youth worker at a residential children's home. He was another who obtained the trust of parents and the Scouting organisation.

Recently, a Scout leader was put on probation for two years for indecently assaulting a fourteen year old boy. Now, in this case, "indecent assault" seems a rather harsh phrase to use. Here we have a Scout leader who is female. I'm sure I've said it before, but I did not know of any fourteen year old's when I was that age who would not have given their year's pocket money to have been seduced by a twenty six year old woman. All those hormones, a copy of Penthouse and a right hand - or left, use to suit. Sarah Hubert, the Scout leader, had a year long affair with the unnamed boy after a kiss and a cuddle on a camping trip. What is so stupid and typical of today's neurosis, is that Ms. H. is to be placed on the sex offenders' list. They had sex at least once a week, either at her parents' house or the boy's home.

It was not without a sense of irony that the judge said he decided not to send Ms. Hubert to jail as "the boy was coping well with his experience". Not really surprising, is it? He is half-way up the learning curve when some are still struggling at the age of thirty.

Last words go to his mum, which I feel should be read in Pythonesque, Terry Jones style of delivery.

"My son's going to have nothing more to do with those Scouts".

Well, that was timely, Maureen's just called up. My mother wants a word with me. What have I done wrong now?

CHAPTER THREE

THE COMPENSATION BANDWAGON PICKS UP SPEED!

I was not aware that gladioli, freesias, geraniums and lobelia originated in South Africa. A young lady from that country, now living in London, is attempting to raise £400,000 in order to buy the last remaining 1,325 acres of land near the Cape that gave the world these varieties of flowers. She has paid a 10% deposit. If she fails, the land will be ploughed after purchase by farmers for the planting of vines. What's the saying? The price of everything, the value of nothing. For once, I wouldn't mind Lottery money going abroad. I wish her well.

The above snippet reminds me of an article I read concerning a series of beach chalets at East Mersea in Essex. Built nearly seventy years ago, and in many cases owned by members of the original purchasing company, the chalets were commissioned for troops during the second World War.

Originally called Sunny Beach and owned by the East Hall Farm Estate, the two hundred huts were bought by Owen Cooper Estates in the late 1940's. The name was subsequently changed from Sunny Beach to Cooper's Beach. Mr. Cooper, the owner, died in 1989. The new owners demolished sixty huts with undue haste shortly after purchase. The current owners, Leisure Great Britain, propose placing yet more caravans on the site and basically want the chalets out of the way. If the remaining chalet owners stay, they would have to move the chalets to another smaller area and at their own cost. Furthermore, the agreement is for one year only.

It's another little twist of the knife in the heart of the ordinary. Chalets were once an integral part of our coastline, unassuming, tidy, well cared for, individual and proud. In short, intrinsically English. We now have a coastline covered from north to south and east to west with hideous, green or cream caravans and mobile homes.

And you could never take to a name like Leisure Great Britain, could you?

Well, I'm into my last full week at work, here in London. Only three more lunch times left for sitting in the park. No excuses not to crack on with the book now.

The cover is not yet designed. I usually contact the young artist around March time. Her name appears just inside the front cover. I give her an outline of what I perceive the cover should portray, and she does the rest and puts it into shape. I've had a quote from the Guernsey Press, who have printed the previous three titles, and I will be confirming print dates with them shortly. We are currently looking at publishing late September. Around May/June I have to contact the main buyer of humour at WH Smiths, to see if, and if yes, how many copies they will take. Their acceptance of the title is vital, as Smiths carry so much weight in the retail market place - weight in the market place, I'm almost sounding professional.

Right, it's the Scotch egg next - home made, and I have to say, Maureen does make exceedingly good Scotch eggs. D'you know, that would make an ideal slogan for a food producer - cakes, maybe ......

I think the last notes I wrote from my car involved my slurping tomato all over my shirt or tie (or both). No such problem this time as Maureen didn't pack any tomatoes. I have, however, got a raspberry crumble and I have been known to spill them before - Mucky Pup!

On the way up this morning I passed many areas of green (I'll avoid the word "fields" in case a developer reads this and re-traces my wheels). Signs stating the words "public footpath" abound. The Wednesday before last a group of ramblers attempted to walk over a restricted path on land belonging to some cove who rejoices in the name of Nicholas Van Hoogstraten. He is a property developer (boo loudly) with a £30 million private estate in East Sussex. I saw a photograph of him in a newspaper late last year. Condescending soul he looks as well.

In this corner of England that looks set to remain forever Van Hoogstraten, the mansion is equipped with a sub basement, in which he decrees that his body, art and antique collection will all be entombed together. The path in question is blocked by a barn, metal gate and a row of old refrigerator units. East Sussex County Council have informed the said developer that the barn should not have been built across a right of way. His response, the council admit, has been to tell them in no uncertain terms that he has no desire to comply. Said council state that they have other priorities as "resources are scarce". Could you see them being scarce if it were you or I? Just a point, but I suspect his council tax is worth a few quid, and let's be honest, money talks!

Van Hoo, as I'll refer to him, considers ramblers to be the "great unwashed" and "disgusting creatures". Last Wednesday's walk, Van Hoo being abroad at the time, was made by a fair number of ramblers, who were joined by seven police officers, the president of the Ramblers Association and the MP for Brighton Kemptown. I've just dug out the cutting from last year's article and perused his photograph again. I have to say, I was never going to like him as he looks the type who would have a continuous smell under his nose, and as you know me to be a fair and just individual, I will allow him the last quote. "The only purpose in creating wealth like mine is to separate one's self from the riff-raff".

Talking of riff-raff, you know the Barratt development I was on about earlier, the one behind us - other side of the railway line - yes, you do. I just thought you were nodding off. What? You were resting your eyes. Fine. Anyway, I drove round there last night. Deep into its bowels I ventured and what did I see? A three-tone Sierra on blocks. Didn't take long, did it? There must be less than half a dozen trees with protective strips around them, saved from the bulldozers and probably to be featured as examples of their caring stewardship. These will no doubt be surrounded by six blades of grass and a sign acknowledging their cherished status.

But enough of this realism. Let's get cynical, suspicious, contemptible. Let's get back to Edith Cresson - that's the French Edith Cresson, and her boys at the Ministry of Silly Salaries.

It concerns me greatly that these high-octane Eurocrats are able to hamper police investigations into fraud through the system of diplomatic immunity, behind which commissioners are allowed to cower. What incentive is there for you and I to be honest, when all pigs are *not* equal. The poor sod in the street cannot claim immunity. Now that is one tradition I would jettison today - well, tomorrow actually, as I'm shortly going down the railway club and we have Brakspeare's ales on and oh, Maureen's driving me there and picking me up later. Isn't that good of her?

Over the past few days, otherwise known in this household as the run-in to the Charlton-Newcastle game, there have been a number of pictures of the Cresson woman. I've had time to study her in more detail, neck upwards you understand. She appears to have eyelids that are permanently half-closed. They give a dismissive, condescending slant to an already hard exterior. No-one can help how they look, but a smile, a twinkling eye may soften her appearance. As I said earlier, we're looking at a serious case of humourless Frog syndrome. She is accused of favouritism in her choice of contractors. Bear in mind that her department's budget for a youth training scheme over the past four years has totalled some £450 million. What I find worrying is that Jacques Santer states that even if the French woman or the other five under suspicion are censured, no individual commissioner will be forced to resign. It is quite frightening even attempting to comprehend the extent of fraud in the EU.

MEP's are allowed £100,000 per annum to spend on office expenses. Some have been found using a proportion of this money to top up their personal pensions - that of course is a pension paid by us all. They are also allowed to claim travelling expenses of up to £200,000 per annum, with just a petty cash voucher and no receipts. They recently voted against the proposal to provide receipts for these expenses. Unbelievable. It's just been announced that a Eurocrat who had his contract terminated after an enquiry indicated his involvement with fraud running into millions of pounds, has been awarded severance pay of £83,000. Makes it all seem so much more worthwhile, doesn't it?

The new parliament building in Brussels has cost £700 million. It contains no fewer than 2,600 offices and many shower rooms, which cost £7,000 a time. There appears to be a lot of backhanders between builders, bankers and MEP's, and for what? Another edifice to the collective ego.

And when money isn't being pocketed by the Euro rich, the recipient for the handout seems very often to be a misguided choice. Take the EU's overseas aid programme. This cost £2.7 billion, of which Britain contributed no less than £530 million, which is enough to keep Manchester United in full kit for the rest of the season!

A large amount of taxpayers money was given over to the Cameroon for building roads into their rain forests. This brilliant move led to logging in a world heritage site, the killing of much wildlife and the destruction of a village. To be fair to Claire Short and her minions, they did protest, but the EU strode on regardless. Environmentalists believe that the Cameroon government and French logging companies worked hand-in-hand in their effort to extract funds from aid programmes. Other effects of EU intervention have seen whole communities ejected from their homelands in Uganda, and the wholesale destruction of farms and forests in Nigeria. And who benefited? Was it the locals or those with money and a downright obsession with making more? ....

Right, Glyn and I are off to Charlton shortly. Kick-off's at 4 pm. We're leaving here about 1 pm so that we can soak up the atmosphere and a pint of best. So, see you when we return. Hopefully with a score line of Charlton 5, Newcastle 0. Okay, I'll settle for 1-0 in injury time.

Byee.

It's 9 pm Sunday. The journey up to London was awful, the traffic through Tooting was nose to tail. In fact, it was so nose to tail that I felt like an honorary member of the priesthood! Still, we did arrive and manage to park some twenty minutes before the match commenced and in the process guzzled a pint before finding our seats. Strange to tell, but the match ball was donated by the Dutch meat board? - search me!

Despite chances at the Newcastle end, Charlton went into the break 1-0 down and it was nice to hear that terrace humour has not vanished with the terraces. I queued alongside home supporters for a half-time burger and chips. It may be unhealthy, GM mutated or high in BSE, but it's obligatory. As it happened, it tasted good and I've suffered no ill effects. Whilst queuing I commented to fellow would-be purchasers that it was the first time in thirty five years that I had visited The Valley. "I thought I hadn't seen you for some time", replied one wag.

The second half saw Newcastle go two up, before Charlton rolled up their sleeves, pulled one back and eventually with the last kick of the match finished up drawing two-all. The match was exciting, Newcastle however seemed limited in imagination and enthusiasm - an observation I've made on several occasions since Kevin Keegan's departure some two years ago. Still, his Fulham are doing very well.

I have to tell you that the journey back was almost as tiresome as the journey up to South East London. What an awful place it is. Peckham, Dartford, New Cross, etc. It gets better across Blackheath and through the "restored" areas of Greenwich, but generally it's deep in rubbish and squalor. Oh to see the sign which proclaims "Surrey" - home.

The main event announced in today's newspapers was the return of the Bramleys and their two foster children, all well, I'm glad to report. Cambridgeshire Social Services immediately stated their intention to take the girls away. That Railton woman, the long neck in charge of the county's social services, made an odd statement. She said, "I hope Mr. and Mrs. Bramley will now lodge their adoption application, there is nothing to prevent them from doing this. We will place our arguments for opposing the adoption application".

Bit funny, isn't it, inviting an application and stating you will object in the same breath?

Footnote to the Bramley story. It appears that despite hundreds of sightings of the family in mainland Britain, not one was genuine. So while the fat controller was lapping up his fifteen minutes of fame, naming and shaming some poor couple who suffered, as most of us have, with badly behaved, selfish little oiks, the real Bramleys were looking after their "family" very nicely in Tralee, Southern Ireland. Just how much egg can one smear across that smug, self-satisfied, self-righteous face. Huh? Mr. ex-vicar!

It's funny how the real fathers of these children are facing up to the situation. Paul Duckett, aged 24, Jade's father, says he wants to be "an active part of his daughter's life". Sounds like an extract from a social work manual, whilst Craig Knott, 26, Hannah's father, goes totally overboard with his announcement that he intends to adopt her. We are talking about a man who has three children, each by different mothers, none of whom he sees, while his current girlfriend is expecting another one. So, responsibility rules with this chap! Then again, knowing how social services work, he's probably got a jolly good chance of adopting the little girl - or all five of them.

So, what else happened today? Maureen popped up the road to a wool sale and William slept in - again. Tomorrow I start my part time routine. I'm really looking forward to getting up at 5 a.m on two days a week only. See you later.

It's Friday. I've been busy settling into the new role. Spent Monday up here in West London, Tuesday to Thursday was spent travelling around the home counties south for the puzzle magazine publishers, and today I' m at the superstore. The staff level here increases every week, along with the number of computers. I think I'm right in saying there are only two desks without them - and one's mine!

Sad to report that the do-gooders can notch up another victory. The Cedar School, an independent primary, situated in east London, is to close rather than give in to new laws banning the slipper and smacks on the hand. All corporal punishment is to be outlawed in independent schools from September. The parents of the pupils are well aware of the conditions before their offspring join, but their preferences in discipline are ignored by the misguided, arrogant lawmakers who take note only of the vocal rabble who side with the villains, never the victims - bastards!

Here we go, Germany is pressing ahead with its plan for a "bill of rights" for the EU's 370 million population. They are using the Euro as a whipping stick to bring countries like ours into line. They say the new currency's value could fall unless countries pool their sovereignty, reduce the number of vetoes and reform finances. They go on to insult the populace by stating that a "bill of rights" will make the people of Europe feel closer to EU institutions being created on their behalf.

Bloody cheek! Who asked them to create these institutions? I can only assume that certain commissioners will be horrified. The last thing they will want is people "feeling closer". An ivory tower is power and power is money.

There is this gradual "drip" process being employed by both our government and those on the continent regarding our currency. Last November there were soundings that the demise of the pound was inevitable, despite the continued promise of a referendum. Dire consequences of our remaining outside are well published. Just before the turn of the New Year, the EC commissioner responsible for the Euro stated that Britain would not continue to be a major power unless we joined. You see, little nibbles at our independence. I presume the hope is that if you tell the same story for long enough, the people concede and accept their fate as inevitable.

An overpaid Frog within the commission argued piously that "we can survive without Britain, but Britain cannot survive without us". I still say its jealousy and no, I can't put my finger on it, but I do feel those abroad wish us to be soul-less, kept, beholden to them . He went on to advance his theory that Britain's reluctance paved the way for Germany to dominate Europe. Well, frankly, they were always going to. Mind you, his enthusiasm for the "harmonisation" of corporate taxes within the EC "was not warmly received by our government". I just wonder what stage has to be reached before ministers realise they are past the point of no return.

The major surprise to me is the lack of opposition from the German people. Are they really so enthralled, so enthusiastic? Are they actually more European than we generally take them to be, or is it a darker force. Is it an unspoken realisation that they *are* to be the dominant landlords, an expectancy unparalleled since the late nineteen thirties. Let's be honest, no-one in their right mind would ever trust them. Only three weeks ago, they stated that "the EU must aim at political unity".

Hang on, yes, here it is! On Monday, 9th November last, a week long "Euro Ready Week" was opened by Baroness Symons, the junior Foreign Minister. The town selected for this joyous little romp was Rotherham, Yorkshire. So, despite reiterating that Britain would "play no part in economic and monetary union unless the benefits were clear and unambiguous, and it was agreed in a referendum"we still have to play the role of the good European. What utter bollocks! Baroness Symons must have had her tongue firmly stuck in her cheek (or somewhere!), for she enthused, "We all have to prepare because the Euro starts in less than eight weeks time. It would be negligent of the government not to be ready for that. What Rotherham has done today is to take the lead and I think other towns should learn from their example and get themselves ready".

Can you believe such utter nonsense? I have to say it's probably the only time Rotherham has ever taken the lead, although I think they were once 1-0 up against Cardiff, but I feel the exercise is totally lacking in substance. Dual pricing in pounds and Euro's for one week, and offering customers vouchers resembling Euro bank notes, cannot be deemed a serious contribution to monetary education. Just seems such a waste of money and trees - and for what? Something the majority of people didn't want in the first place.

Another football team is in trouble. This time, it's an ex-league side - Barrow. Having lost their league status many years ago, they have clawed their way back to the Vauxhall Conference, only to become embroiled in a dispute with a construction company. They are facing a winding up order and although their results on the field have been better of late, their future lies outside their hands. I wish them well, I hate seeing a club go to the wall.

Right, what's on TV tonight? Ah-ha, Parkinson's guest is Caroline Aherne - we'll watch that. Poltergeist? No, seen it twice. What's on *BBC2*. Oh, God, it's that *"Gimmee, Gimmee, Gimmee"*, goes under the heading of "comedy". Not impressed. *"Reeves and Mortimer"* - definitely not! Surprise, Surprise - no, not the Cilla Black show, I mean it's no surprise to find there are more "flies on the walls". *"Airline"* and *"Neighbours From Hell"*. Pleased with the programme's advice on the Leylandii, which by the way are doing very nicely, thank you. Thank God (or someone) for *"Friends"* and *"Frasier"*; all is not lost on a Friday, though Saturday night is probably the most dire in television history.

What is good news is that the two little girls from Hastings have been found alive and well. It was quite remarkable that as the police were giving a press conference outlining their worsening fears, news broke that the children had been found in a house in Eastbourne. A man is now under arrest. As they had been missing since Friday, the chances of finding them alive were receding rapidly. Two very happy sets of parents today.

It's Saturday morning, I've just finished eggs on toast, with a large sprinkling of salt and mixed peppercorns. Yes, it certainly went down well, followed as it was by two cups of tea.

Oh, no! Club 18-30 are in trouble with my favourite embodiment of all that stinks, the CRE, and all because they decided to portray an ex-Robertson's jam staff member on their 1999 calendar. Yes, it's our old favourite, Golly. He is shown selling watches on a beach. So where's the harm in that? Some humourless oik called Chris Myant, a Commission spokesman (shouldn't he just be a spoke?) says, "It really is in pretty poor taste. I fail to understand why a company which is in the business of selling holidays would choose an image that a significant proportion of the population would find offensive". So who are the offended? Very few blacks, I suspect; it's usually the do-gooders with a guilt complex. The good news is that over 2000 calendars have been distributed and according to the CRE, tasteless though they may consider it, nothing they have done is illegal. So yar boo and socks to Chris and his pathetic tribe (oops, smacks of racism, should have said troop!)

There's to be a new television series on *Channel 4* called *"Sex and the City"*, about four girls who play the part of the sexual predator. The *Sunday Mirror* poses the question, can a woman sleep around like a man? Simple answer here, no, because if she did she'd be a slapper. Males can because, well, we're like that (not me, of course, because Maureen's typing this and I really don't need the histrionics, so hypocrisy wins again!).

Well, the fourth round of the FA Cup is over, Swansea is out but Fulham marches on. Interesting little piece in the Sunday Telegraph concerning referees' kit. For the past seven seasons Premiership matches have been officiated over by men in many colours. Who decided to change the strip from the traditional black, still fortunately sported by referees in the nationwide league and the FA Cup?. Gates are up, confidence is high, so why jazz up referees. We already have goalkeepers sporting multi-coloured jerseys. Again, why? Another fashion dragged over from the continent, it seems.

Talking of referees, I read that Paul Alcock, the fellow who took several backward steps before going to ground after a push by Di Canio, is frightened that his career may be over. Now I have seen the incident repeated on television many times and as far as I'm concerned, the very act of physical contact with the referee should see the player concerned banned for at least five years. I'll give Mr. A the benefit of my doubt, but it still looks as if he "milked" the situation, to say the least. He's now saying that he has suffered from disc trouble ever since the incident. He goes on, "All you hear is Di Canio doing this and that, but there is never anything said about the ref - well I was the victim ......!" Oh, yes, another victim. The world's full of victims - doesn't he whinge on? Tell you what, I'll be very surprised if he's not back blowing his whistle at the start of the season......

In the days of "hard men", like Norman Hunter, Nobby Stiles, Chopper Harris, etc. opposing players, sorry, victims, got up and got on with it, but now, oh no, for them a quick phone call to a legal vulture and any mis-timed tackle becomes the catalyst for increased earning power. Within the past three months an ex-Crystal Palace player whose career has now ended, has considered suing Huddersfield Town FC for a tackle committed by one of its players. The charge is "late and reckless". Interesting to note that the word "deliberate" was not mentioned. Another player, this time from Bradford City, has already been given £50,000 as an interim payment for damages over a tackle described as "negligent" by the judge. This case also involved a Huddersfield Town player.

As if all this isn't enough, a young girl, back in 1994, was hit on the arm by a football mis-kicked in a warm-up prior to the commencement of the match. She was in the stands at the time of the incident when she received a broken arm in two places. The club was not aware of the incident for nearly two years. Interestingly, this young "supporter" of Huddersfield Town has thought twice about suing the club, as she thought the action would be against Wycombe Wanderers, as the team was playing at Wycombe's ground. She says that "Huddersfield Town has got enough problems as it is". Her solicitor states that the action could still progress unless a settlement is reached. Alan Sykes, the club secretary, says "We will continue to defend the matter until it is either dropped or we win in court. There will be no settlement. We can't have a situation where spectators are suing. If people attend a sporting event, they do so at their own risk" - exactly!

But football's not what it used to be. The pleasure lay in supporting your local team, or one you had an association with. There is now talk of Bury, Oldham Athletic and Rochdale merging to form a team called Manchester North End. Yes, the three teams concerned command small attendances, but it's the independence that counts. Your own ground, however dog-eared and rambling it is, as a supporter it's yours. I sincerely hope this idea does not bear fruit.

I was sorry to see Dave Bassett sacked at Nottingham Forest. He was always on a hiding-to-nothing. What a pity for the club that Pierre

Van Hooijdonk felt above it all and decided to strike. I'd ban him from playing again anywhere. Loyalty - now what was that?

But for every five moans, there's a chink of light, a reminder of why we like the game. Take Rushden and Diamonds of the Vauxhall Conference. Here is a team, built by one local businessman with a passion for a local side. They progressed to the third round of the FA Cup, before losing to Leeds United. Formed from a merger between two local clubs seven years ago, they present a very professional image and play at a stadium many league clubs would envy.

Max Griggs, the club's founder, said before the Leeds match that "Whatever happens on the pitch, the occasion will be the most important thing". Mr. Griggs is the man behind Doc Marten's shoes and his factory employs a lot of local people in Northamptonshire. Isn't it refreshing when someone like him says, "I enjoy putting something back into the community, when I see the stadium full on a Saturday and everyone cheering, that's reward in itself".

While football's money men continue to dampen one's affections for the game, the same cannot be said of cricket. I know it's as English as Wilkins jam, but I just cannot understand a game when you're 500 runs for one wicket. The other team are all out for 78 and it starts to rain, so the game is declared a draw.

Having said that, the game is incidental when listening to Test Match Special on Radio Four. The tradition of easy listening commenced in the days of Brian Johnson, and Henry Blowfelt is carrying the mantle and continuing to make the commentary entertaining. I have to say from my point of view I rarely tune in when the match is on, but when rain has stopped play, that is the time to listen. Can you imagine the definitive style, the reminiscences, the laid back approach being applied if Test Match Special was covered by a commercial station? It's an appalling thought.

But TV coverage, apart from the World Cup, is to go to *Channel 4* and *BSkyB*. Worrying words emanated from a *Channel 4* spokesman, who stated that "Cricket is becoming sexy and trendy". It's certainly getting more colourful. What was so bad about "whites"? (I've probably just answered my own question by not being politically correct!) *Channel 4* also intend to introduce "fresher, younger, more multi-cultural coverage". Now there's a surprise ....

Final sporting snippet for now, the 185 year old lime tree that resides in magnificent splendour *within* the boundary at Kent Cricket Club's Canterbury ground is dying. There is a colour picture in one of the papers and it is a sight to behold, an absolute gem. Alas, the tree has a life expectancy of around ten years. The cricket club has bought a replacement, costing £3,000, which will be planted behind the barrier some twenty yards away. When the old tree eventually gives up the ghost, the young pretender will be uprooted and positioned in the hole vacated by its predecessor. At least someone had the foresight to address the situation before the only option was to cut down the tree and commiserate over its passing. Well done whoever is responsible.

By now you will probably be aware that I'm not overly enthusiastic about compensation. It is, as they say, a bit of a hobby-horse. There have been a spate of claims recently. It really is an industry in itself and I understand from a colleague who visited a local hospital, that solicitors' cards offering a no-fee compensation claims service have sprung up in out-patients like weeds in your average garden.

Firstly, we move north to Edinburgh, where some lucky blighter called Alastair Morrison has been awarded £122,653 in damages. The thirty-eight year old ex-night shift manager working for Safeways says that "prolonged kneeling whilst stacking low shelves" caused osteo-arthritis. He apparently knelt for periods of up to two hours at a time for several years. He can no longer walk without the aid of a stick, can no longer enjoy snooker (well I never could and nobody paid me!) and he's finding it difficult to lead a normal sex life. Perhaps he should try using his willy instead of his big toe. According to the now "less financially impoverished" Mr. Morrison, Safeways should have provided him with knee pads or "devised a system which reduced the need for kneeling". If the pain was so bad, why didn't he buy himself a pair of pads? If I was ruling in the court of sessions, I would have sent him packing - as opposed to stacking - with the judgement against him for court costs. Can you be charged with being a complete-and-utter-arse? Just a thought!

We now head south west to Wales, where the local police are trying to reduce theft from shops by releasing photographs and names of shoplifters. This particular example, now aged 18, was convicted of theft two years previously. His mug shot appeared in an album of local offenders as part of the force's crime prevention scheme. This young man is then banned from several retail outlets as a result of this policy. Not content with being embarrassed by his nefarious past, he takes legal action against the force for "loss and humiliation" caused by the circulation of the photograph. Guess what? North Wales police were advised to settle out of court, which results in our laddo being £1,500 better off. As well as this little thank you, they have also had to pay his

76

legal costs, which amounted to £1,057. The police will *not* be continuing with the scheme and shopkeepers will *not* have photographic evidence of would-be/could-be thieves within easy reach.

The above figures are nothing compared with a young secretary called Emma Smith, who is aged 24. Her boss, the managing director, forced his unwanted attentions on her, making sexually explicit comments and touching her. Well, okay, it's not very nice, but being awarded £38,915 would definitely make the pain go away fairly rapidly, I would have thought. This award is made up of £23,000 for injury to personal feelings and £16,000 for loss of earnings. Again, how do the powers that be arrive at such high figures? Severe disability through thuggery is often only a quarter of that, but then, this "victim" was a female and the offence fairly minor when compared to a real crime.

We'll stay with compensation for a while. This time last year, a thief with over fifty convictions was awarded £900 damages after being bitten by the police dog that helped in his capture. I would like to know how a case like this ever gets to court in the first place. This "drain on society" is 23 years old and has served three prison sentences. So his record is not unblemished. How does he manage to bring a case like this on Legal Aid? The police also had to pay £5,000 in costs.

The six-foot, sixteen-stone Mr. Mark Coles said (not surprisingly) that he was "traumatised by his injuries" after being bitten twice in 1992. He was now "fearful of any dog he met in the street and cowered behind his wife". He apparently needed hospital treatment after being bitten and walked on crutches for two months. After listening to his bleatings, I'd have made him pay for the tetanus injections and told him to bugger off and live under a stone until he could grow up and stop thieving. The judge, one Patrick Bartfield, awarded the said oik £2,250 but reduced the amount to £900, as he believed Mark Coles to be "sixty percent responsible". Can someone tell me who was responsible, then, for the other 40%?

In the cause of fairness, one to which I know I subscribe, last words go to the plaintiff. "I'm giving the money to charity as I'm going straight". Let's hope he did and does!

The world *has* gone mad. I can rubber stamp its confirmation, which is a lot healthier than a Catholic church confirmation! This one comes without any form of abuse being included in the ceremony .... Anyway, back in 1991, a youngster, aged 11, trespassed onto a building site in Salford, Lancs (I don't care for Greater Manchester) before climbing a tree and subsequently falling off it. He entered the site via a hole in the fence, before collecting conkers from a horse chestnut tree.

His fall from 30 feet up landed him on a pile of rubbish. He spent a week in a coma and now, nearly eight years on, cannot look after his own affairs or domestic situation. Without doubt, we all feel for him. It is tragic. The Prosecution's case is that the property development company failed to block up the holes. My experience of children, and certainly of my own youth, is that as soon as one entrance is blocked, children find another. Upshot of it all is that the court found against the owners and awarded £150,000 damages which will be paid into a trust. What I want to know is, why is the company to blame? What happened to parental responsibility?

There are several unanswered questions in the newspaper report. One, did the parents start their legal action when the tragedy occurred? Two, were they encouraged to take the case to court by lawyers who are basically there for their own good? Three, do the parents consider that any of this situation is down to them? The boy was only 11, after all. It seems that everyone is responsible except for those directly involved.

One more, then I'm going to bed. It's been a hard day and I'm not getting any younger. There's been a growing tendency for members of the police to sue for this and that, you know, injuries sustained, witnessing horrifying scenes, all the areas of the job they didn't think about before joining. It's just a bloody gravy train. Perfect example here - Laura Dyer, a former detective, has recently been awarded £175,792. She has "won" this amount from the Metropolitan Police for "hearing damage inflicting by surveillance earpiece". She told the High Court that she now suffers from tinnitus. Every penny this woman got comes directly off the police budget, so we all suffer. She had claimed £500,000, so at least some sanity prevailed. Unfortunately, £175,792 worth didn't!

What's that? You want another? You're as aggrieved as I am. Well, okay and don't you worry about me oversleeping in the morning - you just enjoy yourself! Last one, then. Here we journey to the Mediterranean climes and palm trees that are Torquay! A Mr. John Boyce, aged 40, is currently receiving psychiatric help after witnessing a number of suicides and attempted suicides at the Municipal Car Park in Temperance Street! Over the past year, the unfortunate Mr. B. has seen two people fall to their death in front of him, and he has had to call the police several times, having seen people preparing to throw themselves off the 120 foot high building. Such is the extent of the suicide problem that the Samaritans have installed a top floor telephone line. Mr. B. has, guess what? Yes, he's been diagnosed as suffering from post-traumatic stress syndrome and has been prescribed antidepressants. This poor man is suffering flash-backs, nightmares and interrupted sleep.

So whilst stating that "the money is immaterial" he is suing Torbay Council, owners of the car park. Funny how money is always of secondary importance. The local council have agreed that Mr. B's solicitors have been in touch and placed the matter in the hands of their insurers. What I want to know is, has anyone questioned why people keep flinging themselves off the top floor. Do they see Mr. Boyce and feel it's the only way out? Frankly, I think he's a pain in the arse and should be ignored. Here's an idea; if he feels so badly about his lot, I know of a nice high car park in Temperance Street, with its own in-house telephone help line. Mind you, if other social misfits, outcasts and all-round sad eggs know he's there, I suspect a queue will have formed already!

Right, night-night!

To use the words of that Derek Jameson fellow, "Morning, morning".

You remember that Van Hoogstraten fellow who's not overly keen on ramblers, well there is an article about him in this weekend's *Telegraph* magazine. Having read most of it, it appears that he really is a most undesirable specimen. I've learned that he once served a 5-year prison sentence for organising a hand grenade attack on a former friend's house. In the interview he offers insights into his life, such as the time he abducted an accountant and kept him in the boot of his car for several days, feeding him only on fish paste! He also has a record for not being the nicest of landlords and of being fairly heartless to some of his tenants. He comments that "whether we acknowledge it or not, 99.9% of people are there to make up the numbers. They are cannon fodder".

The more I read about him, the more I feel that the riff-raff are actually better off without his speaking to them. He must be suffering from a dreadful complex. It's almost hard not to feel pity for the poor soul - I did say almost.

I was interested to read that the Queen Mother underwent surgery for a nosebleed yesterday. She was treated under local anaesthetic at her local "county hospital" in Kings Lynn. To be precise, the Queen Elizabeth Hospital. Can't get much more homely than that! It was just after lunch when she complained about her severe nosebleed. "I've got a severe nosebleed", she probably said. The world then stopped revolving while stock was taken of the situation. I'd have told her to look up at the ceiling and pull in her shoulders. That's what my mother used to say. Can't remember it ever ceasing but it did stop the blood getting on my shirt.

After lunch, eh. EastEnders would have been coming on. I bet that stopped the fun and games around the baronial dinner table. Still, you can only be a party-pooper for so long.

The hospital confirmed that the Q.M. had been treated in the Accident & Emergency Department but had not been admitted. I suspect that if the truth were known, the A. & E. had probably been closed for the last ten years and it had now been re-opened especially for her. Maybe not, but I bet she didn't have to queue the way you do at Frimley Park Hospital, nor did the royal chauffeur have to pay for a car parking ticket the way us lesser mortals do at Frimley Park Hospital! Once again, some pigs are more equal than others!

While I think of it, a couple of years ago William was taken by ambulance to Frimley Park A. & E. He had had a slight accident on his bike in a local field - that's the two wheeled variety, not the two-legged! Someone walking their dog found him and rang for an ambulance. We were duly informed and sped (not over 30 mph you understand) up to the hospital. As he was an ambulance jobbie he was taken straight through the tradesmen's entrance, thus cutting out the tortuous journey through Casualty red tape. I have to tell you that the A. & E. Waiting Room was awful. Nothing to do with the hospital, it was merely the class of patient. There were drunks, druggies, families with eyes too close together and hooked noses (shades of "*Deliverance*" and duelling guitars). The TV was on loud, a family sat in the corner singing. Oh, how times have changed. Give me the days when all wards were like "*Carry On Nurse*" and the short-skirted, saucy wench in uniform smiled provocatively as a male patient groped her bottom, while she placed a thermometer in the patient's mouth - no, mouth! What's that, I shouldn't believe everything I see in old movies. No, guess you're right, but then, nostalgia is tinted with rose-coloured glasses.

One subject we have not touched on so far is the terrible treatment meted out to animals. There are those who cheerfully and wantonly murder, i.e. huntsmen, and there are those who shield behind the solid, respectable face of caring. In this case Mary Chipperfield and her other half, a chump by the name of Roger Crawley, deny abusing various animals in their charge. This awful, arrogant woman, who looks as if she is descended from a long line of Germans, said, "I do not regret anything. I have done nothing abusive to any of the animals". This was after video footage, showing her hitting a chimpanzee with a riding crop and striking a camel with a stick in an effort to get it to stand. There are twenty-one charges laid at the feet of this "woman". Her husband faces a further seven charges. The prosecutor described the videos as showing "vicious beatings" of animals. I will follow this case with interest and not a little anger.

Only just caught this next bit as I was turning the pages. I cannot find it as a major item in any of the press, but I consider it fairly important. Our man of the people, Jack Straw the Home Secretary, has renounced Parliament's right to restore the death penalty. Once again, we are to fall in line with the continentals. Upshot is that should we wish to re-introduce capital punishment at any time in the future, and I'm sure the day will dawn at some stage, it will be illegal for us to do so. As far as I'm concerned that wouldn't present a problem. I would just tell the continentals what we were doing as a matter of courtesy , and if they didn't like it, well tough.

What a pity the good Mr. Straw couldn't do something more positive regarding asylum seekers who commit offences in this country. Apparently, these oh-so-desperate people, wishing to make a new life for themselves in the land of opportunity, are defrauding our benefit system and committing criminal offences by the horse and cart load. So much for our hospitality. And what do we do about it? Well, we don't send them back. No, we are to make them eligible to stay in this country.

Yes, that's right, it's the same country that feels there's a need for 4.4 million homes to be built. It's also the country which is rapidly using up its natural water boreholes and streams to feed new housing developments. We've got more traffic jams than you can shake a stick at, but no, even if these ungrateful peasants have served up to a year in prison, they are to be allowed to stay on "compassionate grounds". Up to 20,000 immigrants will be eligible for this scheme. What gutless people we have running this country. Why do they not stand up and say "No more". If only they realised that they would actually have the backing of the public.

Interestingly, or maybe not, as I write this piece I'm eating a Nestles yoghurt - that's Nessles, not Nes-lay. Some £720,000 has been granted by the EU to researchers seeking to answer the question, "Why does yoghurt go runny?" This research is going to take around three years and will involve Britain, Norway, Sweden and France. The researchers will meet every six months to mull (or should that be Muller) over each other's findings. That'll be nice.......

Here's a name from the past. D'you remember the Pridham's. You don't - think, I'm sure you do. They're the family who just kept breeding without a thought for the rest of us. You know, us responsible people. Nichola Pridham is now 40 and currently up the duff for the twentieth time. Kevin, her husband, is a self-employed joiner. No, no puns there! The couple *only* receive £141 per week in child benefit, which goes to boost his earnings. But get this! They only pay £56 per week rent for an 8-bedroomed council house, or as they used to be, two four-bedroomed council houses now knocked together. They must still struggle financially, but hark, what is this I hear? It's the clatter of pens from the News of the World offering an exclusive contract. Seems to me that the more irresponsible you are, the more you get bailed out.

Seriously, what would happen to the country if everybody was as anti-social as this pair? Well, we'd have even less room for convicted immigrants.

Abuse! Abuse!
That Roman Catholic Archbishop of Wales, who refused to take seriously the allegations made against his former aide, has himself now been arrested. The aide was jailed for 8 years last month for rape and indecent assault. Apparently, a woman walked into a south London police station and made allegations of a serious sexual nature that happened when she was a young girl in the 1960's. Just shows you, doesn't it? Anyway, I have to tell you that I've made a decision. I'm now suing for abuse. In my case, it's because I wasn't, and I want to know why! What was wrong with me? Am I the only unabused child. Surely there must be others out there with whom I can make contact. Perhaps we can form a self-help grope (oops, sorry, group). I mean, I made it easy, standing with my pants down holding a card up inviting, "Abuse here, get your free abuse here". But nothing. Perhaps I was a little too forward. "When was this?" I hear you say. "As a child?" "No", I reply. "Yesterday in Tesco's!"

Right, overacting and surrealism is over.

Good news, the Euro continues to slide in value. Now down to .69 to the pound. I like that *and* it's my favourite number!

Bad news, Volvo has been swallowed up by Ford. Just as Britain's remaining mass-produced joke of a company is now in German hands, the Swedes have lost Saab to GM and now this latest takeover. All you know is that fewer factories and workers will be required in the medium to long-term and a bit like the brewing industry, less choice for the punters.

A chink of light - a woman suffering from lysdexia has had her awarded damages, totalling some £45,000, overturned by the appeal courts. Interesting to note that Cherie Booth, QC, who represented her during the proceedings, agreed with the judges who reversed the decision. It's no surprise to learn that dyslexic associations are up in arms, even if they're not very good at writing down what they mean. I'd still like to know who put these people up to it. The woman in question is a single mother, aged 25 (just thought you'd like to know).

There are some people who take naivety to extremes, never before dreamt about. A Mrs. Jennifer Cross of Plymouth wrote a letter to the *Daily Telegraph*. It is published today. She was obviously driven to write, having read or heard about the Chipperfield case. Mrs. Cross states that she has seen Chipperfield's Circus and was invited "backstage" to see a rehearsal. The lion trainer said that the Chipperfield woman was a "stickler for her animals' welfare". This is a view "confirmed" by Mrs. Cross when she visited the Chipperfield's Hampshire farm. She then leads into an equation between wild animals and cattle. As a farmer she needs to contain her animals in order for them to be injected and therefore presumably considers the Chipperfield's questionable methods to be perfectly reasonable. What a strange analogy! Mrs. Cross concludes that "Mary Chipperfield is less cruel than most of us, but a sitting target for animal rights' activists".

Let me tell you something, oh strange one from Plymouth. This Chipperfield woman who has at present 21 counts of cruelty against her, is without doubt more cruel than myself, my family and anyone I would care to have as a friend. If, however, she is less cruel than you, then I feel we have a problem somewhere .....

It really is quite unbelievable. Another lady, a proper person this time, also writes to the *D.T.* stating that she was appalled to see video clips of a circus employee hitting a tethered elephant. To learn that Mary Chipperfield had beaten a chimpanzee was "horrifying". Quite right. It makes you wonder how that Cross woman treats her farm animals.

Right, it's 7.28 pm on Friday, 29th June, and I'm about to go shopping with Maureen. Where will we end up? Tesco's, Sainsbury's, Asda, Safeway - dunno. Will leave all that to Maureen. Oh, the decisions that woman has to make.

Well, it's just before 9.45 pm and we're £130 lighter. Ended up at Sainsbury's after all. Managed to find a parking space 500 yards from the entrance. At least 20 disabled bays and a large number of Mother With Family spaces available. They always are, but no, if you've got five of everything, you must walk for miles. I feel guilty just having legs! Right, Maureen's unpacking, I've got a curry so I shall bid you good evening, see you tomorrow - oh, hang on, there's a voice emanating from the kitchen. What's that? No, I didn't mention it, but I will. Maureen's asking me if I told you that £14.63 went on pickles and sauces. I suppose she sees my telling you as a public penance. Byee......

It's all food at the moment. Saturday afternoon and I've just returned from Littlehampton - and I'm hungry. Maureen's rustling up some fried potatoes, eggs (free range) and baked beans. Incidentally, the other week when we went shopping, Maureen picked up a pack of Value eggs in Tesco's. Thinking she'd made a mistake, because we always buy free range, I naturally pointed out her error. "Oh, no", she replied, "these eggs are only for baking cakes". I'm sure the battery hens will take some comfort from that! Strange logic.

Littlehampton in January is a tad depressing. It's many years since I've been there. About thirty, actually. The green is as I remember it, but the town looked desolate and not a little desperate. With Tesco and Sainsbury locked in battle at either end of the by-pass, the town's heart seems to be in decline. Safeway and Somerfield vie for business, some thirty yards apart, separated only by a car park.

I sat and read the paper over lunch. The Stephen Lawrence case has reared its head once more. Whilst I have every sympathy with any parents, black, white, whatever, who have lost a child, especially in violent circumstances, the continual flak the police are being subjected to will improve matters not a jot. The words "institutionalised racialism" are about as damning as "every black is a thief". It seems to me that the police are on a hiding-to-nothing, the definitive no-win situation.

Our esteemed England football manager, Glen Hoddle, appears to have put his foot in the disabled goal mouth. Naturally, voicing an opinion, any opinion, opens the door for those to shout "resign, resign" before attempting to understand the meaning of the words uttered. However, Mr. Hoddle does not find a supporter to his beliefs in this writer. I cannot subscribe to his view that people are reincarnated "to learn, and face some of the things you have done, good and bad". He goes on, "You and I have been physically given two hands and two legs and half decent brains. Some people have not been born like that for a reason. The Karma is working from another lifetime. I have nothing to hide about that". Disabled groups are up in arms (no, no punch line). Mr. Hoddle adds, "What you sow, you reap. You have to look at things that happened in your life and ask why it comes around".

Have I got this right? You have an argie-bargie with a neighbour in 1638 - not returning his mower, that sort of thing - and you end up in 1999 with a handicap? No, I can't quite see it myself. What is Karma anyway?

I thought the *Daily Telegraph* was going downmarket and "doing a *Sun*". There's a lead article on the front page that reads, "Prince's relief at Camilla's Outing". For a minute, I assumed the reporter was announcing Mrs. P-B as a lesbian. Turns out they walked out together - not such a good story. Can't imagine the Queen being best pleased if it had been the former!

Just read a short piece on a chap called Richard Dawkin. It gives a good insight into the thinking of a supporter of genetics and cloning. During a radio interview, Professor Dawkin was asked whether he'd clone his daughter. He replied, "If I have someone that I love, and if there was some particularly good reason to have an identical twin, that's all there is, there's nothing new about it, identical twins are clones. Anybody who objects to cloning on principle has to answer to all the identical twins in the world, who might be insulted by the thought that there's something offensive about their very existence." Now I understand what he says, but I fail to understand the logic. The basic difference he conveniently omits is that, at the moment, all identical twins are an act of nature. Cloning by scientists is not a natural act. It has once again been brought about by the tampering of nature by man. He also states that "If I had a dog that I loved and if this dog was getting old and might die soon, to have a young clone of it would be perfectly delightful". I find this attitude worrying. Is it that the man's suffering from a complete lack of imagination, i.e. I know what I like and I like what I know? When our current Muttley dies, much as I think the world of her, I don't want one that's exactly the same. And that's the beauty of human and animal life - it all differs in some way.

If left to people like the Professor, our world would become a very clinical, sterile environment where genetically modified life forms would eat genetically modified food and perform to a pattern set out for them by those who think they know best. Was it not the Germans who had a crack at this sort of thing fifty years ago? Far from cloning Professor Dawkin, I think I'd prefer to have him put down! Can you imagine two of them?

In fairness, however, I feel it is the right time to nail my colours to the genetic mast and support certain aspects of DNA engineering. See, not entirely a Luddite. Surely, we will soon be able to ascertain certain facets of an embryo's make-up, having gathered its DNA whilst its in the making. Oh what joy, to be able to tell whether your little offspring is going to wear ear-rings (if it's a boy), tattoos and nose-rings (both sexes), read the *News of the World*, vote Lib-Dem, spit, worship the mobile phone and enjoy Mortimer and Reeves, etc. Armed with any or all of these idiosyncrasies the decision to abort could be taken without reference - that should help to reduce the birth rate, especially in Basingstoke!

Noel Edmonds, a man I will never forgive for foisting Mr. Blobby upon the world, is launching a new communications company. Called "Freedom" the idea is that the subscriber will pay little or even nothing for their phone calls. We all know, however, that there is no such thing as a free lunch or phone call. Every phone call made on Mr. Edmonds's system will be punctuated by advertisements. I go out of my way to record ITV and Channel 4 programmes so that I do not have to suffer inane, incomprehensible, too-clever-for-their-own-good ads as it is. Does anyone *really* want their chat with a friend, parent, whoever, interrupted with adverts for products "tailored to your lifestyle"? Despite the irritation of BT staff ringing during tea-time to inform me of yet another Friends and Family Discount, Friends and No Family Discount, Family Only Discount that they have to offer, I'll stick with them until something better comes along. Just a thought, why is it that the staff who ring on behalf of BT are always Scottish?

I do hope that Mrs. Cross, the Mary Chipperfield groupie, read an article in the *Sunday Express* today. It tells the story of Trudy, the chimpanzee that was physically abused. Although safe at Monkey World in Dorset, the Grand Dame of Circuses, now convicted of 12 charges of cruelty, is threatening to take the chimp away and sell it to the highest bidder. She doesn't learn, does she? You would have thought that she would be seeking to rebuild her credibility with the public - you know, those who pay to see her freak shows, but no, the stubbornness, the arrogance, so readily displayed in her lack of contrition, shows no sign of abating.

Just for you, Mrs. Cross, farmer of the septic isles, I lay open a few figures. Trudy, the chimp, under the Chipperfield regime, lived alone in a metal cage measuring nine feet by eight feet. Her only companion was a large baby bouncer ball. The Chipperfield woman was videoed taking it away from her. At night, Trudy was forced into a sleeping box, otherwise used as a travelling crate for dogs and cats. The chimp was, in winter, kept in this crate for up to fifteen hours a day. It was this crate that the chimp hated so much and for this reason Chipperfield "thrashed and kicked" the animal. Thankfully, the events were videoed for future evidence.

Trudy's present sleeping quarters are fifty feet long by forty feet wide and twenty one feet high. Quite a difference, I'd say. The outside play area is around two acres in size, with toys, ropes and climbing frames. You know, Mrs. Cross, the kind of activities that keep wild animals amused when in captivity. At least the good people at Monkey World go as far as they can to replicate a natural environment but then, their aims are not ones of exploitation. Do you still say Mary Chipperfield is less cruel than "most of us"?

Incidentally, the *Sunday Express* lists three circuses using big cats, elephants or both. These are, the Circus Harlequin and the Bobby Roberts Circus, both based in Peterborough and Circus King of Grantham. Strange how they all hail from the same geographical area. The last mentioned also features a bear amongst its acts. Another seventeen circuses across the country include llamas, camels, horses, dogs, etc. The amazing thing is that all you have to do is register under the Performing Animal Act of 1925 and look for a local authority or landlord willing to rent you land. What a sad reflection on Britain and Europe's law makers that they cannot get their legislative act together and ban circuses entirely. I suppose there is little backhander money to be obtained and no personal gain equals no incentive - bastards!

Now the centre-fold pictures of the *Express* are ones to make you lose heart. The main photograph is of two Frenchman, unfortunately alive and well, firing off a salvo at migrating birds as they cross France on their way north from Spain. There is a twenty- year-old European law allowing hunting from September to January 31st. Guess what, the French consider this too restrictive. They want the open season to start in mid-July and end on 28th February. No doubt the addition of the extra day in a Leap Year would also be most welcome! Unfortunately, such is the selfish nature of the hunter that all concerns regarding the environmental implications are ignored. The effect is that over one hundred and ten species of bird are considered fair game for an even longer period. Contained within the article are interviews with two hunters. One, named Cyrille, boasts that "two years ago I got 364 thrushes in one morning".

Come the day of the revolution, Cyrille and his equally galling (or should that be Gaulling?) arse-hole of a mate, one Bernard Barbie, will be first against the wall!

Barbie? ..... Barbie? - I know that name. Any relation to Claus, I wonder?

CHAPTER FOUR

WHEN GM MEANT GENERAL MOTORS

Oh, dear, poor old Glen Hoddle. The F.A's support appears to be crumbling a tad. Views for and against his continued employment as England's Manager are being expressed in every newspaper. Frankly, I have no doubts he should be allowed to keep his job. If you are going to sack people for expressing a view - however ludicrous or distasteful it may appear, then those who sit in judgement are walking a very springy tight-rope. Sack Hoddle if he fails at his job, but for no other reason.

Charlton lost 1-0 to Manchester United yesterday, which really grates. Even more painful was the realisation that United scored the only goal with one minute of play left. It must have been gutting for the Charlton players. Still, it's not over until the final whistle is blown.

There are some really sad people around, aren't there. A Conservative MEP called Tom Spencer, a married man with two children, is about to stand down from office. This man is one of the privileged gravy-train trundlers consuming vast amounts of our money. It's like Pak-Man for these politicians. Mere mortals like ourselves can only dream of the riches these people collect along every mile they travel, and every minute they "contribute" to the Euro cause. But this bi-sexual fifty-year-old returns from a weekend in Amsterdam with a "male friend" armed with pornographic material and a small wad of cannabis, automatically jeopardising his luxurious lifestyle. Are these people just stupid or amazingly arrogant?

The Stephen Lawrence juggernaut keeps rolling along. Jack Straw is apparently now under pressure from certain quarters to set quotas for ethnic staff in a whole range of professions. The government are playing down the proposals but I've no doubt knee-jerk reactions in favour of minorities will win the day. And it will do nothing for race relations. The effect always has been and always will be the opposite to their naive and misguided ideals.

I have to tell you that I'm getting heartily sick of this case. Of course it was an unnecessary, brutal killing and of course those responsible should be punished, but can you imagine this case becoming such a *cause celèbre* if the victim had been white? Can you imagine any enquiries or soul-searching six years on? No, and neither can I!

A little over a year ago, the *Daily Telegraph* published the findings of a European Commission survey into racism. I won't bore you with all the details but basically there were four main questions; suffice it to say that Belgium came out as the most racist country within the EU. The UK appeared uncomfortably close to Germany, half-way down the four tables. Surveys are surveys and generally a complete waste of time - unless, of course, you're being paid for either their organisation or commission.

The question I find most interesting is "Do you consider yourself (a) very racist (b) quite racist (c) a little racist - (what? under 5 foot?!) or (d) not at all racist. What are they actually asking? I would really like someone to tell me what is meant by the word "racism". It appears to be an all-em bracing cliché used by left-wingers and do-gooders to describe all those who question any aspect of integration, immigration, quotas, rights, etc. I have never once made a single disparaging remark to anyone, be they black or Asian. Indeed, over the last six years several aspects of work have brought me into contact with many Asian shopkeepers. The fact that I've got on with virtually all of them, no more, no less than one gets on with virtually all of one's own race, does not stop my general view that we are still paying for the mistakes of our forefathers. The white man's arrogance in colonising far-flung countries was appalling and indefensible. These invasions were never requested, it wasn't done for the good of the native population, it was done for two main reasons - white man's greed and religious expansion. But as a white person who grew up in what I took to be a white country, I would not want to find myself in an area which was predominantly black or Asian. This is not racism, this is a natural preference to be with one's "own kind".

When you read that white children have become a minority in inner London, I do not consider that to be for the good of the country. However, we are still a nation of "accepters". The white middle class "accept" - that seems to be our goal in life. We pay taxes, much of which goes on social benefit for those who do not work, those who do not want to work, and those who are asylum seekers. Few appear to want asylum in France or Germany. Why is that? Could it be the wonderful hospitality? No! It's the benefits. And until we do something about it, in they will flood.

The do-gooders complain every time another field is built on but are happy to accommodate yet another group of Bosnians, or whoever have outstayed their welcome east of the EU.

White accepters are supposed to take all the damning reports, all the flak but never comment. When is race ever raised as a subject for discussion on television or radio? I won't say never, but the occurrences must be rare indeed. The money and time that is spent analysing as to just why Asians are not well represented in football, as opposed to blacks, who are, is mind-numbing. Now racism to me is having two applicants for a job - one white, one black. The black applicant has the better qualification, is better suited, has a better personality, yet does not get the job. THAT to me is racism. Now, if both black and white applicants are *exactly* the same in all aspects, then I would expect the white to be given the job (shock/horror - now read on). If I were in Nigeria, India, wherever, and I was the white applicant up against a local native and we were equal on all counts, I would not expect to get the job. It's called human nature. The problem is that left-wingers and do-gooders are obsessive and wherever there's obsession, honesty is always compromised.

Staying with race, but on a lighter note, some little while ago a young black teenager walked into a local newsagents owned by a Sikh. It was early in the morning, around 6.30 am. The youth asked for alcohol, which the shopkeeper refused to sell. Whilst the paperboys sorted papers and the owner's back was turned, the youth grabbed a bottle of lager, hid it under his jacket and quickly made his way out of the shop. One of the paperboys spotted him and instantly informed the Sikh. He ran outside to see the boy heading swiftly towards the railway station. "Come back" shouted the Sikh, "Come back here, you black bastard!" The youth didn't, of course, he broke into a run. Turning round to face the paperboys, all of which were white, he said, "It's okay, I can say that sort of thing". Good on him, and why not? It's just another example of how you feel restrained by the thought police in your own country - and one does need reminding sometimes that this is one's own country.

A lack of racial harmony is not the sole preserve of blacks and Asians. A.A. Gill, the journalist, has long had a running battle with the Welsh. Unfortunately, anti-Welsh opinions expressed by anyone are received with all the humour of the CRE. In fact, not long ago, the Welsh Commissioner for the CRE (no, I didn't know there was one, either) sent off a file containing written comments A.A. Gill had made regarding Wales and the Welsh. Now I'm half Welsh. I'm neither proud nor embarrassed. It's a statement of fact, but I can't get worked up over a few comments made by one person. It comes under the heading "A Personal View", both by me and other proper people and "Blatant Racism" by silly people who have more time on their hands than a Swiss watchmaker.

Mr. Gill states that "Wales is a foodie division free zone. You can easily travel from Cardiff to Anglesey without ever stimulating a taste bud". It may or may not be true, but it's a funny line. On Welsh architecture he comments, "Almost everything that wasn't designed by God in Wales looks as if it was built by hobbits". And on the Welsh town of Flint, he states, "It is a town only a man driving a crane with a demolition ball would visit with a smile". Again, a very funny line, although when recalled in the *Daily Telegraph* the town moves north and is described as being Rhyl, but not knowing either, it matters not a jot. The principle of the comment remains the same.

Mr. Gill also referred to the Welsh as "loquacious dissemblers, immoral liars, stunted, bigoted, dark, ugly, pugnacious little trolls". So where's the problem? You either agree, disagree or fail to give the metaphorical toss. The point is, it doesn't matter - well, not to you or me, but to Ray Singh, the aforementioned CRE's waste of public money, it's a different kettle of Bombay duck. To him, it gives credence to his very being. A justification to the unjustifiable. Sad Singh says, "I have prepared a file containing anti-Welsh material and have decided to send it to our litigation department to see what action can be taken". To see "what action can be taken"? Do you mean stifling freedom of speech? I really like being told by an Asian what constitutes free speech in this country. Bloody cheek! He goes on, "We have no powers to bring a prosecution, but after studying the file we could make a strong statement to the Press Complaints Commission condemning his comments".

There was half a page of letters to the *Wales on Sunday* complaining about said scribe. One moaning minnie called Lyn Jenkins hails from Cardigan. Actually, considering how "Welsh" he wishes to be, it's strange that Cardigan is spelt in English and not "Ceredigion", the Welsh spelling. No matter! After admitting to being "one of those" who reported A.A. Gill to the CRE, he goes on to justify the move. "The group that has taken action consists of a retired *Harlech Television* film producer, an ex-*BBC World Service* correspondent and lecturer at American universities, a consultant engineer, a Swansea city councillor, a doctor, a barrister and myself- a farmer and farm park owner". Farm park owner, eh? There's lovely! He adds that "None of us are stupid". Well maybe not, but you're all very parochial and inward-looking and not a little lacking in humour. But then, when there's only one comedian of local note, whose main prop is a giant leek and engages in the Richter Scale screeching of "Oggi, oggi, oggi", then I'm afraid its a question of "enough said"!

However, our last word goes to A.A. who found the situation "absurd" and added that he could not be "less bothered about the Commission. I believe in free speech and shall not be intimidated".

Absolutely right!

We're going to stay with racial issues for a while because I'm on a roll. You may have seen this. It concerns the Barton Gates Model Railway Club in Gloucester. This very small club was looking to turn a disused warehouse into a clubhouse where they could do what all railway enthusiasts do (including me) - that's right, play trains. Now, a railway enthusiast has always received a bad press. He is looked upon with amusement, amazement, disdain, pity, etc. The one point that all non-enthusiasts would surely agree upon is that we're no trouble. Inoffensive, sad, lonely? Yes. But not rioters. Give us a circle of track and a Hornby-Dublo loco and we're as happy as sandboys.

Can you believe it? The Gloucestershire Islamic Trust, who own a mosque next door to the aforementioned warehouse, have protested against the modellers' plans. They describe the enthusiasts as "Poisonous, unruly and disruptive" and add that their hobby will lead to "crowd trouble, loud music and heavy drinking". This "Trust" has sent 162 letters of protest to Gloucester City Council demanding that permission be refused. The Trust's chairman, one Ayub Bhaiyat, wrote saying "The Islamic community of Gloucester vehemently objects to a model railway clubhouse. If planning is granted it will not be conducive to the harmonious relations between communities that is so badly needed".

What a bloody cheek! (yet again). Who are these people? Nigel Bray, the club secretary, said "We are a group of enthusiasts, we are working quietly to build up our club and I cannot see how anyone could imagine it will be a noisy organisation. There will be no alcohol on the premises and no entertainments".

One of the Mosque's trustees, Anwar Limalia, responded that the Muslim community had not misunderstood the application, "We know this is a model railway club but we are concerned about the precedent that will be set".

Is this where I reiterate "Bloody cheek again" - again! What precedent? I'd have thought there should have been more concern shown for the building of the first mosque. That definitely set a precedent. Frankly, Mr. Limalia, Mr. Bhaiyat, and all you fellow worshippers, if you don't like law-abiding chaps indulging in a quintessentially English hobby in our own country, that's our *own* country, then please feel free to upsticks and sod off - preferably to the opposite side of the Channel. They and the French deserve each other!.....

I'm not a Jeremy Clarkson fan but I remember his comments last October at the Birmingham International Motor Show. He described the British motor industry as being "run by Nazis" and the Koreans as being "too busy eating dogs" to design a decent looking car. Yes, once again there were those who took offence. Why? How? The Koreans eat dogs and, well, if the Germans aren't all Nazis I expect the sympathy vote is still very high.

Timely entry, now, for an article about a Kraut called Hans Münch. This person was an SS doctor and colleague of Josef Mengele. Münch is now 87 years of age and during the interview that took place and was reported in the *Sunday Telegraph Review*, he defends both the Nazis and his experiments. The article is very well constructed and harrowingly readable. He found Mengele a "most pleasant companion", the working conditions at Auschwitz "ideal" and talks of the Jews from the East as being a "dreadful rabble".

One instance of their workaday routine is stunning in its apparent ordinariness. "On June 29th Mengele sent him the head of a 12 year old child. Münch examined it and sent the findings back on July 8th. The final question to this believer in German supremacy is "What does Auschwitz mean to you" "Nothing", replies Münch.

Says it all, really......

Despite all the investment, management changes, ownership changes, British Leyland (sorry BL - oops Rover) is still in deep trouble. BMW got what they wanted, Land Rover and Range Rover. It was just a pity for them that everything else had to come with it. To be fair, it took BMW as owners to restore the famous grille to the marque. I wonder would MG have made a comeback if still in British hands. I doubt it. Not that it's the same, of course. It is merely badge marketing. For the MGF to be a real MG, it would have had to be made at Abingdon, in the same way that traditional Nottingham based beers now find themselves brewed in Yorkshire. It's not genuine, but then most of our life is a sham. The new Rover is to be called the "75". I grew up with the original Rover 75, the 90 and 110 etc. The marketing men of today presume the buying public will rush to pay for the nostalgic title. Apart from the grille, the car could be a Toyota, Honda, or anything else.

The Ford Jaguar S, however, is a different tale. Here we have true "retro". This is the first car in years that I could almost become excited by. I say almost, because hailing from Surrey one doesn't wish to overstate a product. Wouldn't do, not the done thing, what! But I have to say, the lines, the sloping grille, the shape of the rear window, does breach the thirty years since its immediate predecessor was being turned out. Unfortunately, once again it has taken foreign ownership and money to back the model. It is, however, intrinsically English.

Well, it's Tuesday, it's 1.30 pm and the *World At One* has just finished on *Radio 4*. I'm in Essex, Lakeside Thurrock, to be precise. What a ghastly place it is. Apparently, people volunteer to come here and shop. Why? It has all the charisma of a worked out quarry. Presumably, the developers actually obtained planning permission. Still, egg rolls taste much the same wherever. Oh, dear, it appears that Tony Blair has done his bit towards Glen Hoddle's anticipated downward spiral. He's gone public, donned black cap and given Hoddle the thumbs down. Looks like it could end in tears.....

D'you remember the days, and not that long ago either, when flying to any destination was considered a socially well-mannered experience? A group of Irish travellers who were thrown off a flight when the pilot made the decision to ditch them in Norfolk, Virginia, say they were only having a sing-song. Are they not aware that one doesn't have a "sing-song" when on board an aircraft. It's not done. One sits, one fidgets, one reads, attempts to follow the film, or if all else fails, contemplates sleep. Contemplation is as far as you get before you start tutting and fidgeting once more. But it's all done very quietly. This gang of twelve have no luggage. That's gone on to Montego Bay. One of their number says "We didn't do anything, everybody was enjoying themselves, having a few drinks ......" And that's the root of the problem - having a few drinks. There are many instances nowadays of air-rage, assaults on staff, etc. and the common denominator is always alcohol.

Drinks being allowed (sorry) I mean drunks being allowed on planes and would-be drunks being plied with free drink does not help the situation one jot. If it has to be, then ban alcohol on flights. Breath test passengers if they are suspected of inebriation. Why should these complete and utter 100% arse-holes be allowed to spoil everyone else's journey?

Right! It's two minutes past two and time for *"The Archers"*. John, my mate in the Czech Republic, said it's the only programme you can miss for up to three years at a time and pick up the threads of the storyline in one episode. I find most of the characters endearing entertainment, although I do wish somebody would drown Sula's child.

Right, I'm home. After I left Lakeside I had to travel to Beacontree, Dagenham, Romford and Ilford, and I have to tell you that after a day north-east of the Thames the sign alongside the westbound carriageway of the M25 announcing "Surrey" is most welcome. It's also the cue to start breathing again!

I understand that shortly there will be a rival to the Lakeside Thurrock shopping experience. This time it will be south of the Thames at another disused quarry and called "Bluewater". I've just asked Maureen if she would like to go out for a drink after dinner, but luckily she said no, so some money's been saved there! Next question for her is, "As you don't want to go out tonight, my sweet, would you like to run me down to the railway club?" I can then sit with my mate Dave and quaff a few pints, instead of the obligatory one if I'm driving. I know, I'll pay her a compliment first..... No, she won't be fooled by the insincerity, I'll just come out with it straight.

It's the weekend. Spent yesterday up in West London at the car superstore, which is still under-achieving, but then, no-one asks my viewpoints or opinions, or to be fair anybody else's who might just be able to put together a few ideas to increase the throughput of punters. Oh, by the way, Maureen did take me up to the railway club. Wonder how I can ask her next week?

Today, we're sorting out the back garden. After years of having little or no money with which to improve the rear, we are making a concerted effort this season. I'm planning to dig up some of the lawn and lay a shingled path. Fencing will separate about a third of the garden for conversion to an allotment and a greenhouse is on the agenda. As we look across the railway line, the devastation carries on apace. Diggers, cranes, dumpers, etc. continue to roam purposefully around the site. Pile drivers plunge their way into the soil before moving onto their next test bed. The trees are currently bare and I wonder if those along our side of the railway fencing will provide adequate screening. I have lopped off a large number of branches for two reasons. One is in the hope that it will generate more growth, and secondly, that the twenty recently planted leylandii will see more light of day, under a canopy of oak, willow, silver birch and damson. I'm also going to rebuild a dry-brick wall, back fill it with earth and hopefully plant our own - well - plants. I suspect that Maureen will be the greenhouse gardener and I will fit the role of transplanter of seedlings and all-round cackhanded article.

So, Hoddle has gone. MENCAP has asserted its wholehearted support for the Football Association's decision. "It is only right that the English coach pays a just penalty for comments which caused a great offence and fuelled more bigotry towards those who already face prejudice." So, no recognition of someone else's beliefs there, then! A far more reasoned approach, however, came from the lips of Jack Ashley, the Labour peer who is totally deaf. He said, "An aggressive media, a weak Football Association and his own lack of judgement have finished Glen Hoddle, but it is a sad day for British tolerance and freedom of speech". Exactly!

Robin Nedwell, the actor best known for his role as Duncan Waring in "Doctor in the House" has died from a heart attack. This comes two years after Barry Evans, also aged 52, and another member of the cast, died at his home in Leicestershire.

Now, here's one that will run and run. GM, or Frankenstein Foods, as one of the papers termed it, are being allowed to grow in selective areas of this country. There are grave doubts concerning their effects on human life, as so far the produce does not have a history. Chemical companies, such as Monsanto, would like us to be that history. To be fair, the last thing they need is a single tragedy which could be linked to genetically modified foods, but this history has not yet been written. Tony Blair is mind-numbingly blasé when he states that the government is acting on "scientific evidence" and rejects a suggested three-year moratorium.

The Americans wish to force Europeans (and in this case it affects us and the Continentals) to accept natural soya that has in all probabilities been mixed with the GM type. American arrogance is such that they say it is impossible to keep the two separate. Why? Or rather, why should the European powers-that-be accept this situation?

The public are being refused a choice. And this is not a small choice between Brooke Bond Dividend and PG Tips. This is a fundamental choice between a natural product and the product of companies seeking higher financial reward where safety has not been proven. Europe is a huge market. Are we saying that collectively it holds no clout against the American biotech companies? For if that is the case, we might as well become just another state - en bloc.

It is disturbing to read that over 60% of processed food uses soya, but that we cannot be sure whether we are eating GM products or not. Labelling is still not required to differentiate real from chemical. I am fairly underwhelmed with the whole situation.

The Lewisham Twelve, as they are now dubbed, which seems an eminently sensible tag since they hail from Lewisham, are back in their quarters beneath the railway embankment. An airline was eventually found to transport them from Virginia back to this country. They are, however, still whinging about being treated badly and, guess what, they are to seek compensation. I'd have thought their fellow passengers, who'd had to endure their selfish behaviour and a disrupted holiday to boot, would have been the rightful ones to sue for compensation. The good news is that having read of their singing, their demands for drink, their brawling and horrendous language, it is very gratifying to know that they live in south London and not the leafy lanes of Surrey. Just wouldn't do!

You know me, known to uphold all standards, but even I'm surprised by the level of snobbery one encounters. The people who bought our last house came to see us shortly before exchange of contracts and sat drinking tea and indulging in small talk. The female of the couple asked, "You do live in Surrey, don't you?" I nodded in the affirmative. She did not look convinced and continued, "Only I noticed a letter on your hall table and it quite clearly states Ash Vale, Aldershot, Hants' followed by the post code". I then explained we were about two miles from the Hampshire border. I expanded by explaining that the actual border between Surrey and Hants (or good and bad as she obviously saw it) lay with the River Blackwater. I continued by stating that although it said Ash Vale, near Aldershot, this was due to the sorting office being in the Hampshire town. Our post code starts GU for Guildford. She still required reassurance. We pay our taxes to Guildford Borough Council. This seemed to be the deciding factor. You could see the visual relief as her body collapsed in the armchair. "Thank God", she said, "I couldn't possibly live in Hampshire". Now that's snobbery!

As I said earlier, they've now moved, but once, when I had a visitor, whose visit was so short that he didn't alight from his car, she came across and asked if we were going to be long. My visitor, who sat there, engine turned off, looked at me in a quizzical manner. Yes, he was blocking her drive and possibly making it awkward for anyone to back out. "D'you need me to move?" he asked. "Are you going out?" "No, I have a friend coming soon", she said, before adding in her usual clipped tones, "She's a GP, you know". I couldn't resist it. "A *GP*" I looked in mock anxiety towards my friend, still seated. He responded in like fashion. "Not a GP? Here? Surely not!" With that, he started the car and proceeded down the lane, turned round, waved and headed off. My neighbour still never quite understood the reason for the show of juvenile sarcasm. Was there any need to come and tell us at all other than, presumably, to impress us with her friend's title, and not a very grand one at that. She never got to know me well (which is probably good news for her). If she had, she would have learned that people have an opportunity to impress - titles do not. Ah, well.

The name Robert Oliver is well known to many families. He is a paedophile sentenced to fifteen years for his part in the killing of 14-year-old Jason Swift. Since being released he has been hounded across the country. No-one wants him in their town and despite all the protests of prisoners' rights, confidentiality, etc. it seems that his next move is always known in advance - which is good news for families with young children. He recently ended up in Brighton, where he took up with another child molester in the children's section of a library. For the past two and a half months he has been in voluntary custody at a police station whilst authorities seek suitable long-term accommodation. Doctors have concluded that he is, and always will be, a menace to children. There is little doubt that he will always reoffend and he is costing the police authority, i.e. us, over £400 per day. I'd like to know how his daily bill adds up to that much. Pensioners get by on less than that each month. More importantly, I'd like to ask why he served only ten years of that fifteen year jail term. If he is so unstable and such a menace, how does he qualify for a third off? Once again, the villain's considerations take precedent over the victims.

Previous readers will know my concerns regarding the use of mobile phones being used in moving vehicles. An elderly gent of 79 was needlessly killed when a female decided to overtake a van at 70 miles an hour while on the phone to her boyfriend about dinner. A Royal Society for the Prevention of Accidents spokesman said, "This is the sixth road death that has been linked to the use of mobile phones". It still amazes me that the police give this offence such low priority. I pass car after car while the driver is chatting away, totally unaware of surrounding traffic. They never indicate, they veer across lanes, they brake late. In fact, they have all the outward trappings of a BMW driver without a mobile phone! If I and many others can see it, why can't the police? I'd make the fines extremely heavy with a one year mandatory ban and no time off for good behaviour. Ideally, mobile phones should not be able to work in a moving vehicle, and that includes trains and buses. In fact, anywhere within a 500 mile radius of Guildford!

Interest rates fell to 5½% this week. Back in November, we organised a fixed rate for the first time in our mortgaged lives at 6.99%. Looked good at the time but for the fifth month in succession, we've seen our decision become questionable. Bloody typical, isn't it?

I write the following with a mixture of amusement and incredulity. Briefly, (*good, said Maureen!*) an official for the Washington DC city government describes himself as "niggardly". A black colleague (I can hear you tutting already) thinks "niggardly" equals "nigger" and reports his workmate. Dictionary definitions are sought and digested. Upshot is, the niggardly one is sacked for using a racist word - even though it isn't.

But wait! Who's that protesting in the wings? Why, it's the gay rights activists. Apparently, our man with the vocabulary attitude is a homosexual and if there's one set of people you want to upset less than the blacks, then it's his fellow rear-enders. So, decision gets reversed, whites, blacks and homos are all friends again. Last sentence or two go to Mayor Anthony Williams who says, "The recently completed review of the incident confirmed for me that Mr. Howard did use the word niggardly' but that he did not use a racial epithet. The review also showed that one of our employees did misunderstand Mr. Howard to have used a racial epithet."

All that comical time wasted when they could have been discussing cemeteries or lighting, like they do on Ash Parish Council.

Well, Wolverhampton and Dudley Breweries have finally taken over Marston, Thompson and Evershed. Marston's Pedigree beer will continue to be sold but it's just a question of where it will eventually be brewed.

Here's another example of why we British feel the need to question, nay, suspect everything we are told. A documentary on whatever subject has always been the preserve of the truth seekers, be it on the *BBC* or commercial stations. We trusted their investigative findings. They rallied on behalf of the man and woman in the street. However, things have changed. There are now charges of faking scenes and altering circumstances to suit the story or argument. It is a device imported from America. It is cheap, shoddy and hyped. Yes, the fingers point (that's both of them) to America.

Channel 4 is expected to be fined quite severely for faking certain scenes in a documentary about male prostitutes, entitled *"Too Much Too Young: Chickens"*. This follows hard on the heels of another Channel 4 offering called *"Daddy's Girl"*. This programme was withdrawn from transmission just one day prior to its scheduled slot when the producers were made aware that they had been tricked by a couple posing as father and daughter. *Central TV* was recently fined £2 million after evidence emerged that a drugs scene in *"The Connection"* had been staged. Now all this is a very worrying development. To be fair, the scale of *Central TV's* fine indicates that the authorities are not taking it lightly, but it does not bode well for honesty, which is the single most important aspect of a documentary. We must not allow the contamination of fraud, for that is what it is, to cloud the crystal clear waters of investigative journalism. There! That was an almost weighty piece in itself.

Right! Joke time!

Have you heard the one about the rabbits housed in a science laboratory? I only want to hear the word "no" - good, then I will continue. I have to tell you that Maureen has, and is hoping that she can get through this section quite quickly on the word processor. There are, to be fair, only so many times that you can enjoy this joke - and seventy seven seems one too many!

To set the scene: there is a laboratory which experiments on animals. In this particular section of the building rabbits are forced to endure smoking endless packets of cigarettes and all in the name of scientific research. Day in, day out, their fluffy little heads are forced through bars and only at 5.30 pm are they taken back to their cages where they can choke away until the "big man with the nasty sneer" comes back for them at 8.30 am the following day. And let's be honest, it's a fairly long day.

So, it's 5.30 pm and the nasty, sneering man brings all the rabbits back to their cages, roughly throws them in, clips the catches shut, shouts nasty things at his charges, then leaves, having slammed the door. What he doesn't realise is that he's slammed the door with such force that it hasn't shut properly, offering a shaft of light across an otherwise darkened room. While some rabbits sit huddled in the corner, dazed, dejected, despondent, two of the younger males, Bernard and Matthew, still naive and with spirit, see the shaft of light as an opportunity for escape. They jump around rattling their cage until the catch falls open and the wire mesh can be pushed aside. Encouraged by their fellow inmates who force their paws and snouts against the bars, clang their cups and offer words of comfort, they make their way towards the shaft of light.

"Do it for old Red", shouts a long-stay Lop Ear.

"Tell the world of our plight", advises a Belgian Hare.

"Pretty Boy", screeches a Norwegian Blue (one of the rabbits kept a pet parrot!)

Anyway, once into the corridor, they shuffle alongside the wall, breathing heavily until they reach a junction. "This way", says Bernard, as he leads Matthew down a long hallway. Suddenly Matthew shields his eyes. "What's that?" he gasps. "That", replies Bernard, "is our escape route. That is sunlight. I read all about it in a Brer Rabbit book".

The receptionist is just putting on her coat as the two rabbits dive under her desk. The windows on each side of the main door bring a sight which neither rabbit had never before witnessed - daylight.

"Goodnight Miss", says a blue-suited security guard, as the receptionist picks up her handbag and makes for the door. As she enters her world of freedom, the rabbits speed out and hide under the flower beds. They hold their breath as they wait for the whistles that would surely follow once roll call confirmed the laboratory was two rabbits short of a hutchful. So, down the path they go, tails bobbing, snouts close to the ground. Over the hills they travel until tired and feeling safe they sleep all night by a large rock.

The following morning Bernard wakes to survey his surroundings. It's a beautiful day. "What's that", he asks Matthew, who squints in the warm morning sunshine. "I think it's a field of ...... Yes, it's carrots! "It's real, natural food", gasps Bernard. "It's real rabbit food".

They arrive at the field and peruse the carrots. "You're right", says Matthew, "and it's GM free". (Matthew had read an article on the subject while a laboratory assistant had inserted a thermometer up his backside). So they feed on the carrots for over an hour before fully replete, they sit with their backs against a tree, their little bellies full to bursting. Suddenly, a crackling in the bushes, a face comes into view. " Allo", announces a chirpy, big brown rabbit. "You're not from these parts, are you?" Bernard and Matthew sit up sharply. "No", says Bernard, "we've escaped from the laboratory. He points towards the town from whence they came. Pleasantries are exchanged and the brown rabbit announces himself as "Del".

"So, you've escaped from over there, then?" Del's eyes grow wider as the story of Bernard and Matthew's escape and past life spews out.

His head swings from side to side as the two former inmates vie with each other to tell their story. "My head's not worked this hard since I watched McEnroe and Connors", admits Del as the pair finally fall silent, remembering their friends ..... Remembering old Red.

"There's a little do on tonight, if you're interested". Del's eyes light up. "Lots of little girlie rabbits, if you catch my drift, no what I mean, nudge, nudge"(for he is a fan of Monty Python). "Yeah, that'll be great", enthuses Matthew. Bernard nods in agreement. "See you at eight, then", says Del as he hops off whistling "Bring Me Sunshine". (He'd always enjoyed the Morcambe and Wise Show and was cut up when Eric died. Even sent him a bunch of carrots). The Laboratory Two, as they were soon to be known, are picked up at eight, feted like heroes and introduced to everyone who is anyone. They dance the night away and Bernard is one of the last on his paws, embracing a young fawn-coloured doe called Fawn. (Her parents were not endowed with a great deal of imagination). As the MC announces the last dance, Rarebit in Red, Fawn asks if she might see Bernard again and lets slip that there will be another dance tomorrow.

And so to bed. They sleep soundly under the moonlight. They'd eaten, they'd danced, they'd rutted. Early next morning Bernard eulogises over Fawn's firm and fine figure. He can't wait for the evening when they will once again dance, buck teeth to buck teeth. Matthew is worryingly quiet. "What's up, our doc", enquires Bernard. (His mother was from Cleckheaton). "I'll not be coming with you tonight", announces Matthew. Bernard is taken aback. "What, not coming? But we had great fun. There were great girls, great dances, why not?" Matthew twiddles his paws, "I won't be going tonight or any night. I'm ...... I'm going back". "Back? Back? Back to those crates, those long working hours, the shouting, the abuse. How can you think of going back to those experiments?"

"That's the problem", mutters Matthew. "I'm dying for a fag!"

It's very rare that we British can be indebted to the Americans for anything other than the fact that there's a lot of water between us. The announcement that our grocers will still be allowed to sell vegetables in pounds and ounces is due to the USA being an imperial measuring nation. Britain was supposed to become completely metric by 1989. That deadline was extended by ten years to December, 1999. We now have a further ten years grace. It's nice to know that the European law lords have been forced to give up their fight to inflict their system upon us in deference to public choice. Long may we use feet, inches, miles, pints and acres. I fear, though, that now so many of us buy £20 or £30 worth of fuel at a time, the gallon is very much on its last knockings.

I'm glad to see that "*Vanessa*", the *BBC's* answer to tacky American live shows, is itself presenting a very red face. I have to say that I'm not fussed about the woman - brash, self-satisfied, smug personalities hold little interest for me. After the fraud found in documentaries, fraud has now been found in "*Vanessa*". A young girl's "live" proposal to her boyfriend during the programme was apparently dreamed up by the two of them in the canteen shortly before the show went on air. I don't know why, this rather made my day.

Oh, this is a hoot. Cindy doll is to get a dull-over. A sort of Cindy dull! From being a dreamy-eyed, tanned, big-busted gal that you'd like to get to know in real life, Cindy is to become a rather sad sod. From party-goer to party-pooper. The new Cindy will be an animal loving, child loving charity worker. Not surprisingly, those in the charity and church industries welcomed the news with open legs (sorry - arms!). The Catholic newspaper "The Universe" headed its front page article, "Taking the sin out of Cindy". Whoever wrote that probably still enjoys making forays into Africa and converting the natives for their own good. The Catholic aid charity, Cafod, (sounds like a Welsh village) says - and you'll like this - "If she is based on someone at Cafod, then she'll eat a lot of chocolate and have very little social life".

But let's be honest, that's only half the story. The real sin-less Cindy would have been abandoned by her single mother to a convent whose nuns would have abused her, before their fellow male zealots paid good money to inflict further suffering. Cindy would then become a prostitute before being befriended (and abused again) by a bearded, bald and bespectacled charity worker. I mean, if they want reality, let's get it right!

A timely piece on those poor religious souls, whose souls I would not seek to save. The Philippines are suffering from a continual rise in the number of rape and murder cases. The threat of a long prison term (paid for by the Filipino version of you and I) holds no fear. So, capital punishment is reintroduced. Yesterday a rapist was given a lethal injection. The convicted had raped his 10-year-old stepdaughter.

Opinion polls in the Philippines show overwhelming support for the death penalty. The Roman Catholic church, which religiously colonised many of the native population in one of those previous mind-bending invasions, is opposed to capital punishment. In a scene reminiscent of that American woman's execution a couple of months ago, nuns and church workers (boo now!) maintained a vigil outside the prison. Security staff kept them apart from pro-execution supporters (cheer loudly!) who lit candles to remember the victims, and for the benefit of the church, the victims are those who suffered or died, i.e. the innocent. I cannot comprehend how these sad, God revering droids come to their conclusions. I find it strange that they can so easily gloss over the offence, whatever it might be. It may go a long way to explain how abuse in the church is so plentiful and so readily covered up. What is certain, is if they have any political interests, they would all be Liberal Democrats. I can see the billboards now. "Get your half-baked ideas here". "If you like sitting on the fence, this is the party for you". "Support the aggressor, not the victim"..... Bastards!

Footnote: The Philippine justice secretary has just announced another five executions later this month - goodee.

Interesting little statistic this - between 1994 and the present time there have been seventeen major instances of assault on board aircraft. Some have involved individuals attacking crew or passengers, others have involved groups (or packs, as I prefer to think of them). As we said earlier, it always used to be such a sedate and dignified form of transport. Next time I travel I'm flying from Croydon with Imperial Airways.

Meanwhile, once more in the real world my views on the rape of our countryside will not have gone unnoticed. With very few exceptions one rarely travels out into the country these days. What one actually does is to travel from any one suburban area to a less suburban area. Just when you feel you've turned off the beaten track, there is a motorway bridge spanning your road, or a new development site, an out of town retail park, or God forbid, one of those estate agency "for sale" signs, proclaiming "5.6 acres with permission for industrial use".

The point is that planning has run amok. Bribes, backhanders, self interest, have all played a part in the concreting of Britain. The breakdown in marriages, second families and, in some cases, third, have all taken their toll. One split family means two houses, not one. We keep hearing that the country's population has not risen dramatically. Actually, I dispute that. The number of illegal immigrants, those awaiting a decision on their application for asylum and those "welcomed" by the misinformed and plainly stupid are a significant number. So, given that the powers that be are gutless, and will not encourage a decrease in number, we appear to require additional housing, and a lot of it at that.

Why, though, do we have to build on greenfield sites? Answer - because it's cheaper and less tedious for the builder. So alter the rules. Our towns and cities are now devoid of heart these days. Cambridge is a clear example, where those wishing to live there outstrip the properties available. Apparently, Cambridge could be four times its current size if proposals to build 209,400 homes go ahead.

Portsmouth and Southampton are proposing another 56,000 homes over the next twelve years, none in suburban areas. No-one could fail to notice the number of empty properties available. Terraced, detached, old, fairly new, they are in every town and city. Why do we not renovate that which we have? Presumably the powers that be (money) and the lobbyists (money again) behind the building industry is enough to warrant a blind eye.

Last month John Prescott announced that of the 4.4 million homes required to be built in this country by the year 2016, a larger proportion are to be built on ground-fill sites. I take little comfort from this statement. For a start, any official statement is easily forgotten a few months down the line, as another "special case" gets the nod after a face-saving PR enquiry has found in favour of the local authority and builder.

The Council for the Protection of Rural England say that to achieve their proposed housing quota, the land required is the equivalent of 650 square miles of concrete. It won't affect any MEP's or MP's as they can afford to remain physically detached from any intrusive brickwork.

What I find less than palatable is that the Conservative Party accuse this government of "threatening the English countryside like never before". That's rich, coming from them. We *are* talking about the party that encouraged out of town stores, indeed was instrumental in the "whole experience" of travelling from your home town to "do the shopping". This is also the party that sold off more playing fields for development than any other in the nation's history. I would lay a pound to a penny that personal financial inducements played a large part in many sales. These people are not in it for the good of the community, but for self advancement and financial gain.

All these proposals come at a time when 2,000 new homes have just been built on fields around Newcastle and 10,000 are set to be built on fields outside Stevenage.

A very good article appeared last November in the *House and Home Review* in the *Sunday Telegraph*. It gave a list of each county and with it the number of proposed new homes. The London area is expected to support another 600,000. Yorkshire, some 362,000 and Hampshire around 130,000. John Prescott, our man at the ministry, omits to mention in his "Green Man Announcements" that a new town north of Andover is proposed, a mass extension to Micheldever, the joining together of Eastleigh and Southampton and so it goes on. It's not as if any of these towns become better places in which to live.

Basingstoke is fairly close to me, about twenty miles away. That, however, is close enough for anyone. Whilst its council is to be applauded for the preservation of the alms houses and a number of town houses and terraces, they pale into insignificance when placed alongside the modern and unacceptable. Whilst it is easy to reject anything new, it has to be said that the estates built/thrown up in Basingstoke are pretty awful. The planners, designers and all their hangers-on should be forced to move into one of their "epitaphs to the end of society as we knew it". I suspect two of the major growth areas for the town are crime, and its prevention.

Many of the estates are products of the seventies and eighties and suffer from any imaginative contribution or thought. Areas such as Popley, Oakridge and Winkelbury are rabbit warrens. It's not helped by those who own cars parking them on the grass verges instead of the lay-by's provided. The planners have gone for quantity and in that, they have been singularly successful. It is, however, all very short term. The general plan seems to be to build a large batch of soul-less houses, throw in a public house, a parade of shops and all will blossom. A visitation would lead to a different conclusion. Within a few years these areas become run down with more than a whiff of dereliction. Graffiti abounds, half of the parade's shops display only a metal shutter, permanently closed, with only a newsagents and/or convenience store remaining as the estate's focal point.

Getting away from Basingstoke - and one should at great speed - we flit north to Roehampton. A good example of how a leafy, pleasant, very upmarket area was turned into a ghetto virtually overnight. If you stand on the crossroads in Roehampton Lane and turn towards the old village, your eyes take in a cluster of tumbling, individual historic houses, shops and pubs, residing safely in their conservation status.

Look across the road and you take in the awesome sight of the Alton Estate. Here resides a large proportion of single parent families. It is not a nice sight. The high rise blocks stand testimony to all that is awful in society. Large mansions set in beautiful grounds were demolished in order to house those who will never raise themselves above that of the benefit merry-go-round. The manager of a newsagents in the main parade actually has a member of staff riding shotgun (sitting on the ice cream refrigerator by the door) in order to make sure "customers" do not leave without paying for goods. It also facilitates a better view of the aisles. This isn't an isolated affair, it goes on all over the country. The main problem is that more and more children, brought up by single parents in these environments, quickly become socially maladjusted. Theft is the norm and is not a punishable crime. Indeed, we now have instances where parents encourage their children to steal with them, or for them.

Right, that's enough deprivation for one day. A final word or two on housing. The Prince of Wales took a lot of flak from architects and critics over his designs for Poundbury, the village built on his land in Dorset. When I first set eyes on the concept and designs I thought, at last, a traditional development, somewhere people would enjoy residing. This was exciting. Curved roads, individually designed houses set at differing heights and with chimneys. In short, the idea offered a lot to prospective buyers and tenants, so why the baying, why the criticism. The problem is that architects think they know best. Remember when they thought everyone wanted tower blocks? They thought everybody wanted walkways in the sky. These are the same walkways that became the graffiti, needle and condom ridden retreats of the shirking classes.

Such is the architects' arrogance. With all the evidence that their creations have *not* been what the inmates required for their families, they still seek to ridicule the acceptable face of modern development. There is no crime in retaining traditional concepts, with chimneys. Perhaps it was the done thing to criticise Prince Charles, well I like Poundbury and wish that many more developments, including that abortion at present being built behind us, had taken note of what could be built.

I have obtained the latest PR information on the Barratt's Old Farm Place..... It's here somewhere ..... I had it earlier - honest. Oh, bugger! I'll find it when I'm not looking for it, as usual.

Just over four weeks ago, Maureen had an accident in her car. Her insurance broker suggested some years ago that she took out separate cover for claiming against the other party if she was not at fault. Now bearing in mind that the car is third party only, the advice at £12 per year seemed too cheap to ignore. All these years we've paid up, but this year we needed to make use of it. An acknowledging letter is the sum of the communication so far. Of course, Maureen's insurance came up for renewal this week. As the case is "pending", she can only receive a 40% no-claims bonus instead of the 60% she has hitherto enjoyed. I rang the claims people earlier but they are "awaiting correspondence from the other party". If our claim is proven Maureen is in for a rebate for the other 20%. If they deem it knock-for-knock, then she loses out.

A couple of years ago we had occasion to visit Portsmouth. I can't think why, but we did. It was a Saturday. We had changed cars and I tried to ring the insurance brokers to register new details, etc. Could I get through? Could I buggery! Continually engaged. I rang another branch and asked if there was a problem. Some hapless assistant told me it was likely that all the lines were busy and I should keep trying. I did, but to no avail. Eventually, Maureen and I drove three miles out of our way to their office. I went in, Maureen stayed in the car and knitted. I stood while the three sales staff dealt with customers. All the while the phone rang and rang, whilst a young girl flitted around the back, pulling out files, refiling files and never making one attempt to lift the receiver. When it came to my turn I explained that I had tried ringing, that the journey was a waste of my time and in totally the wrong direction from which I was to travel. In short, I went "into one". I then, for good but fair measure, brought into play my spotting of said girl. "Why couldn't she answer the phone, she must have heard it?" "Oh, she can't do that", came the reply. "Why not?" "She's not been trained" came the improbable answer.

I admit to being a little taken aback. "Not been trained?" I repeated. "Christ, how much training above common sense does she need?" The young assistant explained that it was against company policy for new staff to answer the phone before they had been trained. Says it all really!

There is an advert by the Metropolitan Police in today's *Sunday Express*. Two-thirds of the ad is taken up by a photograph of three police officers. An Asian female, a West Indian male and a white male. How very pc. Get it? Oh, never mind! In the blurb it states The Met's wishes to "reflect London's rich cultural mix" and points out that "our Positive Action team's on hand to inform and encourage women and applicants from an ethnic minority background who are currently under-represented in the Met". Funny, but I thought the idea was to employ the best, not try to make numbers and colours fit the frame to please the meek and weak Mr. Jack Straw.

The other day when Simon my cousin came over to dinner the conversation stumbled onto race and the very subject of police and quotas. I said that should I be pulled over, stopped in the street, whatever, by a black or Asian police officer, my attempts to remain passive would be severely tested. Maureen and Simon could not see it.

Indeed, Simon asked how ethnic minorities would ever be integrated if people like me never gave them a chance. Well, I do. But the police are a different kettle of fish. I really would not be best pleased to be told to move on by a non-white officer, having spent fifteen minutes attempting to find a parking space, and yes, I would be tempted to explain, childishly maybe, that if there were less foreigners, we might have some spaces left. I know, I know! Not a hint of racism but a bloody big dollop of it! But reverse the role, I'm an Indian in Bombay and I'm told to move on by a white policeman who was born in India, of parents who hailed from Dunstable. I'd feel just the same. This is not the one-sided issue do-gooders and Liberal Democrats purport it to be. It's life, it's human nature ..... It's also teatime!

Well, that was tasty. I must ask Maureen what it was! Isn't it always the way, you start to read an article and get the feel-good factor, only to continue and end up totally frustrated. Let me explain. Today, it was announced that "Criminals are to have their benefits taken away". Now you'd think that policy would be welcomed by all, wouldn't you (wouldn't you?). Not in some quarters. Jeremy Corbin, Islington's Labour MP, is not at all happy about it. He's concerned that the children of offenders will suffer if benefits are withdrawn. He says that "benefit is a right, paid for by tax and national insurance and this goes very much against the spirit of the universal welfare state".

The point is, Mr.C, that the public do not mind benefits being handed out to those who (a) deserve and (b) have contributed. Criminals do not fall into either of these categories, as a rule. Not surprisingly, Peter Cavadino from NACRO, the National Association for the Care and Resettlement of Offenders, shrieks, "This is a thoroughly retrograde proposal, which will be likely to promote crime rather than reducing it".

Thinking about it, those against the proposals have little to fear. This government's record for bottling out is excellent. Frank Field's social reforms, single parent benefit cuts, the sale of sports fields ..... What a bunch of gutless bastards they are.

So, a number of bishops upset their hierarchy by attending a conference organised by the Lesbian and Gay Christian Movement. Despite the decision condemning homosexuality, taken at the 10-yearly Lambeth Palace get-together last year, a number of these chappies were apparently "ashamed" of the Lambeth vote. These are probably the same clerics seen outside the meeting with their black garb hoisted whilst shouting "I'm free" to all and sundry. Mind you, I think the additional "it's all in a good cause, luvvie" was a tad over the top! Ah, well.

CHAPTER FIVE

A LAND FIT FOR REFUGEES

Another ticket punch in tradition's season ticket has just been made. Fire engines are to be painted white. It appears that red is no longer easy to see, especially at night. One of the few remaining "municipal style" authorities, the fire brigade, has always turned out a gleaming machine, complete with home station name neatly painted on the sides in capital letters. Well, I've now seen a picture of the new white monstrosity - looks like a dust cart with ladders. No doubt somebody justified their position and salary with this unwarranted scheme.

The battle to follow Hoddle continues apace. Many names are in the frame. I think the FA should stop faffing around, bite the bullet and invite Terry Venables back. Give him a free rein and not ring him until we've qualified.

I've just checked the date on the paper and there's still over a month and a half to go before wags in the media pull our legs with this year's jolly April jape. I just felt that I'd slipped forward a few weeks, so incredulous is the article. It appears that the collective guilt suffered by the police is now reaching new levels of implausibility. The "Met" has commissioned a group of (c)rap artists to produce a sound track and video. The aim is to recruit ..... yes, you've guessed ..... more black officers. The finished article will criticise the police and then encourage young black people to enlist. Filming will commence fairly shortly in Brixton. It turns out that 3% of the police force is black or Asian, that's around 900 officers in real money, but far too few for the pinko liberals, I'm afraid. They feel that a figure of 5,400 would reflect the true ratio of non-whites.

Naivity is alive and well and doing very nicely thank you in race relations. Another report by a group of people who really should get themselves a proper job suggests that Britain be "rebranded". They advise the government to "challenge directly the attitudes in which racist behaviour is rooted". Those interested in continuing the white man's burden hope the report is "as significant for race relations as Lord

111

Scarman's report into the 1981 Brixton riots". That was eighteen years ago. Nothing seems to have changed much as far as I can see. If it had, we wouldn't have the overbearing subject thrust down our throats every day.

The author, one Ms. Yasmin Alibhai-Brown says that Britain should be "re-branded as an inclusive concept that embraces diversity and values, the contribution of all its members". She naturally calls for more black and Asian ambassadors, advisers and press officers. She worryingly requests a "government media team to rebut misinformation". I suspect she means a distortion of every facet of society in order to promote ethnic causes. The dear Muzz would also like to see government sponsored research on white attitudes to ethnic minorities. There doesn't appear to be any suggestion of government sponsored research into black attitudes to whites.

Laughably, pathetically and typically, she requires the banning of official use of terms such as "bogus" and "abusive" to describe asylum seekers. Why, when most of them are? Still, this is the land of semi-skimmed milk and GM free honey.

I see King Hussein of Jordan is dead. The signs for peace in the Middle East are about as promising as peace in Yugoslavia once President Tito keeled over. There will be an awful lot of egos to be sated, western as well as middle eastern .....

Any respect I had for Harry Redknapp, the West Ham manager, has disappeared with his signing of Paola Di Canio. The player should, as we all know, have been banned from playing in this country again. Instead, he is welcomed back into the golde n world of premiership football.

Humorous little tale now. A female who failed to notice that she was pregnant, gave birth in the Birmingham branch of Marks & Spencers. The boy, who has got five of everything and is quite healthy, has been named Kyron, with Mark Spencer being his middle names. Thinking about it, Kyron Budgen or Kyron Asda just don't have the same ring, do they? While on names, a friend of a friend rejoices under the surname of card. Have you guessed? They actually named their son Valentine! ..... poor little sod.

There's been another case of appalling, boorish behaviour aboard an aeroplane. Down to drink once more, naturally. Three complete arseholes of the highest order, and they presumably were fairly high, performed their own full monty whilst crossing the Atlantic at 35,000 feet. The film of the same name was being shown at the time. Normally passengers remain in their seats, but of course this brain-dead trio had been drinking. Now we're not talking about youngsters here, one is aged 55 and runs a pub, the other two are 49 and 26 - father and son. What makes it worse, is that the 49 year old is a police inspector and his son, a police constable. I think it should be strong tea for all in future and perhaps take your holidays in the front room, where you can amuse yourself in the privacy of your own home whilst allowing socially acceptable human beings to get on with their lives.

Euro's down again. That's the end of the good news. I'm about to go into one! The NHS is about to pay out £250,000 to a woman who basically suffered sub-standard treatment. During the initial 48 hours in hospital the "little or non-active management" exacerbated the damage already caused. And the cause? She was taking Ecstasy at a night club. The young woman, aged 25, suffered "catastrophic damage as oxygen to part of the brain was cut off". Her counsel explained that she would probably never work again, and that she had left hospital paralysed down one side, unable to speak or swallow. She has since re-learned to speak, read and write. She suffers epilepsy, impaired memory, concentration, speech impediment and has problems moving the fingers of her right hand. She becomes angry and her IQ has suffered. It couldn't have been that high to start with if she was taking Ecstasy. Everyone knows the dangers. As Ann Widdecombe commented, "There has to come a time when people take responsibility for their own actions".

It was argued by the hospital trust concerned that the damage could have been caused by a direct toxic reaction and that no amount of treatment would have made any difference. But no, a quarter of a million pounds worth of hard-earned tax payers' money has gone to this woman. Money that could have been used for much more deserving cases. Not surprisingly, her parents were still "unhappy" with the amount which was awarded on top of "substantial" costs. Naturally, there was the all too familiar warning that this ruling could lead to a flood of similar claims.

The Ecstasy taker concerned, now living independently, returned to her council house after the case. I'm so pleased for her!

These last few years have witnessed the seeds of greed germinating by the acre. Facets of life that would never have attracted compensation are now commonplace. As with the last story, new ground is broken weekly, opening up whole new areas for litigists. Bad news for taxpayers and insurers, good - no great - news for the legal profession, who now openly invite those with an eye to a fast pound to "come on down".

For instance, who would have thought that police officers involved with child abuse cases would sue their own force? Yes, it's that overplayed word "stress" again. It's a bit like having a bad back, try proving you *haven't* got one. Now this particular group of five officers claim they were overworked because of inadequate resources. There was a lack of support and, guess what, yes, a lack of counselling after interviews with the accused's victims. So, naturally, they're all suffering from post-traumatic stress order. What did these people think that police work entailed? Endless days bending the knees and exclaiming, " Allo, allo, what have we got ere, then?"

We've already been subjected to the contemptuous behaviour of one PC, Fiona Paterson, who is reportedly seeking £100,000 for back pain caused by the wearing of body armour. If she hadn't been wearing it and someone had shot her, there would have been hell to pay.

While with the police, there's been the case of Laura Dyer who claimed that the tiny receiver she wore in her ear for undercover work led to tinnitus. Naturally, she sued the Met and went home a lot richer to the tune of £175,000. Not bad for a few days' work. I'm not saying she's lying or that she hasn't suffered. My neighbour has had tinnitus for years, but he just gets on with life. Then again, he's a proper person!

Last month the family of Matthew Harding, the Chelsea Vice-Chairman, who died in a helicopter crash, intimated their intention to sue. They are planning to claim against the Civil Aviation Authority for alleged weaknesses in its safety requirements. The family's lawyers have previously sought record compensation of £120 million against the estate of the pilot who also died. I've just checked that figure. Yes, I'm right - £120 million. They state that they are pursuing all legal avenues in an effort to maximise the value of Matthew Harding's estate. The man was apparently earning some £7 million per annum. I'm sure it's all perfectly legal, but it just doesn't seem right - or necessary.

That Louise Woodward case is another oddity. I have absolutely no idea of whether she was guilty or not. Like everyone else, other than those immediately involved, I wasn't there. Even if she had been found not guilty I would have charged her with obtaining a false accent. Who on earth would want to acquire an American twang (well, other than Miss Woodward, obviously). I mean, it's not mandatory, is it?

Mind you, the Eappens haven't made many friends. They're what you'd call a funny couple. Something doesn't fit. For instance, they've lost their son, which is tragic. You cannot bring him back. I know that no amount of money would ever compensate me for the loss of any of my children, but the Eappens are seeking damages of £3 million, which includes £600,000 that they claim is the minimum amount their son would have earned had he grown up to establish a career! Have you ever heard the like? I find it insulting to the child's memory. It's tacky, it's tawdry, it's truly American.

The greatest outcome from Louise Woodward's reappearance in England is the demise of the pub show. D'you remember? All those locals getting their 15 minutes of glory, following in the well-trodden footsteps of the Waltons and their sextuplets, and Eddie Edwards. I suppose it put the pub on the map for a short while. It always amused me how the locals spoke of "knowing" Louise and being totally convinced that she hadn't committed the crime. How do they know? How could they be so sure? Were they there, lurking under a bed, in a cupboard? But then again, once I'd heard her speak I couldn't really give a toss whether she was guilty or innocent.

We haven't heard too much recently of the Woodwards senior either. That in itself is good news. I'm interested in the story of the alleged misuse of cash. That pub and its new-found clientele raised a lot of money for Miss Woodward's fund. There are now suggestions of false expense claims, high living and new cars. It hasn't gone unnoticed that the fund, which reached a quarter of a million, is showing signs of being down a bob or two. The police are wondering where it went to, and why. Some £180,000 of it to be precise.

The Reverend Ken Davey, Chairman of the Louise Woodward and Family Trust Fund, said, "We will fully co-operate". We wait with breath once more bated.

Another few cases and I'll have got it out my system - for a while! There's a lady captain of a golf club who sought compensation for breaking her ankle whilst on the course. She had a "nasty fall" when slipping on a slippery railway sleeper, one of thirty forming steps which connect the fairway and tee on the ninth hole. "I was in agony for a long time". Fair enough. She's been on crutches for seven weeks - also fair enough. Now she is surprised to find that the club have refused to renew her membership. "It was the last thing I expected", she said. "By claiming compensation I was only exercising my rights". So there we are. Rights! She was exercising her rights. If everyone exercised their rights there wouldn't be enough money left to go round. Did she honestly think the golf club was going to welcome her back with open arms once she had sued them.

This one disgusts me. One of the schoolteachers at Dunblane who witnessed the dreadful tragedy in 1996 has been awarded compensation for severe psychological trauma. Linda Stewart has been unable to work ever since. Of course it was horrific for all of those involved, but you have to get on with life and be thankful that you, or your children, were not amongst those killed. The award has not been disclosed but could be around £500,000. Mrs. Stewart states that "No amount of compensation would help to put things right". Then why ask for it!! It does seem strange that she has received compensation before those families who lost children, but then to be honest, why should they be compensated either?

I end on an encouraging note (that's a first!). The recent case of a student paralysed for life after diving into a college swimming pool was awarded £1 million. This young man climbed over a six foot boundary wall and dived into an open-air pool which had been shut for the winter. No-one else dived into the pool that was far too shallow, no-one forced him. He was not drunk and he made the choice. Thankfully, the case has gone to appeal and the judge has found in favour of the college and overturned the compensation ruling. Of course I feel sorry for him, but as Ann Widdecombe said only a few pages back, "there has to come a time when people take responsibility for their own actions".

It's worth repeating that line if only to reassure myself that there is someone else in this country who doesn't feel that the world owes them a fully financed living, having made complete arses of themselves.

The GM font of plenty gets muddier by the day. It's just been revealed that David Sainsbury still retains control of a charitable trust that pumps millions of pounds into genetically modified crops. How can anyone in the position of government minister still be allowed to retain such strong ties with such a contentious industry? These people are involved for the goodness of their own wealth, although they say it's for everybody else's good health.

School discipline has plummeted since I was a lad. Once again, the Liberals, do-gooders and all-round arses have had their way, but what goes round, comes round, as we've found previously. When standards have reached rock bottom a new direction will have to be found to raise them once more. Discipline will be the new way. I mention this because a teacher at a school in Chatham, Kent, was dismissed for grabbing an unruly pupil around the neck. The child is well known for his record of bad behaviour. Fellow teachers have supported their accused colleague, but no, at a school governors' meeting they decided to dispense with his services. Last month, the case was thrown out of court but still the school refused to reinstate Mr. Singlehurst. Yesterday, shortly before the case came before an industrial tribunal, where Mr. Singlehurst was claiming unfair dismissal, a settlement was reached. So what message did that pupil, and others like him, receive?

While Charlton's victory over Wimbledon was long awaited, over three months since they last won, they are now "only" four points behind Everton. I think Notts Forest are doomed but I don't want to see either Southampton or Charlton being demoted. Everton could go, with no tears shed here. They've been milling around mid-stream for years. A big budget club, a lot of in-fighting and ego taking the place of ambition. If they cannot make a fist of it with all their money and experience, they do not deserve to stay up. Coventry? There's something about that team I like. It's probably Gordon Strachan's passion as much as anything. Blackburn? Yes, they can go. Good talented players like they have, and yet they're still struggling. Thumbs down.

Right, I'm off to the railway club, so that I can have a few beers with my drinking partner, Dave. He has that rare luxury of offspring who always owe him favours. They repay him by running him to the club. Handy that!

It's Wednesday and not a good start. Jack "I'll bend over backwards for the ethnic cause" Straw has informed MP's that the recruitment of black and Asian police officers is not good enough. Naturally, he listed eight forces that employ fewer than ten ethnic officers. I suppose there'll have to be a name change from P.O.'s to E.O.'s. We could have E.O. Brown and E.O. Black working alongside P.O. White! Anyway, it's obviously not good enough for dear Jack. I mean, what does he want? Does he want to move blacks and Asians from where they live, just so he can get his ethnic sums right. This obsession with percentages is really getting tiresome. I bet Mr. Straw will be more reluctant to provide percentages if he were asked the ratio of crime committed by whites, blacks and Asians in relationship to population. I have no doubt that such a request would be considered insulting, immaterial and almost certainly racist.

Why are Home Secretaries so gutless? It doesn't matter which political colour they have adopted, it always turns to yellow when push comes to shove. Apparently, in order to reduce the housing pressure in Kent and certain London boroughs, councils will be forced to give homes to refugees. How can they have it both ways? On the one hand we're told that 4.4 million houses have to be built across our once green and pleasant, now not so green and sometimes distinctly unpleasant land, whilst at the same time, we encourage every bloody refugee from anywhere who states they are homeless and unwanted. What a soft touch we are.

Even when he does suggest the introduction of reforms to make it less of an easy option, the process is fraught with danger, not least from his own MP's who shout, "Rights" when discussing anything to do with asylum seekers but ignore the rights of us poor sods who foot the bill.

It's not as if this latest intake from war-torn central Europe are a particularly thankful bunch. I listened intently to a debate on radio a few weeks ago. Shopkeepers in Dover and Folkestone were not impressed by the boorish behaviour, the lack of respect for women and the petty theft. In general, they are a pretty anti-social bunch. Of course, a spokeswoman for some refugee organisation called Annie (typical name that) laid the blame at the door of the locals for not responding to their plight. Could you imagine the welcome we would receive if we sauntered off to pastures east, expecting anything for nothing. That's what we'd get. Nothing! And quite right too.

It's not going to be a happy year for elephants. The Convention on Trade in Geneva has authorised a one-off sale of ivory, some 34 tons held in Namibia and Zimbabwe. No surprise to tell that the Japanese will be the recipients.

The vote to sell was unanimous. Kenya opposed the proposal, stating that the green light had been given to poachers who were already shooting elephants in the hope that restrictions would be lifted. Michael Meacher, our illustrious environment minister, backed the sales. He said, "This agreement will raise much needed revenue for conservation and community schemes in the African countries concerned".

He sounds as if he's talking about a run-down council estate in Newcastle. The same cliché's, only the location has been changed. The problem as always is that if it wasn't for the Japanese, there would be no market. In retrospect it's a pity we didn't finish them off in 1945. I mean, they're such sadistic sods - you only have to look at their game shows.

I was going to look at the TV guide, but I don't think I'll bother. One gets used to the daily diet of police, hospital, animal, fly on the wall and soaps. Same menu, different day. The highlight for Maureen and I are the comedy repeats. Thank goodness one can still enjoy *"Rising*

Damp", *"Dad's Army"*, *"Allo, Allo"*. *"Whatever Happened to the Likely Lads"* was repeated last year. Don't think I missed an episode. It just amazes me when you read of producers' surprise that a 20-year-old comedy is still bringing in 8 million viewers. These comedies have survived as reliable, repeatable fodder because they are well scripted, well acted and funny.

So, the griffin is finally killed off. My bank, the Midland, is now part of that faceless, meaningless corporation, HSBC, with its unimaginative red and white hexagonal logo. In 1992, when the HSBC (can't remember what it stands for) bought the Midland they stated that the business would be developed "under its own identity". They didn't add "only for seven years, though".

Some witless wonder of a chief executive commented that, "We operate in a global market place and the change will help avoid the confusion that exists as a result of the multitude of names we possess" What claptrap! I don't know of anyone who was confused. Bastards!

I wonder how much General Pinochet has cost the poor taxpayer so far. Way back in October legal expenses had topped £350,000. And for what? With their record on animal rights, we should have told Spain to bugger off and stop annoying us with demands for Maggie's friend to pop over and answer a few questions. I mean he's a nice old gentleman on holiday! No, until they ban bullfighting and all the other dreadful games they conjure up in the name of quality leisure time, they can take a jump off one of those towers from which they take such delight in pushing off their donkeys.

I've always given more than a passing glance when in sight of a Morris Minor. They conjure up all that is good in British design. An extensive range of models, saloon, estate, convertible, pick-up and van. The saloon typifies the Bert and Doris 1950's mode of transport. The estate, probably the last with wooden bodyframe, continues to be seen in Sainsbury's car parks around the home counties south and appears to be very popular in Bournemouth. The convertible is a thing of total beauty, whilst builders and small businesses alike continue to ply their trade using the vans and pick-up versions. They were so beautifully understated in appearance and it is reassuring to learn that some 50,000 vehicles still exist in daily use throughout the British Isles. Oh, for the romance of the British Motor Corporation and all those who sailed within her clutches, and then disappeared without trace. Riley,

Wolseley, Standard, Triumph, Vanden Plas. Gone - and unfortunately forgotten by most.

I saw my first traditional telephone box in black yesterday. New World Pay Phones have started installing them in central London. BT hold the trademark to these traditional boxes known as the K6, but other companies are allowed to use them provided they are not painted red. New World's Marketing Director, Lucas Vigilante, (what a name!) announced that his company were putting fifty in and around London.

I never understood why BT decided to act so outrageously and with such vandalistic tendencies in their pursuit of the wholesale removal of the K6 boxes during the 1980's. Now they are replacing the replacements in certain areas of historic grandeur or outstanding beauty. Nice to see common sense returning, if only for a limited period - I'm not that confident.

Some good news for television viewers, *ITV* is to scrap *"Gladiators"*. What an appalling programme that was/is. The contestants seemed fairly harmless, but the crowd, especially those related to, or friends of the participants, appeared to have been on something. No-one outside of America should parade themselves as the audience did during those "tension wrung, breath taking, heart stopping moments" that well, never quite materialised. Despite the hype engendered by Ulrika Jonsson and her co-hosts, the show never raised itself above the IQ of the audience. Shame, really.

We're now going to spend some little time on animals. First, a story that warms the cockles, etc. A young lady, named Linda Rodwell, has won a highly rated conservation award for helping South African's crane population from certain extinction. A prize of £40,000 is no small amount but she fully deserves it after spending nine years overcoming some fairly hostile reactions to her endeavours. In 1990 the South African government reclaimed land from farmers in order to create a reserve for the Wattled Crane. White farmers used to shoot or poison these birds because they feed on newly planted maize. Black farmers used to eat them. Only twenty birds exist, so her work is vital. I wish her well.

The same wishes cannot and will not be extended to the Countryside Alliance who have just published their annual report. Amongst its heart-tugging findings, it maintains that hunting creates 414 full time jobs in the Quantocks and that the murder of animals (*my words, "hunting" in theirs*) is as vital to the local economy as Rover is to the West Midlands. Frankly, if 414 souls lost their jobs and had to obtain work which did not leave metaphorical drops of blood on their hands, then so be it.

However, by the very nature of their "sport" one could never expect the hunter and his ilk - as opposed to elk (which he would have killed anyway) - to place morality and ethics before money.

Hunting is by its very nature an emotive subject. Those who oppose the killings are viewed by the hunter as misguided townies and soft, therefore, dewy eyed and short in vision, lacking any understanding of the hunter's contribution to conservation. These views contain all the hallmarks of arrogance, as Nazis are to Jews, hunters are to animals. It is a farce to suggest that they kill merely to keep numbers in check. This is pleasure, pure and simple. Surely one of their number could be honest enough to stand up and say, "Yes, I enjoy it". At least you would know where you were.

In March last year there appeared a photograph in the *Guardian* showing hunters from the Devon and Somerset Stag Hunt dragging the deer they had just shot up an embankment. The scene, as described, looked horrendous. The River Exe is the boundary between the League Against Cruel Sports 300 acre Baronsdown Sanctuary, and land legally used by deer killers and their followers. This particular stag plunged into the river, having been chased there by the Devon and Somerset Hunt. If it had managed to swim across it would have been safe. However, it doubled back, doubtless in dreadful fear and panic where it was shot. Both sides saw the situation differently, but the thought of those on one side of a river baying for blood and apparently throwing stones and blowing horns in an effort to disorientate the animal, while those on the opposite bank encouraged the stag to safety beggars belief. It certainly polarises the gulf between good and evil.

The Hunt's Joint Master (shouldn't that be Mistress?) one Diana Scott, said this had been "a normal day's hunting", adding "the deer was despatched quickly and cleanly with one shot". That, I suspect, sums up their total reaction. We chased, we killed. There was no reflection on the misery caused to that animal during its bid to survive. Those opposed to the somewhat one-sided hunt endeavoured to save the animal by jumping into the river and attempting to guide it to sanctuary. The killers followed, jeering, whooping and hollering. Words fail me.

The above story came in the same month that the Tories killed off the proposed ban on fox hunting. Aided by a number of Liberal Democrat and Labour MP's, Michael Foster's bill was "talked out". Why should country money talk so powerfully?

This is another example, and probably the most culpable of a weak, gutless government. Before the last election, candidates or their party faithful, descended in droves on an unsuspecting public. Doorstop questions, high street baby kissing, you know the sort of thing. Well, when the girl from Labour called and asked if she could rely on my vote, I asked outright, "Can you guarantee that you will ban hunting with hounds?" She couldn't quite guarantee that, no. She commented that it was obviously in Labour's manifesto, or pledges, whatever, and that she was confident a ban would take place.   I was not confident in her confidence. I didn't vote for Labour, in fact, I didn't vote for anyone. I would like to have been proved wrong, but we are talking about politicians here so one is right to suspect, and one is right to expect to be continually disappointed.

Killing of animals for fun is unfortunately a world-wide sport. In France upwards of 1.5 million take to arms and dogs before taking to the forests and hills. I suppose we should take a crumb of comfort from the fact that the British killer tends to aim at its quarry. The French shoot at anything. What a pity they didn't employ this obvious enthusiasm during the second World War against the Germans. Not that shooting Germans outside of a war is likely to upset anyone anyway.

Three people have been killed and several seriously injured during the present hunting season. One man was shot in the face as he drove his car in a non-hunting area. A woman beater was shot in the head by a killer who thought she was a fox - no, don't laugh - oh, all right, go on. The previous hunting season ended with figures of 45 dead and over 200 injured. It's a bit of a perverse way of getting rid of the French, but I suppose every little helps.

Drink contributes greatly to this carnage. I have no problem with them shooting each other. In fact, I'd encourage it. But for those of the killing fields, woods and hills, it's very much a day out for the boys and beer. With all the ego's to be sated, drink to be drunk and bullets to be fired, it is no wonder that pheasants, partridges and other game birds are in such decline. So what do the Frogs do? Well, they start on the boar and the deer. Whilst it is illegal to fire a gun more than 300 yards, the high velocity rifles they use have a range of over one mile. Conversely, if we hadn't intervened to save the French some fifty years ago and just left the Germans to get on with it, there may well be a number of species less likely to become extinct. Oh, for hindsight .....

Back in Britain (as opposed to backing Britain, which Labour seem unable to do) we are told that fox hunting will continue until the House of Lords is reformed. Good news for the killers.

I remember writing in the two previous tomes about the cowardly custom of shooting old or tame animals because it's easy, and it's a practice that still continues, unfortunately. A South African lion breeder (bastard!) has sold seventeen lions to a Mozambique hunter (fellow bastard!) So that they can be shot by rich Germans (them again!) and Americans as "trophies". The practice is known as canned hunting. Various animal welfare groups have petitioned for the lions not to be sold. Their efforts have unfortunately been in vain.

The wonderful new dawn that is Mandela's government has failed to take any action on this or other animal issues. There was an outcry when thirty baby elephants were taken from Botswana to be trained for circuses. If only all animals were black. Neither Mozambique nor South Africa ban hunting tame or old lions. White South Africans have bought a lot of land recently in Mozambique just so that they can organise hunts. Not content with this awful sport they show a complete lack of regard or respect for anything or anyone. The Kruger National Park is suffering from hunters who make gaps in the fence, lure out the lions then trap them in cages for their own "sport".

I remember a photograph published in the *Times* during last September of an elephant rounded up along with the thirty others to be sold to circuses. The picture showed a small grey elephant chained to a fence post from its left rear leg. The article drew attention to the fact that some had been shackled, roped together at the knees and whipped. Many of the young ones had been taken from their mother, so their chances of survival were minimal. Amazingly, although one should never be amazed, kidnapping elephants in the wild is not illegal in Botswana. Can you believe it?

Nothing to do with greed, the *Daily Telegraph* published a photograph showing some of the 300 beached pilot whales that lived off the coast of a small island in New Zealand. When the alarm was raised most were dead, but over forty were still squealing, hemmed in by their dead companions. All had to be shot as there was no chance of refloating them. A picture like this still hits home as I look at it now. It all seems such a waste.

Meanwhile, in deepest Devizes, the Joint Master of the Tedworth Hunt, a certain Rodney Ellis, was stopped last November by the police. A breath test revealed Rodders to be almost twice the legal limit. Now the huntsman's story goes like this: he claimed he was forced to drive his wife home from a hunt dinner because she had hurt her leg in a fall from her horse earlier in the day. After the fall she had been taken to hospital and later allowed home. She had then made haste to the dinner. During the evening Mrs. E. decided she warts (sorry, wants, can't read my writing!) to go home. Rodders asks if a friend can give them a lift. The friend could not, so he tells the police that he had no choice but to drive his wife home himself. No other choice? Even Devizes has taxis.

So our man of the fox goes to court before the presiding magistrate, one Lady Johnston, wife of Wiltshire's Lord Lieutenant. Remarkably, the misguided (at the very least) Lady J. announces, "You had just cause in driving because this was a sufficient emergency". With that, good old Rodders is fined £450, plus £100 costs. Cheap, isn't it? What a let off? No ban, no bugger all! Can you imagine if that were you or I.

But now the cream! The good news is that the Crown Prosecution Service also thought it was a let-off and the Court of Appeal has agreed that the ruling by Lady J was flawed and that the case is now to be referred back to the magistrates court. I have no knowledge of the outcome, but I suspect the result will be a tad fairer and that Mrs. E. will have to chauffeur Rodders around for the next year or so. Ho, ho! Or should that be Tally-Ho, ho!

You will have appreciated my respect for the *Daily Telegraph* over a number of years, but in its stance over hunting we are at odds.

The *Telegraph* was quick to re-attach its blood red colour to the mast in its comment of 26th December. It paid tribute to the fact that "By tradition, Boxing Day is one of the high days of the hunting calendar. This year we are glad to say promises to be no different ....." They go on to pay "tribute" to all those who have kept the sport alive and positively "cream" at its rude health. The writer points to the 300,000 souls (shouldn't that be arseholes?) who paraded through the centre of London under the collective banner of the countryside alliance.

There's no mention of the march being hi-jacked by four-wheel drive toting, green wellie and Berber jacket wearing Hooray-Henry's, all of whom have a vested interest in the pursuit of immoral death.

Indeed, the paper devoted two pages in its weekend section to the sport, such was its testimony of support. They were not alone. On the same day, the *Daily Express* ran a one-page article headed "Why We Must Rally to the Call of the Fox Hunt Horn". Written by Frederick Forsyth. Well, under a title like that you know there is little room for doubt or discussion. The article made for an interesting read but never disappointed in the remark "..... hunting people are deeply into conservation. A contradiction? Not if you understand the countryside. That old chestnut always comes to the fore. "Not if you understand the countryside"

What does it mean? I take it as arrogance. You do not have to live in the Chipping Camden's of this world for generations to understand death. This is death perpetrated on an animal that cannot fight back, it can only run. As someone once said, when man invented the gun, hunting received an unfair advantage. Might not have been those words exactly, but the sentiment said it all.

The following day, Sunday 27th, saw a story all too familiar but conveniently ignored by the happy killers. In the village of Kirkbymoorside in North Yorkshire, hounds from the Sinnington Hunt attacked and killed an 11-year-old cat in the front garden of its owner's home. The incident took the number of cats killed by hounds to four since the silly season began in October. Unlike my previous search from that handout from Barratt's, which I never did find, I have retrieved an article, the last for a while anyway, on hunting. Again extracted from the *Daily Telegraph* it shows quite clearly why American children grow up to be the American hunter, who seeks thrills in killing old and tame lions. Unfortunately, with the Americans, they get older physically whilst the brain's capacity fails to mature at the same pace. .In fact, it's fair to say that they just do not mature.

The article commences with reference to a hunting camp in Texas where an eleven year old boy sits with his father in a small wooden hut with narrow "windows" from which they shoot animals. In this case it's deer. The poor sap of a child referred to in the article comments, "We learn that animals have souls in church". His hapless dork of a father adds, "I'm sure they have souls because when I shoot them I want them to go to heaven. That way when I go to heaven I'll have something to hunt". Doesn't that smack of grade A arsehole speak. (Maureen just typed grey day, not grade A - good job I spotted it. Pointed out it wasn't Larry Grayson who was the hunter).

Just after 7.30 a.m. on this Texas plain, as father and son bond in anticipated death (if only it were their own!) a mechanical corn feeder sprays corn 50 yards in front of them. Three doe venture out to feed. Hey-ho, the trigger is pulled, one rears up into the air, flails then falls to the ground - dead! "Good shot, John", says Wayne, the boy's father. "That was fun, dad", enthuses John. I find it amazingly unhealthy to encourage a child to kill so wantonly. This outfit called the Texas Youth Hunting Programme is run by an ex-US army colonel, Jerry Warden. There are even all-girl hunts. Four million deer are killed each year by the likes of Wayne and offspring. Mr. Warden has a lot of blood on his hands and a lot to answer for.

I know what I meant to tell you, I'll just unravel the slip of paper that's in my back pocket. No, it's not the five-pound note that's attached to it. Right! During the week, I had occasion to visit beautiful downtown Ruislip. Whilst there I wandered through the library grounds. There are a small number of animal tombstones. I particularly liked the following:

Peter
(Cocker Spaniel)
Born 23rd June 1922
Died 19th January 1927
The best and truest of friends
The sun in our faces, the wind in our eyes

Sad that Peter died so young, but immortalised with dignity and feeling. The second read as follows:

In memory of the black
corded poodle dog Pierrot
(Japan) the beloved and faithful
companion of Miss Netty Levy
who passed away December 22nd 1916
of heart failure. Aged 14 years
and a half. He will never be for
gotten bye (sic) his sad mistress.

I don't know why, but the above reminds me of an ex-colleague from my days organising car shows. He was a real prophet of doom if ever there was one. However, a more kindly, thoughtful man it would be hard to find. I'll call him Harold. He could definitely pass as a Harold. He and his wife went to the cinema some little time ago to see the film "*Antz*". They left after a short while. "I didn't like it", he said the following morning. "It was all about ants". Mock incredulity abounded. Apparently the title and the insects on the posters failed to give even the most subtle of hints. I remember Harold homing in on a discussion about the film "*Silence of the Lambs*". "That's the one with Hannibal Hector in it", he offered sincerely.

Harold is a creature of habit. Every Sunday, rain or shine, he and his wife go car booting. That is their quality time pursuit. Harold is never without a camera. You name it, he'll snap it. A traffic accident to a shop window display, and even his prize company Astra, they're all snapped with the enthusiasm of a young child. He once managed to capture the end of the rainbow at Slough. He sent the photograph to a science magazine and copped £10, I think, for his troubles. Now, perfection is the name of the game in Harold's life. No artisan has ever worked in his home without Harold literally sitting on the poor chap's shoulders, eyeing every slap of the brush, every turn of the screw. Shortly after having had the bedroom ceiling replastered during the fitting of, well, fitted cupboards and wardrobes actually, he found that his water tank was leaking. Up goes the plumber who, probably distracted by the eagle eye, puts his foot through said ceiling. He then arranges for a plasterer to make good the work. Months of "Has your ceiling been repaired yet"and always being greeted by glum face and negative movement of the head, we at work were one day surprised to hear that, "The plasterer is coming tonight". The following day revealed a sombre Harold once more. The plasterer had apparently arrived, been taken to see the offending hole, tutted, shaken his head and commented that he didn't realise the hole was *that* big. Eventually he, or another plasterer, filled in the hole and plastered to match. Harold was not impressed with the work but accepted it as the best he was going to get in the circumstances. In case you're wondering why he didn't get the original chap back, I cannot tell you. Suffice it to say that listening to Harold telling you a story is akin to Uncle Albert regurgitating a sea-faring story in *"Only Fools and Horses"*.

What I can relate is that as the plasterer drove off, he misjudged Harold's wall, taking the pillar closest to the drive with him. He promised to send round a brickie. The story now moves to the summer of 1997 when months had passed by. Staff at work, including myself, made many enquiries as to the state of his wall. It was the best known wall in the company and not one of us had ever seen it. Eventually the date was set. The brickie had been, estimated the work and a Saturday in September was confirmed.

On the Monday after the anticipated event I asked if the wall had been made good. "No it hasn't", exclaimed Harold, as he threw down his pen in frustration. "Didn't he turn up?" I enquired. "Oh, yes, he turned up, but I had to send him away". All heads in the office turned. "Why?" came the obvious retort. "Because it was Princess Diana's funeral and I couldn't have someone working on my wall when her funeral was taking place. What would the neighbours think?" Having pressed Harold as to whether he was joking, and finding out he wasn't, we then discussed his state of mind and concluded that Harold was indeed a creature of extreme habit.

It was during 1998 that calm and a new end pillar descended upon Harold's Maidenhead side road. Over the years I have known him Harold has come out with one or two gems, including the following. "When you retire you have time to stop and admire the roses. At the moment, every time I pass, the bloody things need pruning". Harold once said to me, "Thank you for leaving it in apple-pie order, I just need someone to peel the apple". No, I'm not sure, either, but sociologists would have you believe there was something deep and meaningful.,

Getting back to the people's Princess, I remember the day Di died. Maureen, Simon my cousin and I were staying in Wales for the week. We arrived Saturday afternoon. I drove, Simon navigated. He took us on a very picturesque tour of Hereford, Worcester and Shropshire and all in an effort to encounter a road that would take us over the border. He eventually miscalculated and we found one! The cottage we rented was in the middle of nowhere, high up on a hill. Remote was not the word - well, actually it was. It was on the Sunday morning when I walked into the dining room/kitchen where I found Simon listening to the radio. He looked up and announced, "Princess Diana's dead".

After breakfast we travelled along the coast northwards. Stopping at Aberdovey, we found a shop with a window already displaying photos of the royal couple in happier times. Black drapes and sympathy cards abounded. As the week progressed oversized sympathy cards and lists were lying on tables to be signed by all. Why? Not one of these souls were hardly likely to have ever met her, so why the sad faces and the tears?   Was this another example of American outpourings being adopted by the British masses. Surely not!

Of course it was a tragedy, for parents and children alike, that's her parents and children, but here in deepest west Wales, pictures unfurled of similar scenes throughout the British Isles, as the flower industry blossomed and well-wishers poured out their hearts and their currency. Gone were the days of well controlled faces masking grief, gone was the stiff upper lip, the understated acknowledgement. Here, in 1997, we witnessed full-blown histrionics. I just wish somebody would have told those concerned that public wailing is just not on.

The Saturday of our return, one week later, was Diana's funeral. All the pubs shut until 2 pm which was fairly pointless since in many cases it was closing time anyway. So much for a pub lunch. We travelled long and hard in search of a break to the journey. We trundled through Crickhowell, only to find it had gone on holiday. The one chink of dim light lay in a pub situated somewhere around Caerleon, near the River Usk. A large unfriendly looking building in need of renovation offered "Food available now". It's at times like this you tend to forgive the nose-rings, the tattoos and the pony tails, and that was just the staff! The food, as I remember, was not awful, but as they say in the priesthood, "Buggers can't be choosers".

I think it was the *Times Weekend Supplement* about a year ago that led with "Diana, was it murder?" If it was, it will doubtless be covered up, but then that's love in the fast lane and we'll probably never know if she was carrying a sprog by Dodi.

Right, I'm comfortable. It's 11.26 pm and I'm in bed. Maureen is watching a soap she recorded earlier, so I'll carry on writing for a short while. Must remember to get the toenail clippings out of the bed before she comes up - only kidding, I've already removed them!

Bed is the place when alone, to reflect, to seek answers to questions posed ever since that character from the world famous novel, the bible, launched himself upon the stage and somebody said, "Ok, it's now 00.00 hours and it's 1st January 0000 AD".

I'll pose one now. When I fart, does my reputation go behind me? Now that's surely a question that needs addressing, as opposed to Renault Clio's Nicole, who needs undressing! The things you think about as you lie in bed. Oh, well. William leaves school in four months. He's got to sit - if he can sit for that long - all his GCSE's. I can't think of what he will do for a job. The one thing I know is that he'll get better marks than we would expect him to get on the evidence of any knowledge gained at school. I have no doubt there will yet again be a rise in the number of A-level passes. We all know it has nothing to do with higher standards, just slacker marking and a desire, nay, desperation to be near the top of the league tables. Let's face it, the most successful students of mathematics, with the most brilliant marks, will doubtless still be under the impression that Pythagoras's theorem refers to the thoughtful ramblings of a dinosaur.

A young lady I know, who shall be nameless, was asked if she was studying Jane Eyre during her A-level English. She thought for a few seconds before replying, "Tell me some of the books she's written".

Hang on, I can't write and break wind at the same time. (As Maureen's typing this she looks as though she has a metaphorical smell under her nose - it's not real and anyway, it was a few months ago). Trouble is, I've got to write with the windows wide open and it's not that hot - certainly not as hot as it is up my backside. I'd walk around for a while if I thought it wasn't going to follow me. I know, I'll wave the covers around for a few seconds. I'll tell you what, if there is a Maker, then all I can say is that it was a bloody good decision not to place the nose and backside too close to each other.

I was in WH Smith's earlier today. There were two women at the book counter. One asked for a copy of "Women on Top". The way these two were turned out, they'd have given Crufts a bad name. I would say that from the title of their reading matter they lived in the realms of wishful thinking.

Maureen is in the bathroom getting ready for bed. She didn't say anything, so it's either wafted out the window or she's losing her sense of smell. Anyway, she won't know anything about this until she types it. Right! Clock's wound up, alarm is set, I'm now ready to turn over and go to sleep and Maureen wants to talk. She says she's just been having a conversation with Glyn about the cars he and Debbie have owned over the years. Okay, it's not that sensational but it's all part of the quality time process we need with our offspring. Time for bonding, yah. Maureen's just reminded me of the time Glyn came home late without his keys. Couldn't wake us so he slept in his car, a red Talbot Samba, which on reflection must have been pretty embarrassing in itself. We found him the following morning lying awkwardly on the back seat. A notice had previously been attached to the windscreen concerning a field the car had been seen in. No, I didn't want to know the details either. Maureen suggested it was a vagrancy notice. Quite witty for her, have I married someone new? No, I look across the duvet, at the beautiful woman who uttered those immortal words. Yes, it's Maureen, the young girl I married nearly thirty years ago. I have to write this crap occasionally as it makes her feel wanted while she's typing this book, and I'm watching football. Ah, married bliss!

Tell you what, talking of duvets, I've got a typed sheet of paper someone gave me as material. It's a short list of courses or lessons given by a government-backed education body, the North Yorkshire Training and Enterprise Council. Courses and lessons include, how to put covers on a duvet, how to park a car, finding the right wine for a dinner party, writing a press release for a local paper, and lastly, checking oil, water and tyre pressures.

All right, woman, I've nearly finished. Why does she always want to turn off the light when I'm in full flow. It was a different story when she wanted to relate nostalgic tales of the offspring. She's thrown me out of kilter - what was I going to say? Oh, yes. I was in the library as well today, what a busy little bee I've been. The object of my visit was to compile a list of clubs so that I can post them details of my talk on - well, anything they'd like me to talk about really. Anyway, I listed down several clubs for my own use and then one or two that might cause amusement. Did you know that there's a "Guildford Manic Depressive Fellowship". You have to ask yourself, if they're depressed in Guildford, then what the hell are they like in Bracknell? There's a "Parkinsons Disease Club", where I assumed membership is limited to those who have been attacked by an emu. What d'you mean, I've misunderstood? There was also a Brass Rubbing Club. I had to double-take on that one - I read it as Breast Rubbing! And finally, there's the Horsley Bridge Club. I couldn't determine whether it was the one over the motorway or the railway line.

God, that woman. Lights have gone out. Goodnight!

I'm writing this in the car, beside the park in Park Royal. It's just gone 1.15 pm and the number of staff at the car superstore continues to rise. The telesales department is now in full swing. The manager is a likeable sort of chap I've nick-named Tin-Tin due to his haircut. He's got himself a good team, comprising Antipodeans and a Canadian. I'm not sure foreign accents cut the mustard when cold selling over the phone, especially cars, but time will tell. Car sales appear to be reasonable but the amount being spent on such items as the valeting bay, offices and the proposed MOT area is considerable. When I question such expenditure I am told that I am not looking at the "big picture". Well, fair enough then.

It's the last episode of "*Dad*" with George Cole tonight. I find the comedy refreshingly dated, you know, married, middle class couple still together, still at home. They appear to share meal times and stories. George Cole, in the role of grandfather, or dad, reminds me so much of my own father. Sometimes in ways, but definitely more in looks.

Most papers ran with headlines concerning GM crops and food over the weekend. Professor Arpad Pusztai, who made public his concerns and was sacked for his troubles, is back in the news with sentiments such as "vindicated" being bandied about. I won't go into details because by the time you read this the story's misinformation, lies and damned lies will have been batted back and forth, and we still won't have the truth.

What I will say is this. Tony Blair will live to regret that he wasn't stronger on this issue at a time when decisive leadership was so important. His continual weakness in not imposing a moratorium on GM crops is unacceptable. I realise that he and the government ministers concerned are under extreme pressure from American politicians, American food manufacturers connected with this money spinner and all those sailing along in the slipstream waiting for the financial fall-out to drop into their laps. Uneasy as it is for politicians to stomach, some decisions have to be taken for public health reasons and not financial.

This subject will not go away and neither will the doubters. It doesn't help when you consider that all research institutes receive grants from the very companies seeking to licence, then sell the product of that research. Do you remember when scientists used to be the good guys?

Well, at least Charlton won, 1-0 against Liverpool. Only one point behind Everton now. So the England manager's job could go to Kevin Keegan or Martin O'Neil. Mmmmmm......

Here's something I, and hopefully you, will find hard to swallow. Despite an EU ban on the ritual slaughter of animals, imposed in 1993 for all of us, but extended to this year for the French, sheep are still being exported for this purpose. Interestingly, it is not because the French themselves are heavily into ritualistic killing (as we discussed earlier, little effort was made sixty years ago with the Germans). However, it is the Muslims who celebrate some religious festival, and for that they need 60,000 lambs, ewes and rams.

Now you might think that having been granted a stay of execution, which is more than that accorded to the sheep, the French government would have used that six year period to sort something out. Something like "it might be a religious festival to you, but to proper people it's cruelty, therefore bugger off and buy a kebab, Mustufa", or something like that. But no, a French government spokesman said, "It is a very sensitive and delicate matter. We have to reconcile the interests of French and EU law with the age-old religious traditions of an important part of the French community". He means the French multi-cultural community of course. And no EU law must be used to force these people to toe the line.

These sheep are hung upside down, often being stabbed up to forty times, having had their throats slit. They are left to bleed to death. I call that barbaric and no religious madcap will convince me that he is doing his god's work. The sheep first undergo a journey from Britain, usually Wales, across the country to Dover, from whence they are ferried to France. They are driven south from Dunkirk to the Muslim sites close to Paris.

The farmers of England and Wales know the market and they know that their sheep are bound for Paris. They should hold their heads in shame. They are as responsible as the unfeeling zealots who kill them. All of this could be avoided if the French government took off its spineless overcoat and stood up to its arrogant population just once in a while. Our government and the National Farmers Union are no better. Christ, how money talks! The RSPCA say that, "With so many Muslims in France taking part, the authorities are turning a blind eye so as not to risk any trouble". Well, that doesn't say much. Tell you what, bet the reaction wouldn't be the same if it were whites performing the same abuse. Then they wonder why your sympathy goes out of the window.

As if all that wasn't bad enough, we now have this plague of Albanian homeless freshly consigned from Kosovo. It's not our war, we should stay out instead of shelling out. Financial hand-outs are bad enough, but now we are to open our doors to even more refugees. One huge block of flats in Barking, Essex, is nick-named Refugee Towers. Out of the 400 people who live there, 145 are asylum seekers (or scroungers). They don't speak English, they can't work, but we can certainly support them and are they grateful, are they buggery! There have been many stories of pickpocketing all over the south-east, verbal abuse of women and girls but apparently we have to put up with it. As one refugee put it, "Life in Italy and France is very bad for refugees, you get no food, nothing. Everyone in Kosovo knows you must come to England because you get everything free".

Will Jack Straw please stand up and be counted!

CHAPTER SIX

"AT THE END OF THE DAY ....."

Whilst I find it rich of the Tories to criticise Labour for raising taxes by stealth, did anyone *really* believe that a promise of no rise in the rate of income tax would mean no tax rises?

Presumably, the Tories hope that the populace is short on memory. The problem is that Labour appears to believe that as the new "opposition party" got away with it for seventeen years, they can as well. The sad fact from the taxpayer's perspective is that *all* governments get away with it because middle England grumbles to itself but has too much self respect and reticence to become engaged in a brawl. No, we wait for five years and then make a protest vote in favour of someone who will do exactly the same thing.

Yesterday the word on the street was "GM is safe". Today, "crops altered by science pose threats to birds, plants and animals". We've still heard nothing from government departments. Presumably they will not wish to upset their special relationship with the Yanks.

These foreigners show no respect, do they? Up to fifty Kurd militants stormed the Greek Embassy in London. During the afternoon, after a peaceful demonstration, they break through the police cordon. Why? How? And then manage to sit in the middle of the road, disrupting proper people attempting to go about their business. Are we now saying that our police force is so inept that it cannot handle and contain fifty chanting, baying souls?

The demonstrators then throw cones before one girl sets fire to herself. The police catch her and dowse her with water. I'd have been sorely tempted to turn my back. Bloody cheek! If they want to demonstrate about their own country, bugger off over there and don't bother us!

You remember the two policemen who danced to the full monty on that flight from Orlando to Manchester, well the jury have cleared them.

Those two, and their pub manager friend, who displayed boorish, intimidating and arrogant behaviour, are let off. Where did they get the jury from? Were they all members of the Howard League for Penal Reform? The good news is that there will still be an internal police enquiry and the judge refused them costs. With a bit of luck, they may have learned something. Probably just a few more dance moves!

It's nic e to see that things are never quite as bad as they may seem. While eastern Europe pulls itself apart, and the likes of Monsanto pull life as we knew it apart, Frinton-on- Sea has been subjected to a massive social change. I refer to the imminent arrival of its very first public house. By a vote of eight (all Labour) to six (Tories, Lib Dem and Independents) the motion was carried. J.D. Wetherspoons will be the first dispensers of alcoholic beverages in the town. Roy Caddick, secretary of the Frinton Residents Association, said, "that's cool Britannia, 8, what England used to be, 6. It's the worst day for Frinton since the Luftwaffe beat up the town in 1944".

You wait until they're invaded by Albanian pickpockets.

On a serious note, and the Albanian problem is a serious note, you can't help wondering why consent was given for the public house. One hundred and seventy letters from residents were sent against the proposal and only four for! Doubtless the business rates will come in handy.

So the *BBC* is to axe *"One Man and His Dog"*. I don't expect the title is politically correct enough for them. I wonder if a subtle change to "One Person and Their Canine Friend" would save the day. Probably not.

Another so. So, our Kevin is to be the new England manager. He might well be called coach, but I prefer the original and genuine. Meanwhile, Mohammed Al Fayed has offered "my Kevin for a passport". Still can't see him getting it somehow. Strange how those who revere British institutions and are clearly seen to be putting something back into the country are denied citizenship, while others who contribute the square root of naff all can just turn up at the Passport Office, and hey presto, they're British.

Another test case. This time it concerns an Iranian homosexual. He sees himself as a would-be refugee. The Home Office considers that he should be refused asylum and returned to Iran. The appeal will centre on whether homosexuals are a "social group" (anti-social group I would have thought!) Iranian authorities feel that homosexuals are "corrupt parasites". Isn't it strange how you can warm to another country's viewpoint so easily .....

Just a thought, but I wasn't impressed with *"Harbour Lights"*, starring Nick Berry. Not one you could take to, bit of an arthritic script I felt.

Some people, huh. They are a sad lot, those who believe in a god and a hereafter. Those poor Methodists are now including a prayer with the words "God the Mother". I've just read that feminists and liberals have been campaigning for some years for the feminine line to be adopted. Their new prayer starts, "God our Father and our Mother". You can imagine this lot being politicians. Their wishy-washy panderings to all about the unexplained would grind real life to a halt. It's been bad enough witnessing the Church of England's "get modern" approach to marriage services (Maureen's *still* looking for that troth I pledged her. I told her to look under the stairs, that's where all the rest of the household rubbish is hidden). Now this lot are deleting the words "giving away", i.e. the bride is no longer being given away by her father, or more commonly now, stepfather, guardian, social worker, brother.

They say it is not a theological shift but that they "want to provide material which people feel comfortable with". Pandering! I am right, aren't I - *aren't I!*?

All that time buggering about, changing, deleting, adding words. Not a statement on important issues, such as GM foods, hanging or Kevin Keegan's appointment. Oh, no, for them a discussion as to whether God is a Mr. or Mrs, or both. Have they ever considered that he or she is black, a lesbian, a trans-sexual - just a thought! To be fair, why shouldn't he or she be black. Your Jesus character may be white, even off-white as he's a middle-easterner, but why should his mother or father be white. What with all these step-parents about, I mean, his mother was supposed to be a virgin. Well, you see, there's a bit of a flaw in this novel. It's all a bit misconceived - a bit like Jesus in fact!

Do these trusting souls ever consider any other possibilities? Perhaps God is a born-again comic, because if he is real he would have to possess a great sense of humour, lumbering us with the Gallagher brothers and Robin Cook. I wouldn't even wish them on Harpenden. Oh, well - I don't know why but I'm just reminded of a joke. Did you hear about the man who goes to the doctor's and says, "I've got something on the end of my willy". The doctor takes one look at it and says, "It's a mole". The patient replies, "That's funny, I don't remember having sex with a mole!"

You see, there are moles and there are moles......

Now this is cool. A roads protester has advertised in his local paper for a tenant to live in his tree house in Dorset while he treks off to India for twelve months to study stone carving. I like that.

Tony "now let me say this to you" Blair, our alleged leader, is still attempting to allay fears concerning GM foods. Over the past week newspapers have given over pages to discussions, questions and opinions concerning the chemical sleaze, but our Tone will have none of it. He's now launched a huge public relations campaign in order to boost confidence. Who is he kidding? Iceland, the frozen food store, have announced that they will only sell food that is GM free. BurgerKing are to ban it from their list of ingredients. These are only the first of what will be many. But no, Tone appears to think a swim against the tide will do him good. I wonder if he will learn before he drowns.

And while we are on the subject of TB, here's a question I'd like an answer to. Why is it that new Labour purports to defend democracy and human rights so scrupulously, but when it comes to the leader of the Welsh Assembly, block votes are the order of the day. Alan Michael is a lightweight. He has the word "follower" written all over him. Rhodri Morgan looks the metaphorical fighter, the battler, someone who would champion a deserved cause, however unpopular. In short, he looks electable as a leader. Certainly the people of Wales consider Mr. Morgan their choice. Poll after poll after poll indicate a large lead over Alan Michael. But popularity and one-man, one-vote, is not to be everything in Welsh politics. In short, politics is everything. A block vote decided upon by a committee could let in the lowly pretender and keep out a possible great force. Nice to see that some things in the Labour Party never change.

I see Naomi Campbell was flaunting a coat edged in wolf fur. After all the publicity, all the pain, what a bitch.

So, a national currency changeover plan is being unleashed on an unsuspecting public. There are those who are convinced that the pound will be replaced by the Euro, possibly in 2003. I think the tide is beginning to turn. The government would have a referendum tomorrow if it felt confident enough, or rather they felt the British public were confident enough - but we're not, and they know it! Oh, yes, and the Euro's down again.

It's Saturday morning and I've just got time to read an article by Tony Blair who writes that, "Genetic modification will become the revolutionary science of the 21st century". He's not listening, is he.

137

This week saw the showing of an *ITV* film *"The Murder of Stephen Lawrence"*. The makers have already been accused of bias by the police. It didn't go unnoticed that one of its producers was the wife of Michael Mansfield, QC, who represents the Lawrences. It seems that the awfulness of Stephen Lawrence's death is now a background story. People are using it as a springboard to further their own demands and obsessions. Witness the "Nation of Islam"'s appearance in the court room. Their attendance resulted in scuffles, affray and ultimately violence. It was not the wisest of moves by the Lawrence family.

Would a film have been so readily financed and produced if the colours of those involved were reversed. I don't think so.

Here's one to rankle. The village of Hambrook near Bristol has requested over many years for a small area of land to be designated as their village green. Newly arrived three years ago are a German couple, who recently decided that as this green area borders their property they would do what Germans always do, they'd annexe the land. The greensward is separated by a small stream, but that's no obstacle to this hardy couple. They say their deeds clearly state that the land is theirs. If that is so, why have they taken so long to fence it off? Krauts aren't usually that backward at coming forward, in fact, the only time they retreat is when cold steel is being shafted up their jacksies. "They don't like it up em". If the land is theirs, why has the local parish council continued to apply for village green status for twenty-nine years? Surely someone on South Gloucestershire Council would have said something if it wasn't theirs. Upshot is, it looks like sorting itself out at a council meeting next month. Whatever happens, the Krauts are unlikely to endear themselves to the locals.

Charlton won 2-0 at Derby and move into sixteenth position. It's looking better.

There's an amusing little tiff going on in South Africa regarding the suitability of a certain beauty contestant. The finals of the competition, called "The Face of Africa" are being held in Namibia. A young lady called Tracey Maitland-Stuart has been selected for the South African finals. There appears to be a problem. Miss M-S is white. Many black South Africans are up in arms and feel that the Face of Africa should be a black one - and they are quite right. You cannot have a white girl representing *any* African state. Not, of course, that the same "rules" would apply in Britain if you reversed the colour situation. Can you imagine a beauty competition in this country and someone standing up and saying that a black girl shouldn't be the face of Britain? Doesn't bear thinking about!

Well, Alan Michael, Tony Blair's champion has won it for Wales - or rather, he's won it for himself. The GMB union block vote is what he has to thank for being the newly appointed Labour assembly leader. You really do feel you're in a time warp, don't you. It's 1999, the first Welsh Assembly for several hundred years and the leader is not even elected on a one-man - oops - one-person, one-vote system. And as we said only a short time ago, that's new Labour for you.

What's on TV tonight ..... Soap, soap..... soap on the other side, followed by a soap..... police...... fly on the wall......animal ...... police. Well, that's much the same as last month. There is, however, a new comedy by Caroline Aherne entitled "*Mrs. Merton and Malcolm*". Have to say I got a tad tired of the "*Mrs. Merton Show*", so won't be watching this new comedy on the box, although I'm given to understand by Maureen who's in the middle of cooking dinner that she will give it a try.

One thing's for sure, it's either GM food scares or the Stephen Lawrence case that's number one headlines in all the nationals all of the time. I have to admit that I'm beginning to suffer from an overdose of the Lawrence bandwagon. With regards to the crop fiasco I hope that Monsanto Chemicals now realise that people are standing up and asking questions and will not be put off by their relentless battle to rule the world. The only difference is that sixty years ago you got to see the Germans coming!

I like grapefruit juice for breakfast. Very acidic, very tasty. I'm just finishing off before I trundle southwards to Chichester, Bognor and Littlehampton. A couple of years ago I was in Bognor on business (well, let's be honest, it's the only time you would go there) and needed to make a phone call. Found a box, but it was inhabited. I waited outside. Occasionally I looked in the direction of the box in an effort to ensure that the chap knew I was next in line. I started whistling after a couple of minutes. You never hear people whistling these days. Anyway, he knew I was there, but his body language was not encouraging. Coin after coin was fed into the unit's orifice, as he gesticulated to no-one in particular. Eventually I tapped on the glass and pointed to my watch. Nothing! I tapped again, raised my eyebrows and waited for him to replace the receiver. What d'you think he did? He turned his back on me and continued talking - bastard, I was not amused.

Now I'm not very good at diplomacy when my dander's up so I

opened the door and interrupted the conversation. He swung around and attempted to pull it shut. I was having none of it. One foot jamming the door and two free hands triumphed over his one free hand. Then, the penny dropped, like his had several times. The gesticulating, the near histrionics. He was French! Read this bit with an accent: "I'm ringing my family in France", he spluttered out. I pointed out that if he ventured a little further along the coast he could catch a boat that went there! In the meantime he still attempted to close the door. I remember commenting something like, "In England we use public boxes for short phone calls so kindly replace the receiver and bugger off"! His hands went into overdrive, one still clutching the receiver. I can't remember exactly what I said after that, but I grabbed the phone and ejected him onto the street. I made several references to his "typical French arrogance, French selfishness, French this and that". Result is, he walked, cursing, back to a Renault and made off in an easterly direction. Dover would have been good.

Ah, ha. Just read the television reviews. James Walton in the *Daily Telegraph* describes "*Mrs. Merton and Malcolm*" as having a "generally low key feel", adding that it "meandered mirthlessly and boringly along for thirty minutes, then ended". So, apparently not the biggest fan. Maureen thought it was brilliant. I was actually upstairs writing and could hear her downstairs. Now when you laugh with no encouragement from a studio audience, it must be funny. I will watch it next week.

The race issue is getting truly out of hand. I ignored entering into any discussion regarding comments made last week in the national papers concerning racism in the National Health. But today we have a plan put forward for "a racism league for schools". This will all backfire. I won't waste time on the nitty-gritty, but the article is followed by yet another stating that, "New duties imposed on the NHS are intended to have the effect of improving services for patients from ethnic minorities". Am I being made to feel second class, or what?

Yesterday, for the second time, the granite memorial stone to Stephen Lawrence was vandalised. I do not condone this action at all, it helps no-one. What I cannot believe is that public money has been spent on erecting a closed circuit television. In this latest attack, the camera was a complete waste of space as there was no film in it. Would someone like to inform me if all other memorials in Britain have CCTV? I wonder if there's a CCTV looking down on the memorial of

PC Blakelock who was killed in the north London riots a few years ago.

On the case in question, it is no surprise that despite Imran Khan, the Lawrence's lawyer, saying "it has nothing to do with money" he is writing to the police commissioner asking for compensation. The investigations continue.

It's Monday. I'm sitting at my computer-free desk in west London. It's just gone mid-day and I'm about to start sorting out all the keys for the building. Tedious, but ultimately satisfying. What tripe! It's not, I'm just trying to save face. It's been a funny weekend. On Saturday we bought a 10 foot by 6 foot greenhouse. We've never had one before, as you know. But Maureen has been on about getting one for months, well, ten years in fact! As usual, the selling price of £239, including base, seemed very attractive. We left, having handed over a cheque for just under £600. This included metal tables, metal compost holder, with work shelf and vented window. I asked the owner, for it is a husband and wife team who run the place, if it is easy to erect. His reply was cautious. He must have seen the words "DIY failure" tattooed across my forehead. (Which is better than being tattooed across my foreskin, which would have been more difficult for him to spot). Anyway, after a quick shifty of all the nuts and bolts and bracing, etc. I decided to ask if they supplied an erection service (no jokes please, if you're reading this before the 9 pm watershed). They did, £95 but that included tables, compost holder, everything. The erecters are due at home tomorrow. Trusting souls, they won't even have cleared my cheque in time.

It was very sad to read and hear that Derek Nimmo has died. Now he was a true enigma. As a devotee of *"Just a Minute"*, I felt I had known him for years. He was really part of one's life without ever physically entering into it. He will be sorely missed.

Oh how the cutbacks continue to affect everyday life. Essex Police Farce (sorry, Force) has been on the receiving end of £7 million worth of government cuts. Their fleet of motor cycles has gone, as has four horses. Notwithstanding suffering the indignity of having a police car sponsored by General Motors in Clacton, and a local garage donating two cars to Chelmsford Community Safety Department, it really shouldn't come as a shock to learn that a local bus company is offering free rides to bobbies! Hedingham Omnibuses are the good eggs who have offered free travel. I suspect the level of morale in Essex police is equal to that of a Russian soldier.

However noble, it does put into perspective the money spent on public services which is paid for by the public, compared with that

141

which goes to quangos, overseas aid or the Millenium Dome. Hang on, telephone's ringing. It's okay, nothing important - or rather, it's not for me. Where was I? Oh, yes. Here's a little known fact that you can drop into a dinner party conversation, "Did you know that Murray Walker dreamt up the slogan, "A Mars a day helps you work, rest and play". No, you didn't, did you. But you do now and I bet you feel a lot better for knowing it.

What a cheek - the Lord Mayor and Mayoress of Bradford (Labour Chappie and Chappette) are to be handed £2000 for employing a house cleaner. The Lib Dems and the Tories used phrases like "It's a disgrace" and "I'm speechless". (Not very good if you're a politician). This couple, Tony and Elsie, much more down to earth than Mayor and Mayoress, already receive £9,900 in the form of a civic allowance, but no, it's apparently not enough. Our Tone says, "You really can't expect my wife (that's Elsie) to work from 7 a.m. until midnight without some help". What a cheek - oh, I said that at the start of this paragraph but never mind, it's worth repeating. The problem is that once again a precedent is set. They'll all be snorting into the civic trough asking for more. As far as I'm concerned, if they don't like the money offered, don't accept the job.

Going back ten years, when I was writing *"From Where I Sit"*, I commented that Sky would be the downfall of TV as we knew it. Sport has virtually disappeared from terrestrial TV, and last week the greed cancer spread further into the front room, when *Sky* launched pay-per-view matches. £7.95 was required from any household that wished to watch Oxford United against Sunderland. The power of the satellite stations and all those who fly with her is enormous. They have the ability to change times and dates of matches. The FA and all those party to these money-making schemes seem to squirm like children meeting a film star. They roll over, bellies up Still, as long as the money's good.

Now you probably have an inkling of my feelings for the Germans. As you know, I'm one to hold my cards firmly to my chest and never give out full vent..... I'm sorry, that must be somebody else's life. Anyway, the next piece should give you an inkling that nothing changes, even if you still have your doubts about the Krauts.

Scotland exported 90 pine trees to Germany. These will grace the newly refurbished Reichstag. They have been grown in Perthshire and are sixteen years old. Once they have been planted in German soil for a very short time, these Scots pines will be reclassified as "German North European Pine". The trees are thirty feet high and are costing £500 each. A spokesman for the suppliers, Bellwood Nurseries, said

"The Germans wanted the trees to be as pure and natural as possible" (we've heard all this before, haven't we?). "These trees have been grown from the seed of the ancient Caledonian pine forest. They have a very good pedigree and an excellent provenance with a blood line that can be traced right back. They are Scottish trees, but after they have been in German soil for a year, they become German "citizens". Under EC law each tree has a passport and under nationality laws these trees can officially be classified as German.

A spokesman for the German Embassy in London said, "I am sure that the Reichstag trees will not lose their Scottish roots". (That surely wasn't an attempt at being humorous, was it? I mean, they're never that quick witted. No, must have been an unintended pun). Anyway, the said spokesman went on, "Their blue/green colours will remind us of the braveheart warriors" - condescending git!

It is sad to see that Southern Ireland is becoming more like Somerset - i.e. full of incomers. In the south west of the country there is one small village where the original population makes up only one third of the total. Not only have the rich and famous sought sanctuary in its larger states, but the Americans and Germans are invading in hordes. I remember when we stayed in Roscarberry, County Cork, during 1989 and 1990, one of the locals complained back then that a path used for generations was now barred to the locals. It had been bought by Germans. Not quite the correct way to get on with the locals, but possibly a very good way to discover a pound of Semtex being stuffed up your jacksie. Germans now count as the largest non-English speaking inhabitants of Ireland. There are nearly 6,500 of the burghers. The Krauts look down on the locals, the locals accuse the Krauts of expansion. Relationships are strained. And that is why we have racial unrest. I wonder if any politician sought out the views of those living in the areas where incomers have made inroads on the housing and job market. Irish politicians could do no better than look to England and observe the results of multi-culturalism..

A middle aged teacher from Cork has started a "Keep Ireland for the Irish" campaign. She feels it will gain momentum as the country becomes "saturated with foreigners". She has my sympathy. Ireland, though, is in a good position to do something about it while the problem is in its infancy. I can just see the Irish government being told by some politically correct government minister that they really must accept so many refugees from this country or the other, and that they should embrace multi-culturalism ...... Oh, yes, I can see that.

What else has happened other than my being given a cup of tea by one of the telesales staff. Oh, yes. Forgot to say, I've been made redundant!

George, one of the directors, nice chap, ever so enthusiastic, earlier requested that we "have a chat" in the meeting room. "Anthony", he said, "I don't know how to say this". He looked at his pen while he rolled it between the fingers of both hands. "George", I replied, "this is me. We all know that when anyone comes in here for a one-to-one, they're never seen again!" I continued. "Just tell me one thing, are these water sprinklers in the ceiling gas jets or just bugging devices?" He looked up. "It's a lot easier to tell you you're redundant", he said smiling, and somewhat relieved. I knew it hadn't been easy to say. Still, that's life. I've got one month's notice, which they would like me to work, and I've lasted thirteen months, which is a lot longer than most.

I'd better start sorting out those keys.

It's Tuesday and I'm giving a talk tonight to a group of scouts in Camberley. I hope it goes well. About two years ago I was invited to speak to a ladies' group at a church hall in Frimley. I duly arrived just before 8 pm and was surprised to find very little parking space available. As I sandwiched my car between two four-wheel drives with bull bars, I thought, "Are they all here to listen to little ol' me?" With a spring in my step and a few notes which I never seem to use, such is the tangent I go off on, I headed for the hall. A neighbour smiled as I opened the main door. That wasn't part of the plan, I thought to myself. I normally talk about neighbours, not to them! "Hello", she said. "I hear you're giving a talk tonight". "Yes", I replied. "Had difficulty parking, car park's rather full". "Yes", she said, "that's because most of us are here for the dog training classes. You're in the small hall"!

I've learned over time to try and look in the faces of all those attending. It's very easy to focus on someone displaying sympathetic body language or laughing in all the right places, but I do make a concerted effort to include all those attending. On this particular night I tried unsuccessfully to include a lady in her late fifties/early sixties who sat, legs clenched together, with both hands firmly grasping a handbag which appeared rooted to her knees. There was no facial change of expression throughout the talk. At the end, the club president rose, offered a few words of thanks and asked everyone to clap their hands in a show of appreciation. They certainly seemed warm and sincere. I glanced towards this lady who clapped no more and no less than other members, as far as I could see, but when asked if there were any questions, was the first to raise her hand. "Eunice, dear", invited the president, "your question to Anthony". "Could you give me your thoughts on the Newbury By-Pass", she enquired. I could and I did. It was just that the question and questioner didn't seem to go together. She never expressed the reason for her enquiry and I did not ask, but I managed to move the subject onto Terry Waite by the time I'd finished answering the question! No, I don't know how it happened, either.

The incident with my neighbour at the start of the evening reminds me of a time when I visited WH Smith's Sloane Square branch in 1994. I was working part-time for another puzzle magazine publisher. Having conducted my business on their behalf with the news manager, I strolled across the store to the book counter and enquired as to whether the book manager was available. The enthusiastic male assistant looked behind him and replied, "He's with a customer at the moment, but I'll bring him over when he's free. Who shall I say wants him?" "The name's Anthony Mann", I replied. His head did a double take and the eyes opened wide. "Anthony Mann? You're Anthony Mann?" "Yes, that's right", I smiled - I did, I remember. His fingers started pointed rapidly in my direction. "Don't tell me, it's a black and white covered book, isn't it?" I nodded. "And *you're* Anthony Mann?" "Yes", I repeated. "It's coming". He snapped his fingers in frustration. "It's from somewhere, isn't it, the book's called, From Somewhere'. No, don't tell me, I'll get it. It's, it's ...... From Where I Sit'". "Yes", that's right. He was fairly beaming at me by now. "And you're Anthony Mann". My ego was on a high. "D'you know, we had six copies sent down here from our main distribution centre in Swindon". "Did you?" I replied, anticipating an order. "Yes", he said, "never sold one of them!" With that metaphorical slap in the face he turned and introduced me to his manager. My confidence was now in need of a sharp pick-me-up to say the least. Oh, well.

That great font of public money, the Millennium Festival Fund, is granting £29,400 to Rushmoor Borough Council (that's Aldershot and Farnborough to us locals). The Arts and Cultural Officer on the council said, "This is brilliant news. It is a great achievement for the Festival, which is a real community event and is supported both by the council and many local ....." oh, I've got bored. Doesn't he go on? The point is, it's never money well spent. Another NHS dentist in the area wouldn't come amiss, but of course there's no money available for them.

As you are prob ably aware, I'm not a great supporter of Red Nose

Day. The fact that Lenny Henry is involved reduces my interest by about 99% and if you don't know me, it has nothing to do with him being black. I couldn't find him funny if he were blue or pink, or white. I do not equate humour with someone making strange, loud howling noises and poking their tongue out. Strange habit, I feel. Anyway, I appreciate there are many who do support the giving of money to their causes. A lot of the money raised is by sponsoring events, very often at school. One headmaster of a Roman Catholic school, whose kiddie-winkies were going to take part, has banned all association. Why? I'll tell you why, because he objects to money being given to pro-abortion organisations. To me, that's the most sensible disposal of any money collected. The head, one Mr. Caffrey, is quite indignant about the issue. "The very fact that Comic Relief has contact with such a group means I wouldn't want a penny of whatever charity money we raise at this school to go to that cause". He goes on, "I commend Red Nose Day for all its good and fun, but you have to look at the bigger picture. As a committed Catholic I believe these organisations are about people control, not life and love".

People control? That's rich, coming from the Catholic church. It has controlled people from the moment they've first clapped eyes on an unsuspecting convert and thought to themselves, he looks as if he's loaded.

Instead, the school will raise funds for the Catholic Aid for Overseas Development, better known as the Catholic Fund for Continuing to Stick Its Unwanted Snout into Everyone Else's Affairs! How could anyone take seriously an organisation - of any religious persuasion - that sets out to change native traditions in a far off land. Up go the missions, on go the clothes (it's wicked to walk about with no clothes on). The men could be seduced by the sight of a pretty girl with big breasts and a backside to match, so off you go to church and by the way, you have to have all your babies, but then more heartache for you means more money for us. Christ, how I hate religion.

The headline on page 9 of today's *Telegraph*, "Straw warns police over race relations" means that I'm not going to read it! What I did note from a list of statistics quoted is that during the period 1981 to 1991 the white population rose by 0.9%, while black groups rose by 31.4% and Asians, 46.1%. They were not alone. Other Asian and Chinese groups rose by 56.2%. Nuff said!

Euro's down again. Oh, and by the way it's cost this country £29 million so far to prepare itself for joining the Euro. I have to say I would no longer bet on our joining. I wouldn't go as far as to say for ever - would that I could - but I feel the tide is turning, the Brussels bulldozer marches on relentlessly, but every Euro dog has its day.

Jack Straw is being very free with our money, isn't he? Equality Jack, or should we call him Black Jack, has pledged £300,000 over three years to the Stephen Lawrence Trust. This trust offers scholarships to disadvantaged youngsters wishing to become architects. And moving on to the jarring effect the case has had on this country, black and Asian families will each receive £100 if they have a police officer to lodge with them for the weekend. Get this. A dozen Human Relations Awareness trainees with Hampshire Police will stay with these families so that they can learn about ethnic communities. We knew the world had gone mad, but just how far can it go?

I read that Lenny Henry, CBE, was at Buck Pal yesterday to collect his undeserved award from the Queen. Hope he didn't stick his tongue out, she might not have been amused .....

Gave that talk to the Scouts last night. They appeared to enjoy it. Very hospitable people, proper people, had custard creams with the tea.

Have you noticed a small but irritating change to Britain's traffic lights? The green arrow on filter lights has been changed, and not for the better. The conventional one-piece arrow is being replaced with a stumpy two-piece affair, reminiscent of the arrow used on prisoners' uniforms of old. I suspect someone was paid highly for something that never needed changing. Wouldn't be surprised if it wasn't another American import.

Which reminds me, I was going to tell you about the holiday we had in America last year. I say holiday, it was for Maureen, Glyn, William and my cousin Simon (well, Maureen had someone to talk to). For me, it was to cover the tracks, literally, for the forthcoming novel. Don't worry, I'll give you all the advanced details of the title in good time - never miss out on a marketing opportunity! Anyway, the basic premise was to cross America, east to west, by train in fifteen days. The tour was organised by Explorer Tours of Wraysbury, and very good they were too.

From the time the schedule arrived we knew it was a case of "If it's Tuesday it must be Los Angeles". But at least everyone was going to get a taste of America as a whole, and that's what most of it turned out to be - a hole!

Having spent a full half hour locking, checking and organising the security lights just prior to our departure, we headed southwards. I dropped off the other intrepid travellers and proceeded to the long-term car park. I have to say, parking at Gatport Airwick proved to be much less of a problem than I had anticipated. Good tip, though - make a note of where you left your car. I did but unfortunately the details I noted were totally irrelevant. My fault, nothing to do with the car parking people. First fright was waiting for the bus which would transport myself and fellow parkers back to the check-in area. I found myself to be the only one at the bus stop *not* wearing a Manchester United shirt. The wearers were loud, God were they loud, so the first thing I did was to look at their luggage. Good news! Their destination was Turkey. Not so good news for Turkey!!

As always, sat bored to death wondering why we needed to check in two hours before departure, I mean, it wasn't a last minute booking, they'd known we were coming for ten months. I'm convinced this early arrivals policy is a not overly subtle plan to entice you to the restaurants and shops on the basis that there's nothing else to do. The journey consisted of seven and a half hours of boredom.

America was in when w e landed, which was fortunate. Found our tour rep, a very pleasant young lady called Kate. Found our coach, which eventually found our hotel in the centre of New York. The hotel was clean, but was undergoing a re-fit. The downstairs reception and lobby area had already benefited from an injection of money, but the higher your floor, the lower the standard. The brown embossed paper, with dark woodwork encased the endless walls. I felt we were on the set of "The Shining" and I swear I saw those two little girls as I turned each corner. New York turned out to be lacking in the "Have a nice day" department. What's happened to all the happy-go-lucky students who served anything you wanted, any time you wanted? The staff at virtually every diner had trouble in understanding English, even when I shouted! The notes I made read, "Service over efficient, no time to browse menu, no manners and still no idea of making tea". This was all a distinct change from our previous visit.

On our second day we had breakfast in a deli, served on paper plates with plastic cutlery. Milk was poured from a half-used quart carton. The top of the Empire State Building was closed (again) above the 86th floor. It was in downtown Chelsea that we had lunch and finally met the first really friendly New Yorker, a young girl of Puerto Rican stock. We strolled into Greenwich Village where I encountered my first punk with nails sticking through his cheek from the inside out! In Britain he would have been arrested for possession of an offensive weapon. But then, I just found him offensive! We visited Grand Central Station, which is grand, we rode the subway and rode the carousel in Central Park, before spending the evening at Pier 7.

Days three and four we were up with the lark (if you can find one). We were off to Penn Station. We had to be there by 6.30 am for a 7.30 departure to Niagara. There was just time to grab a bacon and egg bagel. By now, my English was so English I didn't recognise me. You really resent the thought that you could possibly be mistaken for "one of them", no I don't mean "one of them", I mean an American "one of them". The woman serving the bagel never looked up at the customers as they gave instructions discourteously and were served without comment or recognition. All of a sudden it was my turn to peruse the selection of culinary delights. "Good morning", I said loudly, "May I have one of your finest egg and bacon bagels, please". I enquired this with a smile that would have melted a butter mountain. She looked stunned. I don't think anyone had ever offered her manners before. The service was still surly but the bagel surprisingly edible.

Our train meandered, and that is all their trains do, at a comfortable 45 mph at all times, other than when slowing down. We travelled along the borders of New England and I have to tell you the colours of the trees were straight out of the picture books - that's a coloured picture book! At the border crossing between America and Canada which was our stop - Niagara - the customs officers were reminiscent of all the border guards you see on film between East and West Germany. Someone commented that it was the Canadians' way of letting you know they were not Americans. This protracted tedium took up the thick end of an hour. Customs enquiries completed, the train moved little more than four yards before the station hove into view. It was of little significance as a border crossing and even less of architectural merit. Incidentally, the train conductor announced that for passengers staying on, the next stop would be Aldershot. We all looked knowingly at each other, as you do!

By now, the tour party numbered about thirty. This figure changed occasionally as singles and two-somes joined and departed as their schedule crossed that of the main party.

A small fleet of taxis arrived at Niagara Station and took us to our hotel. We passed a nightclub called "Barely Legal". As Glyn pointed out, at home in Aldershot it would have been called "Rarely Legal". Here in Niagara we encountered the first friendly cab drivers.

What I couldn't believe was quite how tacky Niagara was. It was somewhat reminiscent of a condensed Southend. I mean, how many waxworks, house of horrors and cheap-jack shops do you need? How many flashing neon signs, or bright lights? Well, none, actually but Niagara is full of them. Have to say, I was somewhat disappointed with the falls. I think the main problem is that from the vantage points you actually look down on them. Anyway, we did the tourist bit, donned our plastic macs, got wet aboard the Maid of the Mist - which was exceedingly cheap and good fun. You approached the landing jetty by means of a long concrete tunnel. On your way down you pass those who have just sailed, on their way back up. The tunnel was full of cameras slung around Japanese necks. It was at this point that Maureen gave me a quiet slap. All I said was, "It looks as if another boatload of Vietnamese boat people has just landed". That was all, I wasn't loud.

We ate very well, we ate very cheaply with excellent service, staying in one of the best hotels of the tour. After lunch on our second day there we travelled by coach to Toronto. We drove through the city, which though modern and clean was a little soul-less. Our hotel was in the equivalent of St. John's Wood - a leafy suburb. We spent a pleasant evening listening to jazz in a corner bar.

Days five to seven we spent travelling, then spent two more in Chicago. What a beautiful city. Would go back tomorrow. Clean, understated, civilised and a little more friendly. Unfortunately the beer still tasted like urine, but then so it did everywhere we visited in the States! At Chicago's Union Station, late in the afternoon, we boarded the Superliner train that would take us across the plains to Flagstaff. Excellent service and food, with a great atmosphere. We relaxed in the lounge car as we headed into a storm - a storm which was to bring severe consequences to our timetable. We went to bed and woke up several hours later to find that we had not shifted one inch. The tracks had been washed away the other side of Kansas City and we would have to be re-routed. The problem with American passenger trains is that they take a very poor second place to freight, so you have to wait in a loop for some time if a freight train is approaching, as much of their system is single track.

We had breakfast before finally trundling into Kansas City, hours late. What a dump the place is. It reminded me of Sheffield in the late seventies and early eighties. Amtrak had worked out that as neither the eastbound nor westbound trains could make it through to their destinations, the logical conclusion was to bring them as close together as possible, then bus the occupants between the two trains. Eminently sensible decision! We experienced the best service that rail transport could offer until the changeover. We then experienced what could only be described as probably the worst that was made available. The coaches collected us, and having made a wrong turn and ending up in someone's back garden (or back yard as the Yanks would say) we were then deposited alongside a level crossing some ten miles west of Kansas City. Unfortunately, there was no train, as this had had to wend its way westward to pick up fuel before coming back to collect us.

It was like a scene from *"Deliverance"*. Pick-up trucks came and went, men with oversized hats, hooked noses and eyes close together drove their families, who all looked like fellow products from a failed experiment. The dust bowl that was engendered reminded me of the film *"North by North West"*. It was overcast and threatening to rain. It was not a good time. Eventually, the train arrived. We clambered aboard. The staff were at best cold and disinterested, at worst, abusive and downright bloody rude.

It was during these two days of travel that we encountered Americans experiencing the novelty of rail transport in their own country, many for the first time. As soon as you opened your mouth, they wanted to converse with you. One lady was very surprised to learn that I didn't know her son's best friend, as he was English too. She repeated his name, assuming I would remember someone I had never met. "No, I don't know him", I replied for a second time, but she wasn't going to give up. "I *am* surprised", she added, "he is the Vice President of Capitol Records". I was not going to be swayed, I did not know him. Glyn encountered a similar, friendly but unworldly lady, who announced, "We were devastated by the death of Princess Diana. We're such monarchists". Glyn, who is not quite so dedicated, replied, "Oh, right" and left it at that. But she came back with her next question. "Do you know Prince Charles?" "Er, no, no I don't". "Oh", she replied, "he probably doesn't get out so much these days". Can you believe these people?

We arrived in Flagstaff seventeen hours late and with two hours left to reach and see the Grand Canyon. We did. Our mouths dropped. Now this really is one of the world's wonders. William said it was "all right" but was more interested in finding something to eat!

We took the night train to Los Angeles and to one of the most wonderful hotels I have ever stayed in - and I've stayed in Minehead before so I'm very well travelled! The Hotel Figureroa, Mexican in design, is an oasis in what we felt was a town somewhat overrated. In fairness, we didn't get to see it all, but Universal Studios was excellent.

A minibus collected those of our party who wished to spend a day there. We arrived before opening time. As we had prebooked, we were invited to walk through and wait at a certain point. To be fair, this is where the Americans come into their own. A smart-suited "host" appeared and commenced enquiring if everyone was in possession of a leaflet. This was vital as it had the starting times and locations for all the activities in which you wished to participate, or shows to watch. Those not in possession were advised to quickly locate one of the many smiling staff, who were handing out leaflets just beyond the ticket booths.

The group of early birds had swelled by this time to around two hundred people. No-one rushed, no-one pushed, although a Japanese couple stole around the side, only to be reminded with a smile that they should stay with the others.

Whilst advice was offered on what to do initially, we were distracted by the clip-clop of strutting feet, as they marched relentlessly through the crowd, elbowing all from their path. A tall, long black-haired lady held aloft a colourful cane, as every good tour guide should, before coming face to face with our "host". She was followed by small women and fat husbands, all in their late fifties, sixties and seventies. They jostled for a position at the front. The black-haired one requested that they be let in now. The host, ever smiling, explained that no-one entered the park until opening time. She became louder, though it was difficult to decipher her words. The explanation came from his reply. "Madam, I appreciate that you pre-booked. However, that does not allow anyone in early". I'm sure she stomped a foot in temper. "Madam, it is not meant personally but if you wish to take it that way, so be it". She backed off as he awaited a reply to his disarming reasoning. Now in command, he enquired, "Say, where are you from?" "Rrrrrussia", she boomed. The hunched, wrinkled little women were now with their leader, having made it to the front line, and after handing out a few bruised shins and arms in the process.

"Are you all from Russia?"

"Yes, yah", whatever it is they say to acknowledge in the affirmative. Hands waved around. He looked over his audience.

"Not all", I interjected. "We're from Surrey, England". I can't remember if he heard me, and if so whether it was recognised, but it made me feel better. It was at this point that something had to be said about their appalling lack of manners. "You can see how easy it was to fill the trucks for Auschwitz, can't you? Christ, this lot would have been first on the platform". I looked to Maureen for acknowledgement, but she turned away slightly. Both boys were moving away, Simon was already away! "What?" I said, "What?" I really do hate bad manners.

Some of these tawdry souls dripped jewellery in a most unashamed manner - all money, no class.

After that it all went swimmingly, the weather was - well - picture post-card California. We thoroughly enjoyed our stay, Water World being the topping on a very excellent trifle.

Over both nights we ate at a place called the Original Pantry and yes, I bought the T-shirt! It was a most amazing place, an old style diner situated on the corner of the next block (how awfully American). Its staff comprised of an array of characters one could only dream of seeing in the most unbalanced of psychological American thrillers. Each had a chequered history written on his face. All were over fifty, some positively geriatric. All meals came with a side-dish of coleslaw steeped in milk and a hacked half loaf of bread. I kid you not! The menu was comprehensive and high up on the wall. There were no personal menus on tables. When an item was sold out a waiter would raise a squeegee mop above the customer's head and rub out the chalked offering, so if a space on the menu was "wet" you knew they were "fresh out of it".

Days ten to twelve we boarded our train once more at Union Station, Los Angeles, and made our way through mountains and vineyards to San Francisco where were enjoyed our final three days, and whilst I didn't leave my heart there, I did find it an enchanting city. I particularly warmed to the sight of a "Bristol Lodekka" bus (sad git!). The only drawback in San Francisco was the continuous row of beggars living out of their cardboard boxes along the pavements, pleading with and harassing you for money. Signs enlightening you to the fact that "My name's Joe, I've got AIDS and I've five years to live" may bring the "Aaah" factor from some, just gives me the hump!

Anyway, cable cars were terrific and so was Alcatraz. We flew home to a cold, windswept Gatwick. I eventually found the car and left the car park £86 lighter. William still comes down to breakfast paraphrasing my request for "Three hot teas and a portion of chips, please". What we did find when we came home was that my security checks had not been to the standard we would have wished, as although I did manage the correct procedure with the security lights, I forgot to lock the back door!

Go on, then, ask me what my overall impressions were. All right, then, I'll tell you. I think the average American signs up for Uncle Sam, salutes the flag and is totally unaware of any form of life outside their shores. They have too much land. By this I mean they abuse their extremely good fortune. Having taken everything from the hunting grounds to the animals they hunted, the native Indian has been pushed further and further into a life of hand-out benefit and reliance.

The white American settler now uses this very land to dispose of the cars and white electrical goods as easily as confetti.. (I was going to add "at a wedding", but where else do you dispose of confetti?) Back gardens the size of an English estate were littered. The plains were littered. There were also an unhealthy number of dead cattle observed along the railway lines. The population at large appeared to suffer from a greed culture. Every act of known civility requires a tip. Too many are loud, brash and in desperate need of a heritage. They seem to spend their time either searching for British roots, or even better, Irish ones, or telling you they're sure they've got one somewhere. Strange that a race without roots should have so much power. And your average American believes without question, there is no questioning of hormone treated cattle, there's no questioning of foreign influence and there seems to be no questioning of their own dress sense - which is definitely questionable.

What I'd (we) would like to do is to fly direct to Chicago, mooch around there for a couple of days, then drive to Albuquerque and Injun country, stay in the area for a week and then continue to the Grand Canyon and stay a tad longer. Meanwhile, for this year, it's a week in the Isle of Man and a long weekend in the Czech Republic.

So, Dusty Springfield has died, aged 59. Now she was a truly great singer and yes, I do have some of her records. As one star dies, another gives birth. Victoria Adams, or the mis-named Posh Spice, coughed up a seven pound boy last night. I don't know whether Ms. Adams comes from Essex. If she does I suppose she could be referred to as Posh, after all, there's very little opposition. Perhaps she actually is posh, and the voice we hear is dubbed, in order for her to "get on" or be "one of the girls". It would appear that the only way to get on, especially in the media, is to drop every "t" or "h" along the way. I understand the poor little sod is to be called "Brooklyn" on account of that's where Ms A discovered she was up the duff. I suppose it's a small mercy she didn't find out on a tour of Skegness ..... South Mimms Beckham, Peckham Beckham ..... No, on reflection, Brooklyn's not so bad after all.

Not content to continue with our colonial hold over the Turks and Caicos Islands, the British Virgin Islands, the Caymans, etc. we now require them to legalise homosexuality. It is still a crime punishable by imprisonment. I do not agree with that. For some of "that" type prison would be like a meal ticket to contentment, especially if free condoms are on offer (Howard League for Penis [sorry, Penal] Reform please note). Big Brother is counting you. The next census in 2001 is to include questions concerning homosexual relationships. The word "partner" will appear for the first time, no doubt appealing to all those intent on destroying family life as we knew it. The government want to know how many pinkos are living together. I'd like to see a family section, inviting replies from proper people. This hopefully would convey to homosexuals that we'd rather you didn't reply as this is a "nice" census, and would not wish it to be sullied by those we'd prefer not know about, thank you!

The Telegraph uses that awful phrase "dumming down" in one of its headlines today. I have to say that a touch of irony has surely crept in when a report on the "low level of intellectual challenge" includes the phrase "dumming down". I was invited onto *BBC local radio* a couple of months ago to air my views on the subject of modern phrases - no, I was, really! "Dumming down" is one of my pet hates. What did they say before? What's causing the lowering of standards, bowing to the lowest common denominator. The problem is, we are finding people who are being interviewed in the street coming out with the same clichés as professional interviewers and pundits. There are, I have to say, a number of replacement phrases or words that should be totally rejected in regular speech. Some of these are "family" words. For instance, "upturn", "downturn", "upbeat", "downbeat". What was wrong with "improvement", "loss or retraction", "enthusiastic", "pessimistic"?

To "rubbish" is an appalling modernism, and so is "modernism". To "criticise" should be sufficient. To "trash" is another ghastly import from Uncle Sam's harvest of GM words. To "destroy" is all you have to say. And these days, one does not give priority to, one "prioritises" often with a "z". Ghastly! Another two words which have taken on new meanings and which I find totally incomprehensible, are "spend" and "build". You have a statement from Homebase and it refers to your monthly "spend", total "spend". Do they mean "amount spent" and "total amount spent?"

"New build" is an engineering term which is finding favour. Whatever happened to "newly built?" You cannot have a "build" anymore than you can have a "spend". Nowadays, especially with computers one "accesses" something or another. I was always brought up to understand that one gains access. And whilst at work, one is "tasked" where formerly one was "asked".

A "high of", says the weather forecaster. I prefer, "Today's highest temperature is likely to be ..." You can't have a "high" of...

"Feedback" equals "response"?

And if you were a listener of *"Kaleidoscope"* on *Radio 4* you could not have failed but to try and guess the number of times the word "genre" was used. All the luvvies use it to describe their pet area of artistry. How did they ever complete a sentence before their discovery of the word.

"Upcoming". More American tosh! What happened to "forthcoming", has it gone on an extended holiday as opposed to a vacation! Now "downsizing" has got to be one of the worst American imports. If you mean "redundancy", say so. And if you are reducing the size of your company, say so. But these are now all "key" words - oops, that's another one, like "key factors", "key tasks", "focus groups" and their ilk. Watch the people on TV who use the words "We'll talk it through". And how many people, especially in soaps, are "there for you"? How many people these days need "time out?" The worst offender in this modern parlance is the man or woman who replies, "But at the end of the day ....." They are the true vocal nerd. One chap I know (sorry, Neil) uses the phrase at least three times a minute, and that is no exaggeration, but then in mitigation, he does pay for his round, drinks real ale, tells good jokes and gave up supporting West Ham United when they signed up Di Canio. So he's not all arse!

After news that English food has been forced off the menu at Birmingham City Council's meetings as a sop to the ethnic councillors (white councillors, 99, ethnic minorities, 18) our lads in the forces appear to be faring no better (faring - geddit). Apparently, the Royal Marines receive ration packs that are carried inside their already full rucksacks. These "arctic" rations are dehydrated. The Marine adds melted ice and, hey presto, a ready made meal for one appears. The standard pack, which they are now being forced to use, contains water already, so they are heavier to carry and freeze at cold temperatures. Money has to be saved somewhere, apparently, in an effort to develop ethnic ration packs. There's Halal and Kosher rations and vegetarian food for Sikhs, Hindus and Buddhists. Not surprisingly, the number of requests for the above alternatives is very low, which means the cost is very high. I can see it won't be long before the pink brigade, with limp wrists, get their own rations - as if they don't get enough already! "Oh, Sarge", says a mincing Marine, standing with right foot pointing out and hands on hips, "I can't get on with this packet stuff at all. What I wouldn't give for a succulent sausage and two veg".

156

This is all in an obsessive attempt to break down barriers surrounding the recruitment of non-white and non-normal soldiers. Life is full of compromises and if they don't like joining it, bog off. There, couldn't be simpler!

CHAPTER SEVEN

RIGHTS? SORRY, NOT IF YOU'RE MIDDLE-CLASS!

I knew it was the kiss of death, it's always downhill once the manager of a struggling team wins the "manager of the month" award. Charlton lost 2-1 at Coventry yesterday.

So, the Budget has been announced and initial response has been one of enthusiasm. It's certainly not that good if you work and pay tax, of course. Even worse, if you work and you're self-employed.

We witness the final death throes of Miras. Child benefit, which should be abolished, is naturally increased, but then it never did go directly to the child. Only a politician could possibly be so naive as to assume that the great benefit scroungers do not spend it on Lottery tickets, drink and cigarettes. Child tax credit replaces married couple's allowance, another sop to those with partners. Pensioners come off a little better, although no doubt, like everyone else, once the small print has been analysed and all the minuses of the Budget added up, they'll see very little benefit. Fuel duty is increased - no surprises there - except for the rate. The "knock the motorist" mentality really comes into its own at Budget time. Not that it will have any effect on John Prescott (he of the two Jaguars).

Here we are, a few days after the Budget was greeted with cheer, to find that there are several stings alive and kicking in the tail - or the small print! David Hillier at Barclays Capital estimates that personal taxes will have gone up by £5.8 billion per annum. Luckily, that's not all down to you or I. But what we all know is that virtually all of that increase will be derived from the middle classes who already pay the bulk. As we've discussed before, the middle class is an easy target. They are always at home and it's always the same home. Of course, we do move occasionally but we're easy to keep track of. Those who are rich invest off shore, overseas, whatever. The end result is that the richer they get, the less they pay. The social morass at the bottom of the pit pay little attention to climbing out of their hole; why should they,

everything's paid for them. In short, it's a case of
(a) Rich = make, keep, make, keep
(b) Middle classes = work, pay, work, pay
(c) Benefit claimants = take, take, take, take
So no change there! And certainly no change, not even loose change, for us. And if all that wasn't enough, the EU are seeking tax-raising powers itself. When will the state governments of all countries within the EU wake up and say enough is enough.

Some people - huh. Dr. David Hope, the Archbishop of York, says he will return to the back benches of the C of E if women are made bishops. A spokesman for the Church of England said, "The Archbishop has always said he could not cope with women bishops". Whatever my feelings towards these strange cults, I cannot fathom out how those, at the very heart of Christianity, with all its teachings of equality can fall foul of such a basic premise. And why should the church be exempt from the rules of employment that play - and sometimes plague - such a large part within society's workplace?

Marks & Spencer is to ban GM foods in its shops. This is good news. I just hope it is possible for them to be 100% sure. At least the likes of Tesco, Sainsburys and Safeways, etc. will have to take notice.

Watched *"Mrs. Merton and Malcolm"* last night. Without doubt, it is the finest comedy since *"I Didn't Know You Cared"*, written by Peter Tinniswood back in the seventies. And what a pleasure to find myself genuinely laughing without the inducement of canned, or studio (suitably encouraged) laughter.

Here's a case that's hard to understand. A 59 year old man requires a heart by-pass. He's booked in and prepared for the operation. The surgeon enquires as to whether the patient has given up smoking. He replies that he has not. The surgeon says, "Go home and rejoin the NHS waiting list when you've given up". The chances of the operation being successful while the man is still smoking are apparently somewhat diminished. Ten months later the man dies.   His wife takes out a writ against the hospital, she wins and we, the tax payers, lose the £40,000 she receives. If your heart is in such a bad state that you require a triple by-pass, wouldn't you follow advice and give it up.
I fail to see how the wife managed to win an out of court settlement. I think the principle should be that *all* smokers must take out private

insurance, or pay the NHS the going rate for medical care. Smokers know the risks they take. As usual, these people want their fags and smoke them .....

After a couple of days without resorting to thumping the table in anger, flouncing around and generally being of irritated spirit, I have to confess to a sense of outrage once more. (Is that mock surprise I see upon your face? Oh, no, it's downright sarcasm).

I am heartily sick to the back teeth of this compensation scam. To call it a culture is to give it the credence accorded to the "professional foul" in football.

Two policewomen are to sue William Wilson, the Chief Constable of central Scotland, for negligence in the aftermath of the Dunblane killings. They say there was not a "critical incident stress debriefing". They are looking for £400,000 each! Of course the episode must have been most harrowing for them, telling parents, seeing the dead and injured. I've no doubt it haunts them day after day, but place their feelings alongside those of the affected parents and relatives. Let's get this in proportion, did these two think that life in the police force was all about point duty and dressing up in uniform?

"We didn't have stress counselling so we want money instead" seems to be the attitude. It was interesting to note that while sixteen children and one teacher were killed, one hundred and thirty nine claims for compensation have been met, and there's still one hundred and eleven to be considered. That's an awful lot of people on the sidelines who are gaining money out of this sorry affair.

One man who lost his daughter says, quite rightly, that he's "suffered more trauma than any police officer", but unfortunately goes on to say that he's still waiting for a pay out "for myself". I have to ask again, why? No amount of money is going to bring these children or their teacher back, so what real good will it do them?

The most sensible quote was from Mrs. Isobel MacBeath, whose daughter Mhairi was one of the children killed. She said, "Our family is not suing because we want to quietly get on with our lives. I cannot get my daughter back, so money is a side issue".

The council tax increases will be winging their way across the country as I write. Bloody Lib-Dems. We've just had ours - £108 per month last year, and £115 this year. You can always rely on the "Yellows" to spend other people's money, usually on frippery. The local councils blame central government, and vice versa. All you know is that no-one is going to put up their hand and accept responsibility.

This has been a week for deaths. Rod Hull fell off of his outside perch, Ernie Wise lost his battle with heart problems and a very rich young man called Christopher Dawes was killed in a motoring accident. At 39 he had already sold his company - Micromuse Computers - which he started for £24 million. Christopher Dawes died at the wheel of a McLaren F1 Sports Car. Two other people also lost their lives as the car exploded near Great Dunmow in Essex. This F1 sports car is unusual in that the driver is positioned in the centre of the vehicle, with passengers either side. This limited edition McLaren costs £640,000. I can't see anywhere in the article of a top speed figure, but I think I'm safe in saying that it's faster than an Austin Maestro. The point is, should these cars be on public roads? What's that? No, you say. Something else we agree on - that's good!

Here's a disturbing little piece that raises more questions than it answers. In the *Daily Mail's* "Fifteen years ago" titbit section, it tells the story of the last days of a Mrs. Phillips. This particular Mrs. Phillips was the mother of actor Leslie, probably one of the best loved of all British actors. Back in 1984 she was attacked by three black youths who knocked her to the ground in an effort to snatch her handbag. She did not let go and eventually they ran off. Mrs. Phillips was 92 at the time. She broke her hip and suffered from severe shock. She was taken to hospital, from where she never recovered. A few days later, the coroner recorded a verdict of unlawful killing. Her assailants were never caught. What I find strange is that this little story has taken fifteen years to come to light. Leslie Phillips is reported to have said, "I have suffered in silence for long enough. I kept very quiet about the attack as the police asked me not to speak of it. It seems they are trying to hush it up. I would like to get these little bastards because I don't think the police are ever going to".

Why didn't, or don't, the police want to make a fuss. Why keep it quiet? I bet this never went down as a racial attack. I bet the CRE don't have this in their compendium of racial crimes. No doubt this was merely an assault. Turn the tables once more, imagine the outcry if it were a black actor's mother, aged 92, who was assaulted by three white youths. They'd be found, and quite rightly so. But the emphasis on race, the ensuing paperwork, investigations and questions in the House would eat up several hundred thousand pounds worth of tax payers' money. And all to sate somebody's guilt.

It does make you wonder if there is some cover up where only attacks by whites are well publicised. I'm not suggesting that the CRE do pull rank over media and political statements, but I wouldn't be surprised to learn in the future that their political four-pennyworth was an extremely effective lever to lean on the police in "the wider good of race relations". I don't know, of course, but you'd never trust them not to.

As if we didn't squander enough money overseas as it is, we're now going to start bombing Serbia. Why? Is it anything to do with us? No! Tony Blair's justification comes in his statement that "there are strategic interests for the whole of England at stake. We cannot contemplate, on the EU's doorstep, a disintegration into chaos and disorder".

So when the Russians marched into Hungary, and later into Czechoslovakia, presumably that reign of terror didn't count. Or was it that the Russians proved more formidable opponents? It's ever so easy to be sanctimonious when the opposition is not that tough. So where is the benefit to Britain in all of this involvement of ours? We didn't get Hussein out of Iraq. What makes anyone think President Milosevic is going to say, "It's a fair cop, guv" and come out with his hands raised. All you do know is that it will cost the country a packet, with no real conclusions , with money that will be found for arms and war but can never be found for schools and hospitals back home. Bastards!

Back on the home front, the sad gits who have nothing better to do than complain about adverts have been getting more than their fair share of recognition. Whatever I think of animal welfare, one must never lose one's sense of humour. Unfortunately, 589 poor souls have done just that. They've taken exception to an advert which features a cow uttering the words "when I'm a burger, I want to be washed down with Irn Bru". Thankfully, the advertising standards authority ruled that most people would not be seriously offended by it. Quite right, too. But who are the 589? How could you find that many people. They probably all live in Harpenden.

In another instance, this easily offended brigade objected to an ad for TCP throat lozenges. In this, a man is seen with a tiger whose jaws are around his throat. This ad hit the screen at the same time as a circus performer was mauled by a tiger. What's there to complain about? The circus employee should derive no measure of compassion. That should be reserved for the tiger, faced to lead a life as a captive animal. Although not in this survey, but from a different article, we are reminded of Heineken's Christmas advert shown during December, 1998. It was of a barn, with all the leading characters from that famous novel. Donkeys, sheep, wise men, they were all there. Above the barn and below the star was a heading. "It's a girl", with the message, "How refreshing, how Heineken" below the picture. Now I find that a very imaginative slant on a predictable scene. Mind you, the lager still tastes like urine, but then all lager does. Hopefully if I say *all* lager no-one will sue me. What d'you mean, I'm likely to be sued anyway! What have I said that could possibly upset anyone?

The Church of England complained that the ad was offensive because it was run at Christmas, and "more importantly, because it was selling beer". Would they have preferred the ad to be run over the August Bank Holiday when Mary would have only have been five months up the duff, and don't forget folks, she was still a virgin. Yes, that bible has a lot of explaining to do.

Well, I've left the car superstore, my last day was Monday, 29th March. We had a very pleasant farewell do. I was particularly pleased that the mechanics and cleaners came as I'd got to know them well over the previous months. Those who worked hard and those who just took a lot of money out of the company were all there. It went on until it was time for me and my two fellow workmates to catch out last Underground train. Mark, the builder, Joydeep, my assistant, and myself wended our way to Park Royal Station, bade our farewells and awaited our trains. I managed to catch the last main line train home from Waterloo to Ash Vale, but shortly before 1 a.m the silly grin that I'd worn from mid-evening managed to get hold of the situation a little better and I believe I managed to alter a few of my facial muscles. I thought twice about ringing Maureen and asking her to come and pick me up - you see, always the thoughtful husband - and anyway, I didn't want the phone slammed down on me! So I walked home. I have to tell you, I did have one hell of a headache the following morning.

Charlton lost 1-0 again, this time to Chelsea. It is now looking a bit grim. Southampton look as if they just could squeeze out of trouble again. And I know you'll be pleased for me to report that Newport AFC, County as was, are going well in second place in the Midland division of the Doc Marten's league. Promotion will see them one division away from the Vauxhall Conference. Now that's what I call success. Aldershot Town are languishing in mid-table. Disappointing, really, as I - and many others - expected to see them pushing for promotion this season. They are joint top scorers with 70 odd goals so far but they keep losing matches by the odd goal. Still, there's always next season, or the next.....

It's all backfired just a smidgen. We bomb the Serbs, the Serbs kill the Kosovans and Albanians, and presumably anyone else who gets in the way. Meanwhile, in deepest Whitehall our over-friendly Home Office make arrangements to accept a "flood of refugees". Have we not got enough problems already. Clare Short is just about to squander, sorry, donate, another £10 million to the relief effort. Excuse me for asking, but did we not feel the same sense of anger, enough to start bombing, that is, when the Hutu were knocking seven barrels of crap out of the Tutsi's, or vice versa? No, I'm not overly interested, but this display of concern for people we know nothing or little about does smack of hypocrisy. Is it just "good training" for our chaps, the kind you can't get by low flying sorties over Cardiganshire. "They get awfully miffed if we fire rockets at Aberystwyth". Well, it may be a bit faded, but it's not that bad. Basildon, Bracknell, Basingstoke, now you're talking, excellent areas for target practice and you don't even have to go abroad.

Within a week, we've seen Andrew Gardner, the newsreader who presented the very first *"News At Ten"* die at the age of 66, and also, Lionel Bart. Andrew Gardner was a distant relative, you know, once removed twice over, that sort of thing, of Maureen's father, or mother. Anyway, it's probably the closest our family is going to get to being related to a recent death in the *Telegraph's* obituary column.

Lionel Bart's death was probably of no surprise. He seemed to miss so many years through drink. The world remembers the musical *"Oliver"*, both on stage and as a film. Less well known, and certainly underrated, was *"Blitz"*. The whole stage consisted of an underground station. My parents took me to see it in the early sixties. It was a truly imaginative show and I loved every minute of it. *"Fings Ain't Wot They Used T' be"* was also an excellent show and seemed to sum up his and many people's feelings for a Britain that was going downhill even then. I wasn't aware, however, that he wrote the Tommy Steele hits "Rock with the Cave Man" and "Little White Bull", or the massive Cliff Richard hit "Living Doll". Another piece of useless information is the fact that he penned "From Russia With Love", a wasted talent in his middle years.

Refugees are back on the agenda as we bomb Belgrade - weather permitting! Am I wrong (probably) but didn't we dispose of our earth-shattering clutter at all times of day and night during the Second World War? Perhaps I've seen too many films, but John Mills never seemed to be waiting around for good weather, before soaring into the sky in a mainly wooden machine and bereft of today's technology. We have Serbian civilians being killed, which brings even greater intensification of their killing of Kosovans. By taking in refugees throughout western Europe these countries are helping the Serb leader. Are we not playing totally into his hands? We've already had 9,000 Kosovar Albanians seeking sanctuary (and benefits) over the last year. Will they be building the houses in the grounds of Chequers to accommodate the hordes? Will they buggery!

Now this is a bit rough. A young man called Martin Townsend, aged 19, was driving his VW Golf to his home in Little Stoke, near Bristol, when he espied a young lady prone on the pavement. Karen Newmarch, aged 25, had fallen and there was clearly a problem. So Mr. Townsend stopped, picked her up and rushed her to hospital. On arrival doctors were concerned about her spine and decided that she could not be brought out through the doors of the VW. A bit of chin-fingering and a lot of discussion witnessed the decision to cut open the roof of the Golf and bring her out that way - a bit like a mechanical Caesarian! Anyway, firemen, as opposed to firefighters, tore off the roof using heavy duty hydraulic cutting gear. The young lady has now recovered, but Mr. Townsend is left to literally pick up the pieces. He was only third party insured so the damage is legally down to him. Ben Bennett, the medical director at Southmead Hospital, said "It's regrettable that this chap's car was damaged, but the most important thing was to get to the patient and treat her safely". Yes, but ......

A small crumb of comfort. Charlton won 1-0 away at West Ham.

I do hope this war with Serbia ends soon. Every day it takes up the first six to eight pages of the *Daily Telegraph*, and frankly, it's all so repetitive. I mean, if you've read tales of torture, rape and mass executions once. How many variations on a theme can you have. Solace can be found in the fact that it now takes a lot less time to read the paper. I have to say, it does become brain-numbingly boring after a while. Well, about a day to be honest. I'm just waiting now for someone to say it's our fault.

Another one's gone, then. Bob Peck died yesterday from lung cancer, aged 53. Like many, he was first brought to my attention through that wonderful series *"Edge of Darkness"* in which he starred with Joanne Whalley in 1985. He was a superb actor who enjoyed much success on TV, the theatre and latterly, the big screen.

It's always nice to see a Rupert Murdoch get-richer-even-quicker scheme flounder, and today's news that *Sky* cannot take over

Manchester United will be greeted with relief by all *real* fans. If it had gone ahead, that giant supertanker of the airways would have set yet another unwarranted and dangerous precedent. As usual, this has nothing to do with a boy-made-good from down under wishing to put something back into a team he has followed since he was a callow youth. Oh, no, we're talking power, which equals money. The only winner would have been those with money, while the fans would once more have been made to stump up even higher admission fees. Whatever it is, you know that Manchester United will make the most out of it, so well done Tony Banks and all those who stood up to Mr. Muscle and his allies.

That nasty little person, Mary Chipperfield, got her come-uppance yesterday in Aldershot, when she was fined a total of £7,500 for twelve charges of cruelty to animals. Her husband, that Roger Cawley person, was fined £1,000 for cruelty towards a sick elephant. There were in excess of 200 people demonstrating against this despicable pair. The crowd screamed abuse and hurled eggs and fruit as they left Aldershot Magistrates Court. What concerns me greatly is that this pair of evil, obnoxious sub-specie were still allowed to carry on working with animals.

Apparently the courts have the power to take away her licence and take her off the Performing Animals Register. Why did they not do it? What on earth do you have to do to an animal, or group of animals, before someone says "enough". Frankly, I'd have locked them both up and thrown away the key. Oh, that's after I'd clouted them with a stick. They'd bloody well dance around a cage then! Bastards!

Christ, they're going down like ninepins. It's Anthony Newley's time to be called now. Only 67. One of my first records was "Do You Mind", written, incidentally, by Lionel Bart. As a youngster I warmed to *"The Strange World of Gurney Slade"*. Looking back, I probably liked it because my mother and father didn't. I was always the black sheep of the family; problem was, my parents only had one lamb!

I do not understand the continual clemency afforded to those who err. Here we have the case of a retired man called Anthony Jones, aged 82, who fell out with his neighbour some years ago.

The neighbour, Eric Nicholls, aged 64, a former car dealer, attacked Mr. Jones with his walking stick. Mr. Jones died from blows to his head, back and neck. Nicholls told the police, "As he went down I brought the stick down as hard as I could on the back of his neck. It was a solid blow, like a ball hitting a cricket bat in the right place. I feel a sense of relief that he is dead. I have no remorse". What a strange and calculating thing to say. Although 82 years of age, Mr. Jones cycled, wind-surfed and still went camping. He wasn't what you would call an inactive man. Nicholls was sentenced to 30 months in jail. The judge apparently took into consideration his previous good character, his age and his disability. What he doesn't seem to have taken into consideration is that Nicholls killed someone. Mr. Jones's offspring are considering suing Nicholls. I hope they do, and that they manage to get the sentence reviewed and increased dramatically. Thirty months ..... words fail you!

There are on average six pages a day now being devoted to more stories of rape, execution, massacres and marches into exile, followed by the evening news being taken up by moving pictures of the same stories. Some people obviously "get off" on other people's hard luck situations, but this is really tedium personified. All this pounding of Serbia hasn't made the slightest bit of difference, although we have inadvertently managed to kill a fair number of refugees. Just wait until the Americans *really* get going, then you'll see a massacre - naturally those we're trying to save! You know the Yanks. They never stop with the enemy - to them, anyone's fair game.

Back in the GM field of play, Michael Meacher, someone I've never had a great deal of time for in the past (always found him a bit wishy-washy) is leading the pack with his refusal to kow-tow to the Blair think tank, that is, we pay homage to the Americans and everything American. Our Mr. M. of the ministry is preparing not to reappoint ten of the thirteen members of the government's advisory committee on the release of GM crops. It seems strange to a layman (like what I is) that Professor Nigel Poole should be on the committee in the first place. He is not an independent adviser who knows about these things; oh, no, he works for Zeneca Foods who hold certain opinions of a slightly biased nature. How can we find out the truth when representatives of the very companies set to gain so much at our expense are openly encouraged to put in their four-penn'orth. Public confidence in an opinion will never be forthcoming unless the panellists are independent and without favour. There! You can tell I'm a Librian, fairness runs straight through my heart and down to my roots. What d'you mean, what heart?

There's an article entitled "Democracy and Our Rights" in the local paper. I didn't bother to read it because I'm white and pay taxes, so I don't have any! However, after my churlish reaction, I did feel compelled to read and comment on the little piece entitled "Euro

Twinset". It concerns the tidy and pleasant little village of Hartley Wintney. Not content with being linked or twinned to somewhere called St. Savin in France, the Euro lovers of H.W. are setting their sights on another little jolly. This time they are joining forces with the folk from the Flemish town of Malle. You'll find it somewhere close to Antwerp, apparently. There are 35 souls departing for Malle in June. Mrs. Jean Amos, who is Chairman of the St. Savin Twinning Association, said, "It will add another dimension to the village and will give people, young and old, a new slant on Europe. The more you can do to forge links with European neighbours, the better, as people do not feel so threatened by it". Poor, deluded soul! "Add another dimension?" "New slant?" She must have been on a course, probably attended by the other 34 eager beavers. Postscript is that the people from Malle are expected to visit Hartley Wintney some time next year. That'll be nice for them.

You have to laugh, don't you. A black mother from London is in jail in Belgium (cheaper for our taxpayers than being in prison here) for smuggling illegal immigrants across Europe. Her sentence is three years. Now's there's a campaign group (isn't there for everything) which goes under the name of Fair Trials Abroad. Their director, some misguided mortal called Stephen Jakobi, said the woman would appeal as the verdict was "institutionally racist". What a surprise. Still, never mind, eh.

Right! Have you heard the one about the cowboy captured by the Injuns? No? Well, I shall begin.

There's a cowboy who's captured by the Indians and is taken back to their camp. He's very frightened as the Indians' reputation has gone before them. "I expect you're going to tie me spreadeagled on the scorched earth, until I almost burn to death in the heat and then scalp me", he cries in fear. The Chief looks aghast. "What, good God no", he replies, "you don't know much about Indians, do you?" The cowboy trembles and fitfully shakes his head. "No", says the Chief, "that's the sort of stuff they'll have you believe when they make films about it in a hundred years time. We're very civilised". The cowboy relaxes, the Chief continues. "Of course we're going to kill you, it's only natural, but we'll be spearing you through the heart in three days' time. Until then, you'll be our guest. You'll eat well and we have a very good range of food. Old Rising Son's mother makes a wonderful hotpot". And he goes on describing the array of culinary delights in great detail. The cowboy's appetite for the veritable feast ahead is slightly dimmed by the thought of his impending death.

Just before leaving the cowboy's tepee, the Chief informs him that every morning for the next three days he can make a wish (it's always three of everything, isn't it). Anyway, the cowboy asks for his horse to be brought in. Allan, for that is the horse's name, is brought in and handed over to the cowboy, who also happens to be called Allan. He holds the bridle and whispers in the horse's ear. The horse raises its head in acknowledgement, snorts and turns. Off Allan (the horse) trots. Some hours later he returns with the most gorgeous blonde the Indians have ever seen. To be fair, they haven't seen that many, but she is a cracker. Into the tepee Allan and the blonde go. A few hours later, Allan (the cowboy) bids farewell as Allan (the horse) takes the blonde back from whence she came.

The following day, at "make a wish" time, Allan calls once again for his horse. He stands in front and with both hands, pulls the bridle, looks deeply into his nag's eyes and whispers once more. The horse winks knowingly, raises its head in acknowledgement and once again trots off. He returns an hour later with the most incredible red-head. There's much nudging and elbow-bending in the Indian camp. As she enters the tepee there's prolific chanting of "Gorn my son" and "hand out a portion for me" and other such encouraging witticisms. Eventually she is returned and Allan (the cowboy) relaxes for the evening with a three course meal and a book for bedtime.

On the third and final day (thank Christ for that, I hear you say) he once more asks for his horse. Allan trots in but this time the Indian guard steps out of earshot. (He has to, or we'd never know what is said). Allan spends a fair amount of time preparing the other Allan. The bridle is pulled tight in the manner of someone being held against the wall by his collar. The horse's ears prick up, he knows the message is important. "Look", says Allan, "for the last time, I said bring a POSSE!"

It's Monday, 26th April, and we witness the smiling faces of Kosovan refugees as they arrive at Leeds/Bradford Airport. Didn't it used to be called Yeadon? Anyway, it's nice to know we've got room for an initial 161 of them. There were some twenty wellwishers at the airport, waving banners, sporting the sincere but not generally representative slogan "Welcome Kosovans". Oh, goodie. A senior social worker described their new homes as being as close to hotel accommodation as you could get. There are a few pensioners who wouldn't mind that luxury, but still.....

Well, that's it, then. I think it's all over. A 4-1 thrashing at Everton is, I believe, the nail that tightens Charlton's coffin. A swift return to the

First Division but at least they are still playing at the Valley and not on foreign soil.

So, Jill Dando, the thinking man's crumpet, has been murdered. She seemed a really nice person. I know TV personas can be misleading but she always came over as sincere and unaffected. It seems an odd case but I bet it ends up by being someone known to her.

What have Nestles and Tesco got in common this week? They are both working like busy little bees to eliminate GM materials from their foods. With so much at stake can the government really keep singing the praises of "experiment and see". Even the National Trust has banned crops being grown on its land, and quite right too.

The award for "quickest response" goes to Volvo, the car manufacturers. In yesterday's paper there was a report, with photograph, of a Volvo car being trodden on by the two front legs of a two and a half ton rhino. The damage was minimal - a good advert in itself. Today's *Daily Telegraph* carries a full page ad. It is a mostly blank page, but in the middle is the "torn out" cutting and photograph from yesterday's story. At the bottom of the page lie the words "Volvo. Because it's a jungle out there". Now I think that's very good.

Another dream is shattered. I appreciate that nursing is now only another job, instead of the vocation it became when matrons ruled instead of chief executives, but it's hard to understand the reduction in status now being inflicted on Florence Nightingale. The following illustrates perfectly where political and racial correctness is getting us - it's altering history. Those pumped up, egocentric comrades at Unison are attempting to instal their own chosen star. Delegates at Unison's conference were told that our Flo was out of date and represented "the negative and backward element of nursing". How so? Well, she was white, middle class and a Protestant. Shouldn't these strange creatures be a little more concerned with patient care than considering her unsuitability in a multi-cultural Britain?

Now let's think for a second. If you get rid of your flagship you have to find another. Well, she can't be white, that wouldn't do. Heavens preserve us from somebody else who's middle class. No, we need a name few have ever heard of, which can be resurrected from the annals of nursing history.

Ladies and Gentlemen, please show your appreciation for Mary Seacole. Who? Mary Seacole. She may not be famous, but she's black! She was a Jamaican who also tended to the injured and dying. Now a tug at the heartstrings. M.S. was rejected by our Flo and spurned by the

Victorian establishment. These accusations are probably modern interpretations or slants on a story that may or may not be true. Such is everyone's ability to alter whatever bit of history they don't like.

Unison, no doubt, would love it to be true. They are not looking for a heroine, they are looking for a martyr and they don't come much better than a black one.

It really is quite frightening when you read the confused ranting of Wendy Wheeler, a health visitor. She says, (yes really), "All over Eastern Europe statues of Lenin are being taken off their pedestals, dismantled and pulled off to be cut up. It is in the same vein that the nursing profession must start to exorcise the myth of Florence Nightingale. Not necessarily because Florence Nightingale was a bad person, but because the impact of her legacy - or more correctly, the interpretation of that legacy - has held the nursing profession back too long". I have to ask, how? Why? This Wheeler woman added that Flo's privileged background - she established a hospital using family money - was unrepresentative of the ethnic mix in today's NHS.

Is Ms. Wheeler jealous? So far, she has made no contribution to Unison's demand to change history. Unison now wants to change International Nurses Day, which is currently held on Flo's birthday to a "more suitable" date - Mary Seacole's birthday, perhaps!

So where are all the proper people in this discussion? Even a trade union, with four hundred and forty thousand members, must have one or two, or are they all sheep?

Here we have the true result of the Lawrence family's continued offensive in their fight for "justice". Stop and search activities by the Metropolitan Police are now greatly reduced because officers fear being branded racist. This is a terrible indictment. The result? Street robberies peaked in London during March. Assaults are now being committed at the rate of more than 100 a day. Police officers are now thinking before stopping and searching any black suspect. It's a criminal's charter. So thank you, the Lawrences, you have "helped" so many people with your obsessions. No "wider picture" being seen here, then.

Another one bites the dust. This time it's Oliver Reed. At least he died in a bar.

Well, there's going to be one pervert less in life, although doubtless there will be another one taking his place as we speak, or rather, as I

171

write. A parish priest arrested for indecently assaulting a child, committed suicide by jumping off a cliff in south Wales. What never ceases to amaze me with this religious disease, is that when told, his ex-parishioners were in tears. The Bishop of Monmouth said that Canon Peter Edwards had been "very popular and ran a very successful and flourishing parish". So, not a word about *you-know-what*, then?

Brilliant! Well done, our PM! The extremely hospitable Tone has agreed to take 1,000 Kosovans a week. That is all we need. Sharp landlords will do ever-so-nicely thank you, social workers will be creaming themselves, and anyone within five miles of a counselling job will be in the bluest of heavens.

Tonight is local council election night. And no, I won't be voting. The Lib-Dems always feature grainy mugshots of councillors looking particularly smug, an aspect that does not become them.

Their "Focus - local election 1999 pamphlet No. 2" arrived some little while ago, followed more recently by No. 3. The former extols the virtues of voting Lib-Dem. "More cash for Ash". Well, it has a nice ring to it. There's the usual blurb and self-preening about what they've done since ruining (oops, running) Guildford Borough Council. At the bottom, we're advised that "good councillors make a difference". I agree, but I don't think that many are in the Lib-Dems.

Turn over the page and we have a councillor by councillor break-down of their achievements and ambitions. First out of the hat is Terry Horton. Now retired, Terry is chairman of the Recreation Development Working Party. He's on the Parish Planning and Cemetery and Open Spaces Committees.   He is a committee member of "Churches Together" in Ash and Tongham and is a referee's assessor! He is very concerned with the increasing amount of road traffic, etc. And if re-elected, will continue dealing with them as a matter of urgency. That's nice!

Next is Brian O'Sullivan who's also been on the Cemeteries Committee and is very concerned about development issues, while Robert Pettit says that, if elected, he wants to make Ash Vale a nicer place to live in. Over the page, to the women's section, where Denise Smith and Geraldine Pettit (married to Robert above) are contesting the seats. Denise Smith has been on several committees, apparently - bet one of them has been Cemeteries. It's her ambition to "achieve more for local people. I want to continue using my abilities for the benefit of the local population, while Geraldine, aged 36, (Robert by the way is 47) believes that local councillors should listen to local people's views. Well, that'll be a novelty - no, it'll never catch on. Anyway, if elected, she will "work hard" as she is very concerned about road safety and large scale housing development. Finally, she wants to do her best to make Ash Vale a safer, cleaner and more pleasant place for everyone.

I haven't read such shallow, insignificant drivel in a long time. Each councillor spouts forth a list of what they consider to be the ultimate in change for the better, but when their pledges are considered, nothing of substance is actually offered. We can all be concerned, we can all make overtures regarding road safety and a cleaner environment, but there's nothing above that tells us how they will do it, and why it needs to be done! Ash Vale, a place where I have lived for over twenty years, has always been comparatively safe, clean and pleasant anyway! The biggest problem is the continued development, which as a parish and borough council, they have no control over anyway, as all decisions on this one are taken by central government.

The Conservative pamphlet portrays an equally smug set of photos. They have their own "key pledges", their words, not mine. These should read words include, ensuring that a new mobile CCTV system is introduced to the suburb, banning drinking in public places and guess what - making sure Ash gets a cleaner, better street cleaning service. Their special edition "In Touch" A4 sheet extols the virtues of Conservative's recent successes - or success - recently. One of our councillors is "celebrating" the recognition that the parish of Ash is in Surrey and not Hampshire. No longer will the residents of this parish have to put Ash Vale, near Aldershot, Hants. as their address. Oh, no, we can now face the world and say, "We are in Surrey", followed, of course, by the GU postcode. Well this really is a great advancement for local politics. If that is the extent of their newsworthiness, then I feel that the Tories have come to a pretty pass.

Oh, dear, we've bombed the Chinese Embassy instead of a Yugoslav ordnance depot. There have been phone calls, apologies, hands up, explanations and investigations. I bet someone in NATO said, "It would have to be the Chinese Embassy - Iceland or Tanzania wouldn't have complained half as much".

I can imagine the content of the letter our Tone has sent to Beijing. "Dear All, Sorry about that. Problem was that both your embassy and the depot have red front doors. Doesn't help that you're number 69 and they are 89. Our chaps always seem to home in to a 69! Anyway, let us know the cost and we'll send round flowers for relatives, etc. And let me say this to you, we really are a caring government. Anyway, must go, check that they have the right address for tonight's little sortie. Just hope the weather's good, eh. Let me know when you're popping over, we'll get in a round of golf. Byee. Tony. PS - any chance of a panda?"

Dirk Bogarde's gone now, aged 78, from a heart attack. The second enigma this year.

The results of the local elections have been announced in the *"Aldershot News"*. The Lib-Dems have only managed to secure two parish council seats out of twelve, the others going to the Tories. On the borough front they lost all their seats in Guildford. I wonder if the Lib-Dems will "take on board" their drubbing and "learn from this experience". If they do, it will be a first.

Not good news from NATO today, they've just killed one hundred refugees. Good news for us, though, we're down to four pages of Kosovan news in the *DT*. It still takes up half the news time, however, on TV and radio, with the Israeli elections taking up the rest. Surely something happens in Britain these days.

Not good news for Charlton Athletic, they are relegated. Good news, however, for Southampton, they escape at the eleventh hour and the fifty-ninth minute.

Euro's down again.

Roll up, roll up! The compensation pay-out game is about to start! Who wants to play? Come on down, little lady, and tell me, what's your name? "My name is Lyn Armstrong, aged 52 and I've taken medical retirement from the prison service".

"My word, that's terrible. So tell me, what were the symptoms - no, let me guess, could it be post-traumatic stress syndrome?"

"Well, yes, how did you know?"

"It's been very catching this decade and it has become a major winner for a lot of people. So, what was the catalyst for your compensation claim - sorry, your stress disorder?"

"It's like this, I was guarding Rosemary West and the prison authorities did not help me to cope with the experience. I became ill, I lost my confidence, I couldn't even make a simple decision. (*She's made one decision - to sue the Home Office, but back to the story*).

Rosemary West had to be guarded around the clock as the prison authorities were under great pressure to ensure she did not commit suicide. We were expected to monitor her 24 hours a day, in three 8-hour shifts. Most of the other warders would do a week or two, but I kept being brought back because West asked for me. I think she linked' to me emotionally. I believe that once the prison authorities realised that, they wanted me to guard her most of the time, but I think they forgot about the effect it might have on me. I feel that the authorities should have ensured that there was a more regular changeover of guards. They shouldn't have allowed her to get too close to me emotionally."

This is me now. This woman has had 23 years' experience in the army, followed by working with sex offenders and paedophiles. Wouldn't you have thought that this would have been sufficient grounding for dealing with Rosemary West? Apparently not. Her writ against the Home Office alleges negligence and breach of duty. She is claiming damages for personal injury (not literally, surely) and lost income which could exceed £50,000. As far as I'm concerned she wouldn't have lost any income had she stayed at work. There's a photograph of Ms. Armstrong, head to one side, hand on chin, index finger close to temple. The caption reads "Devastated". Still, a hefty sum in compensation should bring back a smile to her face.

It is a shame that the culture of village life, some would say the very fabric of rural society, is cut away by one interloper. The fact that the interloper is an Indian woman is by the way, beside the point and nothing to do with it. I just felt you should know.

In the village of Heslington, West Yorkshire, the local cricket club have been playing cricket on the green for well over eighty years. During the game and afterwards those involved and those who were not, enjoyed a couple of pints. Wednesday night was training night for youngsters, attracting up to thirty would-be ..... well, quite good cricketers, one hopes. Fathers would watch and sup ale, while their offspring put bat to ball. A good time was had by all.

However, all good things come to an untimely end. In this case the end is one Dr. Haleh Afshar. This person, a political lecturer (sums it up) at York University became the chairman of the sports field management committee two years ago. There's a picture of her engrossed in conversation with another woman. She is carrying a large file of papers in one hand, and pointing with the other. Her whole persona exudes ego and power - bet she struts and all.

There has been an attempt by those for Sunday cricket to pass a vote of no confidence in the doctor at the AGM but this was rejected when she allegedly refused to accept the vote! The cricket club claims she has attempted to raise their rent to £500 per annum. They have been banned from playing on Sundays, alcohol is now forbidden and the junior training is all but defunct. This woman argues that as the land was left to the village as a charitable trust for recreational use, cricket restricts the "rights" (them again) of other villagers and their children. Cricket can at present only be played on a Saturday.

It seems she was elected by students who live in the village and other college related persons. Thankfully, the Charity Commission has now ordered that a fresh annual meeting of the sports field committee should take place in three weeks, in an attempt to sort out the issue.

Who the hell does she think she is? Well, you'll get a good clue from one of her quotes, which is "I only drink very good champagne". So there's your answer - not really a proper person.

That well known extractor of money and owner of vast tracts of our country (how *did* they acquire it?), the Church of England, are to assess whether they should be spending £9 million a year on bishops' expenses. No, not their wages, their expenses. Most of it goes on staff, some 84% apparently, office equipment, entertaining, travel, light, heat and cleaning soaks up the rest. The staff aspect doesn't just include secretaries, there are also the everyday staff expenses that we all endure - gardeners, chauffeurs and cleaners.

The Bishop of Wakefield, the Right Reverend Nigel McCulloch, considers his expenditure of £3,000 pa on lunches as "unremarkable". He can organise or oversee any event costing up to £400 without passing it for clearance. After having saved £10,000 pa by doing away with his chauffeur, he still enjoys the services of a gardener who looks after his eight acres of garden (think of the council estate you could build there). Let's think of the wider issues, refugees, resettlement centre, a gay parent project, oh, it fair boggles the mind!

This poor lost soul is of the opinion that "the Bishop is an important figure in that he has the ability to draw together people from different positions in the community". Says a lot for his self delusions, I fear, whilst the money says a lot about a group of people who may well see the world as a real place, if only they could get themselves a proper job and stop hiding behind the trappings of grandeur.

I would have more respect for this strange phenomenon if they at least kept to their beliefs, but like the present government, it's hard to understand any policy when they twist and turn like twisty-turny things. The highest paid of them all, the Archbishop of Canterbury, George Carey (salary £53,370, plus expenses of course) can't seem to grasp the novel that he purports to follow. I thought it said somewhere in that tome that buggery between chaps wasn't on, although to be fair, I don't think they put it quite like that - there was probably a "thou" and a "thee" thrown in to give atmosphere. Anyway, the nub (or should that be knob) is that by J.C. chatting with homos and lesbians he is on very dangerous ground (especially if he's on all fours on the ground!). If it is in their teachings and beliefs that homosexuals are not on, then stick to your guns. It is no good being intimidated by that loathsome Peter Tatchell, and I have to say, what a quite revolting example of humanity he is, surely he could somehow crawl back into that closet from whence out he came. By talking to them about their part in Christianity, the Archbishop is giving them a false sense of acceptability, and I'd hate them to believe that their predilections were acceptable!

Another "last". This time it's the turn of Britain's last remaining pit ponies to hang up their shoes and retire to an RSPCA sanctuary near Milton Keynes. (I'd like to say it's better than anywhere, but of course it's not really). The Drift Mine at Pant-y-Gasseg near Pontypool will become fully automated and Gremlin, aged 25, and Robbie, aged 7, will be replaced by machinery. The two ponies worked from 8 am to 4 pm five days a week. Their minder, Mike Desmond, a miner at the Drift for 27 years said, "They are wonderful. Robbie and Gremlin are not just pit ponies, they worked hard and were part of the team. I have been looking after them all of their lives. I see them every day at work and I visit them at weekends, and over Christmas, to make sure they are all right.

It's nice to know that there is a Pit Ponies Fund set up to care for these animals, administered by the RSPCA. Mr. Desmond is going to miss these two.

At last. Now we know how it is that pupils all attain such high grades and pass every exam they take, but still cannot spell or add up. The government have been lowering the pass marks. Desperate never to find a long term cure for our atrocious standards in education and social knowledge, it has been revealed that pass marks for 11 year olds have been dramatically reduced. In reading, writing and spelling, the minimum "attainment" mark in 1997 was 52 out of 100. In 1998 it was reduced to 51. This year's examiners have been told to lower the pass mark to 44. Fifty two wasn't exactly setting the world alight, but 44 is appalling. These figures are for average children. The brighter pupils see the minimum pass mark of 75 out of 100 reduced to 67. Less able children's pass marks (or dunces, as we used to call them) are reduced from 28 to 23 out of 100. What a joke!

They might be retired but they are still being rooted out. Another vicar was yesterday jailed for nine months after admitting assaulting three girls, all aged 11. Guy Bennett, aged 66, who was formerly the vicar of St. Mary's in Oxted, Surrey, assaulted his victims over a period dating from 1976 to 1988. School classrooms, trips to the Isle of Wight, you name it, he did it. This man had two daughters of his own. I wonder which bit of that novel he followed to justify his acts of indecency.

A drunken dude called Ian Bottomley, aged 36, caused mayhem upon a flight from Johannesburg to Heathrow last January. He head-butted and attacked staff, injuring three and causing £30,000 worth of damage. The aeroplane used up £10,000 of extra fuel in its efforts to reach London as soon as possible. What sort of prat is it that has to be tied to a seat at the back of a plane. I do not understand, however, the airline allowing him to board in the beginning. He was refused alcohol on the flight, having spent the previous hours beforehand drinking with friends. Threatening to urinate on the deck because the toilets were all being used does not bode well for other passengers. This Bottomley fellow argues that he was attacked by a member of the airline's cabin crew because he complained about not receiving a vegetarian meal. He also added that he suffered from a rare eye condition which made him appear drunk. It didn't go unnoticed that he came from Essex. He may well have had better luck if he had used this piece of information as a mitigating circumstance. Upshot is, he's been found guilty and sentenced to three years in prison. I didn't see any damages being awarded. Why is this? Why should the airline and ultimately the fare paying passengers continue to pick up the tab? All costs incurred should be met by those found responsible, even if it takes them years to pay it off. They might just think twice.

You know, these doctors are greedy. Some are charging pensioners up to ten pounds to sign their bus pass and rail card applications. I was not aware that doctors can charge what they like to sign passport applications and passes. I was also unaware that doctors who visit nursing homes charge a retainer fee. This little scam, from which they do very nicely thank you, can be as much as £600 per month, per home.

I should have been a doctor! Well, gynaecologist really. I can see myself as a specialist in breast implants, or maybe a psychologist, helping women with their sexual problems ..... No, you're right, Maureen would not have been impressed!

Meanwhile, back in the real world. It's a sad state of play when schools and youth organisations stop field trips and expeditions because of the fear of accidents and red tape. The NUT have advised members to boycott all trips where pupils' safety cannot be guaranteed. In their case, however, I have no doubt that they breathe a sigh of relief being able to discount yet another moral, if not legally binding aspect of their work. After all, they've cast off any control and discipline. In fact, I see the day when teachers will only be happy once they receive their monthly pay without having turned up at all.

I digress. Really, you say. I know, but we've all got our little foibles, though in my case, just the two!

But seriously, it is a pity that anything associated with a risk attached should be so easily dismissed due to fears of legal action, should anything go wrong. We have the American litigation culture and all those who have made a tidy living out of compensation to blame for this. Their greedy antics and the equally greedy encouragement of our legal profession have fed the fire and raised the costs - oh, yes, and given those in health and safety a warped sense of purpose akin to that enjoyed by traffic wardens.

The phone just rang - no, of course you didn't hear it. Your's will ring, just give it time!

Anyway, I've just heard that the car superstore where I was contracted to has gone into receivership. A large international firm of accountants is handling the business. All have now been made redundant, save a few sales assistants, one mechanic and the accounts staff. A buyer is being sought but a lot of people have already lost money. A friend of mine, who ran the car cleaning contract, is owed about £15,000. A regional car magazine publisher, with whom they advertised, has lost a similar amount. It is all such a shame but over-expansion and expenditure on frippery has now taken its toll. It won't affect those at the top, who I suspect will move on to pastures new with barely a scratch, but the staff, many of whom have mortgages and moved their on a promise of great expectations, will be deeply resentful, and rightly so.

Perhaps I wasn't too far out with my questioning of priorities, staff levels and marketing practices. Perhaps I, and many other foot soldiers, did see the "wider picture" .....

The Euro's down again, and leaders are calling for calm. Nice to see a bit of panic, an acceptance that not all's well with their funny money.

The following never happened in *"All Creatures Great and Small"*. Here we have the story of two vets, father and son, who were examining a cow when it kicked out and knocked a heavy metal pen against Graeme Richardson, the son. He underwent an operation and had a screw inserted into the fracture. He was in plaster for six weeks and it will still be some time before he is back at work. Graeme is suing his father for "fault and negligence" - oh, yes, and £25,000 in damages. Mr. R. Junior says his father either knew, or should have known, that the Limousin breed of cattle were "fractious" and should have made sure that the pen was secured. Mr. R. Senior said that the lame cow had shown no "propensity for viciousness" adding that the damages claimed were excessive and unreasonable. The case is in its early days, but can you imagine a son suing his father? As a partnership there will never again be the same trust, regardless of financial outcome.

Is it really over? All that murder, rape, NATO bombing, waste of taxpayers' money. I do hope so. It is interesting to read that the rebuilding of Kosova is going to cost an awful lot of money. Britain's share of this expense is likely to run into billions. Could somebody offer an explanation as to why? They've got their country back, we have got out of this the square root of bugger all, except for a bit of target practice (and it looks as if we needed it). Oh, and we also copped a fair number of refugees. I'm sorry (not really) but I fail to see why we should donate a penny to rebuilding this country again. There'll be no thanks anyway. We will be building their flats, giving them toilets and a pound to a penny the colour scheme will be wrong. I wouldn't mind, but they only had an outside privy last time.

Also interesting is the fact that the Americans are to stay in the Balkans for years. With a bit of luck, perhaps the Kosovans won't take to them. No Kentucky Fried Chicken, no McDonalds, no bagels, just think of what they could be missing.

I find it all a bit strange that policemen in certain circumstances will be required to wear a baseball cap for identification purposes. Armed officers will wear either dark blue or black caps, whilst plain clothes officers will wear a garish yellow for easy identification, so that they are not arrested or shot by their fellow officers. I feel this to be just the tip of the iceberg. Presumably, green will be used by those involved with environmental groups or countryside demonstrators. White caps will be worn backwards by the ethnic minority to show equality, brown will be used by all those who ingratiate their way up the promotional ladder, while a nice dusky pink will be issued to all those who are "that way inclined".

Once again, the EU, including Britain, are sticking their noses where they do not belong, nor where they are required. Does Trinidad require a lecture on its legal system? I think not. I don't remember reading of its desire to see us change our ways to theirs. Not only is it nice to see a small country stand up and be counted for its views, it is also gratifying to see it sticking two fingers up at both us and the continentals. The Trinidadians have just hung three men involved in drug dealing. Another six are to be hung soon. The British High Commissioner joined the chorus of EU songbirds who told Trinidad's foreign minister that they were very naughty for using the death penalty. Germany, who holds the EU presidency, sent a further statement to the Trinidad government, which I find rich coming from them. On reflection, however, and to be fair, it doesn't state that the Germans were condemning Trinidad, it just says they sent a further statement, so they could have been offering advice on multiple executions. And there's no denying, they've had the experience! .....

Another one gone. This time it's Peter Brough. One of the worst ventriloquists of all time. I remember an interview with Beryl Reid when she recalled the first time she met Peter Brough, who was sitting with Archie Andrews on his lap, in the *BBC* studios. She asked, "Which one is the dummy?" Only in Britain could a ventriloquist become such a success on radio.

Two million pounds is to be spent on anti-racism campaigns and a new buzz phrase is about to hit the street. Forget blacks and Asians, Turks, Spaniards, Iti's, they are all to come under a collective term. From now on, they'll be known as "Visibly Minority Ethnic Groups". A spokesman, or sucker-upper, for the police, said, "It is meant to avoid causing offence". Asad Rehman, of the Stephen Lawrence Family Campaign (them again!) said, "The police need a radical overhaul of their methods - this shows them concentrating on irrelevant semantic arguments". So no support there, then. Mind you, are you surprised?

181

This is the sort of appeasement Attlee would have championed. I think the slogan "Not English" would be most acceptable. Certainly here in Surrey, anyway!

What was I saying about Brother George, the Archbishop of Canterbury, having tea and crumpets with homosexuals. No, that was a rhetorical question - of course I remember. Our dearly elected government of things minority wish to reverse the rule that makes the "promotion of homosexuality" illegal. Not content with their desire to lower the age of consent for homosexuality, they appear quite happy for schools to accept the social practice as, well, acceptable, if not openly endorsing it. It's just another slap in the face for the family and normal people.

Some Manchester United players never learn. David Beckham went a long way to losing it for England in the last World Cup. Roy Keane does it for his team on a regular basis and now it's Paul Scholes's turn. Not content with receiving two yellow cards and subsequently missing his club's champions league final, he has now been sent off whilst playing for his country. It was appropriate that it would fall to a Manchester United player to be the first sent off at Wembley. I do feel that such is their desire to win, that winning becomes all important and the timing of a tackle a poor second. Still, on these players' salaries, any financial slap on the wrist is just that.

I don't know where John Prescott or his underlings get their ideas from, but reserving the outside lane of the M4 into London for buses and coaches only is half-baked in the extreme. His view that not only will it be better for public transport passengers, but also for motorists, is arrant tosh. Three lanes into two will not go. I can understand that new systems take a while to gel, but eight mile tailbacks of traffic sitting watching the outside lane remain almost empty, is not going to placate those of us who are now paying the highest rates for fuel in Europe.

Good news - the "Vanessa Show" is being dropped by the BBC. Guests, victims and odd-balls who turn out to be actors are bound to reduce credibility. Probably by about 100%, which in this case is to be welcomed. As I have said, she is really someone I cannot take to, always full of herself, so it will not hurt her ego to have both feet replaced on the ground once more. What does concern me is that the Beeb are working with her on a new TV show, provisionally entitled "Talking TV". Matthew Bannister, head of BBC productions says the show aims to "tap into the British passion for TV. The new show would give the audience a unique and immediate opportunity to participate and contribute to the discussion about what they see on British screens". Well, I think they've just sold me a very good reason to spend another half hour in the garden. It sounds to me as if that already empty barrel is being scraped once more.

The CRE are never satisfied, are they. According to the latest figures racial complaints against private sector employees are up by 60%. The unwarranted quango's chairman commented that while it is not an indication of guilt, there is more awareness of people's rights (them again). You'd have thought their chairman and all his little chairettes would be preening themselves that their jobs are safe, but no, he is ever so concerned with the low numbers of complaints from the Bangladeshi's. I don't suppose for one moment that it could just be that they are happy with their lot! Still, I've no doubt that with a few sticks with which to beat the nasty white man, he'll be able to change all that. What better way to start their collective day than sit back and wait for people to complain. Another case, another dollar ...... pound ...... Euro!

The naivety of the Church of England is still boundless. It has been largely in favour of GM trials since April but has had nothing to do with them. (I thought we'd found something in common at last, but thankfully this is not the case). The Ministry of Agriculture is now looking to the C of E to provide test sites. If they say yes, it will be because they think the outcome will provide enough crops to feed their unwieldy herd - and ultimately, the church's pocket. The very fact that they are considering this move flies in the face of everything they should be standing for. Didn't that novel of theirs refer somewhere within its text to "all God's creatures"? If it did, I think they should find that it includes animals, birds and insects, as well as their destroyers, i.e. us.

CHAPTER EIGHT

ARISE, SIR ALEX, BUT PLEASE CLOSE YOUR MOUTH WHILE YOU CHEW!

It seems like only six months ago since the New Year's Honours were announced - well, actually it w as, but why stop the party. It's now the turn of the Queen, with her hand-chosen list of recipients. It was not long before I noticed Sir Alex Ferguson heading the list of sporting heroes. Tony Adams, MBE, well he has served Arsenal and his country for a while, I suppose, and if they have to tag letters to names, then he's as good as anyone. Craig Brown, the Scotland manager - nice chap, I'm sure - but with his country drawing with the Faroe Islands I'm not sure that a CBE is justified. Robbie Earle and Garth Crooks, I just cannot see. Nor Iwan Thomas, he's only 25 and got a long way to go. Gregor Townsend (did someone leave off a y' - perhaps they pay for their Christenings by the letter in Scotland) - again, he's only 26 and he's to be an MBE. Away from sport, we have Julie Walters, Simon Callow and Juliet Stephenson - are they not actors, for Christ sake, just doing their job? Lord Longford's daughter, Antonia Fraser, is a CBE. Norma Major? Yes, from now on it's Dame Norma for all that charity work she does. We could all do charity work if we didn't have to go out to earn a living.

Joan Bakewell, Jenny Murray and Libby Purves are another three, a CBE and two OBE's. Why? Again, they are only doing their job, and I have to say very well, but they're programme presenters. Perhaps there's discount for a job lot!

It's spanking good news in Kosova. The British have liberated the country, don't you know! Boris Johnson, he of the *Daily Telegraph*, is there and fairly relishing the raising of arms and cheering that is accompanying our lads' arrival. The Kosovans' sense of relief will no doubt subside when they eventually become members of the EU. Still, knowing the Balkan country's history, if it doesn't suit them they'll shoot their way out. Mmmm, perhaps they could start with the

Germans!

Staying with Europe, it appears that very few Brits were enticed to vote for the gravy train candidates. Maureen and I had better things to do, like gardening and going to the loo with a book (although this last bit was me, actually). Glyn thought about voting for a nano-second, but carried on with his pint of lager. The turnout was apparently just over 20%, which is just over 20% too high for my liking. I cannot understand how those who voted thought they would be doing any good. I suppose that like those who go through the motions of a trip to church on a Sunday, they just felt it was the "right thing" to do.

Ah, well, it's nice to know that the church abroad is as obsessive and controlling as it is here. Our United Nations ambassador, Geri Halliwell, made comment concerning safe sex during her goodwill tour of the Philippines. I don't know whose script she was reading from, but her words "I believe that if you can't control your fertility you can't control your life and if you're having sex, you've got to be protected ...." is absolutely spot on. No surprise, of course, that the ill-named Cardinal Jaime Sin described condoms as "evil and only fit for animals". I find that statement insulting to animals and humans alike. What right has this person to tell others how to run their lives? The Reverend James Reuter, who is - wait for it - director of the National Office of Mass Media of the Catholic Church of the Philippines, said "This is a free country. We don't interfere in the right of anybody to go anywhere or say what they believe, but we do not need population control and any effort at safe sex is totally, utterly immoral from top to bottom". This rather makes a mockery of the first part of his sentence.

Here's a little snippet I picked up in today's *D.T.* Were you aware that all of our acts of Parliament are preserved on animal hide? It's a sort of latter-day hard disk, I suppose. Every piece of legislation since Henry VII is stored in the Records Office on hide. Soon, however, we will be using paper. The vellum produced from goats' skin *only* costs £28 per A4 page, which is not so much of a snip as a 200 page A4 pad at 99p from Woolies. I wonder how many other countries have stored all of their acts on animal hide. Very few, I would imagine. Still, it was quirkiness like this that made Great Britain so dependable.

Sad to see that our own elections will no longer be graced by Screaming Lord Sutch. The only perpetual loser to gain popularity with every lost deposit. He was never a very successful rock singer, he failed to win a seat, but he was always there. It appears that the private persona was somewhat more subdued and depressed than the stage version. Elections will never be the same again.

Basil Hume, big in religious circles, I understand, has also died.

That's it, time to go upstairs and watch Maureen while she packs our cases. And won't I just moan if I find she hasn't packed my razor. We're both looking forward to a week away in the Isle of Man. I did tell you we were going, just hope it hasn't all changed. See you when we get there.

We've arrived at our holiday cottage in Higher Foxdale, which in case you're wondering where that is, lies some eight plus miles from Douglas. When I say "we've arrived" I mean Maureen, myself and one case. The other is still at Heathrow. The omens were not good last night. Having packed, checked the airline tickets, car hire vouchers and driving licences, we decided to take Muttley around the block. "I've got a key", said I. On our return I realised that the key was for my office above the garage, and not our front door key. Out to the shed I wandered, extracted the ladder and in an effort to "help" the situation, Maureen squashed my thumb between the two metal sections. Less than amused, I scrambled up the ladder, climbed the tiles and plunged head-first through the bedroom window. Turning on the light, I thought "Bloody good guard dog, didn't even bark". I then realised she was outside on the end of the lead with Maureen. I put it down to a sudden rush of blood to the head.

Anyway, instructions were given to Glyn and William concerning the watering of plants, locking up behind them, etc. then we all went to bed. Slept well, except that I still keep dreaming, almost nightly now. Today dawned bright, at least that's what Maureen told me since she was up at 5 am. I appeared in the kitchen sometime after 6.15 am when I'd given up waiting for tea in bed - well, you can only wait for so long! - I watered the plants, explained to the dog what was happening, not that she appeared to be overly interested, and awaited the arrival of Debbie and Tim who were taking us to the airport.

They duly pulled in to view at 7 am. We played *"Butterflies"* with the cars, shunting everything about, until all were in position for the duration of our holiday.

Now Tim, our son-in-law, is a fast driver - fast, but safe. Heathrow was reached in 25 minutes. We bade our farewells and Maureen's last request was to ask if they could pick us up the following Saturday. No, apparently we hadn't mentioned it before, but better late than never. Luckily, they weren't going out.

Check-in and boarding went without hassle, the captain introduced himself and the crew - nice of him - he explained that we would be taking off at 9.05 am and then announced that we would be heading north over Hemel Hempstead and Birmingham before turning left over Liverpool, where we would commence our descent. Hardly up before you're down again, I mused. Maureen commented that she's witnessed that experience many times at first hand!

Breakfast was taken at 24,000 feet. I remember, because I counted, before we rolled onto the runway at the newly rebuilt Ronaldsway Airport. Into the baggage hall we flocked, where the conveyor belt commenced its relentless circuit. Businessmen and women, holidaymakers and those we could not pigeon-hole extracted their cases - others, like us, extracted one or none. After some 20 minutes of waiting the machine was switched off. People started to look at each other blankly, shoulders shrugged but nothing was said - well, we'd never been introduced! A green-suited Manx Airline representative with blonde hair tied in a bun stepped forward and announced gingerly that, "There's no more luggage from the Heathrow flight. Could you all please make your way to the check-in desk". About thirty of us were then informed that the loading conveyor belt at broken down at Heathrow and that all the remaining luggage was still about 300 miles away.

Two male pensioners were behind us. One explained how, only two months ago, his daughter had gone to Cyprus but her luggage hadn't. "We laughed when she told us", he enthused. His companion was equally jolly. "Your daughter will be laughing when you tell her about this". Oh, how we laughed in the queue at the check-in desk. One by one, or in our case, two by one, we gave our names and Island addresses. Manx Airlines explained that the rest of the luggage would be put aboard the next flight, due out at 6 pm, and delivered to all the temporary residences. And no, we did not require counselling or demand compensation. We accepted this irritation in the manner befitting Surrey residents and made our way to the car hire desk.

The jolly lady at Mylchreests Car Hire swept through the proposal form, handed us the keys and bade us farewell. Within a few minutes our Peugeot 106 was galloping its way along the A-road towards Douglas. Occupation of the cottage was not officially until 3 pm and it was only just creeping up to 11 am. Strange to tell, but the railway station was the first port of call to enable me to collect timetables and general fliers concerning the week's enthusiasts' specials. Isn't it funny, what a coincidence, the one week I choose above all others to go to the Isle of Man and it turns out to be the Railway Enthusiasts Week!

Maureen didn't see it quite as such a coincidence, in fact, she went so far as to accuse me of planning it! Would I?

We then purchased provisions and visited a few shops. Unfortunately we were only a few hundred yards from the car when it started to rain. Within a few minutes it was extremely heavy. The walk was curtailed and we drove to Safeways, after which we had a 20 minute jaunt before reaching our farmhouse. So that's brought you up to date. Maureen has just made the tea - well, she likes to play Mum when we go away - and I have to tell you it is now fairly bucketing down, with a wind approaching gale force. Still, we're thinking of the benefits. We don't have to keep getting up to answer the phone only to reply that "he's not in", and then explain that we actually have no idea where William is. And there's no fear that the use of the words "walk" or "block" will excite Muttley into thinking it's time to go out.

(As we're typing this I've had to spell out the above two words in quotes, as Muttley is at present sitting between Maureen and myself and the slightest mention would see ears prick up and manic leaping take place.)

There are three cottages within the farmyard. All very nice and situated on one side of the cobbled courtyard. The opposite side is taken up by stables. There are two ponies that I can see through the rain, heads are over the stable doors and I assume there are bodies to go with them. A young sheepdog appears to be keeping two chickens in line - probably just practising - while to our right is another stable block housing a goat, a calf, an extremely large horse and, on the rafter, a peacock. The view is over South Barrole, a small mountain or large hill, whichever, but it's 1592 feet high. At the moment you can't look over anything as it's encased in cloud, but you've got the general picture.

Bearing in mind that we haven't visited the island for fourteen years very little appears to have changed, which is why we're here. One notable and very irritating exception are the car number plates. The more recently registered cars are disfigured by the use of hideous "foreign" style plates, with numbers in Euro type, hyphenated every two to three letters/digits. It looks as if the Island is full of foreigners - most disconcerting.

Maureen's just been looking through the visitors book. The majority of holidaymakers proclaim the farm experience as "brilliant, great time, very enjoyable and very friendly". There are, however, always the exceptions. One couple from Luton in Bedfordshire leaves the comment, "Mirrors a little high for short people" - sad bastard! Another couple have stamped their name and address in the book. Do people *really* take a rubber stamp on holiday with them? Suppose they must! There are many comments regarding the high standard of finish, the quality and comfort of the furniture, the atmosphere, the superb accommodation - "it's home from home", "it's peaceful and relaxing", they say. But not according to the Masons from Carlisle who note, "Peacock and paying guests do not mix". Ouch!

Right, I'm going to read the papers, wait for the luggage to arrive and then we'll try to find a hostelry about 3 miles away which has been recommended by the owners. Byee.

It's now gone 11 pm. We found the hostelry and I have to say, it wasn't quite us. Maureen said she felt uneasy. I could see her point although I just felt we'd stumbled into the British version of the film *"Deliverance"*. We walked to the bar, looked at each other for confirmation of opinion and then walked out and back to the car, and headed for Peel. We had a nice meal in the Creek Public House. Pity all the tables were for smokers, but there. At least it had stopped raining long enough for us to walk through the deserted town, back along the deserted promenade and peruse the old station building and yard, now the obligatory car park. So to bed, perchance to dream!

Morning, morning! I hope I haven't disturbed your Sunday lie-in, but it's 7.30 am, the sun is attempting to come out of hiding and I've made the tea. What's that? No, it's not a printing error, I've just made the tea. Look, it's as much Maureen's holiday as it is mine, you know. Well, that's what Maureen keeps saying. Today we're off to the Groudle Glen Railway and the Summer Fair which is being held at the local school, here in Foxdale. See you later.

Home once more. Groudle Glen Railway was very good. Pity it rained. Foxdale Summer Fair was washed out, us with it. We came back, changed, had a nice cup of tea and slept. We then visited Port St. Mary, Port Erin and Peel again. Lovely walks along the harbour wall, beaches etc. and still hardly a soul about. It's like Sundays used to be on the mainland. We half-fancied fish and chips but we passed one particular establishment for a second time, only to find that on both occasions it has had neither a customer nor a member of staff in view. The establishment was open, the sign said so, the lights were on and there was fish on the top glass shelving, but definitely the establishment was bereft of human life. So we travelled across the island (all fifteen minutes of it) to Douglas, where we had superb fish and chips at Arkwrights on the Promenade - very tasty, very sweet.

Back "home" now. Maureen's made tea, so armed with packet of chocolate digestives we are about to sit down and watch TV and that makes a change in itself, finding a whole packet of unopened biscuits. I think we could be here for some time, it's a film, so book's going down, see you tomorrow.

It's Monday, it's sunny and it's very, very windy. We've now planned our week so I'll probably not bother you for a while, which is good news for you, I suspect. Right, first stop is the woollen mills - the excitement and anticipation of it all .....

It's been a funny sort of day, really. Well, not so much funny as just bloody awful. We drove the couple of miles to the Tynwald Craft Centre, which opens at 10 a.m., having stopped off for me to examine the remains of St. John's Railway Station. We arrived at the Craft Centre around 10.30 a.m. and soon realised that the word "craft" was something of a misnomer. Names like "Timberland" and "Laura Ashley"do not conjure up "crafts". Many of the shops were still not open and others announced that they didn't open on Mondays. Where were all the owners of the vehicles in the car park? We presumed they were the shopkeepers. Aside from the bookshop, whose owner was very personable and helpful, the general feeling was not one of welcome. Three shops were still being hoovered by members of staff. The Centre's information board informed Maureen of the whereabouts of that elusive wool shop. Yup, there it is, No. 19, opposite Laura Ashley, or so it maintains on the map. Back we went, but for "wool" shop, read "toy" shop. Further enquiries revealed that the former bade farewell over two years ago and nobody bothered to instruct a signwriter.

Hey, ho, off to Peel, where the first thing we saw was a man loading a Hoover onto a pick-up truck. It was mid-morning and we discovered that half of the shops are shut. Why? Yes, you've guessed, it's Monday. Up the main street we walked, only to find a middle-aged man carrying an upright Hoover. What is it about Hoovers and Mondays on this island?

Following a route that delivered us to Sulby Glen Woollen Mills, we remembered too late, yes, it's Monday and therefore it's closed - but then, it is only the height of the holiday season! Incidentally, the sign at the junction at Sulby states, Mill 1½ miles. They are exactly two miles short of reality, either that or the mill has moved "up glen". So, off to Jurby Junk in the north of the island. We'd visited this emporium about fourteen years ago, housed in one of many old aircraft hangars. It was at that time a veritable mine of bric-a-brac, ephemera and relics, as well as an awful lot of rubbish, but it was interesting rubbish. I remember buying Glyn a Second World War helmet and gas mask. He's still got them. Now, however, the "Junk" is clinical, mass-produced, sorted and housed in what appears to be a purpose-built warehouse. It certainly is cheap, but it's not what it was.

We then headed back, taking in the beautiful scenery, before making our way home for dinner. Fully replete we decided to head for the coast and spend a couple of hours "chilling out" but first a phone call home. This is the point at which our holiday was stood on its head. Glyn answered, we were both keen that his first day at his new job had gone well. Luckily I had my BT chargecard with me since a coin box is almost impossible to find on the island, they are nearly all card phones. Try finding a shop that sells cards, that is open after 6 pm. Unfortunately, the St. John's exchange was "playing up" according to the operator. However, I eventually got through, listened to Glyn telling me about his first day, and then seethed to boiling point as he unfurled the nightmare that had taken place at home last Saturday.

You remember me saying that we'd bought William a Metro from the mother of one of his friends. Well, perhaps I haven't, but we did. It was parked at the back of the line in the drive and he could not gain access to it. My car came next in line, with Maureen's Peugeot 205 third. Glyn's was ready to take off in pole position. Are you beginning to grasp the series of events?

At this stage we have only brief notes on certain aspects but the result is clear. William and two friends were going to play pool on Saturday evening, that we know. On their arrival back home it appears that "full moon syndrome" came into play. Taking the keys to Maureen's Peugeot they then pushed Glyn's car out of the drive, reversed the Peugeot and once more pushed Glyn's car back in again. Glyn, by the way, was at a party, not returning until the early hours of the morning. The gang of three took Maureen's car for a quick spin around the block, no insurance, under age and without the owner's consent, i.e. us. Off they go, navigate the first corner, then straight into a fence. Result - panic! So what's to do? Own up, or lie? The latter appeared easiest. Glyn came home about 3 am and surprise, surprise, William doesn't say anything. Glyn is not aware that one car is missing. There is no outside light on the drive at this point and at that time of the morning, there could be two, three or four cars and no-one could tell.

The early morning dawned and William said something to the effect that someone had taken Mum's car. The rest of the news is somewhat hazy at the moment, but all we know is, that we are one car short of a family and the car is in a recovery service yard. Having said cheerio to Glyn, I broke the news to Maureen. She cried, I seethed. You can't string a child up by proxy, can you, so I'll have to wait. Words fail me. I cannot imagine anyone doing anything quite so stupid and potentially dangerous. Whatever possessed them? It's not as though he's the product of a single parent.

So instead of enjoying the evening quietly listening to the gentle lapping of waves in some remote bay, following by a pint in a pub, we travelled to the airport to see if we could get an early flight home. Guess what? The Airport was closed. (We wondered if it was because it was a Monday!) The only sign of life was a security officer who informed me of Manx Airlines reservation telephone number and stated that they opened at 6 am; he added, however, that it was "best to leave it until ten to quarter past" as they like to brew up first! Well, naturally one must get one's priorities right. So, as we can't do anything until tomorrow, we've decided to sleep on the options. There's no alternative, so I might wake up and find it was all a dream .....

No! Apparently not! I'm awake, Maureen's awake and the problem's still with us. Neither of us slept well last night, I find the affair even more incredulous after a bad night's sleep. But we've worked out a few priorities so I'm off to the phone box.

Right, I've rung Glyn, he seems a bit happier, as they say a "problem shared is a problem doubled"! Deborah has offered to have William for the day (although, until he's 25 would be preferable!) and the recovery company are delivering the Peugeot back home at a cost of £180. The police have now released the vehicle after fingerprinting it, or whatever it is they do. The car is being delivered back to our home after 7 pm as Glyn needs to sign for it. Us? Oh, we've decided to stay. I don't see why our holiday should be ruined further by cutting it short. Kids, huh!

It's now Friday morning. The sun is shining yet again and we're off to Ramsey on the electric tramway. The weather has been pretty well perfect after last Sunday's downpour. It rained slightly Tuesday evening, but other than that, super. We've travelled to Port Erin by steam train (there's a surprise), we finally visited the craft shop in Sulby Glen - you remember, the one that's 3½ miles from the signpost and we've looked at many shops in all the towns. Most are interesting, if only for trying to work out who would buy the tat. Some invite you to "come in a browse without obligation". The good news is that it's optional, not mandatory. One shop window provided an entertaining few moments. *All* the displays were discoloured. There was a mix of dull blue and hearing-aid grey, be it tea bags, chocolates or toffee the sun had bleached all of the items. A clue to their longevity of internment was indicated by a packet of dates, which stated "Best before March 1997" - a full two and a quarter years ago. On closer examination I ascertained that the shop, which sported no indication of ownership or trading name, was definitely open. Bananas vied for space with onions, whilst a cabbage lay undisturbed on a lower shelf. We didn't go in.

Whilst returning by car from Ramsey we decided to stop off at some of the east coast's beauty spots, north of Laxey. One, an outcrop called Maughold Head, sports a pretty cluster of houses and a church. On our descent from the headland we walked through the churchyard, looking at tombstones, recognising family names observed elsewhere in street names, businesses and the island's history. A gaggle of black-robed vicars wafted speechlessly around the paths. Some in blue attire lay on the grass amid the gravestones, reading. I was desperate to spot one of their number hiding a copy of GQ behind the sermon he was purporting to read, or was it the latest manual on "How to abuse your parishioners and still make them feel the guilty party". This I took to be "high" church as a peacock god-worshipper, dressed in vivid red, swanned around outside the church entrance (can a peacock swan?). There was a notice pinned by the gates inviting all to their forthcoming annual garden party. I did note that they were providing a bouncy castle for the children. I wonder who was providing the sweeties? .....

I did call Glyn last night. The Peugeot is "safely" back in the drive. It is, however, undriveable. William is still rather quiet and so he should be, having just been told the car's a right-off. He definitely has some explaining to do tomorrow night when we arrive home. Still, it's now time for our journey into the known - Douglas, actually - to catch the tram. See you.

A few notes now from the airport lounge before we depart. Ignoring the unmentionable, we've had a great week. It is a credit to the Isle of Man and its inhabitants that it still acts and behaves as England did fifty years ago. The people are friendly, the service is generally very good, beer is around £1.50 a pint, which is considerably cheaper than most locals in Surrey, and what a pleasure it is to be able to park anywhere without meters gobbling up every penny of your loose change. In all honesty, it's amazing how reassuring it is to know that within yards of Douglas's shops and restaurants there are long lengths of streets with up to two hours of free parking. You visit the bays - no parking charges. In fact, nowhere else, either. I realise this may read like an advert, but it really has been a relaxing! holiday. Oh, yes, and where else can you go and find a telephone box which has a telephone directory that has *not* been damaged, defaced or burnt?

No surprise to you, but I've kept a few cuttings from the week's papers and as there's another twenty minutes before we board, I'll use the time to share these with you - all, right, bugger off and mow the lawn, but I'll still be here when you've finished.

Last Saturday, the *Daily Express* headed an inside article, "At long last, police get to grips with race attacks". The article was accompanied by the now obligatory photograph of Stephen Lawrence. It stated how prosecutions for racial attacks had risen over the last couple of years. Again, the native white is supposed to feel guilty about his colour. I mean, fancy being white *and* British. To the *Daily Express's* credit, it did comment that, "In Brixton the rate of racial violence was far lower than Hounslow with just 32 blacks, 14 Asians and 29 whites attacked. Now, to my mind, 29 is not a lot fewer than 32, and just over twice 14. Does the fact that 29 whites have been on the receiving end cause ripples through political circles, society itself or the dreaded CRE? - does it heck as like! I do so enjoy using these regional phrases from time to time.

On Monday the *Daily Express*, in its comment section, toed the popular media line and vented its disgust at racists. As I have said all along, the vast majority of us do not like violence perpetrated against/by any colour, race, etc. But this drip effect, on behalf of the so-called oppressed, is becoming tiresome in the extreme. The comment, responding to a report by the Joseph Rowntree Foundation, speaks of ethnic families afraid to go shopping or on holiday. Many refuse to allow their children to play outside. I have met many elderly people who have suffered harassment (that's pronounced harass-ment, not har-assment, thank you!) at the hands of black (yes, black) as well as white youths. But then there doesn't seem to be the same ear lent to their plight.

Incidentally, page 17 gave us virtually the same story as that expounded on Saturday. You know, shock horror stories of how minorities "cannot hang out the washing for fear of abuse". Once again, Stephen Lawrence's photograph was featured alongside. The article, not surprisingly, used the opportunity to report the "unsympathetic treatment" by the police and other agencies. No wonder morale and indifference is widespread. Day in, day out, someone's whinging at the white population.

The *Express* goes on to state in its comment that Britain is rightly proud of its multi-cultural society. Is it? And if so, why is it? Britishness and being British has been greatly diluted since mass immigration, the onslaught of refugees, black and not so black, and the blind eye that is turned to those illegally entering our overcrowded island. I stress again that by moving the scenario abroad the result would be the same. Any country loses its individuality of spirit, culture, etc. if it becomes multi-cultural. You go on holiday to encounter different cultures, ideas, standards, etc. Who, other than the Americans, want wall-to-wall McDonalds, Pepsi-Cola, Kentucky Fried Chicken?

I found it somewhat upsetting and more than a tad irritating to learn that civets, members of the mongoose family, are being trapped and kept in appalling conditions so that they can be "milked". These animals apparently produce the musk that is used in a number of fragrances. Thousands of these animals are kept in wooden cages, some three foot by one foot by one foot. They cannot turn around. Rows of these cages are kept in airless, smoke-filled huts in Ethiopia. Musk is taken from a gland at the base of the animal's tale every nine to fifteen days. This process is extremely painful and some give up eating as an alternative to the constant torture. Over two hundred of these "farms" exist in Ethiopia. The above findings are from a survey conducted by "The World Society for the Protection of Animals" and were reported in the *Daily Express*. I won't bore you with the details, but the response from the French perfume companies was hardly encouraging. Ninety seven per cent of Ethiopia's exports go to France (those bastards again!) for its perfumery industry. Now here's where the EU could gain a touch of respectability. Why not insist that all perfumes that contain animal products, or where tests have been made on animals, clearly state "We hereby inform the purchaser that this product has involved the use of animals". It would be too much to expect that labelling similar to cigarette health warnings could be used as a rider. "The animal or animals used may well have been trapped, ill-treated, tortured and eventually killed or left to rot". Incidentally, Chanel, Lancome and Cartier all admitted using civets' musk. Regrettable as it is, at least they replied to questions asked by the above-named charity. Many failed to reply at all. So much for ethics - or rather, so little .....

Tuesday's headline in the *Express* was good. "Commons riddled with racism". Delete Stephen Lawrence's photo, insert Keith Vaz and Trevor McDonald, along with Margaret Beckett and Archie Kirkwood.

Keith Vaz has become the first Asian minister in a British government. Now you know me, not one to be cynical, but you have to ask yourself, was Mr. Vaz appointed because he was the best candidate for the job, or because the government was desperate for an ethnic flag bearer, and there aren't many candidates. As far as I recall, Mr. V only ever comments on the plight of the ethnically under-privileged. He does himself no favours by being so obsessed with the percentages of blacks and Asians employed hither and thither. Much better that he champion the cause of the imprisoned civet than those who life is made so awful by the nasty white man.

Wednesday saw the death of Buster Merryfield. I mention his passing as my mother and Aunty Mabel went to school with him! According to mum, Mr. Merryfield's mother "always wore a green coat". Funny how some things stick in your memory.

Bloody hell, it doesn't get any better. In the continuing effort to placate, fawn, suck up to, appease, ingratiate themselves to the hapless ethnic, DNA tests are to be introduced for all racial offences. This includes abusive language. If I am referred to as a "honky" by some unknown verbal assailant somewhere, can I make a citizen's arrest and demand that the scoundrel be DNA'd. Frankly, I couldn't be bothered, but then I doubt if I would be taken seriously, bearing in mind my colour.

Right! They've called us to boarding control so pens and chocks away - no, not the Cadbury kind. See you later.

Well, we're cruising at 23,000 feet, the stewardesses have just delivered a snack, and quite tasty to boot, so inbetween mouthfuls (you don't mind, I hope) we'll chew over a few more items of news.

I'm beginning to feel sorry for the *Daily Express*. Presumably, it's obsession with race stories is supposed to increase readership. Thursday's edition devotes two pages in which to mull over the secretive, free-masonry fetish that is rife in Westminster. More shock horror. Not content with the usual accreditation of tales to an "unnamed former senior officer of the Commons" they equate the large number of masons to the low number of blacks and Asians. I am not in favour of secret societies and am no supporter of masonry, but it is rare to find two pages of such a non-story in a fairly reasonable national such as the *Express*. Oh, yes, while we're back on the old race issue, the armed forces have obviously had the equality do-gooders breathing down their necks. At a conference on ethnic minority recruitment, General Sir Charles Guthrie, Chief of Defence Staff, stated that they are "on target" to appoint the first black or Asian Admiral or Air-Marshall. General G added that, "We have declared war on racism". I thought everybody had. It's become a *cause celèbre* or a celebrity cause, whatever. Actually, I really do detest these French clichés, I find them so passé! (And so does Maureen, she has to keep changing her keyboard to International mode).

Getting back to the story, it really is quite laughable, all this effort and yet, the end result will be that every promotion will be questioned. Merit or political token gesture?

What's this? Ah, yes. Three Jesuit priests have been arrested following allegations of sexual abuse at a Roman Catholic public school. Five former employees of St. Mary's Hall Prep School have already been remanded on bail, charged with indecency offences. They keep coming out of the woodwork, don't they?

The best news Thursday offered was the announcement that the Bramleys could continue fostering Jade and Hannah for at least the next two years. Social Services will still be sticking their corporate beak in, but it's definitely a better conclusion than was first considered possible. Best of luck to the Bramleys - all four of them.

Yesterday, I read of an eight year battle by a small parish council and a group of Oxfordshire residents to retain their village green. Eighty thousand pounds has been used in legal costs against that labyrinthine organisation, the Church of England. Not content with licking their wounds after a poor showing in the investment market, that all powerful asset-rich leader of the misguided looks to asset strip. The C. of E. wish to build two houses on glebe land that has been used as a green for many years. Five law lords ordered Oxford County Council to overturn a previous decision and allow the land to be registered as a village green. Good news there and good news for around thirty similar objections currently being heard concerning the future of other village greens.

The Church of England, however, is not known for its Christian spirit and true to form, is less than gracious in its response. The Rev. Thomas, a communication director for the diocese, stated that, "The church has been severely penalised for being a tolerant and generous landowner. The church will now take steps to ensure that all other open spaces are sufficiently protected to prevent the establishment of similar rights elsewhere". Pompous arse!

Let's be honest, little land the church owned was ever purchased. Given, favoured, probably just taken. Oh, yes, it gives me such a warm and glowing feeling to know that the "church" has lost out. Glory be their loss. Amen!

There are some sad souls around, aren't there. Two of them wrote letters to "*The Weekly News*". The first, from MS of Bristol, announces, "I suppose I should feel flattered that my husband turned down a slap-up meal with some friends on his holiday to enjoy my home cooking. He really loves my home-made shepherd's pie, with its rich filling and crunchy potato topping and this is what he requested for his birthday treat. I'm sure he would probably eat it almost every meal, given the chance, but I was only too happy to oblige".

Bet they're a fun couple.

Second letter, from the undead, came from Mr. S.R. of Swansea - there's lovely, isn't it! He writes, "My wife has never been particularly fond of the cars I've owned - until recently when I was working away from home and she made the final choice about the colour of the new car we'd ordered. It was a very unusual and striking colour of metallic blue and she really took a shine to the car when it was delivered. I never get the chance to clean or polish it as my wife is constantly giving it the once-over. But I am not complaining!"

Can you imagine wasting a stamp, then walking to the post-box, just to inform all and sundry of the pathetic little world you and your other half inhabit.

Finished eating, trays have been cleared and yesterday witnessed another landmark. Here we have the story of one Beverley Lancaster, whose photograph accompanies the article. She's smiling, and no wonder. This woman is about to welcome up to £200,000 into the family coffers. Birmingham City Council, her former employers, have accepted the blame, so it's all plain sailing from now on. The "blame" is an admission of liability for personal injury caused by, yes, that good old standby, stress! We read how Mrs. L. "wept" as she told how work-related stress had destroyed her life, prompting panic attacks, anxiety and bouts of clinical depression.

This senior draughtswoman had her confidence "destroyed" when transferred to Sutton Coldfield's Housing Office. She was unable to cope with even the most mundane duties. Now we all know that dealing with the "I want's" of the world in a housing department is never easy, and it may well be that Mrs. L. is not the best person to deal with the ungrateful and disgruntled. What is not made clear in either the *Express* or the *D.T.* articles is whether she actually asked for a move to the housing department. Did she tell anyone that she couldn't cope? If she did, was she ignored? It's all water under the bridge now. Since ill health and absences caused her to retire on medical grounds over two years ago, the near quarter-of-a-million heiress cannot do more than one thing at a time.

Stress used to be something that was the sole domain of moaners, whingers and those who knew their rights. Now it's become a desirable commodity - in other words, a nice little earner!

Two retirements in similar circumstances. The first concerns Det. Inspector Ben Bullock, who is involved in the Stephen Lawrence trial. He has become so dismayed by the tactics used by the Lawrences' team to delay the trial that he's obviously had enough. So that was an own goal by Imran Khan, the Lawrences' solicitor. Secondly, we have the case of Don Bramhall, who has sought to retire four days before facing a disciplinary tribunal for making an alleged racist remark. His crime was to offer the opinion, "I'd rather be gay than black" to a group of new recruits. Frankly, I do not share his opinion but to face an enquiry for that! Does all this not smack of McCarthyism in the most extreme form. Whatever happened to that good old standby, a sense of proportion?

No surprise to find that Curtis McLardie, to whom Mr. Bramhall made the remark is pursuing a claim for money - sorry, racial discrimination - against the fire brigade.

This last bit is a hoot. Do you remember Patti Boulaye? She was either on "*Blue Peter*", "*New Faces*" or neither. Anyway, during an interview with the *Guardian*, the interviewer thought she uttered the word "apartheid" instead of "a party". Not content with an apology in the paper, which I remember being quoted on "*News Quiz*" on *Radio 4*, she has now been awarded £15,000 libel damages. Perhaps this would-be Tory candidate may well consider spending a reasonable amount of her bounty on elocution lessons, as this would save any mistakes in the future. There's no give with these people, is there.

And finally, as we approach Heathrow and we've been advised by the stewardess to "clunk click" I see that Morlands, the Abingdon brewers, are embracing a proposed takeover bid by Greene King. Back in 1992 they were fighting off bids from predators but now, having lost MG, the car manufacturers nearly twenty years ago, Abingdon is likely to lose its brewery and around one hundred jobs as well. Two famous brews, Old Speckled Hen and Ruddles, now just a marketing name since the demise of the erstwhile Oakham Brewery in Rutland, will be brewed in Bury St. Edmonds. Following hard on the takeover stakes comes news that Guinness Peat, a company holding shares in Youngs Brewery, is attempting to loosen the Youngs' family hold on the business. Youngs have been canny by reducing the voting rights of certain shareholdings, which means they retain control, and why not. We all know the outcome if this company gets its way. You can bet your last pint of best that mergers, takeovers, closures, will be the order of the day, and once again, the only winners will be the faceless vultures who care not a jot but go home fully loaded, while some poor sod waits to be interviewed in the Job Centre. His sin? He was expendable. Bastards!

It's now Monday morning. I didn't write anything yesterday. Had to sort out the problems at home. First look at the Peugeot 205 confirmed the view expressed over the phone. It is not a pretty sight! William was not allowed to sleep in this morning. He had to accompany me on a visit to the couple whose fence and trees had been damaged. There were three fairly mature conifers, two of which had been uprooted. The couple were very friendly and remarkably poised, given the situation. We now await estimates for fencing and tree surgery. William and his cohorts will pay for this little lot - literally. I walked round the Peugeot after we had returned. It was still in the same condition, nothing magical had happened. Half the front bumper is missing, off-side wing is beyond repair and I suspect the same will be said of the bonnet. I'm not sure of the rules governing insurance when the car has been taken by a member of the family without parental consent. We'll have to ring the insurance company, we also await police reaction. What a great welcome home.

Just called at the PO box and there were some orders for books, which helped to dilute the misery somewhat. Interesting to note that I'm still receiving orders for the first two titles, although *"The Club"* is very much in season with the railway preservation society bookshops. Long may it continue to sell, I hear you say. I'll drink to that - cheers! The full glass is raised but with whose beer?

There's been a twist to the proposed takeover by Greene King of the Morlands Brewery. Wolverhampton and Dudley Breweries, you remember, the ones who bought out Marstons some pages back, are also in the frame. Their bid would be higher and there is a slight chance that the brewery could remain open, whereas there is no chance at all if Greene King get their way.

I won't be shopping in Do-it-All again. The unethical, uncaring prolls who sit back lapping up the cash have decided to apply for licences to sell animals. Named "Petworld" these outlets will be incorporated into all 138 stores. Some PR blurb states that "The company does not consider the purchase of a pet as an impulse buy".

Really? The spoke goes on, "The intention is to provide a unique shopping experience for all the family and these stores should not be compared with supermarket retailing". I'd like to know what is meant by "a unique shopping experience". If they mean that the company has decided that profits can be easily increased by adding to animal suffering, why don't they say so?

There are hundreds of animal shelters desperate to find homes for unwanted pets. One of the main problems is the type of person/family who would consider buying a pet from a DIY store anyway. They generally come from the social class Z stables, "I want somefink macho - Doberman, Rottweiller, Staffordshire or English Bull Terrier". Then, the tattooed, studded, dishevelled and unemployed loathsome oik steps foot into a pet shop, with his cashed giro, and buys a snake. This Petworld outfit already have fifty stores open within the Do-it-All chain. They sell rabbits, guinea pigs, hamsters, cold water and tropical fish, plus lizards, snakes and spiders.

Can you imagine the uncaring, selfish dross that's going to take home any of the latter three species. Whilst I can understand the pleasure some people take in keeping fish, even rabbits, guinea pigs and hamsters, this pet trading should be discouraged. I'm the first to hold up my hands and admit that I bought furry bunnies for my two elder children - when they were younger of course. My problem was that of many parents - I didn't think. No small animal should be kept in a small cage. It's the residential equivalent of a battery farm.

As if to highlight the point, in 1997 there were 180 recorded incidents of cruelty to exotic pets. These included a starving crocodile, two snakes ripped apart by a jealous boyfriend, abandoned turtles, chipmunks and a lizard saved from appalling and filthy conditions in Morecombe. This is a real problem and pet shops feed those whose interest span is measured in hours and who will take out any irritation they are suffering on a harmless animal.

Lizards and snakes may well make "interesting" companions for humans, but they are totally out of their natural environment. Does the purchaser know how they were acquired by the store? Do-it-All and all other pet shops may well check that all their suppliers are bona fide, but it still does not help the poor animal that is caught, crated, shipped and then exposed like a circus act in the hope that some gormless moron is going to shell out for something that will lose appeal once another new craze comes around.

I complained today to the departmental manager at our local garden centre. Garden centres used to be just that. But no, the spreading tentacles that lead to profit now encompass the animal kingdom. Parrots, cockatiels, love birds, as well as those mentioned above, flutter in small but doubtless legal cages. Larger, single specimens, perch on, well, perches while the human form looks on attempting to imitate the bird's song or squawk. I would outlaw the ownership of birds entirely. No-one should keep winged pets in a cage as like fur, it looks so much better in the wild.

I never thought I'd see that great northern sport of the working classes, rugby league, become customised, Americanised - in other words, cheap. Never did I imagine that teams such as London Broncos, Leeds Rhinos or Lancashire Lynx, would be doing battle with the likes of St. Helens, Wigan and Castleford. They too, for all I know, may include a second string to their bow but they are not commented upon in today's sports pages. Incidentally, is there still a Bradford Northern, or has today's leading team - Bradford - dropped the Northern?

Where is the thinking, the logic, the justification behind the addition of a macho animal name or animal-related name in the case of the Broncos? Are more fans going to pay to watch them perform? I can't see it myself.

Now if it were women's rugby and they adopted names like the Halifax Whores or the Dewsbury Dykes ..... What about the Castleford Kits-Off, or the Featherstone Fannies? I could definitely become a fan of the Salford Slappers! ..... But then you know me, I can debase any serious conversation!

Meanwhile, back in the grim world of reality, that Mandelson creature is attempting to claw his way back into power and influence, or should that be money and effluence? Anyway, he looks set to become Labour's unofficial roving ambassador for Europe. It's always the same, they know how to look after their own. Head down for a few months, then hey presto, a well-paid position - without portfolio - to ease their way back in, become accepted once more and within a year, be given an official title. It's like the political version of "time out" in sport - only more lucrative.

It's Wimbledon. All the angst, all the drama and all the prima donnas. The media keep on about "our" two male hopes. Surely only Henman is really "one of us". Rusedski presumably has some British connection, but can we really accept someone as "one of ours" who speaks with such a loathsome North American accent and wears his baseball cap backwards? I think not.

Talking of tennis, which we very nearly were, I was amused to read of the judge who postponed a four day trial as it could have run into Friday, the day he had booked off to go to Wimbledon. I like the man's style. He said, "I won't be doing anything this Friday apart from sitting in Wimbledon, watching tennis. I arranged to take this Friday off and I start four weeks' holiday immediately afterwards. Unless I can send the jury out first thing on Thursday morning, I can't start the trial and it would not be right to make everyone feel that they had to rush it".

Robert Conway, defending the accused, said he did not object to the case being put back to December, but added, "Wimbledon is on my doorstep, but I can't get tickets". The good and witty judge replied, "They are only given to the deserving". All good stuff!

What were we saying about compensation? It has been disclosed that in 1998 the armed forces awarded £27 million to servicemen for "injuries sustained during service". I would ask if the world has gone completely mad but the question was asked at least three times only last week. The whole of that wasteful war in Kosovo *only* cost £43 million. What a waste of our hard-earned money. Someone has got to grip this compensation racket by the throat and shake the life out of it. Attitudes have got to change, and change fast.

There is an advert on TV every morning from some legal practice inviting would-be litigants to ring in with their story of woe. They cite examples, along with still photographs, of Joe and Judy Public, whom they have helped receive great wads of readies. It's all so easy. Why work when you can have a bad back. The company's ace is to inform the would-be money-grabbing bastard that it's a no-win, no-fee deal. The vultures end their spiel with, "Remember! This could be the most important call you make today" then the telephone number flashes once more. It may be legal, but it is certainly immoral.

Well the sad story with our car is now developing into what can only be described as a farce. As it happened, the old Peugeot should have been re-taxed today, 1st July. But due to the bodywork bulging and the battery flat, we have decided to wait and see what action the police will take before proceeding. Naturally, the third party insurance doesn't cover us unless we wish to prosecute, and with the greatest will in the world, I can't prosecute my own offspring. I can't remember, but did I mention that we had bought William a Metro? (Maureen's just said that I have). Well, he's lost that - we're taxing that for ourselves and he will have to think about getting himself something once he's started to earn money - and he's repaid us.

Now, Maureen's back at work so she needed transport immediately and as she said, she'd tried for five years to get out of driving our old Metro, and here she is, back in another one - albeit not Kermit Green this time! So, the car is taxed and Maureen has to go to Guildford for a meeting. She's also taking a colleague from work. Off they trot to the car park in Farnham, where Maureen works. Once settled in, the car is reversed from its space, first gear is found and Maureen prepares to leave. Now by the side of where she parks is a pedestrian entrance, alongside a pay machine. As she moves off, a young chap, running into the car park through the pedestrian entrance, runs straight into her Metro, somersaults over the bonnet, arms flailing, elbow smacking the screen, and promptly lands in a crumpled heap out of sight by the offside front wing. As Maureen and her colleague put hands to mouth and take in the situation, the young chap pops up, as if in reverse gear, waves his hand at Maureen, exclaims, "Sorry", and continues his run across the car park and into the High Street.

A woman who witnessed the incident came across to see if Maureen was okay. She was *then* but it took its toll later when she rang me from work. But, hey! She's okay now. No counselling, no histrionics, no litigation, just a few scratches from the chap's shoes on the bonnet, which will be polished out. Easy to say now, but try finding the time later. I mean, let's face it, it's only a Metro.

Good news followed, though. We had a policeman round to have a word with William and as there was nobody else involved, they're not going to be charging him with any offence, like wasting police time, driving without ..... that sort of thing, so I'm now off to bed. Oh, you're staying up for a while. Remember to turn off the light!

So, Louise Woodward's parents have now been charged with offences of dishonesty following a police investigation into the trust fund set up on her behalf. There'll be a few people who will wonder where their contribution went.

Talk about being in the wrong place at the wrong time. There's a Mrs. Bradshaw from the Bristol area who just happened to be in a local Asda store when an eight foot pane of glass fell from the deli counter and sliced off the right toe of her big foot. Her husband and 3-year-old daughter were with her when it happened. She has received a letter of apology and a bunch of flowers but "intends to pursue compensation"..... Naturally! It was an accident. I think I would have just been glad it hadn't been my daughter who was injured.

For all its faults, and like Britain it has many, America has earned a few Brownie points today. I read with satisfaction that eighteen states have now scrapped kilometres on their road signs and re-adopted miles. Fairfax County, Virginia, yesterday abandoned the rule insisting that all building plans be submitted in metric.

It was an interesting little article, insofar as it outlined the millions of dollars spent over two hundred years in an attempt to impose metrication, but people power and choice have won the day. It is expected that all states will revert to imperial measurements very shortly. Shell Petroleum spent a small - or not so small - fortune converting pumps to metric and what happened, the American public avoided the service stations, so Shell had to shell out again to have them reconverted. It's nice to know that in America the public literally voted with their wallets. We have no choice or chance of reconversion here. The yes-monkeys kowtowed to Brussels and the public were dragged along, but never without a profit being made somewhere.

All jobsworth's are contemptible, boorish, humourless oiks at the best of times, but those at London Buses (London Transport, as was) who decided to prosecute a nun for travelling one stop further than her pass allowed should be handed over to the Germans for target practice. Sister Virtus Okweraoha had put in a fairly hard day at her office, i.e. getting up at 5 am to pray, then working at Bolingbroke Hospital as a voluntary chaplain. Off she goes by bus to visit a hospital patient, falls asleep, misses her stop and is awoken by a bus inspector, Angela Kelly (boo loudly). The intrepid inspector confiscates the sleeping nun's travel card and refuses to accept payment of £5 for the excess travel.

Poor Sister Virtus then receives a summons. At Horseferry Magistrates Court yesterday she pleaded guilty to the "offence" and was given a six-months conditional discharge.

Who authorised the summons? The case cost London Buses several hundred pounds in legal fees which the court directed them to pay. Their application for £1 in compensation, a fifth of that offered on the bus, was rejected as well.

London Buses then had the audacity to state, "We are not questioning the sister's honesty or suggesting that she tried to cheat us. All we are saying is that she broke the rules and falling asleep is not an excuse we can accept". Small-mindedness, stupidity and an assumed abundance of money are all too prevalent at L.T. - sorry, L.B.

The Germans, bless em, are muscling in on Finland, which makes a change from marching in, although I suspect it's only a matter of time. Anyway, were you aware that the Finns took on the chair for the next six months in that merry-go-round known as the EU Presidency. You didn't - well, you do now!

Apparently, the working languages used throughout this expensive money-making charade are English (naturally), French and the language of those in the chair. Now whether anyone likes it or not, those are the rules. Germany, along with Austria, are not best pleased to find that German is not being used. The Austrians are presumably sucking up in case the deployment of German troops in Kosovo raises national fervour within the fatherland sufficient to cast an eye around the borders and declare, "Well, we might as well take it now, it's only Austria".

Chancellor Schrîder has informed the Finns of his displeasure. But they've refused to kowtow, stating the established practice that I mentioned earlier. As usual, it's one rule for Europe and another for the Krauts.

Well, Wimbledon's over for another year. "Britain"'s Mr. Rusedski bowed out along the way, but our true Brit, Tim Henman, made it to the semi's - which is quite an achievement for one of our boys. It was refreshing to note Steffi Graf retiring with dignity and grace. No hyped up last goodbyes. As she said, having lost the women's final, "It was Lindsay Davenport's day". She really is too nice to be a German. I suppose someone's checked?

Not so nice, however, is that overpaid whinger, Nicolas Anelka. At least we now know the answer to the question, who put the arse in Arsenal? The quicker he moves to Italy - or anywhere east of Dover - the better. He says he's desperate to wear the shirts of Lazio and the French National Team. He feels that "English people don't like me. In the end it's only a natural reaction. I'm beginning to go off English people myself". The point is, Mr. A., that we English do not take kindly to those who moan, berate and generally criticise all and sundry. The quicker you and your management bugger off, the better. Like your Dutch counterpoint, Mr. Van Hooijdonk, the only time we wish to see you, is when you are playing in a team that's being beaten by one of ours. There! A bit *Sun*-like, but I've got it off my chest!

I had occasion to visit Butlins at Bognor Regis on business yesterday. You can spend a fortune rebuilding, repainting and generally tarting up, etc., but it's still a holiday camp. To be fair, that's the reason people have decided to stay there over the years. It's just that walking around the place you do feel a time warp coming on. It's not so much the place, as the visitor. Judging from the epidemic of flat-vowel syndrome a goodly number hail from the West Midlands. It is still a fascinating accent to listening to, but you can see why (well, hear why) few are taken seriously. Tattooed men with beer guts and ear-rings played basket ball with youngsters, whose attention was being distracted by other attractions. Fat women, several of whom must have been single parents, shouted loudly at others within their party yet only a few feet away. I suppose it comes from living in a tenement building and seeking to gain the attention of their uncontrollable offspring, as they set fire in the courtyard to yet another Ford Escort, unaware of whether human life is still at the driving wheel or not. Now you know me, never the snob and not one to generalise, but I did feel that the place was frequented by a sub-specie of pond life.

Outside, a couple of families sat on suitcases, waiting for the bus to take them to Bognor Station. At least two males sported caps worn backwards - nuff said!

And you wonder if there are not better things they could have spent their benefit on, like paying someone to tow away that Ford Sierra, dumped in the weed-strewn pit that started life as a front garden. Or what about rehousing the two long-haired Alsatians that bit the baby at No. 13 shortly before you left home, but who will have surely fended for themselves during the two weeks you have been away.

Maureen and I have just returned from taking Muttley along the canal and across the ranges. At the top of our road is the church, with a hall alongside. On Monday night it is band practice and, by the sound of tonight's offering, the church is guaranteed a booking every Monday for the foreseeable future. We encountered only two other couples out with their dogs. Despite being ten years old the Mutt has a lot of running left in her. In and out of the bracken she wades, snout to the ground and tail in the air. You can generally see the tail, even if you can't see the body. It curves three quarters way up, similar to a dodgem car at the fair. Coots were sitting on their nests on the "Flash" (a widened area of canal) close to the boathouse. The water was still, a mist was rising across the firing ranges. Very pleasant.

The only programme I shall be watching tonight is "The Royle Family". I missed the whole series first time round so we're restarting at Episode 1 tonight. Talk to you tomorrow.

Morning!   It's tomorrow. I'm off to beautiful downtown Bournemouth later. I've just returned from the newsagents, where not only did I collect the *D.T.* but I also bought a copy of the local paper as something caught my eye.

Unless you live locally, you will be unaware that a thoroughfare called Lysons Avenue connects Ash Vale Station with North Camp Station. Along one flank lies a 1980's built estate, or rabbit warren, whichever you prefer, and on the other, industrial buildings of many shapes and total lack of design. Close to the North Camp end, two small woods provide a pleasant relief from either development. Today's *Ash Mail* announced that the woods are to be developed for industrial use by some company called "Hartlake Developments of London". There have been many protests from residents, councillors and Friends of the Earth. Guildford Borough Council, ever eager to increase forced contributions, or business rates, as it's better known, approved applications for the site. Bore hole testing took place well in advance of consent being given, so the words "foregone" and "conclusion" could well be applicable. Despite all the concerns regarding traffic, schoolchildren, etc. the planning committee were informed that the area had long been reserved for industrial use.   It really is a pity that council greed is so unaccountable. Which brings me on to another point.

It was timely that whilst searching for another sheet of notes which lay somewhere but are still elusive, I should stumble upon Barratt's handout, you know, the one I was looking for some time ago. The *Ash Mail* also reports on its front page that Barratt's are to build an extra 33 flats on the land they have razed to the ground behind us in "Old Farm Place". The extra space has been found and given the green light by Guildford Borough Council as, surprise, surprise, the previously planned doctor's surgery, shop and community hall will not be built. What a nice little bonus that turned out to be! And far more saleable, too. Barratts are, however, paying £250,000 towards a new community centre in Ash Vale village. This community centre will replace the old wooden structure that resembled a set of over-sized stables. Also to go will be the portakabin used by the parish council and the Citizens' Advice Bureau, so everyone's been bought off quite nicely.

Now, to the Barratts' handout. "Old Farm Place", Ash Vale, near Guildford, Surrey - a *superb* collection of two, three *and* four bedroomed homes. There are three photographs accompanying the blurb. One shows a pub in North Camp (at least two miles away) and viewed between shrubs and trees by the side of the main road. Reality would produce a somewhat different perspective. The second exposes the would-be buyer to the tranquillity that is the Basingstoke Canal. The third shows a photograph of the "Standard of England" public house, which *is* in the centre of Ash Vale, in all its outside floral glory. The caption reads, "Traditional inn, typical of the area".

The text informs the prospective punter that, "Barratts Premier Collection homes have won many national awards for excellence. Their cottage style architecture beautifully reflects the dignified homes standing in the quiet streets and avenues of Ash Vale - a much admired village in its own right. To the south lies the attractive Ash Green, reaching the lower slopes of the picturesquely named Hog's Back". Talk about milking a situation. I'd like to find someone who admires the village in its own right. For village, read suburban sprawl. The only reason Ash Green is still attractive is because Barratts haven't yet been allowed to build on it. Still, there's time.

Honestly, I've never heard such tosh. If you look across the railway line or drive around this new estate, it definitely does not strike you that cottage-style architecture has been the intended result. Since when were blocks of flats transferred to the cottage-style department? Quiet streets and avenues? Everywhere is blocked with traffic. There's 440 - oops, 473 new homes with today's announcement - so they're not going to help the situation at all.

The PR people must be desperate. They go on to inform you that within the "variety of local shops" there's a Budgen's! I have to tell you that that is nothing to write home about. As you know, from the Forward, they used to have a deli, but that's closed now. Actually, I must tell you. One Saturday a couple of years ago, during June, Maureen and I had occasion to require some meat and salad for unexpected guests that were soon to arrive. They weren't unexpected after they'd phoned us to let us know they were coming, but you get the point. Anyway, the deli was closed. All the haslet, ham - everything - was covered up. It was only 3.30 in the afternoon. We enquired. The deli wasn't open as the girl "who does it" is a tennis fan and she'd gone home to watch Wimbledon. Apparently there was no-one else able to serve.

Back from the tangent - the handout then extols the virtue of Guildford, 8 miles away and Aldershot, two miles away. Funny how it says, Ash Vale, near Guildford, in its introduction! If you turn over, there's a map with more photos. An outside view of Farnborough Recreation Centre, a couple of chaps teeing orf on the green and an inside view of Princes Mead Shopping Centre in Farnborough. What a pity the caption reads, "The Wellington Centre Shopping Mall", which for those of you not of local disposition, is actually in Aldershot, so they got their geography wrong there as well.

After further information regarding recreational activities, ease of rail access, road access, bus travel, etc., the piece signs off "Everything you need to enjoy life at Old Farm Place is here". Not only is it a cynical distortion, it is quite stomach-churning reading the ingratiating soft-sell.

It's still not fashionable to say it, but oh bugger it, let's be brave! I find the whole world of homosexuality murky. Yesterday, Mr. Justice Latham announced that "Homosexual prisoners, intent on indulging in what would otherwise be unsafe sex should be prescribed condoms in jail" He basically countermanded a directive refusing to supply them, saying that the prison service had "misinterpreted policy". A homosexual inmate called Glen Fielding has campaigned long and hard (no pun intended!) for access to condoms in jail.

Now I don't understand that. All "normal" prisoners are denied sex for the tenure of their sentence but Fielding and his cohorts feel that because they are fortunate enough to be "banged up" with members of the same sex that they should be allowed. Frankly, if they want to have ..... I was going to say sex, but it doesn't feel right. Okay, if they want to ..... you know ..... then let them. But don't hand out condoms. Let them take their chances and hope that the chances aren't very good. I mean, it's not very nice, is it. Could put you off your chocolate digestive for life.

You remember Beverley Lancaster, the Birmingham City Council employee who sued for stress after changing jobs. Well, she's now got her reward. £67,000 in compensation. Not as much as she had hoped for, but not bad for staying at home. Do you remember how work-related stress destroyed her life, prompting panic attacks, anxiety attacks and those nasty little bouts of clinical depression, well today I imagine a great weight has been lifted from her shoulders. The award is to cover her pain and suffering, loss of past and future earnings - and prescription charges.

Unison, that trade union dinosaur, still steeped in one-sided logic, welcomed the decision calling it a "significant breakthrough in employment law". "Significant breakdown" is surely more relevant. The repercussions are horrendous. Another green light has now been given for more "get rich quick" merchants to become stressed out. In this case they will be supported by both the union and the legal professions. "Stress will not be regarded in the same way as physical injury". It's the sort of quote to make you shudder. We all end up paying for it. Compensation does not come free. And there's more good news for Beverley. An expected prognosis on her prospects are apparently "optimistic". Well, well. She's recently managed to start doing some part-time work. Presumably, it's not stress related - yet! I read on and this piece looks a bit suspicious. "However", says the quote, "it is unlikely that she will ever get a job that will earn her more than £4.50 an hour". A psychologist testified that because of the mental damage caused by her experience in the housing office, she could suffer a relapse at any time - and wouldn't that serve her right!

I've just walked into the kitchen having driven back from the newsagents - and a very nice day it is too. Maureen is having a cup of tea with her toast. To be honest, I've sat down since I can't stand and write very easily. Anyway, although it's not front page news in the *D.T.* it is in the other nationals. Some chap from Yorkshire has donated his organs for transplant but he stipulated they can only go to a white person.

Up to now, I've never thought much about the subject. Donating organs is something other people do. Generally speaking, people who have enough time to bugger about filling in forms. This will become more than a storm in a teacup, because the "offence" is against the ethnically challenged. You never know whether it's "in" or "out" to say coloured or black. Never mind, I've been mulling over the implications whilst I devour a bowl of Frosties. Frank Dobson has put everything else on hold and ordered an immediate investigation. Mr. Dobson - cooee - it was *one* donor, not a thousand. All the medical authorities seem to be in agreement that *no* would-be donor should be allowed to make conditions. Once the organs are in the hands of the hospital they are their property and they can do what they like with them.

Now this is beginning to make me think. This case caught the headlines because it's a good story with which to bash white sensitivity. What would have happened if the donor had said, "no homosexuals" or "no weather presenters". Well, you never know, he or she may have had two rotten weeks of weather in Pwllheli when the outlook was described as sunny.

It conjures up all forms of exclusion. For me, up until now if asked, mine could have gone to anyone, but not now. Oh, no. The list of those not to be given my bits and pieces would be far longer than those who could be saved. No priests, vicars, social workers, employees of the CRE, anyone who finds *"Reeves and Mortimer"* funny - the list is endless! Look, tell you what! I'll start the ball rolling. A few names of those I'd rather my testicles, or whatever, do not end up dangling from. Then I'll leave a space where you can add your own pet hates. At least you can say that you contributed to the book - but no royalties!

So, without further thought:

Lord Longford, Lord Archer, Eddie Edwards, Little or Large, Cannon or Ball, Lenny Henry, the Duchess of York - mind, I probably haven't got an organ big enough! Right, over to you, your go.

What's that? The real world wants to know when I'm returning. Coming, dear.

Good news of a kind, Kevin McGuggan, from Dundee, who had subjected a plane full of people to the vicious spectacle of his drunkenness has been jailed for two years, which means he will probably be free by the time you read this. The toss-pot attacked staff and head-butted fellow passengers. One stewardess had to spreadeagle herself (probably quite attractive, given other circumstances!) in front of a door in an effort to stop him kicking it open. The aircraft was travelling from America to Gatwick at a height of 33,000 feet at the time. Any suspicions, throw them off. It would be nice to see the aggressor inconvenienced for once, instead of proper people.

Right, that's me, I've got a skirting board to put back under the sink. It was removed some two and a half months ago when the new dishwasher was installed. I told Maureen it would only be a five minute job - just didn't tell her which year. See you on the next page.

CHAPTER NINE:

ALL'S WELL WITH THE NHS - UNLESS OF COURSE YOU'RE ILL!

Guy Mitchell's death was announced today. It knocks you a bit, when you remember that "Singing the Blues" was recorded in 1956 - 43 years ago. Even worse is the fact that I can still remember the words.

Breakfast is over and I'm sitting in the office above the garage looking out over the railway lines. Barratts' workers are closing in. The area of trees felled and cleared last year left, as I told you, one massive scar. Months of inactivity had witnessed a green covering beginning to take hold. There was even a slight resemblance to an open field. It was, however, to be an Indian Spring. To my left portakabins, portaloos and security fencing have sprung up. Several weeks ago building material, bricks, sand and large grey concrete pipe sections were distributed around the site. To my right, diggers and dumper trucks loaded with aggregate now converge early in the day. They scurry around while the constant "bleep, bleep" of reversing vehicles echoes where formerly bird song and crow cawing were the norm.

Muttley barked a minute or so ago - a deep, guttural "woof", which means that she was not happy. Such outpourings are generally reserved for night time but a fox has just this second climbed up the embankment and is currently walking unhurriedly along the track towards Ash. This particular fellow is quite a regular. I think he must have a den just the other side of our garden boundary, as most nights you can hear rustling in the undergrowth before he appears up onto the ballast and walks one way or t'other. You know it's the same one as his rear haunches are more mottled, more shaggy. His back is reddish-brown but the cream towards his flanks is distinctly lighter. We haven't yet got a name for him, although being original of thought *and* a supporter of all things traditional, we're considering "Albert Reynard Mann", adopt a fox, or what!

Right, that's it, I'm off to visit Bracknell, Windsor and Slough. Weather's good so have a nice day!

It's 4.43 pm and I'm back home. There's a note on the kitchen table from William, who was still in bed when I left. It reads, "Hi Dad, gone to Aldershit. Back later". He'll presume that it covers him for the rest of the day and probably most of the evening. He's taken to fishing once again. Much as I don't go along with killing or harming something you have no intention of eating, I have never stopped him or suggested he refrain. There, you see, Anthony Mann, the epitome of fairness. I feel a slight preening coming over me!

Had lunch with a friend yesterday. She was saying that her sixteen year old daughter's friend's dad suffers from M.S. He is divorced and was waiting for the district nurse to call round to help him wash and get him ready for bed. She turned up drunk. So much so, that the daughter and my friend's daughter, who was there at the time, did it all themselves. Bearing in mind that they are only sixteen or seventeen, I think they showed a responsibility above their years. A drunk nurse, huh? Well, that's care in the community.

I recall another friend of ours relating a story of how a hospital outpatient department rang after her father had failed to turn up for the previous day's appointment. My friend was at her father's house at the time and told the enquirer that her father had died only yesterday. The hospital staff's response was, "That's as maybe, but it was inconvenient, no-one told us!"

Another lady Maureen and I know was very upset when a community nurse, while discussing her husband's terminal cancer, asked jauntily, "So where will he go to die?" Not good, is it?

We're about to take Muttley out along the canal and over the ranges. Sincerely hope that band has stopped practising. I remember some time ago reading in the parish magazine that two boys had been observed creeping into the church, turning their backs to the congregation, pulling down their pants, "mooning", then running out again. We know both of them!   I had a word with William about this.   I said it was very dangerous to moon in a church as these priests can be as quick as lightning! Only joking, Mr. Vicar, only joking.

The Church Warden came round to complain about William, who had sworn at him and had not given his name when asked. He can be very stubborn. Problem is, he still has to find a cause to be stubborn about but he's got time on his side. In an argument once, when he was much younger, he said that he hoped we would both die in our sleep, then he could go back to his real parents. If only, we thought, if only. But as I said, he's a lot better now - well, up to two weeks ago, that is.

Forgot to tell you, but last Saturday was William's Prom Night at school. Yes, another American import, but there we go. He looked smart in black jacket and neatly creased trousers. I never thought the day would dawn, or in this case set, when he would ask to borrow a tie. He and five others hired a stretched American limousine, which toured slowly around Aldershot, allowing them to wave at anyone and everyone. They thought they were the dog's endanglements. He came home at about 1 am. Organised and marshalled by teachers and year heads, it was apparently a great success. Before taking their GCSE's all the pupils voted for the school "Oscars". There were several categories. William was nominated for "Most Fancied Date", "Best Physique", "Best Backside" and "Loudest Pupil". He won the latter two.

Today I'm off to Watford, Rickmansworth and Uxbridge. Yes, I get to visit all the exciting places. Next month I'll be taking a copy of this book's cover and having a word with WH Smiths' book buyers at the same time. Tonight Maureen's drafting a letter to the new humour buyer at WH Smiths' head office. He's asked me to include a synopsis of this book, a copy of the previous two and a set of reviews. I spoke to him about a month ago and he didn't seem disinterested when I attempted to "sell" the title for Smiths' Christmas stock. His decision, as I said earlier, will be vital.

Reviews are strange things. You ask a newspaper if they would review a book and then it is totally out of your hands. You obviously have no control on the thoughts or the words that will be used. Plaudits or damnation, you have no idea until you read about it. I try to organise the publishing of a review to coincide with a book signing session. Some sessions are good, and some are, well, not so good. I suppose curiosity drags a few souls across the floor to enquire "What's it all about?" You dare not look anyone in the eye, as they treat it as a threat and hastily beat a retreat, or turn to look at something in which they were never interested in the first place. Smile warmly and they think you're a bit odd, smile confidently and they assume you have an ego the size of Asda - or Wal-mart as it will be.

I've just been collecting photocopies of reviews for inclusion in the package that's going off to Smiths. It's interesting to remind oneself of the differing reactions expressed by reviewers. There's one here from the *Wandsworth Borough News* concerning "*As I Was Saying*". The reviewer states that "During the course of the book he proves once again that he is rude, insensitive, arrogant, self-opinionated, sexist and worse. He is also decisively anti-Europe and anti-Midland Bank - He is also very very funny". That's a nice one, isn't it!

The *Croydon Advertiser* described the same book as "page after entertaining page". I received good reviews for both titles in the *Aldershot News*, *Surrey Advertiser*, *Wales on Sunday* and several others. I tell you this because whilst you never become blasé, it hits you like a wet haddock across the gills when you read a review which can only be described as cool at best and downright disgusted at worst. I refer to the *Farnham Herald's* review of "*As I Was Saying*". Paul Merrill, the reviewer, stated that I was prejudiced, narrow-minded, banal and offensive. He considered that "from start to finish it is one long bitter diatribe against any minority you care to mention. It's presented in a way to make it unintelligible, constantly jumping from subject to subject without warning. There are touches of humour in places, but you have to get through an awful lot of tasteless oysters to find a few pearls". OUCH! Mr. M.'s final line is "It's the ideal Christmas present for someone you genuinely don't like. Better still, donate the £5.50 cover price to an AIDS charity and leave it on the shelf". I think that's another ouch!

I can't pretend that I wasn't a little disappointed, especially when I had been invited for a signing session at WH Smiths in Farnham that weekend. I have to say it turned out one of the best supported sessions I have been involved in. Makes you wonder about Mr. Merrill, though. I think he must be a very sensitive soul.

But, ever onward. Today Libya admitted liability for WPC Yvonne Fletcher's death fifteen years ago and is to pay compensation to her family. In this case, quite right.

The organ donor furore continues. Frank Dobson is still swashbuckling at the idea of racist motives, but then he would. I listened to a discussion on *Radio 4* concerning the subject. One contributor explained, or rather let slip, that this wasn't the first instance of a donor's family making conditions, as he knew of a Muslim who offered his organs "only to other Muslims". I have not heard this declaration on any programme since or read about it in the papers. Obviously didn't cause the same level of fuss because it's the "other way round". Frankly, if the story had come to the fore on its own merits it would not have made me get that upset. If that was what the Muslim concerned wished, then it was his choice. The fact that hospitals are so short of donors should put it in perspective.

Naturally, the BMA have been discussing the moral, legal and every other aspect of the situation all day long. They've come up with a very cunning plan. A plan so cunning, even Baldrick wouldn't have thought of it. They propose to work on the principle that we are all would-be donors unless we have a card saying that we object. In other words, you can only opt out of being a donor. I'll have to think about that.

Now here's one that could just make you a little upset. Some chappie who is serving a 20 year prison sentence for attempted murder is suing the Prison Service for damages. Colin Morton, aged 42, was convicted in 1992 of trying to kill Mr. Harry Cole, aged 65. After throwing Mr. Cole into a cold bath he slashed his throat in an effort to make him say where he kept his money. Morton got away with £300.

So having told you of his crime you can understand that there are nicer people in the world. This one has the temerity to seek £1,200 compensation, claiming his bed is uncomfortable and that he has disturbed nights and suffers from back pain. He states that the Prison Service did not listen to his complaints quickly enough. His figure of £1,200 is reckoned at £10 per night for sixteen weeks, the time during which he has suffered discomfort. His claim, and you'll like this, has been placed through his Legal Aid solicitor. How do people like that manage to obtain legal aid? Personally, I'd take the mattress away and tell him to sleep on the floor. Didn't he contribute just a little to his own discomfort? Obviously he thinks not.

Just as I've got used to remembering by bank account PIN number, the system is about to be made redundant. Today sees the first cash dispenser free from such vintage trappings. Not even a keyboard for us lesser mortals to tap into. Stella, as the device is nicknamed, uses three high-definition infra-red cameras that see into the customer's eyes and determines their identity from the iris. This Stella thing (you can tell I'm not overly keen) greets the customer by name and asks, "Would you like cash or a statement?"

This piece of Big Brother technology "learns" customer habits and after a while will ask you if you'd like "your usual". It will wish you a happy birthday, remind you of outstanding bills and offer advice on the weather and Internet shopping. Very shortly it will provide information on mortgages, car loans or even sort out your personal financial affairs. You will even be able to have statements beamed by infra-red directly to a personal organiser or pocket computer. I'd still rather walk into the bank and talk to a human being.

The actor Jack Watson died today. I first came across him in the film *"The Hill"* with Sean Connery. I did not see *"This Sporting Life"*, another film in which he starred until the 1980's. It was a cracking film.

He was apparently a very modest man in real life. His obituary in the *Daily Telegraph* shows a photograph of him, alongside Richard Burton, with whom he acted in the *"Wild Geese"*. To me, he was the epitomy of the British trooper. He popped up on TV and in films on a regular basis over five decades. Never the star, but always the professional.

Bloody kids! It's always the same. I come home from work - or anywhere - check to see if there are any messages on the answerphone and observe that the phone is not sitting on the receiver. It's one of those walk-about types. Every time the same thing happens. Instead of just being able to make a cup of tea, I have to press the Intercom button and walk about the house listening for the bleep from the handset to get louder, enabling me to locate it. There is no pattern that you can follow for this. It can be anywhere. Under a pillow, on the settee, down the back of the settee, under the settee. It's at times like this that we find the redundant remote controls for the stereo system and television that packed up years ago. If no luck in the small sitting room (I hate the word "lounge") I start to look in the big sitting room. If not there, I get decidedly irritated and flounce upstairs shouting obscenities to absolutely no-one. But it would be William if he were there. We search the landing as it has been known to be under the dog or the dog's bean bag. (Perhaps she made the last call). If not, I search William's bedroom, our bedroom (why should he be in our bedroom?). I realise why the following day when there is only one sock left in my drawer. He now has the pair.

It is amazing, I mean it's not much to ask, if you use the phone kindly put it back. The request is always met with a sleepy "s'pose so". Luv him!

I'm just reading the local paper. It does make you laugh. Hart Borough Council, they look after the Odiham, Church Crookham and Fleet area, refused permission for a nursery to expand its operation. Their grounds were that it would be "harmful to the character, landscape and setting".

A government inspector has ruled against the council on appeal. These councils have a nerve, don't they? They are quite happy to turn down an extension to an existing countryside activity and equally happy to grant permission for new technology office buildings in the countryside, not to mention residential estate after residential estate. Bastards!

Further to my jottings yesterday, that only *Radio 4* commented on the "Muslim organ for Muslim consumption only" debacle, I have to say in fairness that the *Telegraph* quotes a leading transplant surgeon in today's edition. He says he has experienced ten examples of conditions being applied. Not only two Muslims but Irish kidneys marked "Roman Catholic not Protestant". Did any of these cases reach the national media? Of course not. They weren't white enough!

I'm going to take a break now and sit in the shade. The garden is looking very colourful, well, green, with sightings of yellows and whites - sorry, reds - assume I said red. Mustn't mention white in case the thought police are out and about.

A small nursery in Aldershot closed recently. The couple have retired to Pagham Bay and the site is to be cleared for housing. To be fair, you could never park more than 8 cars comfortably within its confines but it was a very friendly establishment. Before the couple left, I enquired as to whether they would sell me two wooden crates. Mrs. Bennett, the co-owner, asked what I would be doing with them. I told her they would look good on a railway platform porter's barrow that we have in the garden. Filled with flowers I thought they would look just the ticket. "What about the pots inside them?" she enquired. "Oh, I wasn't going to take them", I replied, not wishing her to think of me as greedy. "That you do", she said, "if you take the crates you take the pots. I've got enough of the things and we only have two weeks to go". Sold! Two crates and about one hundred pots for sixty pence. Today I'm going to pick out the wording which is getting rather faded, and then varnish them.

Elsewhere, the fruits (and vegetables) of Maureen's labour in the greenhouse are paying off. Our beans are growing, the lettuces, cabbages and potatoes continue to sprout, but no sprouts. I planted some shallot bulbs. Don't quite know what you do with them, or when, but we'll enquire. Someone must grow them locally.

The poppies, cornflowers and the country mix have been very successful. The collared doves have started to build a new nest further down the garden in the oak tree by the allotment. Last year their nest was very close to the patio. They bred two young ones in August. They hung around for some time. I suspect they could well be the same pair.

During 1997, on a very hot summer's day, Maureen and I were lying on the sunloungers. Maureen was asleep, I was dozing. Even though my eyes were shut a shadow was cast as something flew close by. Moving my head slowly I observed a curlew standing only two feet away, between our sunloungers. I tried to gently attract Maureen's attention. Unfortunately, she woke with a start and exclaimed, "What, what?" Before she could get a good look, the bird had flown. "What was it doing here?" she enquired. "Oh, probably mistook you for a mud flat", I scoffed. Oh, how we laughed ..... I made my own tea that afternoon.

Right, off to the sunlounger with me. And then, to take Muttley up the canal for her evening constitutional.

Brilliant! Guess who forgot to record *"Friends"*. I'm writing these notes before the start of *"Frasier"*. It was a pleasant walk along the canal and over the ranges. Only saw one couple with their dog along the whole of the route. Tail up, snout down, sniffing everything, well Muttley is mostly terrier. I just wish she would refrain from sniffing other dogs' doings. I said to her, "You don't see your mummy or your daddy doing that, do you?" She took no notice.

Maureen's taking up evening classes again this year. Over the past couple of years she has gone to English Language and English Lit classes and done very well with her GCSE's - and it wasn't me who said, when told of Maureen's grades, "They probably mark higher if you are a mature student"!

I'm flicking through the adult education catalogue, just to see how much we'll be forking out. On page 8, under contents, is an invitation by Guildford College of Further and Higher Education, for would-be pupils to join their "Basic skills/EAL (English as an additional language) courses". The blurb states that the course was previously known as the ESOL. Are they sure it wasn't the RSOL class? I know, cheap jibe, but it's late - only ten minutes to *"Frasier"*.

They ask, "Are you resident in this country?", "Is English your second language?" "Has dyslexia caused you problems?" There's no mention of counselling so far, but I wouldn't hold my breath. It goes on to tell how you will have an "individual learning programme which will be discussed in confidence with you before joining the scheme". You can join these classes at any time. There is an opportunity to achieve qualification and progress to other levels/courses. Now guess what? They are free! A small registration fee of £15 per academic year and you can attend up to three basic skills/EAL classes within the area.

Next is the page dealing with "learning support" - for adult learners with specialised needs. Now that's what I call a growth industry. Every parent interviewed on TV seems to have a child with needs.

It goes through all the political correctness concerning their commitment to students with learning difficulties, sensory impairment, mental ill-health, physical disability and any combination of these.

Advice and guidance will naturally be given. There may also be specialised classes.

We then learn that Surrey County Council Community Services is aware that it has always been difficult for deaf and hard of hearing students to obtain information about classes. (Why, they can still read, can't they?) Anyway, they are setting up portable loops (portable loos will be next!). I can see it now, we cater for all, including the incontinent and those with bowel problems. Laxatives will be distributed during the coffee break for those concerned that the next half hour could be a difficult period - oh, and for those with periods .....

They haven't finished yet. They state once again their support for students with disabilities and are keen to extend access to their classes, going so far as arranging priority parking spaces close to the entrances, or moving a class to ground floor accommodation. I don't know why they don't offer a one-to-one service in the student's home and be done with it. I don't wish to sound uncharitable (what do you mean, that's what I sound like) but this reading is somewhat tiresome. You feel that the author has tried so hard not to upset anyone and include everyone, I'm sure they don't mean to sound sycophantic, but it all seems more than a little weasly.

Naturally, all courses are ten weeks for £15. I'm just reading the fee structure. A = full fee, B - over-sixties reduced fee, C = unemployed person's fee. What's A? Able-bodied? Oh, adult. I don't object to our over-sixties being given a discount, on average about £10 cheaper per course. The unemployable, of course, obtain a mighty 50% discount. Why? And why are they allowed access to mid-afternoon classes when they should be out looking for work. Christ, don't we pander to the great unwashed. There are ten week courses entitled "Your child's behaviour". The words "bloody awful" spring to mind in our case. There. That didn't take anything like ten weeks to sort out!

There's lot of arts and crafts and pottery, computing and cookery - it's all here. Dog training. I know a few from Aldershot who would benefit from that course. And they'd get in for half price!

Dancing in all forms is catered for, yoga and PE. This one would suit me it's called "Gentle Exercise". I could just about cope with that. After sports they list the general health options. Did you know there would be an in-depth Oil Day - £20 and no reductions. Or, at the Effingham Centre, you can "Improve your diet - juice for health". There's even "The art of juicing fruit and veg". This is a one day course, £13.50 and no reduction, one pound fifty of which is for your materials! Maureen will go to that one, she loves a good marrow.

Alongside aromatherapy classes is listed "Indian head massage". That's nice. Just read the small print about fees and discounts. Regarding the C = unemployable, it states, "Persons in receipt of Job Seekers' Allowance, Income Support, Family Credit, Housing Benefit, Council Tax Benefit are eligible for a 50% discount on a maximum of two courses running at the same time".

I have to say, it really doesn't seem fair on those who work and pay their taxes. If I join a class, I'll pick one with no reductions against it. At least I would have some idea about the person you are sitting next to, and you know me, can't abide snobbery.

One minute to ten - *"Frasier"* - byee.

Saturday morning has dawned, eggs on toast were very pleasant sitting under the gazebo. What a hoot. I've just read that our esteemed leader, Tone, now thinks he'll have another go at banning hunting with hounds, once the other house is in place, referring to the House of Lords. If he is so supportive, why did he not vote when Michael Foster's bill was going through Parliament?

There's a lot in today's papers concerning those who live in the countryside and support animal murder. They are once again shrieking that the government and townies are against them. That is not the case. It is only hunting, oh, and feeding cattle animal by-products that cause BSE, oh, and the continual use of battery hens, not to mention allowing hundreds of acres to be used for testing genetically modified crops which will disperse its pollen across the rest of the civilised world. In short, not much to complain about at all.

It's the language of the hunter that exposes the closest trait to those of the Germans - arrogance. They all expect demonstrators to keep within the law, yet assume that by marching in hordes and in 4-wheel vehicles they will intimidate the government into submission and finally go to ground. Much the same as their quarry.

The quotes from those affected by the possible ban on their plaything is quite staggering (no pun intended). David Maclean, a Conservative spokesman, said, "This is the last straw for the countryside" and that country people should not be the real victims of "class warfare". A slight stretching of the issue, I feel. The National Farmers Union meanwhile sit on the fence and say that if the landowners wish to hunt on their land, they should feel free to do so.

The *Telegraph* reminds us of a comment by the Home Secretary made last year concerning a possible ban. "We do not see a mandate for it. This has always been treated by the Labour Party as a Private

Members' measure". I think that shows a rather yellow strain of gutlessness myself.

It's rather funny that the election of sixteen new commissioners in the EU was seen as an announcement that might wake up the slumbering Euro. Nobody knows these non-elected by-products, with the exception of Chris Patten. He will be in charge of "external relations" and head the commission's foreign and security policy. A lot of swanning about there, then.

Race rears its head today, in Liverpool, Norwich and France. In Liverpool, the police authorities have gone completely doolally. These are the repercussions that such inward looking, soul seeking investigations bring. A 78-year-old pensioner wrote in paint before the Euro election "Don't forget the 1945 war" and "Free speech for England". The way we are going on I feel I could be the last. Will this book be withdrawn for sale for abiding by that very maxim? Now the above two phrases do not constitute racism. Well, not to you nor I, but Merseyside Police's new Chief Constable, Norman Bettison, said at the time of the pensioner's arrest, "We are cracking down on anyone found committing offences against racial or minority groups". This is appalling. This chief constable has appointed full time thought police, sorry, "racial incidents officers". Have you ever heard of such tosh. That type of policing polarises views and it does not endear any group of people to each other, least of all the police.

And just to labour the point on behalf of the police Inspector Jim Fitzsimmons added, "We take seriously any racist behaviour which comes to our attention and we appeal to our communities to join with us in the fight against racism". What sanctimonious twaddle!

Meanwhile, in darkest Norfolk, the Lawrences of London are receiving honorary degrees from the University of East Anglia. So, like other honorary attributees, they wear the caps and gowns of people who have worked hard for that "honour". Their little hand-out is for "demonstrating through their courage and determination that individuals can advance the cause of justice and a more equitable society". I'm not saying a word.

Over to France where the "race" obsession is swiftly getting underway. Now whatever I think of the French, and it's not a lot, I have to admit that they know how to stir up a national anthem. Rarely, are anthems sung with more gusto and passion - other than our own, of course, when England beats the Krauts. Anyway, some charity campaigner rants on that the Marseillaise is an "incitement to racism" with some of its words. Let's hope the French government can summon up some resistance to such a call, you know, slightly more than they could muster up sixty years ago.

I was never happy that the Midland Bank changed its name (and its ownership) but what alternatives are there. The NatWest, or as I prefer, the National Westminster Bank, no, they're not for me. Were you aware that they are spending profits on fringe organisations such as Stonewall. In case you are not aware, Stonewall consists of a group of homosexuals who campaign for greater rights instead of quietly getting on with their grubby little scene behind net curtains, out of sight from nice people. Apparently, the bank sponsored Stonewall's equality dinner back in May. Amongst the guests were Chris Smith, Culture Secretary (naturally!), Jack Cunningham (why?) And Mo Mowlem (again, why?). Oh, and I've just read, Paul Boateng - well, at least he speaks nicely. I just cannot understand why anyone who does not have "those leanings" would want to be associated with a homosexual and lesbians' night out. Now bear in mind that Stonewall aim to give rights to these people to adopt children, which would not be a course of action guaranteed to win the Labour party votes, I would have thought. The good but misguided Dr. Jack outlined the government's intentions to increase homosexual rights, however, and to repeal Clause 28, which stops the promotion of homosexuality in schools.

Again, not a great vote winner outside of the pinko brigade. I find it amusing that the National Westminster consider this unwholesome group to be in the same category as Afro-Caribbean business ventures. They are all considered minority groups and are therefore worthy of customers' money.

Some person called Tommy Hutchinson, who regales under the title, "Corporate Affairs Director", said that his bank was also sponsoring Stonewall's fringe event at the Labour Party Conference in the autumn. I treat their Tommy with suspicion. He says, "Our customers are very diverse and we aim to recognise all the groups with which we do business". Oh, yeah. I'll remember that next time our railway club wants a loan. The man must be myopic. The gains from these with "strange tendencies" will be more than offset by the withdrawal of accounts by proper people. Apparently a number of customers have closed their accounts now that they have been informed of the bank's financial support for Stonewall.

Stonewall ..... Stonewall? Isn't the name just a bit macho, sort of aggressive and strong, not really in keeping with its flock. I would have thought Pink Paper Maché Partition would have been more appropriate.

Talking of strange, a number of personalities were asked which photograph epitomised their face of the century. David Bowie chose a snap of Peter Mandelson holding a rose. It's an eerie looking pose of an eerie looking cove. With head leaning slightly to one side, the moustache and the red rose held between both hands makes him look like a cross between Hitler and the pianist from the 70's pop group "Sparks". Strange choice.

I find it hard to understand how pupils can obtain A-grade GSCE passes in English while making mistakes with their spelling. A government report states that on average a candidate makes one spelling mistake every hundred words and that punctuation mistakes are widespread.

Not surprisingly, Dr. Sue Horner, QCA co-ordinator in English, says, "Pupils don't just get Grade A's for spelling and the technical accuracy of their work, they are also marked on their ideas and how to express them". She did accept that "correct English is very important and that there is room for improvement". Such as deleting the words "like" and "stuff", liberally sprinkled in every sentence, I would imagine.

Going back to her first quote, I don't see how, if you make mistakes, you can then obtain an A. In line with most people outside of the education authority and government, we suspect that pressure is brought to bear on those who mark the passes, so that it looks as though the standards are rising. But being marked on your ideas and how you have expressed them is like giving the markers an open season. Now Dr. Bernard Lamb of the Queen's English Society has put his finger on it. He says that a lax approach by examiners and teachers is to blame. Quite right.

When all three of ours were at school I always had to ask why spelling mistakes were not corrected in history, geography, science, whatever. The answer was always the same. "We don't wish to undermine the confidence of the pupil by the amount of red ink on their pages". What a cop out. But that's typical of the teaching profession, a title that should be tested under the Trades Description Act. They pass the buck on everything - discipline, bullying, British history, spelling ..... But then, when you're actioning key tasks and prioritising your meetings, in order to placate the racially obsessed and the gender bender freaks, where is the time to teach children about worthwhile subjects?

William is out looking for a job, I suspect. I hope so, anyway. The house is empty, save for Muttley. The telephone is now back on the receiver and I have finished my wanderings for the day. There are several messages on the answerphone - all girls, all for William. No job offers, mind you. Some of the messages left by his male friends on occasions make them sound like complete retards. They're not, it's just that no attempt appears to have been made to open the mouth fully and construct words into an acceptable and understandable speech pattern, whereas the messages left by girls are entirely different. Theirs are identifiable, happy sounding voices that inform the listener of who they are and who the message is for. What a difference.

We need William to get a job as soon as possible, if only to enable him to pay back some of the money he owes. Maureen is not best pleased at ending up with a Metro, which is now the second car. We've had it taxed and tomorrow it goes for its MOT.

Right, joke time!

A man is having trouble obtaining an erection. He's tried everything. Yes, including the tried and tested Viagra. The doctors have tried, the prostitutes have tried - nothing. He is recommended to a hypnotist who offers him some hope. "I can help you", says the hypnotist, on hearing the man's tale of woe. The good news ends there as the hypnotist says, "The treatment will cost £250 per session and a session lasts one erection". "Two hundred and fifty pounds?" repeats the customer, in astonishment. "The thing is, I'm supposed to be taking the most beautiful girl in the world away for the night, and she is gagging for it". He talks himself into hypnosis and out of £250.

Under he goes, out he comes. "You are now ready for an erection", says the hypnotist. "Great", replies our Romeo. "But what do I do, how will I know?" The hypnotist is a calming influence. "When you want it to rise, you just say 1 - 2 - 3. When your session is over and the young lady is asleep and you are both sexually sated, you say, 1 - 2 - 3 - 4. Is that clear?" "Yes", replies the man, "Yes, yes", for he is eager and anxious to try out his new-found rigidity.

Come Friday, cometh the man. Off he and his girlfriend go, up to Henley for the night, an excellent candlelit meal, excellent service and gentle background music. They hold hands over the table, they are replete. She motions upstairs with her eyes. They fairly run up the stairs, the anticipation, the breathlessness, it's all there. The key slides gently into the lock. They enter the room and view the four-poster bed with anticipation. She raises an eyebrow and then turns and kisses him lightly on the cheeks. "I'm just going to the bathroom to slip into something more comfortable". Her voice is silky, her eyelids heavy with sensuality, her breath sweet. (She sounds nice, doesn't she?)

Into the bathroom she wafts, her hand turning on the light as she enters. Our desperate one drops his trousers and exclaims "1 - 2 - 3!" The girl turns quickly and enquires, "What's the 1 - 2 - 3 for?"

A gamekeeper at the Holker Hall Estate in Cumbria has just been jailed for three months for laying illegal snares to kill badgers. John Drummond, the offender, is no better than the fox or stag hunters. Police found corpses, bones and skulls of animals which had obviously suffered excruciatingly painful deaths. The report includes one instance where the badger dragged its snare, which acts like cheesewire cutting through the neck, until it hanged itself over an escarpment. I read the above and then studied the photograph of Mr. Drummond. Words cannot describe the disgust and contempt I feel for the ..... I was going to say "man", but that would be to impose a status on him to which he would never rise and never deserve.

Three months should be three years. He has left his job by mutual agreement, which means we will also be paying for his upkeep until he is once more employed, so what's new?

It's interesting that the Church of England is to offer "baby blessings" without the "strings of attachment". The idea is to allow non-believers to have their child baptized. No water or candles, the minister holds the sprog, utters its name and presents the parents with a copy of the gospel to use as a "guide".

Still can't see the point myself. Here we have the foundations of a long-running argument that I have with my father and which never seems to be resolved. In other words, I can see the point and he can't! He tells me that I was christened - I don't remember, but I believe it to be true. Maureen and I had both Glyn and Debbie christened. Why? I suppose because it was traditional and I had never bothered to question the role of the church in any depth at that time. I had always looked at churches as nice pieces of village architecture. By the time William was born my views had been more firmly established. He was never christened and frankly, if the other two were still under the age of consent, I would attempt to have them de-registered.

As far as I'm concerned no child should be baptized, christened or whatever until they reach the age of consent when they can make up their own minds. My dad always asks, "Well, what difference has it made, that you were christened?" He also asks if it has had any adverse effect on me. I reply "no", he says, "Well, then" and sits back in his normal self-satisfied way.

The point is, that by its very nature, religious beliefs are exactly that. Beliefs. If reality ever entered the equation there would be mass soul-searching, but your average parishioner doesn't question his cult. How many of those christened within the C. of E. change brands? How many Roman Catholics change to Calvinist, or Wesleyan to Buddhist? Of course there are exceptions, but in the main, and the mass majority are in the main, people continue within the religion of their forefathers and mothers. It appears to be very much a personal heritage, part of one's own roots. That I find is the greatest pity. Unless they get that much advised "life" they will never consider the possibilities of another avenue of belief, or more realistically, that there is, in fact, bugger all out there. Just life and death. And when it's over, that's life I mean, then there is nothing else. No-one, absolutely no-one can prove to me, or you, or anyone else, that there is a life hereafter or thereafter, or that we will definitely come back as an aardvark, or something else.

Believers are bred to believe in whatever it is as the only true religion. The sheep element is bewildering and extremely worrying. I was never taught anything about atheism. I learned about the Fab Four, God, Jesus, Mary and the one with the pseudonym ..... oh, yes, the Holy Spirit. They were all worthy subjects for discussion. You accepted their presence, just as Mary accepted her presents (didn't know I was going to say that!).

Religion should be discussed in schools, not taught, as a quirky little by-product of life. If anyone wishes to follow any of these beliefs or cults, then at the age of sixteen they should be able to join a club. Whatever one thinks of their beliefs at that stage, at least you know they have considered the matter on its own merits and on their terms. And not because they are the products of their parents who were the products of their parents, who were ..... Here endeth the lesson.

So, racism in the police, schools, armed forces, NHS, pot-holing - *pot holing* - oh, no, but it will be tomorrow. Well, now we have racism in the church. The photograph on page 10 of Wednesday's *D.T.* shows the Right Rev. John Sentamo with ..... yes, Neville Lawrence. D'you remember when Suzy Lamplugh went missing, her mother became a household and media name, championing every cause which could accommodate her snout. Are we not in danger of an updated re-make? Déja vu all over again! Be that as it may, the Right Rev. Jonners has told the General Synod that it needed to shed its monochrome image.

He says, "When we first went to church in the early days there was an atmosphere. People would look at us as if to say why are you in church?'" I am sure our man is quite right. All that does is to illustrate just how shallow, insincere and hypocritical a large number of white Christians really are. So no news here, then!

What I find particularly sad is that so many blacks rolled over and accepted Christianity in all its branded forms when the missionaries arrived. Why didn't they stand up and be counted instead of transferring allegiance to someone else's god? In a way, the Right Rev. is still falling for the white man's teachings because he has no more way of knowing the truth than you or I. I suppose it's out there somewhere, but probably not as we know it.

Anyway, back in Lambeth the Right Rev. says that, "There is a block on black clergy becoming bishops. They get to a certain stage when they could move up but they are left at the bottom" (so that was the stage he was talking about). He says, "The church has to address this". That's another modernism, isn't it. Address. Everything needs addressing, but I disagree vehemently with his request for schools to introduce anti-racism classes and the keeping of registers to record racist incidents. Can he not see, is he so naive to understand that it would be totally counter-productive. With this Bishop's lack of foresight, as opposed to the Jesuit priest, who would doubtless display his lack of foreskin, he should be a politician or a traffic warden, perhaps. They're probably short on their ethnic target!

However, he was applauded by the 570 strong attendees, as was Neville Lawrence. Another idea that was *warmly* received was the concept of - wait for it - a "partnership" between police and the church to encourage black and Asian members of the congregation to join the police force or become magistrates. But this didn't stop here, oh, no. He wants trained volunteers to support victims of crime with church buildings being used as neutral places where racial incidents could be reported. So we don't mean all victims of crime, only victims of alleged racial incidents. Well, that's all right, we'd hate the ideas to be far-reaching.

Another call was for ethnic Anglicans to be more visible within the life of the church - well, what's wrong with turning up the lights! I know, I know, but I couldn't resist it - it's just difficult to take all this eye-wash seriously because all the time you know that legislation and media overkill just hardens opinion.

It's just the same with the disabled. I always felt sorry, and still do really, for anyone who is disabled, but the number of "impaired" people claiming "rights" really does nothing to make you support a cause, however worthwhile it might be. It's back to OBS (Orange Badge Syndrome). I've never seen so many able-bodied disabled shoppers parking legally in disabled bays. I count their legs - yep, two, both working in unison. Not the far end of the car park for them! Oh, no, a hop, skip and a jump and they're in Sainsbury's. Me? I'm still passing the mother with child, over eighteen months and under four, Mother with baby, under eighteen months, Pregnant women, Single women on benefit, and all the others who get a discount for life. Where are the bays indicating Middle Class Tax Payer (poor sods). That's right, we are the unmarked graves at the back!

As Maureen is typing this, she's just told me - well actually as she's typing it she might as well tell you directly -

"There's a large board on the wall outside Tesco, with outlines of several types of trolleys available. There are trolleys for disabled in wheelchair, mothers with a young child, mothers with twins (probably different fathers, although it's not stated), mothers without children (for the likes of me - this is your common-or-garden trolley for those not in the know), and lastly there is even a trolley for a mother who has a disabled child". Why don't they just have one symbol for all the disabled - a trolley which has three working wheels and one gammy one?!

The "Paranoia's Society" membership is increasing daily. *Why is it, who told you*!!! It comes to a pretty pass when parents inform a headmaster that their children feel uncomfortable and exposed being filmed on video in their PE kit. We are talking of a primary school sports day. Mums and dads take photographs and videos, that's what they do when watching Jack and Jill run around, though not necessarily up a hill. The headmaster says, "Though there has never been any suggestion of anything untoward happening at our school, I couldn't ignore parents' concerns, particularly in this day and age, so I asked parents if they would co-operate and refrain from filming at our school sports day. Most of them complied".

The request was apparently made by a couple of families because they feared that the forthcoming event would be used as an excuse by paedophiles to film children. Frankly, I find this namby-pamby attitude appalling. I suspect that the "uncomfortable feelings" of these children were instilled by paranoid parents. Glad to say, not everyone submitted to the headmaster's ill-judged request. Several parents ignored the plea and complained to the school governors. As Margaret Morrison of the

National Confederation of Parent/Teachers Associations said, "If parents cannot take videos of their children at a school sports day because of the fear that pictures may fall into the hands of paedophiles, then the world is a very sad place. What will be coming next? Will parents be banned from filming their children's school play?" Quite right, Mrs. M.

We have another winner. Step forward, please, Mrs. Sharon Oliver from Essex. Sharon has now been awarded £4,500 by the Central County Court because she was not shown how to pick up a box of sausages! This incident happened five years ago. A customer asked for a packet of sausages - she probably said something like, "Could I have a packet of those sausages which aren't on display". Sharon from Essex couldn't find any on the shelves, and so walked to the storage cage in the chiller room and extracted a four kilogramme box. But ..... oh, no, ...they slipped through her tiny pinkies, causing "slight damage" to the soft tissue of her wrist. I suspect that's bruising to you and me. Anyway, Miss O., a former legal secretary (didn't go unnoticed) claimed that the arrangement of the cages was ramshackle and that she was untrained in picking up boxes in the low temperature of the chiller room!

If she felt the need to be trained, why didn't she ask? There's no mention of her being lacking in the tongue department to the tune of one tongue, or why did she feel the need to go and extract the box herself? Would she have felt silly informing the customer, "I'm sorry, but I can't pick up sausages, I've not been trained". The horrific result of the wrist injury? She cannot perform very easily such functions as opening packets of biscuits. I've got news for Sharon, the opening of biscuit packets is a complete mystery to most people. You pull, you tear and you end up after thirty seconds holding a piece of wrapping no bigger than a quarter inch by a half, and the biscuits are holding firm.

Tesco representatives at the court said she should have asked for help, but the Assistant Recorder found Tesco liable. I find that decision appalling. Still, it was a nice little earner for Sharon from Essex. Ladies and gentlemen, a round of applause, please.

On a more serious note, the case of Mr. Arthur Banks is quite awful. He consulted his doctor in February because there was something blocking the food going to his stomach. This problem first appeared back in December. On 31st March he visited the Pilgrim Hospital in Boston, Lincs, where it was discovered that he had a growth and that it was malignant. Mr. Banks was told he needed an urgent operation. An appointment was set for 22nd May. The hospital phoned him the day before and cancelled this appointment because there was no surgeon available. He was then rebooked for the 8th or 15th June, but these dates were cancelled as there were no intensive beds available. The next appointment, 21st June, came and went because there was still a shortage of beds. On 29th June, having heard nothing the day before, Mr. Banks duly arrived at 9 am as requested. He underwent a full day's pre-op tests and awaited his transfer to surgery before he was told there was no bed available again, and he might as well go home. Can you imagine how thoroughly dispirited and downhearted one would be. An operation of any nature is a fairly traumatic experience. You get yourself worked up, before many false starts, but eventually you are there. Most people, having undergone the pre-op tests, would expect the operation to follow immediately. He finally gets the call to appear on 6th July. Having removed a rib to get to the growth the surgeon then tells him it is far too advanced and is now inoperable.

Mr. Banks has now lost five stone in weight and hospital staff tell him he could last a few weeks, or several years. As he says, "Individuals are not to blame but this whole country has been let down". The hospital's acting chief executive has written explaining that they had a series of emergency admissions, so beds were a little scarce. I am sure that made Mr. Banks feel a lot better.

Can you imagine a member of the Royal Family waiting any longer than the time it took to get them from where they fell ill to a private room. But then Mr. Banks, aged 74, a former police officer, has paid all his taxes and insurance throughout his career. He wasn't born with a silver salver up his backside. He wasn't a leech on benefit, or a.... or a....

It has been a great week for the Euro, or to be precise, non-supporters and critics of the Euro. Continental Europe speaks as per the Labour Party with one controlled and united voice. All try to encourage enthusiasm but it won't wash, it's now down to its lowest point ever and that news gives me a very warm feeling.

German Euro sceptics (at last we have found some) are rallying support to keep the door open, should the mark be required - or hedging your bets, as we'd call it. German investors see their hard-earned savings being jeopardised by the loss of the mark. How much egg can a Federalist face take, I wonder. It is, however, a question one cannot answer as politicians have many faces.

Maureen and I spent the night scanning the papers for a replacement car. Yes, that Metro replacement for the Peugeot 205 has failed its MOT in the grandest of styles, i.e. to the tune of £400. Problem is, add that to the cost of the car, = £500, take away its true value (even with an MOT) and you are left with the £100 you started with. So a decision has been made. The second we find a car to buy, both the Metro and the Peugeot 205 are to be sold to one of those advertisers in the paper who requests "All cars considered, with or without MOT".

We are still awaiting a response from the claims agency regarding the accident Maureen was involved in last January. Problem is, no witnesses.

We looked at several Golfs and Polos, most of which were quite expensive and quite high-mileage to boot. But we're off to see what we can find, so I'll let you know later how we got on.

It's now four and a half hours later. We looked at a VW Golf and a Polo in Woking and we almost saw a Fiat Tipo, which had just been sold. We were umming and ahhing over the Polo and drove away, having offered the obligatory "We'll get back to you" line. Anyway, halfway back, we stopped off at a phone box, having made the decision to buy the car, because time is not on our side and I'll be away again for three days come Tuesday. Which means, Maureen will have to catch the train to work, as the most important comment the MOT tester made regarding the Metro was, "Don't drive it, it's unroadworthy"! Having found that phone box I rang the young lady who was offering the Polo. No reply. Isn't that typical. So, home we came to have a cup of tea and mull over the situation, only to find a message on the answerphone from a number I had rung the previous night. This lady had a Peugeot 309 for sale and she rang back to say it was still available. At this point you wonder, why wasn't it sold? So having made the return phone call we trundled over to Church Crookham where, lo and behold, we came across an extremely nice example, in Cherry Red, one owner and full service history.

Including car tax which expires next May, the cost was £500, which has had to come out of our savings. This amount will be handed over to us in dribs and drabs each week by offspring number three. Oh, yes, forgot to tell you, he now has a job and we will now have his money!

It was on our way back from Woking and just after we had made the abortive phone call that we passed the Keogh Army Barracks. Maureen recalled being invited there many years ago when she was a member of the local British Red Cross Society. Maureen will now relate this story herself while I sit back and have a glass of beer.

"Having carried out our medical duties, two friends and myself began crossing the parade ground on our way back to the car park. When we got to almost mid-way, a huge bellow rang out across the scene. It was reminiscent of a lion's roar when disturbed at its kill. All three of us shot up in the air in alarm. We could not see where this loud-hailer-like din had originated. Suddenly I espied a peak-capped head looming out of a top window of one of the buildings surrounding the parade ground. This was the source! Again, we were roared at. Apparently we had to vacate the ground as quickly as possible. Scuttling to the other side, we asked an army cadet what had been our sin. You must never saunter across the parade ground - it's sacrosanct!' We thought, What a horrible lot, shouting like that at ladies'!"

I cannot understand for the life of me how anyone would volunteer to go into the army. The thought of someone shouting at you to "get up you lazy good-for-nothings", etc. leaves me cold. Wouldn't it be nice to face the blood-red exterior of a man in peaked cap with a heart of stone bearing down on you, and say, "Thanks all the same, but if it's all right with you, I'll catch you up a bit later, I think I'm getting one of my heads" - on reflection, I think it might be funnier if someone else said it!

On our arrival back home in both cars we realised that although Muttley represented the sole form of life in the house, William had returned at some stage as the butter was on the worktop, the lemonade was left out of the cupboard, with the cap *just* holding the bottle top. I wouldn't mind, but he always complains that the drinks have gone flat. The bread was open to the elements and a plate and glass lay on the kitchen table.

The message indicated on the answerphone was not, strangely enough, for William, although we have received three for him since the commencement of these notes.

So, another one bites the dust. Morlands Brewery in Abingdon, which as I said earlier, strenuously fended off unwanted bids from predators in the early nineties is now to be swallowed up by Greene King. The Abingdon brewery will definitely close and Old Speckled Hen and Ruddles will be brewed in East Anglia. Frankly, I do not think breweries should be able to retain the titles of erstwhile brews. Few well known names emanate from their original town. It's all a marketing scam reliant on English nostalgia.

One finds it hard to pinpoint a more disingenuous, greedy and unfeeling chap than Martin Rose. This is the man who was in collision with a car driven by Trudy Lucas. Mrs. Lucas, her husband and 10-year-old son were killed in the crash. Only their 8-year-old daughter survived. She has suffered appalling injuries and is still undergoing operations. This Rose cove has instructed his solicitors to claim compensation for loss of earnings - £250. No, there are no noughts missing - just £250. The solicitors said they did not wish to cause the daughter or her family undue pain but feel that Mrs. Lucas's estate should pay. I don't know how this man or his solicitors have the gall to instigate a claim, given the circumstances.

Here we have this Mr. Rose, who has previous convictions for drink driving, failing to provide a blood sample after refusing a breath test at the scene of the accident. It is alleged that Mrs. Lucas pulled out at a junction and drove into the path of Rose's van. Three people were killed, a little girl is left an orphan and this appalling example of greed requests £250. With his record, he is lucky to be alive. This is one Rose that doesn't come up smelling so sweetly.

Now as you know, I've never been one to undersell Aldershot. It does quite nicely on its own. That sorry concrete heap that describes itself as the Wellington Centre, something the good duke would not have been proud of, has few shining beacons of class within its confines. One of these is Maher's the bookshop. They have been in the building for just on three years but are now to close. Not due to lack of popularity, not because they are losing money. Oh, no. Apparently, it "does not fit in with the new concept of the centre". The extension to the Wellington Centre, or Phase 2, will become Aldershot Galleries, the UK's "first town cut-price designer retail outlet". Sounds like a contradiction in terms - "designer" and "cut price". This little gem of a concept will be produced by courtesy of the Bank of Kuwait. They are apparently keen for the bookshop to stay, but only as a cut price store.

What a bloody cheek! Cut price equates to tat. I'm very glad to say that Tony Maher, the M.D., has refused to go down-market. The result is that three full time and two part time jobs will go - not to mention another outlet for the Trouser Press!

It says little for the burghers of Rushmoor Council that Aldershot aspires only to the level of cut-price and proceeds no further. On a scale of 1 to 10 in a fictional good town guide, I would put Aldershot at -2, and that would be generous.

Poor Mr. John Greenway, the Conservatives' Home Secretary spokesman. He committed the most heinous of crimes in parliament yesterday. He publicly identified three muggers ..... I'm desperately trying to bring myself to say it ...... Oh, all right, I'll repeat it ..... black muggers. Not my words, you understand, but those of poor Mr. Greenway. They jumped into a vintage taxi parked outside his home and robbed the driver of his bag, money, wallet and driving licence. So is it sack cloth and ashes or an unheralded acceptance of someone merely stating a fact? Opinions are divided but it doesn't need much guess work to assess the percentage terms.

An MP called Iain Coleman, Labour Hammersmith, describes Dear John's comments as a "gratuitous insult to black people". But then his type would. Never let a truthful statement get in the way of racial hysteria. Ann (I'm warming to her) Widdecombe said, "Too much political correction destroys, rather than promotes good race relations". Isn't that what I have been saying for a few pages, now? Well, maybe not in such concise terms, but pretty damn near!

Well, that's it, it's the call of the wild - or to be precise, the calling of Muttley to dinner. Will it be duck and rabbit, game and carrots, beef and heart? They all smell the same anyway!

CHAPTER TEN:

RAMSGATE AND CROISSANTS DO NOT MIX

Foxhunting is like a religion to a hunter, I now believe. All rational and logical thought goes clean out of the window and unfortunately such is their obsession that when things go against them, they take away their toys. Take the case of James and Charlotte Townsend. They play a large part in a company called Ilchester Estates. They may even own it. What is clear is that the company owns Fleet and Chesil Banks in Dorset. They had accepted an invitation by English Nature to designate the area as a nature reserve. This agreement is now cancelled because of the Prime Minister's proposal to outlaw hunting.

The pair have written to Baroness Young, Chairman of English Nature, whinging on about losing confidence in the government's understanding of countryside management issues. Frankly, with all the pressures on farming, building and the like, I wasn't aware they had any. Still, they drone on. Listen to this. "The Fleet and Chesil Bank owe their diverse landscape in part to management policies which result from the commitment of generations of owners to all activities conducive to conservation, including hunting and other field sports. Recent political statements have made us realise that English Nature will be required to observe a ban on hunting and other field sports, regardless of the environmental and conservation benefits". They use the word "reluctant" in withdrawing from the agreement. It appears, then, that if you won't let someone hunt, they won't allow a piece of land to be preserved for posterity. There is an intransigence which matches the hunt supporters' arrogance.

English Nature considers the area concerned to be one of only three in the country which embraces such important geological features and rare species. Their future is now put at risk because of the hunting issue. The single and small-mindedness of the hunting fraternity is at times beyond belief.

Tony Blair is going to have to be strong, very strong on this issue. He must not give in to the hunters' intimidating "class" call. They will unite and threaten, they will puff out their collective chests, go red in the face and crack their whips. They must not be allowed to win. For to win, is to allow needless killing.

I've just read the above case again to check one or two items and it does seem powerful. In fact, it seems so powerful I am sure someone else has written it!

I like this next little piece (not that I haven't liked all the other little pieces - never undervalue your own efforts!). Anyway, Yvonne Amor, who lives with husband Richard and their two daughters in a splendid little twelve up, sixteen down, in deepest Cornwall had the bailiffs round recently. No, not Bert and Doris Bailiff from Acacia Avenue, Leatherhead, but official ones.

You see, husband Richard had been fined for traffic offences but ignored warning letters instructing him to pay the fines. Probably thought he was above it all. The court lost its patience and sent around the two bailiffs, one Jayne Thompson and her colleague, Simon Nutt. They were to seize goods to the value of £433. Remember, the Amors live in a 17th century country home and plan to open it to the public. On arrival the bailiffs were confronted with Yvonne storming into the hall and inviting them to "get out of my house". They didn't, so off goes Yvonne to get the family's double-barrelled shotgun. While aiming it at Jayne Thompson, she phones the police and says, "I will get violent if you don't remove them. There is this silly cow who stinks of cheap scent. She is polluting the atmosphere. She stinks like a tart. I am surprised these people have not had their faces filled in years ago by people far less civilised than I".

She's got balls, the metaphorical variety that is.

Jayne Thompson told the court, "It (*the gun*) was pointed at me. I thought I was going to be shot. Mrs. Amor kept referring to my perfume and my weight and calling me a whore. I was absolutely terrified".

The police arrived and handcuffed Mrs. A. while one of her daughters waved a hockey stick at the officers involved. The other daughter, aged fifteen, is said to have tackled a police inspector.

Mrs. Amor, an unsuccessful Conservative candidate, admitted abusing the bailiffs. She said, "I do have a slightly florid turn of phrase when I get going. I am sure I was extremely offensive".

She was given a dressing down by the judge and was convicted on two charges of threatening the bailiffs with intent to cause them to believe unlawful violence would be used against them. A tad long-winded, but accurate. Yvonne Amor was jailed for nine months. As she was led away from the dock, her daughters screamed, "She did not do it". Yvonne Amor turned (I'd like to think she turned, anyway) and said in refined tones, "Remember, you're an Amor". A bit like a Womble, but with more class. Yvonne's husband, Richard, commented, "The only thing that is keeping her going is the thought that the bailiffs will burn in eternal damnation!"

You've got to hand it to people like that. They do know how to grab a sticky situation by the jugular. Not for them the handing over of a cheque and worrying if it's going to bounce. Oh, no, a full confrontational, or nothing.

This week saw the news that a field of genetically modified trees have been damaged. By whom I know not and I care even less. In an article today there came suggestions that these trees, or their scientifically generated offspring, would be forever devoid of wildlife. No bees, butterflies, moths, birds or squirrels. These sterile plantations will be deliberately engineered to secrete toxic chemicals through their leaves, enabling them to kill off all caterpillars and other leaf-eating insects. Resistant to all herbicides, all ground flora would be eliminated.

Monsanto (them again) and Shell say these *man-made* (my words) trees will grow faster and reduce the use of chemicals and energy used in papermaking. Now you and I know that claims of savings are in 99% of all cases absolute tosh. I remember with the advent of computers, claims abounded of the savings in paper that would be made. I have never seen such paperwork as that generated by computers.

Monsanto and Shell are not in the business of ecological care. They are there to make a profit for their shareholders. Why can they not have the guts to admit it? A spokesman from Monsanto offers this dollar's worth of PR, which I am not swallowing. "Increasing the productivity of tree plantations safely and sustainably will help meet the world's wood needs without increasing pressure on native forests". Would you believe that? No. Who is he kidding? Does he honestly think the loggers will cut back their destructive activities in the rain forests?

Environmentalists are not unnaturally concerned and sceptical. Other than profit I see no argument for the plantations' creation.

Mrs. Blackbird is still collecting worms, several at a time, before returning home just the other side of the railway fence. The blue and great tits have made few appearances since the arrival of the squirrel in our garden. Quite out of the blue, or to be more colour correct, out of the green, he chewed the nut-holder to smithereens. All the remaining nuts fell onto the grass, which pleased Muttley enormously.

Tomorrow I am going to London to collect the magazines I will be distributing along the way during my tour of Kent and Sussex. I am once again starting my six to seven week tour of the holiday camps, leisure centres, etc. Three days a week working my way along to Cornwall and then from Cornwall north, ending up at Cheddar. Not bad - quite nice, really!

Right, got to go. Maureen's just shouted that dinner's ready. Think I'll open a bottle or two. Beer, I mean, not wine.

I'm speaking to you from Ramsgate. I'll cut out the beautiful downtown bit. It's Thursday morning, whereas it should have been Wednesday. I'll explain. On Monday, whilst waiting for a phone call before going to Hammersmith to stock up with the puzzle mags, I decided to take off the two seat covers in the Metro, as well as taking out the radio. I finally found a man to take the car away for £25. He is also taking the Peugeot 205 for the grand sum of £50. Anyway, I unclipped the first of the spring tensioned fasteners from under the seat, when it flicked back and caught me in the pupil of my right eye. The tension was extremely strong, the pain was excruciating. I visited our local health centre who, without looking at my eye, suggested that I make my way to the Eye Clinic at the Royal Surrey Hospital, Guildford. It was like a severe headache in the eye and my vision was extremely blurred.

Parking in the hospital's pay-and-display car park I walked what seemed like a route-march to the Accident & Emergency Department. Booked in and waited for an "assessment". The nurse was very pleasant and informed me with great enthusiasm that I was very lucky. No, nothing to do with the eye, my luck was due because usually the wait to be seen could be anything between four and five hours, but today, it was only "an hour or so". It wasn't always thus, was it. After what seemed like an eternity I was examined and given some ointment. The cost of waiting is now an important part of the hospital's funding. The car park information board advised me that parking for an hour would cost me 80p, £1.50 for two, and rising. If the average wait is between four and five hours, the hospital is doing very nicely, thank you. What a squalid tactic.

When I booked in, the receptionist asked me if I had been to the hospital before. I replied that I couldn't afford the car parking charges. Don't suppose that helped my case. I find it abhorrent that one should be forced to pay to park in a hospital car park. It is, however, indicative of today's greed. If I do have to visit the Outpatients Dept. again, I will park in Tesco's on principle, and walk. At least we shop there!

Upshot is, I set off for the concrete patio of England, otherwise known as Kent, a day late. Have you ever been to north Kent? Faversham, Sheerness, Herne Bay. Don't bother! I'd like to say that Aldershot fares well in comparison, but they are not quite that bad. Margate is still as tacky as ever, with that ghastly tower block still standing testimony to someone's pay packet. Wherever you seem to be, either on train, car or foot, it follows you. It's like the Mona Lisa, you turn round and it's always there, staring at you, in all its greyness.   I moved on quickly, having concluded my business, along the coast to Ramsgate. Funny place, really. Some extremely tasteful and interesting examples of Georgian terraces, Victorian back streets and a pleasant harbour, but it's full of scruffy, loud teenagers, gathering in the streets, which needed a good clean as well. In short, it's messy. Won't be going back.

Well, it's Thursday morning, as I said, it's 7.20 am and I'm on the headland. The sun is shining, the sea is beautiful and calm and I am about to cross back over the road to my hotel to have breakfast. Apparently, it's only continental. The girl didn't tell me that until after I had agreed to take the room. Croissants, bagels or crumpets, she offered. The crumpets I assumed were some kind of sop to those who didn't want to go totally European. The way I see it, if you don't *do* an English breakfast, then it should say Bed and Continental Breakfast. I told her somewhat frostily that if I were on the Continent I would expect a Continental breakfast, but I am in England. It cut no ice but I really could not be bothered to shop around, and to be honest, the town didn't appear to be teeming with reasonable B & B/small hotels anyway. Right, must go, me crumpets await!

So, what sort of day have you had. Expecting an answer from you is the same as expecting an answer from the dog. "Evening, Muttley", I say, "so how was it for you?" That's right, she hardly stirs. A slight flickering of the tail, but that's all, and that's if she really feels active.

I've moved down the coast somewhat, visited a few holiday camps and parks, seen a lot of sea and I'm currently residing on the bed on the first floor of a terraced B & B close to Littlehampton Harbour.

It's clean with a firm bed and is reasonably cheap. There is, however, a peculiar smell of petrol up the stairs and on the landing outside my door, although I can't smell it so much in my bedroom. There's no light bulb in the bedside lamp but there are twelve tea bags.

There is a full English breakfast. I did check. Tomorrow, I shall continue my way to Bognor, Chichester and Hayling Island. I trundled through Deal today. Now that is a fascinating little town. An architectural gem to boot. That, however, is where the good news ended. Human life seems to be encroaching more and more onto Camber Sands. High fences, pylons, etc., all the usual paraphernalia that manifests itself from man's intrusion on anything remote. And what's happened to Pevensey Bay, where once there was a wilderness there is now an Asda, a retail development of the Comet and Halford's kind and a housing development most authorities would be glad to host. It is really an extension and out of town shopping area for the ratepayers of Eastbourne.

What's happened of note this week? Oh, yes, another Kennedy went AWOL. There really should be a health warning issued on baptism with this family.

I found it amusing to read that the Tories are aggrieved by the tobacco industry's aggressive marketing techniques. A chap called Gary Streeter (no, I've never heard of him neither), the Shadow International Development Secretary, has written to British American Tobacco. He sounds off that its advertising in Africa and elsewhere abroad was an "obvious evil, at best indiscriminate and at worst targeted (at children)". It wouldn't be amusing were it not for the fact that Kenneth Clarke, the ex-Chancellor, is deputy chairman of British American Tobacco and Margaret Thatcher is a consultant with Phillip Morris. Other than for money, how do people like that get involved with companies and industries so heavily implicated in the manufacture of the most common drug the world has ever witnessed.

I see that up to 500 protesters spent two hours destroying a field of genetically modified oil seed rape on land owned by AgrEvo. I like good news.

A.A. Gill, he of the anti-whoever ilk, has upset the Germans, I see. I don't even know the man, but I like him! Right, I'm off for something to eat.

I'm back from having something to eat - and drink. A pint at the Cob and Pen and another at the Nelson. My landlady has just given me an alarm clock. My wristwatch strap broke some months ago and I have never quite got round to getting it repaired. I always make do with the clock on the car dashboard. Problem is, it's difficult to get it out of its casing and even more difficult to get it to balance on the bedside table! I did have the foresight to take one of the bedside clocks we have at home. Unfortunately, I left it behind on the bed. Having handed over the said clock, she asked what I did for a living. I rarely say that I write as it always seems a touch pompous, and generally, the reply is, "I've always wanted to write a book" and a conversation ensues as to why they haven't. Having told me that she likes puzzle magazines (that's a couple of free issues before I leave tomorrow) she told me that one of her sons works for a motor manufacturer. "He often goes to Blackpool and he takes me with him. We stay in four-star hotels, there's me, him and his friend". At this point she moved her lips but nothing audible came forth. "Sorry", I said, "I didn't quite catch what you said". "He's .....?" Again the moving lips. I craned my neck and frowned in puzzlement. She looked over the bannisters, came back in, closed the door and whispered, "He's a poof - has a partner". She finally imparted, "Not my son downstairs, no he was a Marine". She explained that her husband chose not to recognise their son's homosexuality. She said she couldn't cast him out and enquired as to whether I could if he were my son. I said I couldn't say as it fortunately hadn't happened. I reasserted my good fortune. She said he apparently "came out" (her words) or "come clean" would be mine, although it's a contradiction in terms, at his father's funeral, introducing all to his partner at the same time.

I admired her loyalty but I can't say I would be quite so accepting. I find it all rather cringe-making.

There's an interesting report in the *Express* today concerning the case of a thief who took pictures of himself and his girlfriend in a stolen car. Said thief then crashes his car but leaves the camera, which belonged to the owner, in the footwell of the driver's side. The car was written off, but the owner, when salvaging bibs and bobs, found the camera and had the film developed. The police immediately recognised the little oik. The sad aspect to this humorous little piece is that at 29 years of age the oik has learned nothing. He has a long history of car theft but is given two years' probation and a two year driving ban. He should be locked up. The photograph of him with two fingers raised outside the court says it all.

And now for some good news. The highlights of the Two Ronnies shows were superbly refreshing and even better news, there's still no sign of Little or Large, Cannon or Ball, and long may it continue.

Not content with ending the Royal Tournament as a traditional spectacle, we now witness the proposed demise of the Pegasus Flying Horse insignia. Contractions and mergers mean that the Pegasus will fly no more. Another bit of England's air space gone.

Shock! Horror! ..... The Passport Agency (Office as was) has lost its charter mark. This is the mark awarded for excellence in the public service and the Passport Agency has had it for seven years. This little scheme, and no doubt a good salary for those involved, was introduced under John Major's "leadership" - so *that's* what he gave to the country! It's actually sheer bunkum as the charter mark does not add to nor reduce the queue for passports. No-one is sacked and a Mr. O'Brien, Jack Straw's lackey, or Immigration Minister, whichever you prefer, said, "We do not operate a blame culture". That's right, go on taking the salary. It seems to sum up the government, pointing the finger and taking responsibility is not very politically correct.

Mind you, Mike O'Brien is not the sort to sit anywhere other than a fence regardless of situations. He is quite happy to push refugees on anyone, widen the burden and hope they will go away. If moving them to the seaside was a subtle hint that the next stop was home, then it was obviously lost on those concerned. As taxpayers know to their continued cost, refugees don't go home - and I use the word "refugees" in the broadest of terms. There are now more than 1,500 of them lolling around the Kent coast. It's hard enough getting paying visitors to take a holiday in any of these towns, but when you are sharing your hotel with Sri Lankans, Afghans, Albanians and Kosovans, none of whom speak English - oh, with the exception of the words "rights", "entitlement" and "benefit", it's just not on. Our tourism minister, Janet Anderson, is even entering the fray. At least someone can see what the situation is doing to our embattled tourist trade, especially in areas like this. I mean, it's not as if you are going to get hordes of Americans "doing Sheppey" or "doing Thanet" in the same way as they "do Windsor".

Further to our chat earlier concerning women priests and the hostility it causes, a new Bishop of Exeter has been installed - or whatever you do with them! This chappie is a supporter of women priests and has a wife who is in training to be ordained. Already, church traditionalists are turning on him and his wife referring to his appointment as an "act of aggression". Every other facet of life entitles one to sexual equality in the work place but as I have said before, the church appears to be above it all. Any more crosses available?

It's with a smile that is wry and a laugh that is mocking when I look at the smug face of Neil Whitehouse. This is the fellow who risked his and everybody's else's life aboard a plane bound for Manchester from Madrid by refusing to switch off his mobile phone. The arrogant arsehole has been sentenced to one year in prison. I am looking at the photo of him again. I am smiling again. He was described by the judge as stubborn and arrogant but apparently looked suitably shocked when told of his sentence. I'd have paid good money to see that!

Asked to switch it off by a steward, he replied "Why, are we going to get lost?" I'd have added another year for sarcasm. As you know, sarcasm is not something I can empathise with. For reasons unexplained in the newspaper article, he has not worked since his arrest. He was earning £35,000 per annum. A spell inside might relieve him of some of his problems concerning other people's safety. It doesn't help, though, when his father says, "The sentence is a bit harsh, there will probably be an appeal" ..... And a claim for compensation, stress, harassment. All of a sudden, it will be the captain's fault!

Getting back to genetically murdered (sorry, modified) food, I find it rather disturbing that despite the major supermarkets' pledges to sell GM free food because "that's what the customer has told us they want", GM free does not actually mean GM free! It means just a little GM. To my mind, it either is or it isn't. The EU (them again) is set to allow labelling proclaiming GM free, when the product contains up to 2% GM material.

And a food commission report is urging those who make the rules to insist on a 0.1% maximum. The arrogance of the Co-op is in line with the mobile phone prat. They are happy to allow 2% of its GM free products to be genetically modified. They consider the figures "realistic". Is it me, have I missed the point somewhere?

It's like everything, though, we can only take it on trust. We cannot know what we are eating. Monsanto and all the others who would use us as guinea pigs still hold the aces and must be laughing all the way to the many banks in which they deposit their disputed gains.

I now also realise that I and many others have been conned in the free range egg scam. As all purchasers of these eggs would agree, we buy them because we do not want to associate ourselves with the appalling trade in battery reared chickens. In essence, it appears that our trust has once again been misguided and our money taken under *almost*

245

false pretences.

The pretence is that the chicken has a field to run about in. That is what the purchaser assumes. They lead a healthy, stress-free life, pecking around until the sun drops behind that row of elm trees away in the distance and they are called in, each by name, to be safe from the fox until dawn breaks and a whole new world opens up once more. That, as I said, is the pretence.

According to a very well written piece in Thursday's *Daily Express* free range birds live in huge barns which accommodate some sixteen thousand chickens. The density was brought home by the analysis that it is equivalent to twelve birds to a square yard and a bit. (The article used the word metre, but I can't be doing with it myself). To me, it's a square yard and a bit! More simplistically, it works out at two chickens to one page of the *Daily Express*! Now that brings home what free range really means. Because there is access to an outside area, their eggs are allowed to be sold under that emotional banner. There is, however, little incentive for the chickens to venture into the outside world as their drink and nest boxes are all inside. Their eggs are still collected on conveyor belts and their food and water piped in from vast hoppers. These barns are artificially lit for up to sixteen hours a day, so that the birds keep on laying. This is no life. This is exactly the kind of reason why we, and thousands of others, choose to pay more for our eggs. Were you aware that bullying, due to stress, is commonplace? Birds' beaks are routinely removed due to damage caused to each other. At just over a year and four months a free range chicken is killed. A battery chicken lives for an average year and seven months. The free range chicken is also likely to be fed more antibiotics than its battery cousin. Illegal drugs are found more in free range chickens than the battery variety. I didn't know that either.

I remember seeing the "Freedom Foods" quality mark on egg boxes. Like a fool I actually trusted the labelling. I assumed that because the RSPCA said it was okay, it actually was. The article goes on explaining - or exploding the myth. It really says a lot when the Minister for Agriculture admits "the legal free range standard is no guarantee of good animal welfare".

So who is there that the public can trust? Certainly not the Min. of Ag. or the supermarket who will sell you anything in an animal friendly packet if it thinks it can make that few extra bob from you. And certainly not the farmer, whose ratio of care to profit has let him down time and time again. Sadly, not even the RSPCA who will sell out for small gains over the years. I feel this particular organisation needs a thorough overhaul and a more aggressive management. Show the public what is wrong with animal welfare. Bring it to their attention. As the Americans would say, "in your face".

This particular article has taught me a lot. I hope others who attempt in a very small way to show some compassion also read the article as it was a real eye-opener. It was also very debilitating to find that once again, the consumer was being duped and that they were paying more to be duped. So if possible, buy all your eggs from a local farm shop and hit the supermarkets in their fleece-lined pockets. It's the only way.

Remember these names:- Eric Forth and David Maclean. They are the two Tory MP's who wrecked the proposed bill to end fur farming. As yesterday was the last day of parliament before the summer recess, it had to be agreed by close of play. By employing delaying tactics this uncaring, arrogant pair of half-wits killed off the chance to save a lot of animals from suffering. I view their action, and it has happened time and time again, as a gross abuse of an MP's privilege. They are elected to represent their constituency, not play with life for political kicks. This "Forth" person, MP for Bromley, said, "I don't think the people of this country should have laws foisted on them". I do not understand that statement. The people of "this country" have irrational and unfair laws foisted upon them daily, but when a bill is presented that engenders cross party support, oddities such as these two use parliamentary time to filibuster. I trust their constituents will take a dim view of their representatives' trite concern.

Just a little statistic here - the Stephen Lawrence Enquiry has cost the British taxpayer over £4 million - money well spent? Thought you might like to know!

Here's some good news that might help me when the book goes on sale! Lord Justice Sedley found in favour of a group of Christian fundamentalists who, it was claimed by the police, were "obstructing a highway and causing a breach of the peace'". The good Lord said that there was "no lawful basis for the arrest or the conviction". He added, "There was no suggestion of highway obstruction, nobody had to stop and listen".

I particularly warmed to his summing up when he said, "Freedom of speech is not worth having unless it can cause offence. The irritating, the contentious, the eccentric, the heretical, the unwelcome and provocative all have a right to be heard". Well said! - not that any of my rantings could be classified as such, you understand! I'm merely making an observation or two.

As I passed the television in our small living room the local news was on. My attention was drawn to a proposed development of many fields and woods at Winchfield in North Hampshire. The new housing development, which would completely destroy wildlife, is planned by, yes you've guessed, Barratts. They used phrases like "It's totally in line with government thinking". It makes you wonder who is in charge of development - the government or the builders. Building developers are a cancerous growth on the countryside. Still, I suppose with all these refugees to house .....

Some parents never learn, do they? I've just followed a car into Farnborough. A woman was driving, with a child, aged about four, standing in the rear footwell with both arms spread across the tops of the front seats. A sudden jolt and he would have shot through to the front and probably injured himself quite severely. Still, the driver was wearing a baseball cap, which says a lot for her, doesn't it?

The following is a particularly good reason to justify never responding to a request to vote at a local election. West Oxfordshire District Council has a policy of free parking within its towns - Chipping Norton, Burford, Carterton, Eynsham and Witney. No doubt the good residents of these towns appreciate their council's policy. After all, free town centre parking invites shoppers to town centres and not out of town supermarkets. The logic and refreshing foresight is completely lost on the government, however. Grants worth over £500,000 will be withheld unless West Oxon. D.C. paint more yellow lines and install pay and display car parking. Apparently, under plans drawn up by Johnnie (Two Jags) Prescott's distinct anti-car department, free parking "conflicts with government policy". A chap called John Rider, who is a senior transport planner at the Government's Office for the South East, said, "The availability of free parking close to the town centre must be considered as a serious deficiency. It is important to remember that the size of the allocation (of funding) will to some extent reflect the degree to which the objectives in the plan accurately reflect government policy".

In short, he is saying, "Do as we say, or lose your money". There is no such thing as local government unless you place a higher emphasis than I do on chairing the Lighting and Cemeteries Committee!

Here's a figure to make you stand up and think - or if you are already standing, slump down into that armchair. Were you aware that last year 432,324 genetically modified animals were used in scientific and medical research? That's up 95,000 from the previous year. Whilst everyone is aware that research equals suffering, George Howarth, the Home Office minister, glibly concedes that "it allows new areas of research to be explored". I don't care whether it helps cancer, M.S. or any other disease or illness, it is morally wrong to inflict suffering on any animal just to ease our suffering - bastard!

Stand up please those Ofsted inspectors who criticised a school for instilling manners into its pupils. Turnfurlong First School in Aylesbury, Bucks., lays down certain rules in social graces. There is a "no talking policy" ensuring that pupils do not speak when they are eating. Whilst the parents of children at the school are delighted that someone is at last insisting on certain standards, along comes the Ofsted gang of nerds and considers the rule "inappropriate". They counter that the ruling will have a "negative impact" on pupils' social development. Have you ever heard such utter drivel? Jan Tyson, the headmistress, said she was dismayed that her attempts to teach good manners was being criticised. As she said, "There's nothing worse than sitting opposite someone who is eating, while they are speaking, and seeing every morsel being chewed in their mouth and possibly spat all over you".

I'd like these "inspectors" to explain how teaching manners can be interpreted as "negative". The school is also critical of the Ofsted team's whole approach to its inspection, referring to it as intimidating. The school, however, does itself no favours when you learn that eight out of the fourteen teachers have been off sick for stress-related illnesses. It never seems to take much for them to "do a sicky".

However, it seems a shame that Jan Tyson wasn't the headmistress when Alex Ferguson went to school. She could have taught him a thing or two about the closure of his mouth when chewing. And wouldn't it have been to the good of all if footballers had been told at school that "spitting isn't very nice". Oh, for the days of blazers and straw boaters.

The government really is trying to be all things to all people. The problem is that that avenue leads to either no decision or a bad decision being taken. For instance, their obsession with children's rights. They want test-tube children to have the "right" to find their biological mother and father, when their very being was only made possible by the donation of eggs or sperm. This is fraught with danger. Would anyone welcome the possibility of a doubtless legally-aided attempt to extort money some twenty or thirty years after being born. This is one area where absolutely no information should be given to the child concerning donors. The number of would-be donors will plummet and the number of frustrated, hapless couples wishing to have children, will rocket. But then, rights have overtaken reason.

I see that we have an epidemic of pickpockets working out of the east end of London. There has been a 64% rise in offences since April. These groups take advantage of off-peak rail travel. Oxford, Reading, Windsor, Gravesend and Tunbridge Wells (? Tunbridge Wells) have all been targeted. All the pickpockets concerned are Bosnian women. They specialise in robbing tourists, the elderly and those in wheelchairs. Apparently, their knowledge of the legal system and their "rights" is extremely good. They also groom children of seven or eight to do their work with, or for them. Being under the age of criminal responsibility, the women know these children will not be charged. The police now have a list of 160 Eastern European women who are wanted for these offences in London and the south east. However, if just one is caught and successfully prosecuted, will they be deported? Will they buggery. Remember, they have rights!

They're a rum lot, this countryside rabble. Not content with threatening non-compliance of the law, should hunting be banned, they are likely to disrupt the PM's holiday in Tuscany next month. Now whatever I think of T.B., and it's not much, he and his family are entitled to some time away from the office. No-one deserves to have that precious period interrupted by demonstrating oiks regardless of cause.

That epitomy of a Tory arse, Douglas Hogg, does nothing to re-establish confidence in the party to which he belongs. Bearing in mind the previous paragraph, he and other pro-hunting Conservatives are expected to step up their campaign by disrupting business in the Commons. Mr. Hogg, a keen hunter, said "If they take away my foxhunting, I shall take away their time". However strongly he feels about a ban, it is amazingly childish and a complete affrontery to the electorate of this country to act in this unforgivable manner. He joins Messrs. Forth and Maclean as being the definitive holes in the arse of puerility.

Meanwhile, in a field in deepest Norfolk, Lord Melchett & Co. were destroying large chunks of a field full to the gunwales with modified maize. Several vehicles were damaged by the field's owner, William Brigham, and his brothers, John and Eddie. The maize was being grown on behalf of AgrEvo - remember, that's AgrEvo.

I cannot fathom out either the government's or the chemical companies' attitude. They still fail to understand the concern of the public. If it were a level playing field (one that hadn't been sold off for development) where the modified crops could be genuinely tested in isolation, then there would be more support for the trials, and subsequently less destruction. The problem, unanswered as far as I can see by any pro-organisation or government department, is how you stop non GM crops becoming contaminated by pollen. As has been written previously, no-one can guarantee immunity from cross-pollination and until they can (*if* they can) then all crops should be destroyed.

Only recently we have seen reports of damage to wildlife in America. The Monarch butterfly has been wiped out in areas of GM grain. Bear in mind that the Americans have planted up to 20 million acres of the stuff. With that investment they will resist very hard *all* reasoned argument, *all* overwhelming scientific research and *all* attempts to stop the erosion of choice.

I applaud the Melchett fellow and all those who flailed with him. I wish I had the courage to join them. I happen to believe that Michael Meacher is probably the one honest light in the flickering, murky world of GM engineering. He at least seems to speak without a forked tongue and with genuine concern for a possible catastrophe. What riles me is when he explains that Britain has been *told* to plant test crops by Brussels. Again, who *are* these unelected toadies that can allow the possible risk to British citizens' health. Who is working them? Is there money being passed from these companies with a heavily invested interest to ministers gullible and greedy enough and without foresight?

I am writing all this from the English Riviera - well, Paignton to be precise! I am one of the few inside a small public house. Most of the tourists are sitting at the tables with their stud-eared offspring, awaiting the passing of a local carnival - can't wait to miss it! There is very little with en-suite available in the town centre, so I have drifted out to the suburbs. The room is comfortable, there's a TV but no remote, and no bedside light. Does this qualify for counselling?

I finished my pint of Bass some time ago, and have surveyed the bar area on a number of occasions with a view to a refill. The throng waiting with empty glasses and first-time punters is quite horrendous - a bit like a bank really, there's only four bar staff serving. The English disease of silently queueing has just been broken. A tattooed Bulldog of a man, with a cross hanging from his left ear, has just exploded. "I've just stood ere for twenty minutes. 'Ow much f...... longer ave I got to wait?" It's funny, isn't it, but having offered a meek apology, one of the bar staff explained that this chap was indeed next! After that explosion it was always going to be his turn! I think I'll wait a little longer.

Last night I stayed in Torquay, was suitably impressed. It has cleaned up its act considerably - litter-ally! The gardens and frontage along with the harbour are clean, bustling places, with very pleasant cafés and bars. I supped in a Wetherspoon's pub - didn't know who owned it until I was asked for my money. One pound and ten pence for a pint of Thwaites. Now that is good value. I followed it with a pint of Director's, at £1.39. I'll be heading home tomorrow afternoon, calling in at Exeter en route to pick up some more magazines. Next week, Cornwall. That's nice!

It's always the way, you don't visit somewhere for years, and then you're back again within a few days. After having spent the mid-week on the Torbay coast, I have just returned from a day trip to Kingswear. This time, however, I wasn't driving. My mode of transport was a 1950's built Mark 1 coach, one of eleven in red and cream, or blood and custard as we enthusiasts refer to it. The twelfth coach, in chocolate and cream, was the support coach and the locomotive in question was a Great Western Railway King Class, No. 6024. What a magnificent sight it looked from our coach window at the rear of the train as she wound around the coastal route west of Exeter. She fairly stormed through Starcross, Dawlish and Teignmouth. Like the rest of July, today, Sunday, has been a cracker. The holidaymakers on the promenades, beaches and in the sea, turned almost as one to watch the grace and speed of the shining green king. As I have said before, I can think of no other activity that generates such friendliness and association between passenger and passer-by. Mums, dads and children all wave without hesitation to a steam-hauled train. The sheer volume of people watching, the smiling faces and the waving, made one feel very much part of something special.

My cousin, Simon, Dave and Kevin from the railway club were my fellow travellers and a good time was had by all.

Right, I've got to be up early tomorrow as I am traipsing all the way down to deepest Cornwall. Night, night.

The seagulls are screeching and squawking this morning. I'm sitting in my room in a small B. & B. overlooking the harbour at

Mevagissey. It doesn't have an en-suite but it does have a parking space, which are as rare as hen's teeth in this village. Last night I ate at the Fountain Public House. I have to tell you that the mixed grill was without doubt excellent, as was the company of a charming couple from Sidmouth (Wilmslow, Cheshire, originally, but now retired to the south coast). You know, spoke nicely, proper people! The St. Austell ales fairly flew down the hatch. I am currently nursing a slight headache - too much sun, you understand!

Today I continue my travels around the various holiday centres and parks in my quest to dispose of the puzzle magazines. She is a very nice landlady and I am looking forward to breakfast. She has already offered to "see me back out, as the road can be dangerous"! Sweet.

Maureen has started typing the first chapter of this book. I have to dictate from my notes as there's no way she can read my writing. We have just three weeks to knock it into shape before the final disk wings it way to the Channel Islands for printing. I have still not heard from W.H. Smiths, although I'm aware that the humour buyer is on holiday until the weekend. We will await an answer in anticipation and with more than a slight sense of anxiety.

Right! Did anything else happen in the rest of the world while I was enjoying the rarefied heights of steam travel. Let's see now ..... Well, lookee here! Carol Vorderman has a new look, and what a transformation. Now this is one makeover that turns her mumsy, middle-aged contented look into a very sensual lady who belies her thirty nine years. "Please, miss, I think I got all my sums wrong, so I expect you will have to smack me?" "What? Across the knee, oh, very well then, Miss Vorderman". (Maureen tutted disdainfully whilst she was typing this section, referring to me as "slightly sad". Well, I like our Carol).

Meanwhile, reality calls once more. Well done the Children's Society. This liberal minded misguided bunch of saps have just decided to allow homosexuals and lesbians to adopt children. Not surprisingly, pink christian groups clapped their clammy little hands while proper people denounced the move. I suppose the Church of England's hypocrisy should surprise no-one. But one of its spokesmen commented that "There is no place for homophobia within the church and this move brings the charity into line with others, but the church will continue to teach that a stable married environment is the best place for bringing up children". Talk about hedging your ecclesiastical bets! Mind you, when the government, in its usual lily-livered way advises that people should

253

not be banned from fostering because of their sexuality, it makes you wonder just who is going to take a lead on the subject. When will someone have the balls to stand up and say, "Excuse me, but has anyone sought the views of the public and reflected on how they feel about this?" Of course not.

I'll just mention it in passing, but in the first six months of this year, 580 gipsies from the Czech Republic have sought asylum in Britain. This compares with 512 for the whole of 1998. I do hope someone will take all these free-loaders into account when Barratts, Wimpey, etc. submit yet another planning application for a meadow outside Dorchester or Cambridge, citing "desperate local shortage of housing". Just a thought.

The all-embracing Church of England is advising parish churches to "welcome offenders, including paedophiles, into their congregation". Their report goes on to advise that "congregations may be one of the few places where sex offenders can mix with a welcoming community. We have a duty to welcome people into our congregation, especially offenders who may have no family. Offenders will have to agree to sit away from children and not loiter when they are at play".

It's strange they advocate the separation of paedophile and children in the pews, when very often much of the clergy have the same tendencies.

Last word to the church - no, I'm not becoming gracious - but their comments form an excellent tool with which to dig a pit for their hapless souls. "Churches", says the report, "should not ostracise paedophiles but offer themselves as therapeutic communities'". Need I say more?

Well done the Appeal Court. They have just ruled that transsexuals may have their sex-change ops on the NHS. A test case brought by North West Lancashire Health Authority has been lost. Appeal Court judges described the health authority's refusal to pick up the tab as "unlawful and irrational". This means that the authority must pay £200,000 in legal fees out of its medical budget, which would have been much better spent on patient care than overpaid legal bods. As usual, a test case is a sign for a deluge of cases if the decision goes against all logic, as this one has. British taxpayers will doubtless be very happy to pay for up to one thousand transsexuals' ops, the cost of which is some £8 million. How do those with the power to say yea or nay come to the conclusion that these people should be NHS cases when dental treatment for the masses, fairly important, I would have thought, costs the earth.   Still, they are a minority and minorities must be cosseted.

It must be a real bummer walking around with a willy when what you wanted - what you really, really wanted - was an extra large pair of tits!

It will be of comfort for the C. of E. to know that they are not the only ones to support unwarranted cases. Shelter, the support group for those who will not help themselves has taken up the case of a group of people in East London. This "family" of eight, as they call it, live in a two bedroomed flat. There are two adults plus six children who live there. The adult female describes the conditions as "hell". Three of her children, aged ten, eight and six, are from a previous relationship (don't even think of mentioning marriage), while the others are 22 months old and twins of 11 months. Tower Hamlets Council has told them that it could be between five and ten years before they become a priority case. What I want to know, why get pregnant for a fourth and fifth time when you and your "partner" and three children are already living in hellish conditions. Is nobody responsible for their own actions these days? Apparently not.

Shelter is, of course, taking up the family's cudgels and appealing for a change in rules, allowing for more affordable housing. Better still, why don't they hand out condoms or self-sterilisation kits?

It would make a change to find the newspapers who report on these matters actually asking relevant questions of the aggrieved, instead of merely reporting their plight as if it is someone else's fault.

So, the findings of the Southall rail crash investigation are concluded and the case proven. Seven dead, one hundred and fifty one injured, and all because the driver was foraging in his bag as he careered through red lights. Great Western Trains have been fined £1´ million. In the old days the *real* Great Western Railway used a system called AWS which automatically brought a train to a halt, should it go through a red signal. This latter-day imitation of a railway company also has safety devices fitted. But on the day in question they were not working.

It is reported that these train operating companies, along with Railtrack, put the profits of shareholders before safety. Commuter trains are now more overcrowded than in BR days. Why? Because stock is being cut back from the twelve coach trains to eight and eight to four. The passenger levels either remain the same, or in many cases have increased.   We are back to the old argument whereby successive governments price motorists off of the road and market the benefits of rail travel, the price of which is increased several times above the rate of inflation on promises which never materialise.

British Railways should be a public service paid for out of taxes, run by railwaymen with the passenger (not customer) in mind. Safety issues would be more accountable if those responsible were not sidetracked by profit.

Good news. Nicolas Anelka is finally on the move. Thank Christ for that! Well, I say Christ, it could be Norbert or Digby, it's just that Christ is a better known figure for some reason. Anyway, after suffering Van Hooijdonk going on strike at Notts Forest, we footie fans have suffered the unsavoury antics of the Anelka family and their part in the great greed trail. I read that Alex Ferguson is having the same problem with Roy Keane, and Leeds with Jimmy Floyd Hasselbaink.

Roy Keane is apparently demanding £2 million per annum. No player should be allowed to break a club's wage structure, however ludicrous it is at present. Let him go, let them all go. There has to be a stand against these people. No single player should ever be bigger than the club. The fans will not forgive the manager for this. They see greed as a betrayal of their favoured side, be it Manchester United, Macclesfield, Leeds United or Luton. The principle is the same. Thankfully, nothing unites supporters like an egotistical money-grabbing half-wit attempting to hold a club to ransom.

I see that GM soya is blamed as a cause for herpes. The Ministry of Agriculture, Fisheries and Food are to investigate the claims made by a leading British surgeon that her daughter developed large cold sores which would not respond to treatment. The daughter has since undergone a number of tests which have revealed she is not allergic to ordinary (proper) soya. It goes without saying that pro GM scientists pour scorn on the allegation and put the cold sores down to an "allergic reaction". It makes you wonder if people are paid to toe the line. As we've discovered, little research these days is independent and test results can be interpreted to prove whatever is required by those who pay the piper.

No avenue is safe from the litigant these days. A golfer was blinded when the ball she attempted to hit out of the rough rebounded off a stone and ricocheted into her left eye. It's bloody awful luck in the same way that I was temporarily blinded two weeks ago when the car seat hook flew into my pupil. I couldn't, and wouldn't, have gone in search of the cover manufacture and attempted to prise dosh from them because the hooks were at the end of an elastic cord "overstrung for the purpose of attachment", or some other wordy claim dreamt up by lawyers eager to earn commission on a no-win, no-fee deal. This woman was dreadfully unlucky, but no, she is suing the greenkeeper, Mr. Duguid, for £200,000. The case rests on her submission that the course was badly designed and maintained. Mr. Duguid commented that the golfer, Mrs. Milne, was wasting her time. "What am I supposed to do - go round the whole course and pick up every stone?" Exactly! Perhaps he could counter-sue for injury to feelings and harassment, etc. Oh, no, please don't, I was only kidding.

In the same way that a footballer should not be bigger than the football club he plays for, no presenter should be bigger than the company he or she works for. Des Lynam gets as near to being the exception that proves the rule as one can get. However the *BBC* word it, it is a loss, another nail in the coffin of terrestrial sport. Still, they do retain the rights to the Oxford and Cambridge Boat Race. It hasn't gone to *Sky* - yet. All these people now paying a fortune for football via satellite will one day wake up when the price of pay-per-view begins to bite. When the *BBC* and *ITV*, *Channel 4* and *Channel 5* have all relinquished their ability to provide adequate sports coverage and *Sky* have total monopoly, does anyone honestly believe it will be a cheap option, because that is the point, there will be no option.

All the talk of potential murderers, rapists, violent offenders being locked up for the public good comes to nothing when you read that a 12-year-old girl has been sexually assaulted twice by convicts released early from prison. Both attacks were made within nine months on the girl by a murderer and secondly a rapist, who were unknown to each other. The murderer, Neville Parry-Roberts, aged 37, had previously been jailed for life in 1985. He served twelve years before being released on licence. Why was he not made to stay in prison for life? He was allowed out and then convicted of indecent assault and jailed for fifteen months, which he obviously didn't serve, as nine months later he attacked the twelve year old girl.

The rapist, Michael Callaghan, aged 20, was released with 188 days of his sentence still to be served. He attacked the twelve year old and five days later a woman walking her dog. He has now got an 8 year sentence to serve, plus the remaining 188 days. So by the time you read this, he'll no doubt be out again, once more a menace and a threat. If only those responsible for the relaxation of a prisoner's sentence were also responsible for crimes committed between the date of release and the original set date, we might witness a more reflective and realistic attitude towards releasing prisoners.

Now here's one claim for sex discrimination I wholeheartedly back. Rachel Anderson is Britain's only female football agent. In 1997 she was banned from the Professional Footballers Association dinner because she was - a woman. She is the only FIFA licenced agent in the world and represents thirty five players. Mrs. Anderson was actually asked to leave the table and wait in her hotel room. In 1998 she wrote to the PFA requesting a ticket for that year's dinner. She was refused.

I find it remarkable and insulting that Gordon Taylor, the PFA's Chief Executive, instead of apologising in the most humble of ways, as he should, said "It would not be acceptable to his members to waive the rule barring women. I hope you will not take offence at this". What else is Mrs. Anderson to take? Delight?

As this "do" is a private function, you can apparently bar whom you like - which is fine if the rule is put to good use - drunks, improperly dressed attendees, people from Harpenden - but because she is a woman it's fairly unbelievable. The case now rests on whether the dinner *is* actually a private function or whether it should be placed in the *public* section, as tickets are on general sale. What is the PFA so scared of? Is football so conceited that it thinks it can remain a purely man's game. Females like watching football, clubs are happy to take their money at the gate, but be involved - oh, no. I sincerely hope she wins her case.

Now here's one for thrill seekers. A South African rancher is hoping to stage a motorcycle rally. Nothing in that, you think. A three thousand acre game farm near the town of Ellisras in the northern province will be the venue. Those partaking will pay £30 each for colour coded pellets of paint, which they will fire at their "quarry". No, not the impala, zebra or kudu, but prostitutes hired to run around the bush at £20 per hour, hoping (or not, as the case may be) to avoid being splattered. Revellers are invited to enjoy an "unusual weekend in the wild". What subsequently goes on between hunter and painted is entirely up to the "consenting, fun loving adults".

A bit of adult fun? Not according to the humourless and possibly sexless Rev. Theo Van Blerk, who is the leader of the local Dutch Reformed Church. He describes the comings and, well comings, as "disgusting and shameful". But he and his ilk would. He's having a meeting with other miserable clerics who are attempting to stop the event. He says, "This is an open attack on the traditional Christian lifestyle we still cherish in this area. This is a God fearing town and we are determined to keep it that way". Says it all, really. It may be *his* way, but it is not so for all people. Has he looked around him? No. He and his sort never do. The world, oh blind one, is changing. People now question your god and the majority of us no longer fear him, thank Christ. Ooops! Mind you, it's a thought, isn't it. Living so close to Aldershot, on the one hand, and the army ranges on the other, perhaps I could start up Tony's Painted Stunts - after all, there's very little difference between riding a two-wheeled bike and a two-legged one .....

Talking of dogs, I stayed in Newquay overnight. I have had my breakfast and I'm just making these notes before my trek around 19 holiday camps and parks in the Newquay area. The hills here are certainly alive to the sounds of those occupying caravans, mobile homes, not so mobile homes and tents. Fields that were once green play host to hordes of travellers. Cream, fawn and hearing-aid grey coloured boxes sprawl endlessly, linking Perranporth to Newquay, Newquay to Mawgan Porth and so on.

I digress. Last night, after dinner (a roast) I walked around the town and was amazed to see quite so many dogs. There were two distinct varieties. The first, canine, either Alsation or English Bull Terrier. They all wore leather studded collars with accompanying human bulldog at the end of a leather lead. The owner is generally bullet and bald-headed, aggressive in stance and in motion. Earrings, crosses or both dangle from the ears, the chest is heavy and bared, the jeans require washing, the boots, hob-nailed and the belt studded to match that of the dog's collar. Wrap around dark glasses perch on bulbous noses. The cheeks are podgy, the eyes pig-like and the gut oversized. They're not really my type.

The other dog comes in a group of three, all dressed in short black dresses that just cover the bum. Breasts are just held in. The three walk arm in arm, a mobile phone in one hand, a bottle of alcoholic drink in the other. They clip-clop in high-heeled shoes and talk loudly, expletives flying, especially if they think it will shock the passer-by. The general standard of the resident and tourist appears to be that of pond life. I can think of nowhere where the two are quite so easily matched. As far as I could ascertain, the best dressed people were the bouncers outside the doors of the many nightclubs. In short, not a place I'd visit without being paid.

Then again, perhaps it's slightly better than where I was a fortnight ago, in Thanet. Sandy Bruce-Lockhart, leader of Kent County Council, has expressed his fears to Barbara Rock, the new Immigration Minister, that health, education and immigration services are at breaking point in the area.

Residents in the towns of Dover, Folkestone and those in Thanet are feeling increasingly swamped by more than 5,000 asylum seekers who have gathered in the area. Sandy B-L says it is becoming a "tinder box for racially motivated violence after being overwhelmed by an influx of refugees".

Why should these people's lifestyle be upset by those we didn't want in the first place, but continue to suffer due to the liberal, gutless reactions of this government and the one before, and the one before .....

As if we haven't rolled over enough, Newham Council in east London is designing a block of flats for elderly Asians, where none of the loos face Mecca. The £3.2 million sheltered development will also incorporate extra kitchen ventilation for curry smells.

Are we allowed sheltered accommodation for white people only? No, I thought not. Funny that.

CHAPTER ELEVEN:

OF FOXES AND MEN IN RED

Tony Blair and family go on holiday to Tuscany which, as you know, I do not have a problem with. However, a stretch of beach up to five miles long is to be cordoned off for security purposes. This deprives the local population of their rightful amenities because of the visit by a foreign head of state. If I was a local I would be more than slightly miffed. Seriously, if I were the PM I would insist on the exclusion rule being lifted immediately. Either that, or go to Skegness.

I see that Lord Watson, a Scottish MSP, is to introduce a bill outlawing hunting with dogs in Scotland. Also banned, if successful, will be the "digging out" of foxes by terriers. It is destined to be a hard fought battle with the countryside hunters snapping at the heels of every politician. They are threatening to ignore the bill if it becomes law, or move their hunts to England. Scotland currently has ten hunts. Even if they move south of the border, it will cause them necessary hardship, which is good news. They may begin to feel threatened as a specie, which will also be good news. And the arrogance that goes with this lobby might also be diluted, which would be very good news.

A good example of their arrogance and disregard for the law that goes against them is revealed today. English hunters have stated that they have no intentions of stopping at the border if a fox "makes it into Scotland". Michael Hedley, Master of the Border Hunt, said "We have been following this route for 170 years and it is ludicrous to suggest we stop now". Where have I heard this prattle before? Something Orange, something Loyalist, something concerning marching? Worryingly similar vein, I feel. Anyway, I wish Lord Watson and his supporters well.

The quicker men have the same rights as women the better! Judge David Bryant made a very reasonable point yesterday when he commented on a case which collapsed in his court. A 16 year old girl had made rape allegations against men which were without foundation or substance. The judge considered that such women should be entered on a register which could be the "obverse of a sex offenders' register". He said that the defendant had gone through an "extremely unpleasant case" and was concerned that other people could suffer similarly.

I do not see the problem with this. Women who cry "rape" can ruin someone's reputation for good. Why should they be free to accuse, run, and then accuse again. This particular girl has a history of similar accusations against men. Not only has she put someone's freedom in jeopardy, but she has wasted legal time and not a little public money.

There has been a series of cases where women have either withdrawn their allegations or have been found to have made them up. You would have thought that regardless of sex, all sides would support such a move. But no, "outrageous" and "unhelpful" were words expounded by women's campaign groups. One group called "Rights of Women" said, "Statistics show that the likelihood of rape cases getting to court is very low, let alone securing a conviction. Given that the law is already so weighted against women, we should be looking at protecting rather than targeting (that word again) the few, if any women making false allegations. It's outrageous". See, I told you. Now they're denying that *any* women make up false allegations. I don't understand it. Unfortunately, reality is never allowed to enter the argument as these women are so anti-male that no amount of evidence would convince them that a female could be wrong and a male just could be right.

The situations mentioned are unlikely to ever befall the women who are so obsessed in this view. They go out of their way to make themselves unattractive. You know, lank, straight hair, no makeup, no dress sense and roll-ups. No wonder they can't get a man. Isn't it fortunate that I never generalise!

Whatever one's complaints may be about the government, you could never accuse it of shying away from a rights issue. Anybody's rights, that is, as long as they're not those of a proper person. There are now plans afoot to extend criminal injuries compensation to homosexual couples. Coming hard on the heels of the government's plans for thirteen weeks unpaid leave for parents (of which more in a minute), supporters of the limp-wristed and normally challenged feel that homosexuals should be given time off if bringing up children. (We've already been into that appalling option and it's still as repugnant). They want "same sex lovers" - what an awful title - ("queer bastards" is so much more tasteful, don't you think) to be regarded as children's next of kin. That would mean a complete overhaul of pensions, wills, tax issues, housing and adoption. Currently, married couples and cohabiting couples enjoy the benefits of these financial and social rulings. I would change the rules so that only married couples enjoyed the benefits.

That might help the family unit to make a stand against these showers of oddballs - and many probably have.

If these people really cared for the effect they had on children, perhaps they would consider what it is like for a child to admit to having two dads or two mums. The response from fellow pupils at school could shatter a child's confidence for life. Do they really want to take that chance?

Anyway, why should a child grow up knowing that his "Goodnight, Dad", "Goodnight, Dad" will be followed by these two people turning off the downstairs lights, locking the door and saying knowingly, "We could always go to bed early". For a child to be in the same house as adult guardians of the same sex *having* sex is really quite revolting. I am sure Ann Widdecombe would agree. Other than the abortion issue, she is almost a proper person.

Now then, Stephen Byers's announcement that up to thirteen weeks unpaid holiday could be taken has not gone down well in all circles. What is it with these people? Already under the financial cosh, tied up in EU and British government red tape, and basically nailed to the floor, small businesses cannot stand the latest, ill-thought attempt at improving the family's lot. Remember, that's thirteen weeks for each child. Where is the incentive to restrict the number of children you have. Once again, it's a sop to the benefits scroungers and those who contribute the square root of bugger all.

Despite Michael Meacher making noises that appear to support suspicion, if not downright hostility, to GM crops, ministers are set to back a move which could see the authorisation of commercially grown GM crops across Europe. The oil seed rape will be used in animal feed - who eats the animals? We do. Naturally, the name AgrEvo comes into play at this stage. Can someone explain why Tony Blair and his cronies are so desperate to push through this GM technology. It's sad when a British government takes so little notice of the public's concern and goes ahead because we "don't want to be left behind in this area". Once again, safety is not an issue, but money certainly is. There must be a fair number of pockets being lined with ill-gotten gain, almost as many as there are doctored reports, I guess.

Slightly less serious, but equally irritating, the EU logo is to be allowed on our number plates. Who would want them. The letters GB are also allowed but not with a home flag or Union Jack. To compensate for the space used, the actual letters and numbers will have to be 10% smaller, which the police contend could make them harder to read.

It will doubtless be only a matter of time before those without the revered EU logo are outlawed and the offender fined for not showing Belgium enough respect. You may laugh .....

It says a lot for our country and the "rights" of responsible people to curtail the nefarious activities of their offspring. Mike Brundell attempted to restrain his errant 15-year-old daughter by holding her wrists. The girl, Georgina, had been out late at night. Her mother has been waiting up night after night. Georgina reported her father to the police and *he* ended up at the police station for six hours of interrogation. Mrs. Brundell sought the help of social workers. She said that she explained that her daughter was going out with a coloured man ten years older than herself. All the social worker could ask was "Do you have a colour problem?" What a bloody cheek! I know of Asian families who find the thought of their son going out with a white girl to be the most heinous of crimes that one could commit, but of course, that is the other way round.

Anyway, I thought social workers were there to help, not judge. Mrs. Brundell says it's the worst thing she could have done. Georgina is currently with foster parents as she refuses to toe the line and come in at 11 pm. Caring parents are all too rare these days but although Mr. Brundell is not going to be charged with any offence against his daughter, the odds of being right by doing right are stacked against the middle-class, white family.

Last words to Mrs. Brundell. She explains, "Her friends were not nice. Just because they came from not terribly well off families doesn't mean that they have to act the way they do. Their behaviour was really quite nasty. We are not an exotic family, we are old fashioned. I just want to protect my children, I want to be able to keep them on the straight and narrow. We are being shamed all the way along the line, but if we can get our daughter right it will have been worth it. I don't agree with child abuse or hitting a child really hard, but I'd like to be able to ground my daughter when she's been bad and I don't want her to be able to turn around and say, I want my rights'. I want the right to be allowed to be a good parent. I want to turn back the clock. Is that so wrong".

No, it's not. Unfortunately, government officials and social workers have other ideas and these do not include the traditional family unit.

Some little while ago we decided to move our gas and electricity custom to Saga. Following our decision to use their telephone service, Glyn says that it's now like living with the cast of "*Last of the Summer Wine*". Things are actually moving as we have just received a letter from Southern Electric informing us of their "sorrow" that we have left, as our "custom is important to them". The letter goes on to state how efficient they are and invites us to fill in a questionnaire as to why we are leaving. I have. And I cited price in all the reply columns. According to the third paragraph of their letter, they will shortly be offering exciting new products and services. How can electricity be exciting? I'm sure it won't be long before I read that it's sexy. Anyway, these will include discounted insurances and a number of special tariffs tailored to "suit your lifestyle". If we are not satisfied with our new supplier we can return any time by phoning the Welcome Line. Isn't that nice!

I drove back from Cornwall last Wednesday evening in the pouring rain. It only stopped, or rather the windscreen wipers only started to squeak as I approached Fleet Services on the M3. It is now Sunday evening. Glyn and I have had our first shot of football, i.e. we watched "*Match of the Day*". Chelsea won and Charlton won. Today, still good news. Manchester United could only draw at Everton, one of the favourites for the drop. Can't see it myself, I think this year's relegation battle could throw up a few surprises. That is Watford not going down. It could be the season when Coventry City finally surrender their premier position, but then I've been wrong on that one for the last thirty years. Sheffield Wednesday are another that I feel could struggle this season.

Whilst I think of it, is their manager, Danny Wilson, the father of Ashley in "*Coronation Street*". They do bear a striking resemblance to each other, don't they. Oh, you can't see it, well fair enough then.

An article in today's *Sunday Telegraph* confirms that street crime in London has now risen by some 35% since the Lawrence Report was published in February and police have thought twice about stopping black people. I know it has been discussed before, but the fact that the papers consider the subject worthy of continued comment says a lot for the harm it has caused.

Glen Smyth, Chairman of the Metropolitan Police Federation, said that officers are "increasingly reluctant to tackle suspects from ethnic minorities". He added that the "anti-police culture" in the Home Office under Labour was undermining the fight against crime. Appointing the former squatters' rights campaigner, Lord Bassam of Brighton as a minister was "like putting Dracula in charge of a blood bank".

Well done, MacPherson. Your report has certainly helped the safety of Britain's citizens, black and white.

Any reticence felt that this government wasn't all GM crazy are dashed when one reads that Lord Sainsbury, he who has invested millions into the industry, is to be in charge of drafting new laws to boost GM technology. This move is appalling and an affront to every living soul in this country. Sainsbury, a shopkeeper by trade, has written the report which proposes new planning rules to foster the growth of biotechnology companies. He has been closely involved in a number of companies that produce GM crops. It is only a few months ago that the government stated that Lord Sainsbury would play "no part" in GM food policy, so that didn't take long to turn round, did it? How can someone like him view the industry independently with all that potential profit at stake?

Only last week the Department of Trade and Industry announced that Lord Sainsbury's report related to medical research and that he had not visited any company involved in GM foods. It now appears that these denials were slightly wide of the mark.

What really grates is to read that our good lord's report indicates a change in planning regulations that currently prevent local authorities blocking the development of the industry. These are the bulldozing tactics of bullies. Where are you now, Michael Meacher? Speak up! Or are you being worked from up the backside by the unseen, murky fist of fate?

Any doubts one may have about over-reaction to these scientific advances are brought into context by the announcement that genetically modified fish are being developed by the Americans and Chinese. English Nature, advisers to the government, suggest that these fish should only be released into British waters if they are made infertile. Even if agreement were reached between interested parties for that premise to be implemented, would you trust scientists to toe the line? Their preoccupation with knowledge is akin to a burglar ignoring an open window.

Again, other than for profit, why would anyone wish to inject salmon with a gene that makes the fish grow at up to fifty times its natural rate in the wild. Previous tests on fish and chickens have found that those with "growth promoters" average 22% larger than naturally reared species. Any release is bound to have an impact on the wild population of any given specie.

It wasn't until a report last week that the nation at large was informed of previous British experiments with GM fish in Loch Fyne, Argyll. These experiments had been terminated due to concerns that the "rules of containment" were not strong enough.

Some of these salmon have escaped into rivers and shown distinct changes from natural varieties. The most startling revelation is that wild salmon have continued to decline in the affected waterways. So what's in it, then, for a government who is obviously more informed than you or I. There has to be more to it than money, surely, and please don't insult me by mentioning "feeding the world", for that is a very oversized, genetically modified red herring!

It was sad to read that Helen Rollason has died. There was no concealing the fact that Nikki, her 16-year-old daughter was the catalyst for her amazing strength and fortitude and but for her, she may well have died some time ago. Miss Rollason was a very brave lady and her daughter can be justifiably proud of her mum.

Two on consecutive days, huh! First, it's Lord Archer, who quite reasonably commented that years ago "your head did not turn in the road if a black woman passed because they were badly dressed, they were probably overweight and they probably had a lousy job".

The trouble that little line has caused. Headlines or major stories in all the papers, plus taking up half of the one o'clock news on *Radio 4*. Condemned with relish by all as another gaffe. Why? He was only stating an observation that he, and probably many others, made all those years ago. The *BBC's* holiday presenter commented that Lord A. is "either particularly naive, particularly ignorant or showing his colour". Unfortunately, that is a stereo-typical response from one who should know better. Even Ken Livingstone, whom I normally admire (not always agree with, but admire) refutes L.A.'s memory of the early days of mass immigration. The way I remember it, L.A. is right. However, blacks and Asians were still uncommon in Battersea during the fifties and early sixties. Bus trips to Harlesden and Peckham provide me with similar memories.

The day after, comes Prince Philip, no stranger to foot and mouth syndrome, who observed that a fuse box in a high-tech electronics company looked as if it had been put in "by an Indian". Naturally, there was a place in the Press for the offended, the shocked and the disgusted to overstate their case. The remedy for these sad individuals, those who are so easily offended, shocked and disgusted, is to direct their affronteries to more important issues, such as, will Tommy Archer be convicted of vandalising the GM crops, and will Caroline Bone eventually find true love?

I am writing this piece from a headland overlooking Weymouth. The street lights, which came on for about ten minutes, have now been turned off again. The sky is light once more and that much hyped eclipse is over for a while. Yes, it got cold, yes it got windy, but it didn't, however, get very dark - all a bit of a let down really.

The doom and gloom merchants got it wrong, however. I haven't spotted any dead bodies, the earth is continuing to rotate and ice cream is still being served at the kiosk opposite. Yup, all seems pretty normal.

Also overstated, apparently, were claims made by Monsanto. This untrustworthy company claimed in an advertisement that its GM potatoes and tomatoes had been given approval in twenty countries, including the UK. They also stated that their hideous technical processes, or genetic engineering as they put it, were an extension of traditional breeding. Also untrue were claims that the testing of GM foods had been going on for twenty years, whereas it is closer to sixteen.

A Monsanto spokesman said, "We regret the fact that these statements were not in strict conformity with the Advertising Standards' Agency code. It was not our intention to mislead or deceive. (*Oh, right!*) and we apologise to anyone who might have misunderstood our statements" (*you mean, taken in by lies*) {author's italics}. The ASA appears to have all the backbone of a jellyfish and is under fire for its soft slapping of the genetically modified wrist. I wonder who pulled the strings there?

Now here's a case that should never have reached the courts. In 1994 Sarah Field from Cheltenham was surrounded by four men in combat attire as she and her husband attempted to enter a rock festival. They jeered and jumped on her car. They were so aggressive that Mrs. Field feared for her life. Unbeknown to her, a complete twat called Roger Gedge crept under her front bumber to stop her from driving off. Gedge and his four accomplices had spent the day drinking alcohol. One had spent his dole money on lager and cider before they took a bus to the park. (So, who paid for their alcohol and bus fares - was that us again?)

These five "people" had attacked the car in front of Mrs. Field with an advertising board, so the scene was set for further confrontation. One of the thugs tried kicking in the windscreen whilst he was bouncing up and down on her bonnet. Another was on the roof, attempting to punch in the sun roof. It must have been horrendous. In panic, she drove forward, over a bump, totally unaware that the "bump" was the Gedge person. His legs were jammed between a wheel and the bodywork as she accelerated away. The other thugs gave chase, yelling and bawling at her. Gedge had to have his leg amputated and according to his legal eagle, can now only do light work - which is an improvement from what he did five years ago! He was a self-confessed "New Age" traveller, or scrounger to those of us who supported him financially.

Mrs. Field was 22 years old at the time and for Mr. Bacon, Gedge's QC, to accuse her of "exaggerating" the attack, is insulting in the extreme. This thoroughly unpleasant man stands to win some £500,000 in compensation if he is successful in court. The judge will decide tomorrow. I'd like to know how there is a case to answer, although one thing is for sure, it will be us who ends up paying for it. Surely it should be the other way round. Mrs. Field should be able to claim for harassment, abuse, physical and psychological aggression, etc. She and her husband eventually abandoned their car and ran for their lives, while those out of their heads on drink, continued attacking the car with iron bars, fists and feet. Nice people.

The pro-hunting lobby is made up of some strange characters. Take the Duke of Buccleuch, who declares that, "This is 95% about class warfare and 5% animal welfare". I don't know of *any* anti-hunt supporter who considers the issue to be about class. I am beginning to believe that this class argument is a sympton of "burning martyr syndrome" and a cop out to mask the real issues concerning animal suffering.

You can't sack a black or Asian actor and expect to get away with it, even if it's justified but then, when did justification ever have a role in a racial issue. The actor, Saeed Jaffrey, has been sacked from the cast of *"Coronation Street"*. Frankly, I'm not surprised, his acting was woeful. He is wooden, over the top and appears to be reading his lines. He asks, "Would they have treated a British actor like this?" I presume he means a white, British actor. Well, actually, yes. Hundreds of white

269

actors have been killed off, left town, etc. ever since the first soap appeared nearly fifty years ago. In the same article that announced your demise, I also noted that a replacement Asian actor is likely to join the cast as a screen relative. So how can there be a race issue with your departure? Dear Mr. Jaffrey, this has nothing to do with your being Asian but merely your inability to pass muster as an actor in this particular programme. Yes, I have seen you in other films and series, and have considered your acting of a perfectly reasonable standard. Still, if you want to take it personally.....

The heading on page 15 of the *Daily Express*, "Can Hague be Hunky?" is a hoot. His wife, Ffion, wishes to change his image to one of a family action man. Now this is sad, when the leader of a political party has to get his wife to re-invent him. Tony Banks was right. William was a "foetus", is a "foetus" and always will be a "foetus"! Mr. Banks's assertion some time ago that "If the Catholic church had seen him first, their ideas on abortion might well have changed" is a line that always makes me smile. It might not be word-for-word, but the sentiments are there! How refreshing, how Tony Banks.

Roy Keane is still of the opinion that he is bigger than Manchester United. The problem is that he could be proved right. The Club have apparently increased their offer to £40,000 a week. The Irishman is also to be guaranteed a £2 million testimonial and other win bonuses. In total, some £12 million could be winging its way Keane-wards over the next five years. The floodgates, if he does sign, will be open for every other player to ask "What about me?" Say the figure again - £40,000 a week and Keane is still thinking it over. I'd tell him to bugger off in no uncertain terms. If ever there was a justifiable case of cutting your nose to spite your face, then Keane's your man.

Aha, sanity prevails - well, it's back on a day excursion anyway! That Gedge person who was run over as his accomplices attacked Mrs. Field's car is to be awarded the square root of bugger all. The Recorder, Iain McLaren, rejected the ex-New Age traveller's claim for compensation. He told Gedge that payment for damages "would not accord with common sense" however serious his injuries.
It still rankles that Gedge's lawyer, that nice Mr. Bacon, QC, argued that Mrs. Field had been negligent in not seeing him crawl beneath her car and had failed in her "duty of care" by not stopping when she sensed something was under her car. Can he be serious about this? I know he

has a job to do, i.e. defending worthless oiks, but even he must occasionally feel that enough is enough and not take the case. Would he have put this argument if *his* wife had been in Mrs. Field's place. Of course not. There's a group of drunken yobs stomping on your bonnet, kicking in your windscreen, pummelling your sun roof, and you consider as you attempt to extricate yourself and car from the situation, "what is that bump? I wonder if it is another one of those lovable rogues stuck under the offside front wheel".

Fortunately, Mr. Bacon's defensive pleas fell on extremely deaf and just ears. The Recorder summed up by saying, "One has to sympathise with any man injured to the extent of the claimant (*I don't*) but my judgement is that English law provides him with no remedy". Leave to appeal was also refused.

What does rankle is that Legal Aid will foot most of the £50,000 bill - that's you and I, once again - while Mrs. Field's insurers will have to stump up 15%. That's £7,500. Why?

Who advised the Gedge character to initiate proceedings? Who *authorised* the case which was reliant on public funding? With a bit of luck, Mrs. Field will get over the awful event in time and Gedge will always have his memories - with every step he takes.

I wonder how well Jack Straw will keep the lid on his beloved asylum seekers' lack of social graces in Dover. The headline, "Asylum seekers stab eleven teenagers" is not a surprise, it was just a question of when. The Home Office is to hold talks with council leaders in Kent. I have no doubt whatsoever that the gist of the conversation will be "We don't want any backlash from the public, so play it down, call it isolated incidents - two sides to every story". The Kosovans will come out smelling of roses and as white as the cliffs they're living on. The nation will be portrayed as right wing extremists, intent on confrontation. Send them back, they are not wanted!

Interesting, isn't it, that Tony and Cherie Blair were quite happy to ignore the requests by animal rights groups not to watch the Palio horse race in Sienna. As usual, a horse was hurt during this hideous practice. Animal right activists in both Italy and Britain have petitioned for the race to be banned due to the number of horses injured or killed. The race is conducted over the cobbled streets of the town. Since 1970 forty three horses have died in the race. Wouldn't you have thought that the Blairs might have put the animals' welfare before their own desire to witness the spectacle, instead of appearing to give it their seal of approval. No, neither would I, really!

They seem to be immune in all walks of political life, don't they. Nothing seems to be learned concerning the public reaction to GM crops. The government have announced that another four test sites covering one hundred acres will begin production shortly. These will be followed by another eighty sites next year. I wonder how much ear-bending the Americans gave us this time. Hopefully, it will end in ruined crops and frustration for all those hell-bent on quick profits.

I've just read the above pieces having unpacked my travelling case here in deepest Cornwall. Yes, I'm still hopping from holiday centre to holiday centre, distributing puzzle magazines, checking stocks and re-arranging displays. I'm back here in Newquay before moving east towards Bude and Barnstaple. Home Thursday evening. I'm staying at a farmhouse just outside of Newquay and very attractive and traditional it is, too. A sign of the times, I suppose, the view from the front porch is one of rolling hills, bales of hay, agricultural equipment and beautifully made stone walls. From my bedroom window at the back of the house I look across the roof of the newly opened Safeways Supermarket. The development is a typical out-of-town site, adjacent to a roundabout, from which another spur extends some twenty yards before losing its way in a field. You just know that within a very short time that field will be another retail park development. Alongside Safeways is a small field which already has a sign declaring "Retail development land for sale". There is a public house just the other side of the roundabout, so I shall pop up there later and grab a bite to eat. In the meantime, I'll tell you of our weekend in the Czech Republic.

Maureen and I intended going over some time ago, as I mentioned. Friends of ours, Peter and Madeleine, during a conversation expressed a desire to join us. Outcome was that, last Thursday evening they arrived at our house, having journeyed from Somerset, and we travelled up to Heathrow together. We stayed overnight at a Travelodge, which was found after great difficulty at the end of an industrial estate in Heston. It's rare for a hotel to be quite so well hidden. I even drove past it and found myself in a lorry park, before realising my mistake. Good rooms, a good night's sleep, well I slept well anyway, before we drove to the long term car park at Heathrow early on Friday morning.

The flight was uneventful, save for the delay caused by the luggage conveyor breaking down (we had to carry our own suitcases through to the boarding area). We sat on the tarmac for about fifty minutes due to our losing our flightpath. Still, we were treated to the dubious delights of a party of twenty-somethings, all male, from the West Midlands, whose exuberant, childish behaviour fortunately never turned nasty, but

272

you always felt a couple of alcoholic drinks could tip the balance.

Two of them hadn't started off in our good books back at passport control. I wasn't aware that the lady in front of me said quite forcefully, "We are all queueing, you know". The reference was made to a tall, muscular man who wore a cap, peak backwards, which speaks volumes, and another young man who pushed their way in. They explained that they were late for their flight and retained their new found space in the queue. They turned out to be two of the group from the West Midlands. Aware now that people were pushing in, I espied a Frenchman creeping up on my offside. He asked me if he could "go first" as he had a flight to catch. I reminded him that we all had a flight to catch. He showed me his boarding card, 06.50 it read. Quick as a flash, Maureen showed him ours - 06.50 again! I informed him that he really must not panic and that in England, we queue and it's really bad form to push in! I used the words "fortitude" and "stoic". I urged him to take a leaf out of our book and remain calm. I smiled as I told him that he would catch his flight. He smiled weakly but stood behind us!

Arriving at Prague airport I duly held up a yellow A4 cardboard sign which proclaimed, "Fat Bastard Tours - a division of Pink Helmet Inc". John was there to meet us, preening self-assuredly and becoming ever-more like his hero, Basil Fawlty. Outside in the coach waiting area behind a line of super-duper double deckers, luxury single deckers and various upmarket people movers, lurked an unclean, Toyota Hiace 9-seater. Yellow A4 card sheets were attached to the front, rear and side windows, announcing "Fat Bastard Tours and Déja Vu Tours". As John says, with a Déja Vu tour, you only think you have seen all the sights - twice!

Everybody aboard and in good form we travelled south to Bohemia. It's about as far as travelling from Guildford to Chichester and then doing another sixty miles across the sea, or in other words, Guildford to Yeovil. The village of Bechyne is a typical Czech town, a mix of old world charm and Russian built grey slab flats. Luckily, the two are rarely alongside. The old town stands intact with very few concrete additions. Bechyne's population is around 7,500, so it's not what you'd call a big town. Mondays are much the same as Sundays. The town square comes alive very slowly, the cobbled roads vibrate to the sounds of souped up and not so souped up Skodas, Ladas and Trabants, along with a smattering of newer Octavias, Golfs and Audis. By souped up, I mean the colour coded wheel hub-caps and four inch faring mounted above the boot edges.

In typical style John rang ahead on the mobile phone and ordered drinks to be ready for us in the bar on our arrival. They were. Hana, his girlfriend who owns the restaurant and pension (B & B to you and I) runs it with her daughter, Gabi. This time they were assisted by another Gabi (Gabi 2) who is a rather beautiful law student, filling in part-time. I wanted to take her home to England as hand luggage, but Maureen said no. She was very nice about it, but I felt she would not change her mind on this one!

Peter and Madeleine were clearly impressed with the place. Peter was clearly impressed with Gabi 2, too. Their good impressions were a relief as there is nothing worse than waxing lyrically about somewhere and then finding that your enthusiasm is not shared by your fellow travellers. The restaurant can seat 45, all meals are prepared freshly and all washing up done by hand - Hana and Gabis', both 1 and 2. There are no dishwashers.

Due to John's involvement, menus are in both Czech and English. I have to tell you it is a pure delight (a very self-indulgent one, I know) to find that in this distant land you can find a meal entitled "Mel's mixed grill". It's number 22 on the menu. Unusually, all the dishes have accompanying "stories" to them, which is fine if you are English, but I don't think the humour would translate very well. Those years of austerity seem to have dented quick-wittedness. I'll give you an example-

No. 15 - Soup of Today
- please ask our highly trained staff, they know where to go and find out the facts about this sort of thing.

No. 16 - Soup of Yesterday
- no longer available under this heading. Try Soup of the Day, it's probably the same thing.

No. 17 - Soup of Tomorrow
Please allow 24 hours for preparation or telephone the day before, but then it will be Soup of the Day anyway, so save money on the phone call and just come on over.

Get the picture?
What they are not very good at in the Czech Republic is tea. Maureen always takes a box of eighty Yorkshire teabags as they only provide one in a pot for four, and it stays there after they have replenished the water. You also have to ask for milk and make it plain

that you do not want milk in your lemon tea, as some restaurants appear quite happy for you to do so! Still, what Gabi 2 lost in teamaking she made up for in long legs, large bust and a button nose. If she had understood enough English, I'd have offered the hoary old chestnut, "I dreamt about you last night". She would have replied "Did you?" And I would have uttered the punch line, "No, you wouldn't let me". The exercise, however, would have been lost about half-way through the first line. It wasn't helped that her boyfriend kept popping in and overseeing her conversations with customers and guests. He is actually so tall that he has to duck under the door when entering and exiting. John also informed me that he was a Black Belt in something or other, which was another reason I decided not to pursue the possibility of Gabi staying at our house if ever she happened to come to England. Anyway, what would I want with a 20-year-old when I have my love to keep me warm? That's right, isn't it Maureen? Why is she hitting those keyboard keys quite so hard as I dictate this bit to her. Women! One long change of life!

Anyway, back in Bechyne. On Saturday morning, it was decided that Fat Bastard Tours would hit the road at around 10 am and travail the southern towns of Chesky Budovice and Chesky Krumlov - both interesting historic towns in their own rights. On the way we would stop off at a castle constructed so as to mirror Windsor, now restored and a veritable priceless gem, with gardens and sculptures galore. FB Tours parked right in the gardens away from the other tourists who had to park at the bottom of the hill and then walk up. I have to say I had some reservations as to whether the valiant steed would have been clamped as it stood in rustic (sorry, rusty) isolation amongst the castellated splendour. Apparently the word "tour" is fairly universally accepted and a sticker in the window, regardless of any prefacing words, works wonders.

Our journey to the castle was, however, interrupted some five miles short, when we became aware of the temperature gauge shooting to red at an alarming rate. It was while we attempted to overtake an ageing Skoda that this catastrophe occurred. We stopped. John, Peter and I alighted, the women sat inside. John and Peter looked at the water being expelled with great velocity from under the nearside, halfway down the van (oops, sorry, people carrier). I stood alongside, hands on hips, uttering comments like, "Cor" and "gosh" and tutting. I was, in all honesty, pretty useless. Both Peter and John fingered their beards and uttered words like "typical", "shit" and "bugger".

It transpired that the rubber tubes which ran to the rear in order to provide heat had burst. According to John who had taken to lying on a mat, one had a tap at the end of the metal pipe which, given the right tools, could be turned to the shut position. He had the tools. The other, however, was not so well endowed. While John attempted to cut back the rubber pipe, Peter and I went in search of bottles. We had parked alongside open land, the main road was raised above the surrounding countryside. I asked Maureen if she would join us in looking for bottles. She declined. Typical! She and Madeleine alighted and stood a little way from the van, distancing themselves from any involvement. Again, typical! They did what women do best in these circumstances, chatted.

Peter located some bottles in a dried up stream bed. They were sitting on a metal grille. Dressed in shorts and sandals, along with short-sleeved shirt he was ideally placed to get himself dirty. Well, he had spent many years in South Africa and has been used to shooting anything that moves. His wanderings with these bottles in search of water brought a cry from some woodland. "Over here". Maureen assessed my attempts at clambering along the bank as looking like a "nancy boy". I have to say I'm not very good at getting dirty! I remember I once got grease in my fingernails - you must have read about it in the *Evening Standard* surely!

Peter had stumbled upon a lake. Upon it, not in it. It was covered in algae and one approached it by scrambling over a wall and under broken fencing. He scrambled, I handed over the bottles. I felt it was far better that he grazed his knees than me dirtying my trousers and trainers. After all, I'd only just bought these trainers, £17.99 Ascots, from Shoefayre in Aldershot. I don't buy rubbish, you know!

Armed with nine full bottles of water we made our way back to the minibus - *that's* the word. John said he needed a bung which with our combined years in the motor trade should not have been hard to come by! This bung, however, should be able to stop water from pouring out onto the road. Once more our brave hero in shorts extracted from somewhere upon his person a knife of many uses. He set off into the bushes once more. John was still lying under the van, I could only see his legs. I bent slightly, hands on knees, feeling I should be contributing something other than "Ah" and "uhm". I even tried to look interested but I'm not very good at lying. It was at this point that John's face emerged from beneath the vehicle. He looked up at me. "You weren't joking, all those years ago, when I drove 200 yards from your house, having bought a car only for it to break down and you say to me, It was all right when I bought it'. I always thought that behind that faáade of ignorance was a con-man. Now I know that you were just a complete wuss."

The wooden bung was inserted. No tears were shed by the Toyota as it was pushed further up its orifice. We realised that we were nowhere near a monastery as the slightest whiff of a bung would have brought them running. "Me next, me next!" (In Czech of course).

Within half an hour we were once more on our way with our temporary repair holding good. "Whittling Willis's Willowy Wonder" won the day and the thanks of his fellow travellers.

The tour was completed and we adjourned to the restaurant for a meal on our return, before relaxing in the bar. On the Friday night we had been joined by another couple - American - who left early Saturday morning, so our meeting was brief. The fourth and final bedroom was taken by an 18-year-old Irish actor, called Gavin, an extremely pleasant and presentable young man from Derry. (Londonderry to some). We discussed the Irish question long into the night. What it did prove was that it is possible to discuss, excuse, mull over a contentious and passionate subject without fists flying and tempers fraying. Not once did the conversation get out of hand, despite fairly large quantities of alcohol being consumed.

The following day, Sunday, Hana and Gavin joined the merry bunch of sightseers as we headed south-west to the mountains and ski country, where Hana has a house within the boundaries of a National Park. The only problem is time to restore this former hunting lodge. Another good day, with great food at ridiculously low prices (by English standards). The average Czech wage is £120 per month. The exchange rate is $2\frac{1}{2}$ pints to the pound. So good news there!

I questioned with John the fact that out of the B & B's two toilets only one had a key. "I know", he replied, "last week we had a German family staying for a few days and they literally reserved a toilet for themselves. They took the key with them when they went out so that no-one else could use it, and when they left the key went with them". Isn't that bloody typical! Their selfishness meant that the three rooms had to share one toilet. Just who do they think they are? Well, above us, obviously!

John explained that he offered one American couple the option of speaking to them in American English or "proper" English. The Americans were curious to know the difference. "Well", said John, "if I address you in American English, I'd say, the Czechs drive on the left hand side whilst the English drive on the right hand side of the road', whereas in proper English, I'd say, the Czechs drive on the left hand side whilst the English drive on the correct side of the road'". The point was hopefully taken.

A modified (and to be patented) bung replaced the temporary version, a Jubilee clip was tightened over the pipe and an otherwise faultless series of journeys were made. We stopped off at a local brewery, where we seven travellers alighted for beers, coffee and tea. It cost the equivalent of £1.35 for the lot! Earlier, deep in the mountains, we had had a meal for seven, main course, beers, etc. The total cost was £10.45p. Very cheap if you're a tourist.

We left at lunch time yesterday, Monday, for a trip to Prague and a tour of the city, before making our way to the airport for the 8 pm flight back to Heathrow. A good time had been had by all. John is framing book covers from this and the previous titles and hanging them on a wall in the restaurant. As he said, "I'll put them up the day before your next visit, and take them down the second you've gone!"

I was going to give you his address, wan't I. It's the "Pichluv Dum", Pension and Restaurant, Nam.T.G.Masaryka 141, 391 65, Bechyne, Czech Republic - telephone number, 00420 361811075. Just ask for John if you want to have a meaningful conversation in English, or say nothing, and listen to someone jabbering on in Czech! Before I leave this subject, I extol the virtues of another couple of dishes from the English selection. Remember, all main courses are around the £2 to £3 mark, with soups at about 40p and starters and desserts from around 80p to £1.

One of the starters is Tuna with Lemon. As John explains, "No dolphins were harmed during the preparation of this dish - there weren't any in the kitchen at the time!"

No. 25 has a quaintly long-winded appendage. It's Breaded Pork Steak, in the Viennese style, but made locally. (75KC, which is £1.50). *"Note: Vienna is about 200 Km away and therefore our dish is fresher, because we make it here and you would have to wait ages if we had to go and get it, but it would give you time to order the Soup of Tomorrow. Transport charges extra. There is also a Vienna in the USA, but it would be ridiculous to go there, and anyway, they don't know the first thing about cooking. Actually, Fred's Diner isn't that bad, the breakfast is really quite good and his coffee great, by American standards, as much as you can drink for $1. Anyway, we don't offer a Soup of Next Week - yet - so just order the Wiener Schnitzel and get on with it!"*

No. 35 is Fillet of Fish - seasoned with rosemary - *"A genetically engineered boneless square fish, commonly known as freezer fish. Everyone agrees it's very good. John likes it with salt and vinegar, wrapped in newspaper, but Hana won't do it and she won't tell him who*

Rosemary is either".

Their range of potatoes is both excellent and sometimes non-existent!

No. 40 in the list of side dishes is French Fried Potatoes, which adds, *"Not quite accurate because they are Czech potatoes and fried here!"*

No. 41 - Roast Potatoes - *"These are potatoes exposed to extreme temperatures in a confined space"*.

No. 42 - Baked Potatoes - *"Lowered whilst still alive into boiling water - no, sorry, that's lobsters isn't it"*.

No. 43 - Fried Potatoes - *"Yesterday's boiled potatoes but marketed under an exciting new name"*.

No. 44 - Mashed Potatoes - *"As boiled but subjected to severe punishment using a devillish device imported at great expense from England, only to find that we could buy a better one right here for less money. Typical that, isn't it!"*

No. 45 - Croquet Potatoes - *"These have been bashed around the lawn using a wooden mallet to line them up and knock through loops, but I could be wrong"*.

No. 47 - Raw Potatoes - *"As boiled but cheaper and quicker to serve"*.

No. 48 - Potato Surprise - *"Don't know what this is yet but it could be nice"*.

No. 50 - Diet Potatoes - *"None at all, absolutely nothing. Bugger all, but just think of the calories you are saving"*.

Me, again. Hope the above gives you a "taster" of what to expect. John is quite happy to drive, be tour guide and take money from visitors whilst trekking into the great unknown.

But be quick! Within a few years the Czech Republic will be part of the EC, prices will rise, red tape will strangle society and the Germans will have bought up half a country they considered rightfully to be their own anyway.

Hope John is pleased with this plug. Very few caterers and B & B's have such free publicity - well, it's not exactly free, it's £5.99's worth anyway, providing someone buys the book. Well, you did, you couldn't have fingered through this far. What's that? Someone loaned it to you? Should be a law against that sort of thing!

Right, I'm off to the pub before they stop serving food. Byee.

CHAPTER TWELVE:

AND FINALLY

It's Wednesday night and I'm staying at the Bay View Hotel in Widemouth Bay, near Bude in Cornwall. I've already eaten, watched *"Fools and Horses"* and I'm back upstairs in my room, overlooking the beach.

There was a timely piece in today's *Daily Express* concerning Roy Keane, who still hasn't signed a new contract with United. The columnist reminds us that "If Manchester United want confirmation that Roy Keane's statement is only a smokescreen before he leaves for masses more money, they only have to remember what happened when he went to them five years ago. Keane was at Nottingham Forest and he'd ducked and dived for weeks about whether he was staying or going. Then he did a front page article in the Nottingham evening paper pledging his love for the city and his loyalty to the club. He even signed a new three-year contract. Inside two months he had left".

Brian Clough was manager and he was infuriated by the matter.

Keane had got money up front from Forest for the new contract and then another wedge from United for joining them. Money as ever dictates loyalty".

That piece was written by their columnist John Wragg. I altered this short article not a jot. He is absolutely right and it puts Mr. Keane's ambitions into perspective somehow.

Today's *Express* also highlights the futility of awarding "blue flags" for clean beaches, mainly because they're not. Earlier this month a young girl died from an E-Coli infection. She had been holidaying at Dawlish Warren. There had been other outbreaks of the E-Coli 0157 strain among tourists in the area. Every food outlet has been checked and found to be exempt from blame. Now the resort beach flies the blue flag, indicating cleanliness. How is it so, when the outfall pipe discharges untreated sewage from 12,000 people straight into the sea? What a farce. It now appears that the "stringent" laws used to enforce and monitor standards aren't as stringent as we would like. The

Environment Agency has used a legal loophole which enables South West Water to discharge raw sewage close to a beach. Many visitors complain of faeces, sanitary towels, condoms and toilet paper swirling about in the sea or thrown up onto the beach. The publishers of the Good Beach Guide advise bathers not to swim in the sea at Dawlish.

Are visitors expected to read guide books as well as swotting up on the merits of a blue flag? Clearly, a blue flag beach can mean a brown flag. How did the Tidy Britain Campaign award a flag of any colour when there is clearly a cleanliness problem. Although there is no evidence that anyone has been "paid" to award a flag, it does cross your mind for more than a second!

See, I told you so! Tension is running high between locals and Kosovans in Dover. As you know, teenagers have been stabbed and slashed by "refugees" with Stanley knives. The local MP offers empty words, while the government promises to meet to discuss the problem but can't sort out a date yet! Parents are claiming that these foreigners are running amok with knives and razors. On parent said, "The police have told us that the culture of refugees is different and we have to respect that". What a disgrace. Doubtless that loaded claptrap was sent from the Home Office to Dover so that the mouthpieces and puppets would not upset those who are laughing in our faces. Hallo, Number Ten, is anyone in? Or even alive.

Two pieces of good news, now. Firstly, protesters have destroyed another field of GM sugar beet, the trial crop had been planted on behalf of that Monsanto company.

The other piece marks a joyous occasion. D'you remember my mentioning a couple of chapters ago, or several chapters ago, there was the case of the German couple living in Hambrook, near Bristol, who decided to increase the size of their front garden by incorporating the village green. You do remember? Thank Christ for that. I thought you were going to ask me to turn back page after page until we found it!

Well, the good news comes in the form of photographs - and you'll like this - taken during the Second World War by the Luftwaffe. These have come in very handy and prove beyond reasonable doubt that Thomas and Isabela Gehrke have been pulling someone's bells. The disputed land was in use as a village green during the war, just as locals said it was. Bloody Krauts! Not content with moving in, they try and take land which isn't theirs without a by-your-leave. What's worse, they think you won't notice. I'd give a lot to be at the "handing over" ceremony when they have to take down their fence and retreat, just like they did in Russia, France, Belgium, Poland .....

When will Social Services and their masters get it right. They never manage to find a happy medium, although Doris Stokes caused a titter occasionally! D'you remember reading of a 48-year-old father who smacked one of his daughters at a dentist's because she refused to go into the surgery. After much publicity caused when the police were called and the father was subsequently arrested and convicted of assault, the debacle over smacking raised its rump again. Readers and listeners were invited to air their views on the subject. Radio phone-ins, daytime TV chat shows all raised the subject; endless analysis brought yes/no votes and as usual, there was an overwhelming vote of confidence in parental rights to smack - not abuse, but smack their children.

This poor chap not only has to suffer the indignation of being charged and convicted, but now finds his three children aged 8, 6 and 1 are the subject of a Supervision Order. The 8-year-old daughter is apparently very distraught, having heard the news. Her father commented that he and his wife were worried that they would now be questioned about the slightest scratch found on their children. They are to appeal against the decision which gives rise to his feelings that this is a witch hunt.

Talk about over the top! This little piece of S.S. histrionics comes in the same week as another division of this Big Brother outfit is blamed for allowing a 13-year-old girl in its care to die from a drugs overdose. Despite being in "safe accommodation" the young girl was free to come and go and ply her trade as a prostitute in Kings Cross, London.

Poor old Black Jack Straw. If anyone is whiter than white over race, then tis he. But even he has succumbed to being reported to the CRE for comments made concerning travellers. All he said, in a radio interview was, "many so-called travellers seem to think that it is perfectly okay for them to cause mayhem in an area, to go burgling, thieving, breaking into vehicles, causing all kinds of trouble, including defecating in the doorways of firms and so on and get away with it". It is true. He did not say *all* gipsies or *all* travellers. Whilst the CRE is apparently not going to take the matter further, they couldn't resist having a go themselves. They said, "The CRE actively opposes any stereotyping of gipsies and travellers because this can damage race relations by creating and reinforcing prejudice." I assume the spokesman has never come into contact with the owners of mansion-style caravans hauled by brand new Mercedes and four-wheel drive vehicles who explode upon a community and leave a wake of destruction.   Ask the shopkeepers how well-mannered the children were. Ask them how much stock they lost and what the reaction was when tackled. Observe the disgusting state of a recreation ground, field or park after police have eventually gone through all the statutory red tape in order to evict these people. Someone, anyone, from the CRE should be made to clear up the damaged trees, the uprooted bushes, the soiled nappies, the dogs' turds and everything else that is left, once they have departed to create mayhem once again a few miles down the road.

I doubt if these CRE wallahs have ever come into contact with anyone outside of their own kind with views that mirror their own. If they had, they would never allow themselves to enter such a dubious quango. The only other outlet for the lack of foresight would have been the world of the traffic warden. Pity they are not able to take the place of a rabbit or baboon in a science laboratory.

Not that Jack can rely on the support from either the Lib-Dems or the Tories on this one. Not surprisingly, the Lib-Dem Home Office spokesman, Richard Allen (no, I'd never heard of him either) accused the good Mr. Straw of inflaming prejudice. He said, "A responsible Home Secretary should be in the business of calming inter-community tension, rather than inflaming them". If he means hushing up any problems in favour of the travellers, why doesn't he have the balls to say so? - Because he represents the Lib-Dems, that's why.

Very disappointed in Ann Widdecombe, who was becoming my shining star of the West, but is now in decline. She said, "Mr. Straw ought to remember he is a statesman, not a Labour politician grubbing around for votes". Liked the use of the word "grubbing" but not the sentiment. Sorry, Ann, nil points!

Sad to tell that a fifth of all crime being committed in this country is by women. The number sent to prison has doubled over the past six years. The majority of crimes are drug offences, shoplifting, fraud and wounding. It is a pity, because most of us hoped that as avenues in business opened up for women, their natural femininity would soften male attitudes. In other words, the very worst aspects of the male ego would dissipate and a more compassionate view of work and life would unfold. This has not proved to be the case. The sharp suit, severe hairstyle and ego to match is no longer the male preserve. Women have copied all the wrong aspects of the male psyche. Their manners have also declined. No longer demure but loud, brash, tarty and with a fag in hand. They strut unsmiling with name badge prominent to indicate power. Sad that in so many cases women have failed to get to grips with the responsibilities they have so eagerly sought. Don't take my word for it - seek out the views of women who work for women - that'll give you some idea.

Eighty eight per cent of all A-level takers recorded pass marks. We really must have a wonderfully educated bunch "coming out" this year. I did hear tell that someone (probably up north) only got a B in one subject. Surely not! I thought A was the minimum acceptable passmark nowadays. If you think I'm just being sarky, wait until next year. Remember, only 12% to go and everyone has passed.

It's an absolute farce. There is no way in the world that given the standard of education pupils receive at this time, that they would have achieved these results in the 1960's.

"How do you know?" I hear you ask. "Do you have proof?" Please, one question at a time. Well, yes, actually I do. Maureen took Human Physiology & Health at GCSE level in evening classes two years ago. She felt she did reasonably well but knew one question had let her down badly. She had no idea how to answer and wrote very little. Also, another question stumped her; again she waffled her way through it. To Maureen's surprise, she was awarded an "A" pass. It's common knowledge that only six marks are awarded for grammar and spelling in any subject and listening to most youngsters, one can see that even twelve years of schooling have failed to make an impression on the rudiments of speech.

And then you read that teaching is losing its credibility as a profession. Well, well!

I feel sorry for the couple in the Marlborough area who sold their beautiful thatched cottage with a view to moving closer to the town centre. They paid a £500 deposit on a brand-new home being built within a very private development.

Village Green Homes of Newbury, the developers, were asking £279,125 for the home of their dreams. Now they reserved the home eight months ago, completion was due in late May. Various hold-ups caused completion to be put back until now - mid August. Despite that, Mr. and Mrs. Francis were encouraged by the developers to choose their kitchen and fireplace and to draw up details with decorators and electricians. Earlier this month they received a letter explaining that as prices in Marlborough had risen significantly over the past few months, the builders - Village Green Homes - "regret that we hereby attach a revised price list ..... for your consideration". The new price has been increased by just over 25% to £350,000. There was going to be a "gesture of good will" by Village Green Homes which would reduce the price to a mere £328,737 - still £50,000 more than the original asking price.

The Francis's cannot alter the sale price on their thatched cottage. Upshot is, they've had to move into temporary rented accommodation until they find another new home. Legally their £500 deposit only holds the sale of the house, *not* the price. No, I didn't know that, either.

Christopher Vokins, a director of Village Green Homes of Newbury, the one who sent the letter, said "The properties were revalued more than two weeks ago and that it was as likely as not that they would increase in price." He did admit that Mr. and Mrs. Francis were not informed that this would happen. He added, "Fortunately for us, but unfortunately for any prospective buyer, the value has increased substantially. Other buyers were aware that house prices were rocketing and we still have five of them proceeding with purchase. We have done nothing more than acknowledge receipt of their deposit. There was no exchange of contracts".

This is sheer greed and a very dirty trick. The builders' material costs have not increased, their site cost has not increased. Village Green Homes of Newbury should have said nothing and accepted the price they offered, to be the one relevant on completion. I would say, typical greedy builders, but I might get stamped upon by the Commission of Building Equality - there's bound to be one. So remember, always buy "Wilkin of Tiptree" jams but don't buy a Village Green Home. With Wilkin of Tiptree the price is clearly marked on the jar.

This is a hoot, literally. Passengers awaiting the 8.08 train from Tonbridge to Redhill were informed that it was delayed due to the driver being held up whilst shopping with his wife (at 8.08 in the morning?) The announcer, last Wednesday, said that the driver was late because some of the shops they planned to visit had not opened on time. At 8.27, when the driver had still not turned up, it was decided to call in a stand-by. Unbelievable! Please note that the service concerned is run by Connex, which is French-owned .....

Do you remember a little while back, when I had a sore eye and I visited the Royal Surrey Hospital and stood there bemoaning the passing of the Cambridge Military Hospital. Our local paper, the

Aldershot News, tells of a letter sent by the leader of Rushmoor Borough Council's Tories to the then Prime Minister, John Major. This letter was sent on 20th February, 1995, by Councillor Geoff Woolger. At that time, the proposed closure of the Cambridge Military Hospital was provoking fierce reaction. No-one wanted to see it close. The idea was to transfer the military staff to the Frimley Park Hospital, where a military wing would be attached. A petition of over 40,000 signatures was due to arrive on the PM's desk during that month. It has now come to light that Mr. Woolger sent this letter pleading "Please, please do not give any credence to the crowds with their banners. I think your officers will find that many of the signatures on the petition are repeated time and time again".

Now Councillor Woolger has been around the political scene for many years. He was elected to work on behalf of the electorate. Writing to the PM to ask that he ignore a petition from people *he* knew to be passionate about the proposal, is quite outrageous. He says, "I know it looks bad .....". It certainly does. I wonder how the voting will go in the next council elections. Makes you wonder if the people who vote for him time and time again will think twice this time. I do hope so.

Time for a little levity! Did you hear about the snobbish potato family, the Maris-Pipers? Well, Mr. Maris-Piper sits his three daughters down and says, "It is time for all three of you to go out into the big wide world and find a husband. I expect you to come back one year from now and bring into the family a potato of whom I can be proud. Remember girls, they must be as we are - of Yeoman stock. "Yes, father", came the reply in unison. And off they go.

One year on, they return to the family home. Mr. Maris-Piper is standing stiff and of upper lip. He is proud and awaiting his daughters' news. The first steps forward. "I have found the potato of my dreams", she sighs. "And who is he?", asks Mr. M-P in severe tones. "Why, he is a King Edward". They all rejoice. "You, daughter No.2?" She steps forward. "Father", she beams, "I am to marry a Jersey Royal!" There is much hugging and tears aflowing before Mr. M-P invites daughter No. 3 to tell all. "Father", she announces, "I wish to marry John Motson". "John Motson", bellows the father. "You can't marry John Motson". "Why?" asks the daughter, now in tears and distraught. "Why?" "Because", exclaims the father, "John Motson is a Commentator".

Forgot to tell you, but I came home last week from my three days at the coast, to find that the small line of trees across the railway line, that Barratt promised to keep as a screen, have gone. Well, all except six. So much for the twenty foot boundary. I contacted Guildford Borough Council's planning department who agreed to send their tree chappie on a site visit. They promised to phone me back. I told them I didn't expect a reply. The last time I rang and discussed the chopping down of trees, one of their heads of planning promised to ring back and let me know the outcome, but I'm only a ratepayer so I never received that phone call. Out of interest, Maureen once wrote to Councillor Fox, the erstwhile leader of Guildford Borough Council, to ask questions about the proposed estate. She even included an SAE. Guess what? Still no reply.

Well I did receive a phone call back. It was to ask me for further details. Later that morning a subsequent call was made to confirm that Barratts had indeed cut down trees which should have been retained. I drove round to the site and found a "hard hat" who was naturally not the person responsible, he was only the Assistant Site Manager who was carrying out orders. The orders, it transpired, had been given the previous week by the Site Manager who was by now on holiday. The Assistant Site Manager confirmed that a GBC tree chappie had called and was to "make a report". I phoned Barratts area office and received an apology from their area manager. I explained that an apology was not an instant replacement for a number of trees. I now await (or rather I don't) a phone call from GBC to inform me when they intend to replace them.

The post has just arrived. I'll just tip onto the table all the crap that's with it. You know, the crap you've never asked for. There's a flyer inviting me to eliminate roof-rot for ever. There's a special carpet cleaning deal for "people in our area and no job's too small"; a carpet warehouse are having a seasonal sale - probably flood damage; Peugeot are extolling the virtues of their range of vehicles; there's a slip inviting applications from would-be paper girls and boys and finally, a flyer from the Co-operative Funeral Services. It comes under the heading "Community Announcement". Apparently there is now a branch "near you". They can offer a "quality, understanding service that meets your needs". They have a 24-hour service line and funeral bonds can be arranged. (What are they?) I think they should freshen up their slogans. What about "You die, we try", or, "It's never a prob - death's our job!" Then again, "Death made easy". Or you could always learn from the Americans - "Burials R us".(Can't type the "R" backwards).

The name Tony Martin will be in the news for a while. He is the farmer who shot a 16-year-old burglar at his farmhouse in East Anglia. He has suffered "dozens" of burglaries over a fifteen year period.

Local people have been telling the Press of police inadequacies when dealing with any local crime. As Mr. Martin's mother noted, "There are a hell of a lot of the police down at his farm now!" The morning this story broke I was travelling from Mortehoe to Ilfracombe and was listening to a debate on *Radio 4* concerning the levels of policing in rural areas. The police spokesman told of how, over the past few years, more and more rural police stations had been closed. Part of the conversation rounded on just how far householders could go when defending their family and property. A legal eagle confessed that it is all a very grey area. I ended up being none the wiser as to my rights, should anyone force their way into our house. As usual, it seems the only clarified rights belong to those of the perpetrator.

It is a sobering thought that rural crime costs £100 million per year. Over thirty thousand vehicles are stolen from rural areas during the same period.

What a shame that Britain will be losing a certain Mr. Pritchett to Australia very shortly. He currently resides in Borough Green, Kent, but has lost faith in this country. Mr. Pritchett was cleared of "wounding with intent" after shooting two burglars with a 12-bore shotgun five years ago. He said do-gooders had destroyed Britain and that "I am sick of the way law abiding citizens are treated here. The politicians pander to the minority and the majority won't stand up to them. There is a lack of discipline, a lack of morals and a lack of ethics in Britain now". Couldn't put it better myself, although I've spent a couple of hundred pages trying!

It will always be a tragedy when a young boy of sixteen is killed when burgling. But you have to accept that it would not have happened, had he not set out to take what wasn't his. He and two accomplices, one of whom was badly injured by gunfire, travelled from Nottinghamshire to East Anglia with the express intention of taking items that were not for sale. They and their kind had already de-stabilised Mr. Martin after years of worry due to the burglaries, so they were 100% to blame for the result. You never know, this could be the catalyst whereby the government actually stands and looks at crime from the victim's point of view - although I wouldn't put money on it.

Instead of charging Mr. Martin with murder, he should be commended for bravery and awarded automatic compensation for trauma and stress against the two survivers, even if it takes them the rest of their lives to pay it off.

The Tories' desperation to be taken seriously is not well served by the likes of David Liddington, their Home Affairs spokesman. Commenting on Jack Straw's very reasonable assessment of travellers, Mr. Liddington says, "Jack Straw is fast becoming the second most gaffe-prone member of the Cabinet after the hapless John Prescott". I assume Black Jack's remarks were the only excuse the Tory had for denegrating both the Home Secretary and John Prescott in the same mouthful. Whatever I think of Mr. Straw's lamentable ability in tackling immigration and the Scroungers' Charter, no-one could accuse him of being gaffe-prone. I have no objection to politicians upholding a view or commentating on any issue. It is the childish ill-informed and unjust criticism for the sake of it, which niggles me. No, "niggles" isn't a racist word - don't even both looking it up in a dictionary in the hope of finding a connection. No, dear reader, I'm not talking to you, it's that person behind you who's looking over your shoulder. Oh, they've gone now.

An article in the *Daily Express* cited a perfect example of Jack Straw's analysis of the problems - travellers not Romanies - create. Four years ago, Swindon Council set up facilities for a 20-van site with running water and electricity. "New-age travellers used the site". The local village of Chiselden witnessed increased crime and vandalism. The site, which cost £250,000 to prepare, is now empty, save for the rubbish these itinerants left behind. The council has now got to spend £15,000 of ratepayers' money in order to clear the site of rubbish and burnt-out vehicles.

Whilst the Home Secretary should not be castigated for his remarks, which in themselves were very ordinary and unremarkable, merely a statement of fact, he cannot escape criticism for his latest pleas regarding the benefit seekers in Dover. He is looking for local councils to accept asylum seekers. If they do not do this willingly they could be forced to accept them. Why? Did the local population offer to take them into their community? No, of course not. Once again, local leaders and the local people have no say in a matter that affects them greatly.

While Jack Straw accuses Ann Widdecombe and the previous Tory administration for the collapse in the Immigration Service, the Tories blame the government. Will no-one stand up and be counted? In this case Michael Howard, the previous Home Secretary, Ann Widdecombe and the present Home Secretary are all as guilty as each other and yet, it is all talk and no do. I suspect in all three cases it's brought about by a desire to posture in public but close the door at the end of the day's work and hope the problem will go away. I have absolutely no doubt that the cutbacks forced upon the Immigration Service by that awful Tory government caused that crisis in the first place. However, the Labour Party have been in power for over two years now and if the Home Secretary, with all his muscle, cannot get to grips with the situation while you and I pay up and look unhappy, then he should hand over the reins to someone - anyone - who can.

Fame and fortune has certainly gone to the Beckhams' heads. I see that a film to be made about them by *ITV* has been dropped because the couple made such unreasonable demands. These include a fee of £50,000, the right to sack staff working on the programme and editorial intrusion. They also demanded 40% of income derived from sales of the film abroad. It is very sad when people begin to believe their own legends and amazingly arrogant that they automatically feel their demands will be met without question. Well done *ITV* for saying no.

Some people get caught due to the strangest of occurrences. David Smith, aged 45, who is/was a youth court magistrate held images of naked boys on his computer. His home in Rochdale was burgled. The burglar tipped off the police concerning the content of the computer and Mr. Smith was arrested. Well, that's his career down the river. He is now listed on the sex offenders' list and is on probation for twelve months. And all because the burglar had a conscience. Just makes you wonder what he was looking for in the first place?

I was very pleased to learn that Hillgrove Cat Farm, which breeds cats for animal experiments, has at last closed. Only when the last experiment has been conducted on animals will the battle have been won. Apparently, concerted and continuous action by protesters finally won the day. The idea of pressurising one establishment at a time seems to be a winner. The time factor is regrettable but if staff feel intimidated and threatened, then so be it. They certainly show no remorse or they couldn't work at these awful places. I listened to PM News on *Radio 4*, a scientist was being interviewed. He deemed it horrendous that staff should receive threats to themselves, their family, their property, etc. It's not nearly as horrendous as the actual harm suffered by the animals in question. I have absolutely no concern or compassion for anyone who is involved in the legalised torture of animals. If these so-called researchers and scientists have to be "frightened" out of their work then once again, so be it. They certainly have not got the moral fibre to walk away from it themselves. I wonder how many go to church and pray for all God's creatures?

Jack Straw has announced that crime will rise by 20%. However, you will only *think* it's rising due to a new system of calculations. So that's all right, then! This will be of little comfort to Tony Martin, who is charged with murder and grievous bodily harm. The police have already received threats of harm to Mr. Martin and the burning down of his property. Who are these people? Do they condone burglary? Would they feel so outraged and in need of retribution if someone burgled their house - bastards!

That nasty, unfeeling white man is doing it again, B'wana. "What?" I hear someone in the background ask. Well, in Redditch, that epicentre of flat-vowel syndrome, the local amateur operatic society had the idea of reviving "Showboat". They planned to stage their production in the council-owned Palace Theatre. One minor problem! All 45 members are white. Joe Brennan, the Society's president and producer, was about to commence rehearsals when he received a letter from Liz Hume-Dawson of the Palace Theatre. She wrote, "I am sorry to say that it is considered inappropriate for actors to black up, because in the light of Redditch's multi-cultural (that word again) community, some people may find it offensive".

Mr. Brennan said, "I am flabbergasted", and went on to say that he did not intend to turn his actors into charcoal black "minstrels", but to use a soft brown make up to distinguish between the cultures. The local Labour controlled councils (knew it!) amenities committee will discuss the matter further, while Phil Mould, the council leader, said members would be gauging reaction from the Afro-Caribbean community.

Why didn't they do that first, if they felt the need to? I ask once again - who was here first?

I'm off to the pub and time is getting short. Are you going to join me for one last drink at the local, before it's turned into a Worm & Carrot themed bar with all the atmosphere of a dental surgery. Shall we walk, it's a nice evening. What's that, why isn't Maureen joining us? Oh, she'll be catching up with the soaps. Apparently over the last few weeks I've encroached on her quality time, all the typing and retyping, but as I said to her, "This time next year we'll probably still be as broke....."

Right, after you. What'll it be? - fine! You grab the stools and I'll order the drinks.

Aaaah, that's better. What's that? How much further is there to go in this book? Well, we're almost there, I'm running out of pages. I had reserved phrases like "He's the life and soul of the crematorium" and "Christ, Jesus would be tearing his nails out". But I couldn't find anywhere to put them - oh, I just have.

As I read, take notes, write, re-write, etc. certain trends become apparent, or reassert themselves. It's ten years since I wrote *"From Where I Sit"* and the world still revolves very slowly. Britain has waved goodbye to its history, which is no longer taught or its interest sought. The decline of animals, birds, fish and insects continues at an alarming rate. Trees throughout the world are being felled at such a pace that another fifty have gone in the time it took you to read this sentence. We have prisons controlled, if not yet run, by the prisoners. Children are committing suicide due to the pressures of schooling and their desperation to attain high grades. Law and order is a completely sick joke. The country is strangled by Brussels red tape, to which we have added another two boxes for good measure. I could go on (please don't, I hear you say).

I tell you what it is, if I stand back and attempt to see the wood for the trees (those that haven't yet been felled) the overriding word that rears itself time after time is "honesty".

The country is no longer honest with itself. Who can you trust? When I was young you trusted the establishment. We had local councils, comprised of amateurs (ratepayers' association) who represented their electorate out of a desire to contribute. Where have all the philanthropists gone? It is now an avenue for the politically ambitious and those out to maximise expenses. The more committees you sit on, the greater the financial reward.

Only this week a local councillor claimed in the paper that he and his fellow elected members were "good value".

Every town had character, built of local materials. They were recognisable, they were not suburbs or sprawling communes that will be tomorrow's focal point for terror. The municipal authority controlled the town's buses. They were painted in the corporation colours, neatly lined out with a coat of arms proudly displayed above the town's name. It wasn't owned by "First" or "Stagecoach" which have all the appeal of a blackhead. The municipal dustcart collected your rubbish. It was not a profit-making centre owned by a contractor, and in many cases a French conglomerate. Our water was included in the rates and again, not owned as ours is locally by a French conglomerate. Gas and electricity may well have been the preserve of the local utility companies but I never remember anyone complaining about the quarterly bills.

Illegal immigrants were dealt with promptly, i.e. they were sent back. The police was an authority I was brought up to respect. Along with everything else, it's all changed. In general, I would not trust the police. There are many individuals within the police force who are good and honourable people but as a collective organisation the corruption, the indiscretions and the cases of them beating their own dogs give little in the way of confidence.

Again, with a few exceptions, you wouldn't trust an MP, in government or not, even less a minister and even less an MEP. You certainly cannot trust those in Europe. When you consider that on top of a British MEP's salary of £45,000, he or she can accrue £152 per day for parliamentary business within the EU, and £76 per day outside. They have life assurance covering private and political life, business class return flights to Brussels or Strasbourg, £25,800 per year to cover expenses such as telephone, postage, computer and fax costs. That's not forgetting the £74,500 annual allowance to cover expenses for the employment of assistants. Then of course, you mustn't forget the £2,000 extra travel allowance for costs incurred in the performance of duties. If you are ill, medical cover will enable you and your family to be reimbursed to the tune of £20,000. And if you leave after three years, you get three months' salary or after five years, you receive six months. And that's before you start on the salaries and expenses of the commissioners, those who are unelected yet control the puppets' strings.

Such is the scale of fraud and mismanagement within the EU, and such is the secrecy and self-advancement, that I foresee the problem growing like Topsy. It is a legalised mafia, a self-perpetuating body out of responsibility but not out of control. And it will continue to gobble up countries in its efforts to expand its control. Czech Republic please note. Stay away. This organisation could be dangerous to your citizens's health and wealth. The EU invites everyone with a tempting, shiny apple, but once bitten, and a core full of maggots infects and the cancer becomes untreatable.

Despite all EU citizens being denied duty free goods, due to the ending of the "perk", it wasn't the end for some. EU commissioners are exempt under the Vienna Conventions of 1961. They will still be able to purchase 400 litres of table wine, 90 litres of spirit and 20,000 cigarettes next time they go tax-free shopping. If they can be so immoral on an issue of relative unimportance, one can see how allegations and mistrust can arise with little difficulty when it comes to multi-million pound contracts.

Our own politicians lie, let down, fail and for a number of reasons there are few with convictions instead of ambitions. If there was even a hint at honesty without monetary consideration would we *really* be planting GM crops.

Like slaves, our colonial past shackles us, despite the little known fact that more white people are victims of racially motivated crime than blacks or Asians. The fact that 52% of race victims in Bradford were white and 35% were Asian is not in keeping with the front page message foisted upon us day in and day out.

Animal laboratories kill 5 million animals per year because they are surplus to requirement - that's not including those who were subjected to torture in the name of scientific advancement. No licence is required to kill these animals. The Home Office recognises it is a problem but says, "It's impossible to accurately predict demand and actual supply" so there's no hint of government involvement there. Seems quite simple to me. If the practice was abolished, there'd be no need to predict demand and actual supply. How can government after government ignore what's going on behind closed doors? There were photographs in the *Sunday Telegraph* dated 22nd November, 1998. One showed rows of rabbits restrained by their necks, like a yoke. This is not right. A second picture was of two small monkeys clasping each other for comfort. Their eyes spoke a thousand words. That photograph will live me forever.

If man wishes to experiment, he should experiment on his fellow man. We have prisons full of murderers, rapists and other undesirables. Let them take the brunt of these "justifiable" experiments.....

What's that? You fancy a packet of beef and mustard crisps.

Back again. Yes, I know, these Brannigans crisps are very good and they're not greasy, are they. What's that? Playing fields, well of course, you're right about these. This government made such play about the Tories selling off playing fields for development, and then bemoans the lack of facilities for our future athletes. And what have they done about it? Huh! Very little. Over the past ten years 5,000 sports fields have been sold for development and as we sit supping our pint, the good citizens of Sherborne are agonizing over the outcome of an appeal against the county council's decision to sell Fosters Field; this has been used by generations of children and all for the building of a measly 107 homes. Once again, you cannot trust a party in opposition to be committed to any pre-election pledge, policy, etc, once it's in power.

Yes, please, I'll have another pint, that last one was very agreeable.

Well, we've put back the publication of the novel until next March. William's got a job with a roofing company for a few weeks, and I'm off to the Isle of Wight tomorrow, Bank Holiday Monday. Oh, I know what I forgot to tell you - Debbie and Tim came over last week and announced she was expecting. I'm going to call it "It", short for "Git". They haven't got a name for It yet, but she had her first scan on Tuesday, and brought over the photographs. Tim has done whatever you do on the computer and promptly E-mailed copies to his parents and relatives. Neither Tim nor Debbie know what sex IT is and do not want to know until it is born. Apparently you cannot tell from the scan at this stage whether it is hung like a donkey, or a slapper born in true Aldershot style, with its legs raised, knees bent!

This pint is going down as well as the last. Despite everything that's gone on during the months, over the years, come the new century, come the new Millenium, people will still have one conversational ace up their sleeve when discussions and opinions dry up and silence is about to loom heavy. Forget the EU, foxhunting, law and order, the Channel tunnel, the only question worthy of an answer is, "And where were you the day Des Lynam announced he was quitting the *BBC*?"

So, as we come to a close, remember, the next time you are shopping in your favourite supermarket and you think "jam", remember, "Wilkin of Tiptree" - they're the ones for you!

What's that, you've got to go? You're right, I didn't realise it was getting that late. No, I'll just head on back by myself - the fresh air will do me some good.

Well, bye, then .....

Nice person, and I never knew your name. Perhaps we'll meet again. Aaah, ten to eleven, Muttley will be wondering if I am ever going to take her out. If only human satisfaction was on a par with that of a dog being shown a lead, we might all be more contented. Good night.

From Where I Sit ...

"Set to become a humour classic ... the find of the year"
- WH Smith's Bookcase

"Liberals with a heart condition beware"
- Croydon Advertiser

*"An amusing collection of personal experiences,
anecdotes and memories"*
- Surrey Mirror

*"The book earns the author full marks for humour,
determination and street-wise common sense"*
- Aldershot News and Mail

Available from Trouser Press, PO Box 139, Aldershot, Hants, GU12 5XR
Price: £4.95, post free, or through any good bookshop
ISBN - 0-9516501-0-6

As I Was Saying

"Courageous enough to write what most of us think ..."
- Surrey Advertiser

"A humorous look at life as it really is"
- Croydon Advertiser

*"Rude, insensitive, arrogant, self-opinionated,
sexist - he is also very very funny"*
- Wandsworth Borough News

Available from Trouser Press, PO Box 139, Aldershot, Hants, GU12 5XR
Price: £5.50, post free, or through any good bookshop
ISBN - 0-9516501-1-4

The Club - An Everyday Story of Trainspotters

"There is humour found a-plenty in Mel Rees's novel, The Club'"
- Sunday Express

"There is an honesty about the characters that is refreshing ... the story is highly entertaining, I struggled to put it down"
- Railway Magazine

"The author has discovered a rich vein of comic drama, a highly readable story unfolds ....David Shepherd's appearance adds a further touch of authenticity to a believable story"
- British Railway Modelling

"Light-hearted, barbed but not vicious and entertaining - don't blame me if you find yourself in the pages"
- Railway World

Available from Trouser Press, PO Box 139, Aldershot, Hants, GU12 5XR
Price: £4.99, post free, or through any good bookshop
ISBN - 0-9516501-2-2